CAMBRIDGE
UNIVERSITY PRESS

Marine Science
for Cambridge IGCSE™

COURSEBOOK

Matthew Parkin & Paul Roobottom

CAMBRIDGE
UNIVERSITY PRESS

Shaftesbury Road, Cambridge CB2 8EA, United Kingdom

One Liberty Plaza, 20th Floor, New York, NY 10006, USA

477 Williamstown Road, Port Melbourne, VIC 3207, Australia

314–321, 3rd Floor, Plot 3, Splendor Forum, Jasola District Centre, New Delhi – 110025, India

103 Penang Road, #05–06/07, Visioncrest Commercial, Singapore 238467

Cambridge University Press is part of the University of Cambridge.

It furthers the University's mission by disseminating knowledge in the pursuit of education,
learning and research at the highest international levels of excellence.

Information on this title: www.cambridge.org/9781009089760
© Cambridge University Press & Assessment 2022

First published 2022

20 19 18 17 16 15 14 13 12 11 10 9 8 7 6 5 4 3

Printed in Great Britain by Ashford Colour Press Ltd.

A catalogue record for this publication is available from the British Library

ISBN 978-1-009-08976-0 Coursebook Paperback with Digital Access (2 Years)
ISBN 978-1-009-09638-6 Digital Coursebook (2 Years)
ISBN 978-1-009-09639-3 Coursebook eBook

Additional resources for this publication at www.cambridge.org/go

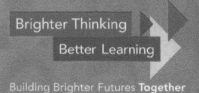

› Contents

> How to use this book

Throughout this book, you will notice lots of different features that will help your learning. These are explained below.

LEARNING INTENTIONS

These are found at the start of each chapter, help with navigation through the coursebook and indicate the important concepts in each topic.

GETTING STARTED

This feature contains questions and activities on subject knowledge you will need before starting the chapter.

MARINE SCIENCE IN CONTEXT

This feature presents real-world examples and applications of the content in a chapter, encouraging you to look further into topics. There are discussion questions at the end which look at some of the benefits and problems of these applications. The feature also provides the opportunity to extend your learning beyond the syllabus.

KEY WORDS

Key vocabulary for the syllabus is highlighted in the text when it is first introduced. Definitions are given in the key words boxes throughout and can also be found in the Glossary at the back of this book. Any key words marked with an asterisk (*) do not appear in the syllabus and are therefore not required knowledge but are useful terms for the subject.

COMMAND WORDS

Command words that appear in the syllabus and might be used in the exams are highlighted in the exam-style questions. In the marginal boxes, you will find the syllabus definition. You will also find these definitions in the Glossary at the back of the book with some further explanation on the meaning of these words.

ACTIVITY

Activities give you an opportunity to check your understanding throughout the text in a more active way, for example, by creating presentations, posters or role plays. They also provide the opportunity to extend your learning beyond the syllabus.

PRACTICAL TASK

Practical tasks focus on developing your practical skills and cover the essential practicals that are listed in the syllabus. They include lists of necessary equipment, safety considerations, step-by-step instructions so you can carry out the experiment and questions to help you think about what you have learnt.

Questions

Appearing throughout the text, questions give you a chance to check that you have understood the topic you have just read about.

WORKED EXAMPLES

The Key Skills chapter has Worked examples which show you the practical application of key data handling and practical skills.

SKILLS TIP

These tips help you with key data handling and practical skills in the Key Skills chapter. You will find references back to them in the Practical tasks throughout the rest of the book.

REFLECTION

These activities ask you to think about the approach that you take to your work and how you might improve this in the future.

SELF/PEER ASSESSMENT

At the end of some Activities and Practical tasks, you will find opportunities to help you assess your own work, or that of other students, and consider how you can improve the way you learn.

> This design tells you where information in the book is extension content and is not part of the syllabus.

SUMMARY

There is a summary of key points at the end of each chapter.

CASE STUDY PROJECT

Case study projects allow you to apply your learning from the whole chapter to pair or group activities, such as preparing posters or presentations. They provide the opportunity to extend your learning beyond the syllabus.

EXAM-STYLE QUESTIONS

Questions at the end of each chapter provide more demanding exam-style questions, some of which may require use of knowledge from previous chapters.

SELF-EVALUATION CHECKLIST

The self-evaluation checklists are followed by 'I can' statements which match the Learning intentions at the beginning of the chapter. You might find it helpful to rate how confident you are for each of these statements when you are revising. You should revisit any topics that you rated 'Needs more work' or 'Getting there'.

I can	Needs more work	Getting there	Confident to move on	See Section

> Introduction

Studying marine science

Marine science is the study of our oceans and seas. It is a subject that has elements of biology, chemistry, physics, geography, and geology. Marine scientists learn all about the different forms of life that live in the marine world and how they interact with each other. They discover the chemical and physical properties of the oceans and how these affect life. They study the different forms of coastlines, the seabed, and how geological processes shape our world. Importantly, they learn how humans interact with the marine world, how we rely on it for food, and how we can reduce the damage that we are doing.

Why should you study marine science? There are many reasons. Some people study marine science to help them to progress onto a career involved with the marine world, but many people study the subject for interest. The organisms that live in our oceans are fascinating and marine science allows people to study them in more depth.

About this coursebook

This is the first edition of our Cambridge IGCSE™ Marine Science Coursebook, which provides full coverage of the Cambridge IGCSE Marine Science (0697) syllabus for examinations from 2024 onwards.

The chapter order generally follows the same sequence as the topics in the syllabus. The various features that you will find in these chapters are explained in the previous two pages.

Many of the questions you will meet in this coursebook test if you have a deep understanding of the facts and concepts you have learnt. It is therefore not enough just to learn words and diagrams that you can repeat in answer to questions; you need to really understand each concept fully. Trying to answer the questions within each chapter, and at the end of each chapter, should help you to do this.

Although you will study marine science as a series of different topics, all these topics in fact link up with each other. You will therefore need to make links between different areas of the syllabus to answer some questions.

As you work through your course, keep reflecting on the work you did earlier and how it relates to the topic that you are now studying. The Reflection boxes ask you to think about 'how you learn' to help you make the very best use of your time and abilities as your course progresses. You can also use the Self-evaluation checklists at the end of each chapter to decide how well you have understood each topic, and whether you need to do more work on each one.

Practical skills are an important part of your marine science course. You will develop these skills as you do experiments and other practical work related to the topics you are studying.

Careers in marine science

We hope that you will find this marine science course and reading this coursebook interesting, and that it will inspire you to pursue your interest in the marine world to a higher level. The world needs inspiring, enthusiastic people to educate others on the issues that face our oceans. Studying marine science can offer many career opportunities. Some people choose to work in industries such as tourism and fishing, others choose to work in environmental research and conservation.

Tourism

Marine tourism brings many employment opportunities. One of the aims of ecotourism is to educate visitors. Marine scientists may give talks to visitors, act as guides, and produce information leaflets. Employers in tourist resorts need staff in hotels who can understand the natural world, and explain the ecology of the area to visitors. Marine scientists are also involved in the development of resorts to assess the impacts on ecosystems. Many tourist resorts are close to areas of scientific interest, and to support these areas there are often conservation projects and aquaria. These need people to work on research projects and captive breeding programmes.

Visitors can learn about marine organisms at an aquarium.

Fishing industry and aquaculture

The fishing industry offers many career opportunities. Employers include government agencies, university departments or private industry. Marine scientists research the health of fish stocks and help set fishing quotas. They are also involved in the development of sustainable fishing methods. The crews of fishing vessels also need to understand the best methods of fishing and how to ensure that fishing is not harming the environment. Aquaculture is a worldwide industry that is growing to meet the demand for seafood. Aquaculture enterprises need staff who understand the process, can investigate ways of improving it, and assess whether pollution from aquaculture is harming local ecosystems.

Energy industry

The worldwide demand for energy increases every year, offering jobs to marine scientists. Fossil fuel companies need people with an understanding of the geology of the Earth to help extract oil safely. As renewable fuels become more important, there is a need for scientists and engineers who can design, install, and operate renewable energy systems. Journalists with an understanding of marine science can raise public awareness about environmental issues and the energy industry.

Conservation

Marine scientists are often employed in conservation, both in research and in the running of projects. People with a knowledge of marine science are needed to assess the ecological health of habitats and the sustainability of species. Active conservation workers who manage areas and run breeding programmes are an essential part of any conservation project. Teachers and guides may be employed as education workers at conservation sites. Sometimes marine scientists are employed to raise awareness of conservation issues, and fund raise through social media.

Careers in marine science

Tourism

Fishing industry and aquaculture

Energy industry

Conservation

Key skills for Cambridge IGCSE™ Marine Science

- learn about the process of scientific investigation and the type of data you could collect

- select suitable apparatus to use in marine science investigations

- understand experimental techniques to use in marine science investigations

- recognise the difference between accuracy and precision

- plan investigations

- record observations

- present data in the form of graphs and charts

- interpret experimental data and make conclusions

- evaluate investigations and identify sources of error.

MARINE SCIENCE IN CONTEXT

An introduction to practical work

Marine science is a practical subject. Everything we know today has been developed through the process of scientific enquiry. This means a sequence of:

- making observations

- forming a hypothesis

- carrying out experiments or enquiries

- collecting data

- testing the hypothesis against the data collected

- developing a theory.

We can repeat this process over time. For example if some observations do not quite fit the theory, then we can form a new hypothesis and test again.

There are many things we still do not know about marine science. Scientists continue to use this process of scientific enquiry to learn more about our seas and oceans and life within them.

Types of observations

There are two general groups of observations: quantitative and qualitative. As a simple rule, if we can record the observation as a number then this is quantitative data. Any observation that we record using words is qualitative. Qualitative observations can also include the use of diagrams or other images.

Quantitative data

Quantitative data describes numerical data (the word relates to quantity).

Some measurements of number are discrete data, meaning they exist only as whole numbers. Examples of this include numbers of living organisms – a group of organisms is made up from a whole number, there cannot be any in-between values (such as fractions) of a living organism. You will use discrete data when counting organisms in Chapter 5.

Other measurements are continuous data, meaning there can be in-between values. Lengths and distances are good examples of this. When organisms grow, their length gradually changes and a measurement is only limited by the measuring equipment. You will use continuous data for Practical Task 0.1 in this chapter.

Qualitative data

Qualitative data describes data by grouping the data into categories (the word relates to quality or categories). The term categoric describes data that can be divided into groups.

Some qualitative data give very limited possible outcomes such as true and false, or positive and negative. Other qualitative data has more possible categories, such as a range of colours in simple experiments, or different types of living organisms.

KEY WORDS

observations: an aspect of the world around us that we notice

hypothesis: a suggested explanation of an observation that we can test through experiments or further observations

data: information such as numbers or descriptions relating to measurements or observations

theory: an explanation of observations that has been repeatedly tested and confirmed through observation and experimentation

quantitative data: data recorded as numerical values

discrete data: numerical data that can only be recorded as whole numbers or integers

continuous data: numerical data that can have 'in-between' values

qualitative data: data recorded as words, descriptions or categories

Experimental techniques, apparatus and materials

Practical equipment

You will need to be able to identify, use and plan the use of a variety of scientific apparatus.

Table 0.1 lists some equipment you are likely to use during your studies, describes their use and gives advice for using the equipment appropriately.

Apparatus	Uses	Good practice
balance	• measuring the mass of a sample • The precision of a balance is the smallest interval the balance is capable of measuring to, e.g. to 0.1 g.	Use the 'tare' button to reset the balance to zero when a container is placed on the tray. If there is no tare button, or you need to make repeated measurements using the same container, then record the mass of the container first.
beaker	• larger container with a flat bottom and usually a small spout for pouring • good for containing or heating liquids	Any volume markings are only approximate. Volumes are maximums, e.g. to contain 100 cm³ you might be better using a 250 cm³ beaker.
bungs — bung — test-tube	• sealing the contents in a test-tube • Some have holes for thermometers or tubing to go through them.	Warming a sealed test-tube is dangerous and can result in the bung popping off or the test tube exploding.

Apparatus	Uses	Good practice
clamp stand clamp — stand	• holding equipment in place	Take care not to tighten clamps too much as this can break glass.
compass N NW NE W E SW SE S	• locating North and for identifying directions	Compasses are affected by magnets so avoid magnets or electrical equipment that may create magnetic fields.
dropping pipette	• moving small volumes of liquid into a test-tube	Never squirt liquids at other students as they may contain harmful chemicals.
evaporating dish	• wide shallow dish to allow rapid evaporation of liquids	Take care not to overfill to avoid spills.

Apparatus	Uses	Good practice
filter funnel	• directing a liquid or gas into a container e.g. pouring liquids into a container to avoid spills • or inverted funnels can direct bubbles of gas into a test-tube or measuring cylinder • used with a filter paper to separate a solid that does not dissolve from a liquid	Dry solids consisting of small grains (such as sand) can also be used with funnels.
filter paper filter paper	• used with a filter funnel to separate a solid that does not dissolve from a liquid	Take care folding and using the paper. If you make holes, this will let solids through.
forceps	• picking up and moving small objects	Pointed forceps can easily puncture skin – use rounded forceps where possible to reduce this risk.
hand lens	• viewing small objects to make the feature larger and easier to see	Place the lens close to your eye rather than close to the object.
lamp	• a bulb in a holder with a switch, which is used to provide light in experiments	Some bulbs may get very hot – take care to avoid burns. Always ensure your hands are dry when operating electrical equipment.

Apparatus	Uses	Good practice
measuring cylinder	• measuring the volume of liquids • When filled with water and turned upside down they can be used to collect and measure the volume of gases. • Available in a range of sizes – smaller measuring cylinders have more precise intervals (e.g. 0.1 cm^3) compared to larger measuring cylinders (e.g. 2 cm^3).	Use the measuring cylinder closest to the volume of liquid you need to measure, e.g. to measure 5 cm^3 use a 10 cm^3 measuring cylinder. Always clamp measuring cylinders in place when inverted to avoid them tipping over. When reading volumes from a measuring cylinder, read to the bottom of the curved surface (this is called the meniscus).
microscope	• observing samples that are too small to see with a hand lens	Start with the lowest magnification and then increase the magnification when the sample is in focus. Follow all instructions from your teacher on safe use.
mounted needle	• holding specimens or samples	Take care not to injure yourself or others with the sharp tip.
petri dish	• A shallow round dish which has vertical sides. They have slightly larger lids which are used to cover them. • Can be used for a wide range of experiments.	Sealed petri dishes may result in harmful organisms or gases being produced – only remove these seals if instructed to by your teacher.

Apparatus	Uses	Good practice
quadrat	• a grid used for identifyingan area of habit at to record the number or percentage of organisms present	Never throw a quadrat without looking where it is going.
ruler	• a straight measuring device used to measure short distances in cm or mm	Carefully line up the '0' to one end of the measurement to ensure an accurate length is recorded.
spatula	• moving small amounts of solid	Tap the spatula while over the container to remove excess solid that may spill when moving the spatula.
spotting tile	• A white tile with small indentations that is used to hold small volumes of samples, usually liquids, and observe colour changes when reagents are added.	Take care not to add too much liquid to each indentation, especially when other liquids need to be added to complete the experiment.
stopwatch	• timing in experiments • Use to record the time that an event takes to complete, or to identify when to record measurements.	When taking multiple readings over a period of time, always leave the time running – never stop the time and restart for a sequence of results (e.g. every minute for 5 minutes).
syringe	• accurate measurement of small volumes of liquids (or gases) • transferring liquids or gases to containers in sealed experiments • Syringes should not be used with needles.	Liquids can come out very quickly – take care not to squirt at other people, especially near their eyes.

Apparatus	Uses	Good practice
tape measure	• measuring long distances or marking lines to investigate	Take care not to trip over tape measures when in use.
test-tubes	• Small and large test-tubes can contain small samples of material to investigate. • These could be solids, liquids or gases and may include small living organisms.	No markings to show volume, so they are not suitable for measuring volumes. Use large test-tubes to heat liquids as small test-tubes can result in the liquid boiling too quickly. Do not point a test-tube at yourself or any other person while heating.
test-tube holder	• holding test-tubes while heating	Never touch a hot test-tube immediately after heating – it will remain hot for some time.
test-tube rack	• holding test-tubes upright before and during experiment	Use test-tubes that fit in the holes for the rack being used.
thermometer	• recording the temperature of substances • Many thermometers use a liquid in a thin glass tube that expands as it gets warmer.	Different thermometers have different ranges of temperatures they can measure, e.g. −10 °C to +110 °C. Glass thermometers may contain toxic chemicals which can be released if broken.

Apparatus	Uses	Good practice
wash bottle	• squeezy plastic container usually holding water • washing or rinsing other containers and equipment	Nozzles are very thin resulting in water coming out fast – this can splash other chemicals out if not careful.
water bath	• heating, cooling or maintaining a constant temperature in experiments carried out in test-tubes or beakers • You can make simple water baths from large beakers, hot (or cold) water and a thermometer. • A thermostat and heater can maintain a constant temperature in an electronic water bath.	Containers may need support to stop them floating in the water bath, e.g. test-tubes in a test-tube rack. Use ice to cool water baths below room temperature. Always use dry hands when operating electrical equipment.

Table 0.1: Scientific apparatus for marine science investigations.

Practical methods

You will need to be able to use the apparatus listed above to carry out a range of practical methods. The following practical tasks will help you to understand the practical techniques that you will need during this course.

PRACTICAL TASK 0.1

Measuring distances

Introduction

The standard unit for distance is metres (m).

Depending on the scale of distance measured, we often use smaller units (such as cm, mm, µm) or larger units (such as km).

µm	mm	cm	m	km
0.000001	0.001 m	0.01 m	1 m	1000 m
(10^{-6} m)	(10^{-3} m)	(10^{-2} m)	(10^0 m)	(10^3 m)

Table 0.2: Metric units used to measure distance.

CONTINUED

SKILLS TIP 0.2

Take care lining up the zero value to the edge of the object.

Record the distance carefully using the smallest interval on the measuring item.

Measurements can be recorded to the nearest half interval. For the ruler in Figure 0.1, the smallest intervals are in mm, so the most precise measurement that we can record with this ruler is 0.5 mm.

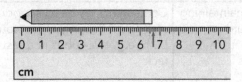

Figure 0.1: An enlarged ruler showing how measurements can be recorded to 0.5 mm.

We can measure distance in any direction. When describing the depth of the sea we usually measure vertically down from the surface of the sea.

Marine science investigations where measuring length may be important include:

- Measuring tidal amplitude (see Activity 1.3 in Chapter 1)

- Changing light intensity in photosynthesis experiments by moving a lamp further away (see Practical Task 4.3 in Chapter 4)

- Measuring the profile of a shore (see Practical Task 5.3 in Chapter 5).

KEY WORDS

light intensity: the quantity of visible light; this is greatest at the surface of the ocean and reduces as depth increases

photosynthesis: the process by which plants produce carbohydrates from carbon dioxide and water using energy from light

profile: the angle of slopes along a shore

You will need:

- a ruler

- a tape measure.

Method

1 Use a ruler to measure the length and width of this book. Record your results in a copy of Table 0.3 to the nearest mm.

2 Use a tape measure to measure the length of the room you are in. Record your results to the nearest cm.

3 Choose the most appropriate measuring equipment to measure the length, width and height of the desk or table you are using.

Results

Item measured and direction measured	Distance / cm
book (length)	
book (width)	
room (length)	
room (width)	
desk/table (length)	
desk/table (width)	
desk/table (height)	

Table 0.3: Measuring distance results.

Questions

1 Fishing regulations often require fish or other marine organisms to be a certain size before they can be caught. Suggest how the length of round or irregularly shaped organisms can be recorded accurately.

2 Why is it important that you check that your measuring equipment is the stated length?

3 What difficulties might we find when measuring the height of high and low tides?

PRACTICAL TASK 0.2

Test-tube investigations

Introduction

Test-tubes are ideal for carrying out small-scale simple experiments. Test-tubes can hold small volumes of substances for investigation. They are usually made from glass so are transparent to allow a clear view of the contents. Test-tubes can be sealed using a bung. This makes it easier to mix the contents without spilling.

SKILLS TIP 0.3

When using liquids aim for 1-2 cm depth of each liquid. This should be enough to make observations easily, without overfilling the test-tube.

Marine science investigations where using test-tubes may be important include:

- Investigating pH (see Practical Task 2.3 in Chapter 2)

- Food and nutrient tests (see Practical Task 4.1 in Chapter 4).

You will need:

- 2 test-tubes

- a test-tube rack

- white flour (e.g. corn flour, rice flour, all-purpose flour, etc.)

- iodine solution

- white vinegar

- universal indicator solution.

KEY WORD

solution: formed when a substance (solute)

Safety: Wear eye protection to prevent any accidental splashing of any substances in the eyes.

Iodine solution is harmful – avoid contact with the skin as it also causes staining to skin. Avoid inhaling any vapour.

Method

1   Add a small mass of flour to a test-tube (enough to give about 0.5 cm depth). Record your observations of the appearance of the flour in a copy of Table 0.4.

2   Record your observations of the appearance of iodine solution.

3   Add two drops of iodine solution to the flour in the test-tube. Record your observations of any changes.

4   Add white vinegar to a second test-tube (approximately 1–2 cm deep). Record your observations of the appearance of the vinegar.

5   Record your observations of the appearance of universal indicator solution.

6   Add 2–3 drops of universal indicator solution to the vinegar. Record your observations.

SKILLS TIP 0.4

When recording observations from test-tube reactions think carefully about the words used to describe what you see – for example the word 'clear' means you can see through a solution, but it does not necessarily mean it is colourless as you can have a clear blue solution. If a solution has no colour you should write 'colourless'.

Results

Substance	Appearance or observation
flour only	
iodine solution	
flour and iodine solution	
white vinegar	
universal indicator solution	
white vinegar and universal indicator	

Table 0.4: Test-tube investigations results.

CONTINUED

Questions

1 How could you check your results for these experiments?

2 Why do the actual masses and volumes of each substance in this investigation not affect the results of this investigation?

3 Compare these results to the results for Practical Task 0.1. How do the results differ?

PRACTICAL TASK 0.3

Separating techniques

Introduction

Mixtures are substances that contain more than one chemical that we can separate by physical processes. Two important separating techniques are filtration and evaporation. In this investigation you will separate a mixture of salt and sand by using these two techniques. You will dissolve the salt in water and then obtain the salt back as a solid.

SKILLS TIP 0.5

Patience is important in science. To get good results in this investigation you will need to allow enough time for both the filtration and evaporation to complete – avoid shaking or poking the filter paper as this may allow some sand to get through. The evaporation will result in large salt crystals if you leave it to complete over several days.

You will need:

- sand and salt mixture
- a filter funnel
- filter paper
- a beaker
- an evaporating dish.

Safety: Wear eye protection to prevent any accidental splashing of any substances in the eyes.

KEY WORDS

mixture: two or more substances mixed together but not chemically combined – the substances can be separated by physical means

filtration: a practical technique used to separate a solid from a liquid

evaporation: a practical technique used to separate a dissolved solid from a liquid

dissolve: the process of a solid mixing into a liquid

Method

1 Pour some water into the evaporating dish to measure a suitable volume that can be held in the dish. Pour this water into the beaker.

2 Record the appearance of the sand and salt mixture in a copy of Table 0.5. Add some of the sand and salt mixture to the water.

3 Stir well to dissolve the salt. Record the appearance in your results table.

4 Fold the filter paper and place into the filter funnel. Hold the funnel over the evaporating basin (a tripod or clamp stand can be used to hold the funnel in place).

CONTINUED

5 Carefully pour the salty sandy water into the filter paper, making sure the water does not go over the top of the filter paper.

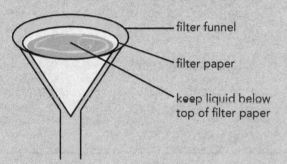

filter funnel

filter paper

keep liquid below top of filter paper

Figure 0.2: Using a filter paper and funnel.

6 Wait for all the water to pass through the filter paper. Record the appearance of the solid left in the filter paper, and the solution that has passed through the filter paper.

7 Leave the evaporating dish containing the solution in a warm place for a few days to allow the water to evaporate.

8 After a few days you should be left with pure salt crystals in the dish. Record the appearance of your crystals.

Results

Substance	Appearance
sand and salt mixture	
sand and salt mixture in water	
solid substances left in filter paper	
solution remaining after filtering	
salt crystals after evaporation	

Table 0.5: Separating techniques observations.

Questions

1 Describe how the speed of evaporation of water could be increased.

2 Suggest how the salt could be made even purer.

3 Describe what measurements you would need to record to calculate the proportion of salt in the sand and salt mixture.

This Practical task links to Skills tip 0.1.

PRACTICAL TASK 0.4

Heating and cooling samples

Introduction

Science investigations often require heating and cooling to investigate the effect of temperature. We use a thermometer to measure temperature. We measure temperature using the unit °C (degrees Celsius).

KEY WORD

degrees Celsius (°C)*: unit used to measure temperature in the metric system

Water baths can be set up in several ways to maintain experiments at a constant temperature. You can make a simple water bath using a beaker on a tripod over a Bunsen burner as shown in Figure 0.3. In this example the thermometer needs careful monitoring as the temperature of the water bath can change quickly, and the Bunsen may need moving from under the beaker to stop heating the water bath temporarily.

A more efficient method is to use a thermostatic water bath if this is available. This contains an electric water heater. A thermostat turns the heater on and off to maintain a constant temperature.

CONTINUED

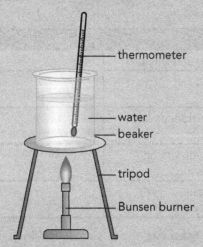

Figure 0.3: Setting up a water bath using a Bunsen burner and tripod.

- thermometer
- water
- beaker
- tripod
- Bunsen burner

You can make another simple water bath by using a large beaker and adding hot water (e.g. from a kettle) or ice to adjust the temperature. You may have to add extra water during the experiment so there needs to be enough space in the beaker to hold any extra water. This method can produce water baths that are colder than room temperature.

SKILLS TIP 0.6

If using a Bunsen burner never hold the bulb of a thermometer directly in the flame as this can break the thermometer.

Marine science investigations that may require the use of a water bath include:

- Investigating the effect of temperature on the solubility of a solute in water (see Practical Task 2.2 in Chapter 2)

- Investigating the effect of temperature on gas solubility (see Practical Task 2.5 in Chapter 2).

You will need:

- 1× large beaker or container

- 1× large test-tube

- 1× clamp stand

- access to hot water, e.g. from a kettle (use water which has cooled a little from boiling)

- ice

- salt (sodium chloride)

- thermometer (capable of recording at least −10 °C to +20 °C)

- stop clock or timer.

Safety: Take care with hot water as it can cause burns.

Clear up any water spills to avoid slipping.

Method

1   Set up the equipment as shown in Figure 0.4 below.

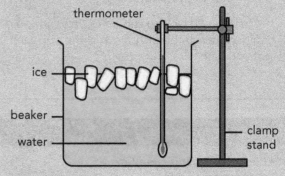

- thermometer
- ice
- beaker
- water
- clamp stand

Figure 0.4: Setting up an iced water bath.

2   Add 40 g of salt to the beaker of ice and water and gently stir to mix.

3   Add distilled water to the large test-tube to a depth of approximately 3 cm.

4   Start the timer and record the temperature on the thermometer in a copy of Table 0.6.

5   Record the temperature every minute until the water begins to freeze, then for another 5 minutes.

CONTINUED

Results

Time / minutes	Temperature / °C
0	
1	
2	
3	
4	
5	
(you will need more rows to record all your results)	

Table 0.6: Results for cooling water in a water bath.

Questions

1 How could you check your results?

2 How could you present these results in a graph?

3 How could you adapt this method to investigate the effect of mass of salt in water on the freezing point of the water?

4 Why might using a freezer be difficult for this experiment?

This Practical task links to Skills tip 0.1

PRACTICAL TASK 0.5

Using an electronic balance

Introduction

An electronic balance can be very useful to precisely record the mass of equipment or substances. You need a balance that can record to a precision of at least 0.1 grams (g).

SKILLS TIP 0.7

When using an electronic balance always make sure this is set to zero (often using a 'Tare' button) before starting, and checking the display reads 0.0 g.

Marine science investigations that may require the use of a balance include:

- Investigating the effect of temperature and mass of dissolved salt on **density** of water (see Practical Task 2.6 and 2.7 in Chapter 2)

- Investigating the effect of temperature on gas solubility (see Practical Task 2.5 in Chapter 2).

You will need:

- an electronic balance
- 1× large test-tube
- 1× test-tube holder
- a Bunsen burner or spirit burner (or access to an oven)
- sodium hydrogencarbonate (baking soda)
- a spatula.

Safety: Take care with Bunsen burners or heating equipment to avoid burns.

Method

1 Use a balance to record the mass of the empty test-tube in a copy of Table 0.7.

2 Use a spatula to place about 1 cm depth of sodium hydrogencarbonate in the large test-tube. Record the mass of the test-tube with the sodium hydrogencarbonate.

CONTINUED

3 Use a Bunsen burner to heat the sodium hydrogencarbonate. Observe any changes in the test-tube. (If you do not have access to a Bunsen burner or similar, you can place the test-tubes in an oven set at 100 °C for an hour, but you may not be able to make any other observations.)

4 When you can no longer see condensation in the test-tube, stop heating and allow the test-tube to cool for a few minutes.

5 Re-weigh the test-tube and its contents and record this mass.

Results

Item(s)	Mass / g
Empty test-tube (A)	
Test-tube + sodium hydrogencarbonate (before heating) (B)	
Sodium hydrogencarbonate (calculate: B – A)	
Test-tube + sodium hydrogencarbonate (after heating) (C)	
Sodium hydrogencarbonate after heating (calculate: C – A)	

Table 0.7: Results for using an electronic balance.

KEY WORDS

density: the relationship between the mass of a substance and the volume it occupies: density = mass ÷ volume

condensation: the process of a gas turning into a liquid, visible as droplets of liquid on a surface or as a cloud in the air

Questions

1 Describe any observations you made in the test-tube during the experiment.

2 What happens to the mass of the sodium hydrogencarbonate during the experiment?

3 Suggest what has happened to the sodium hydrogencarbonate in the experiment.

This Practical task links to Skills tip 0.1.

PRACTICAL TASK 0.6

Measuring gas production

Introduction

When experiments produce gases, it can be useful to measure the amount of gas produced to monitor and compare the rate of the reactions. At its simplest level you might count the number of bubbles of gas produced, but this can be difficult if there are many bubbles, or if the bubbles vary in size.

A more quantitative method to measure the amount of gas is to measure the volume of gas produced. This can be carried out using a gas syringe, but many schools do not have access to this equipment so a simpler set of equipment using measuring cylinders can be used instead.

Avoid using the term amount when discussing any measurements. Use a more precise term to describe an appropriate measurement such as mass or volume.

CONTINUED

SKILLS TIP 0.8

When reading volumes from a measuring cylinder, read to the bottom of the curved surface (this is called the meniscus) as shown in Figure 0.5.

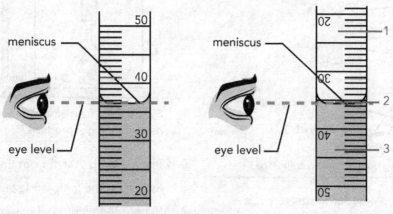

Figure 0.5: Reading a volume in a measuring cylinder.

KEY WORD

meniscus*: the upward or downward curve at the surface of a liquid where it meets a container

Marine science investigations that may require measuring gas production include:

- Investigating the effect of light intensity on the rate of photosynthesis in an aquatic plant or macroalga (see Practical Task 4.3 in Chapter 4).

SKILLS TIP 0.9

When setting up inverted measuring cylinders to collect gases in investigations, leave enough space in the container for the displaced water. Lower your hand into the water while setting up the measuring cylinder to avoid spilling water.

You will need:

- an aquatic plant
- 1× funnel
- 1× beaker or container large enough to contain the funnel
- 1× 10 cm³ measuring cylinder
- 1× lamp
- 1× clamp and stand
- a stop clock or timer.

Safety: Take care not to touch electrical switches and equipment with wet hands.

Clear up any water spills to avoid slipping.

CONTINUED

Method

1   Set up the equipment as shown in Figure 0.6. Make sure the tip of the funnel is below the surface of the water.

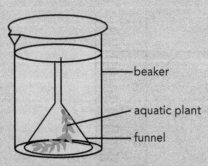

Figure 0.6: Setting up a funnel to collect gas.

2   Fill the measuring cylinder to the very top with water.

3   Place the palm of your hand over the top of the measuring cylinder to contain the water, Then, tip the measuring cylinder upside down and carefully lower your hand and the measuring cylinder into the water as shown in Figure 0.7.

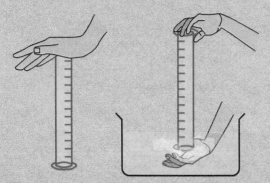

Figure 0.7: Moving the measuring cylinder into the water bath.

4   Carefully remove your hand while keeping the opening to the measuring cylinder under the surface of the water so the water cannot escape. Then move the measuring cylinder over the top of the funnel and clamp in place, as shown in Figure 0.8.

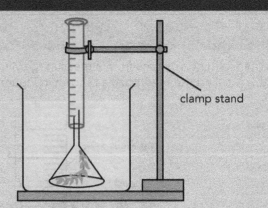

Figure 0.8: The measuring cylinder is in place to measure the gas produced.

5   Place a lamp 10 cm from the beaker.

6   Switch on the lamp and start the stop clock.

7   Record the volume of gas collected in a copy of Table 0.8 every minute for 5 minutes.

Results

Time / min	Volume of gas collected / cm^3
0	
1	
2	
3	
4	
5	

Table 0.8: Volumes of gas collected over five minutes.

Questions

1   Why is it important to make sure the measuring cylinder is held vertically?

2   If some air gets into the measuring cylinder while setting up the experiment, what could you do to take this into account without setting up the measuring cylinder again?

3   What could you change in this experiment if the volume of gas produced in 5 minutes is greater than 10 cm^3?

This Practical task links to Skills tip 0.1.

PRACTICAL TASK 0.7

Using a microscope

Introduction

Microscopes allow us to see objects much smaller than we can see with just our eyes. They contain lenses that magnify the image. The magnification depends on the combination of lenses used in the microscope (see Figure 0.9).

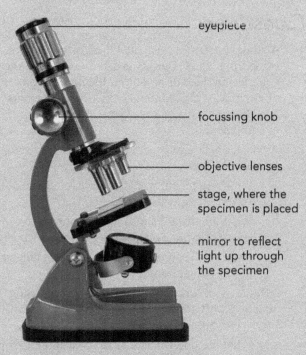

eyepiece

focussing knob

objective lenses

stage, where the specimen is placed

mirror to reflect light up through the specimen

Figure 0.9: A typical microscope used in schools.

You place an object for viewing on the stage, usually on a glass slide. Use the objective lens with the lowest magnification first to view the sample, with the stage set at the highest position. Then move the stage down using the coarse focus dial until you can see an image through the eyepiece. Use the fine focus dial to adjust the image so it is fully focused.

When the image is in focus you can change the objective lens to a higher magnification. Then use the fine focus dial to adjust the focus again if necessary.

SKILLS TIP 0.10

Never touch the glass lenses on a microscope, only use a special lens paper to clean the lens to avoid scratching or damaging the lenses.

Marine science investigations that may require the use of microscopes include:

- Drawing and measuring cells (see Practical Task 3.2 in Chapter 3).

You will need:

- a light microscope
- 1× glass slide
- small piece of paper.

Safety: Follow all instructions from your teacher regarding the safe use of microscopes.

Method

1 Tear the paper to produce a rough edge exposing the paper fibres.

2 Place the torn piece of paper on to the slide and place this slide on the microscope stage.

3 Carefully adjust the focus until you can see the edge of the paper – you might need to move the slide on the stage to observe the edge of the paper.

4 Draw a diagram of the paper fibres using a sharp pencil.

SKILLS TIP 0.11

If you have a mobile phone with a camera, you might be able to take a photograph of the image as seen through the eyepiece. This may make it easier to draw your diagram.

CONTINUED

Questions

1   The magnification is calculated by multiplying the magnifications from the eyepiece lens by the magnification of the objective lens. What is the magnification you used to observe the paper fibres?

2   Why is it difficult to see the paper fibres in the rest of the paper?

This Practical task links to Skills tip 0.1.

Using a compass

We use a compass to find direction using the Earth's magnetic field. The needle on a compass is magnetic and points to the North pole of the Earth. When the needle on the compass stops moving, rotate the compass so the needle points to North on the compass.

The four main directions on a compass are North, East, South and West. Exactly halfway between each of these directions are North-East, South-East, South-West and North-West. These make up the eight-point compass directions.

In the same way, exactly halfway between these are additional directions – the names of the additional directions are based on the directions shown by the eight-point compass, as shown in Figure 0.10.

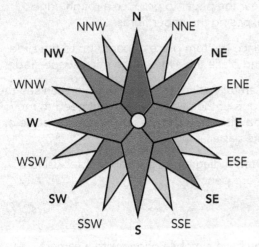

Figure 0.10: The directions shown by a sixteen-point compass.

To use a compass, hold the compass horizontal so the needle can move freely. Turn the compass so that the needle is pointing directly to North. The directions on the compass are now the directions from that location.

Questions

1   A student needs to calculate the density of a cube made from wood. Density is determined using the volume and mass of an object. Identify two pieces of equipment needed to take these measurements and state the units of measurement for each piece of equipment.

2   A teacher hands you a small jar containing a sample of seawater.

   a   What equipment would you use to measure the volume of the seawater?

   b   What are the units for this measurement?

   c   What additional equipment would you need to test a small sample of this water using universal indicator solution?

3   You are asked to carry out an investigation using aquatic plants and you are told that the plant will produce bubbles of gas when light shines on it.

   a   What method can you use to collect the gas produced?

   b   What equipment could you use to control the temperature of the beaker containing the plant to prevent it getting warm during the experiment?

   c   Identify a risk during the experiment. Describe how you could reduce this risk to make the experiment safer.

KEY WORDS

compass: navigation equipment that contains a magnetic needle that always points to the north

magnetic field: a region of space around the Earth in which a magnet experiences (feels) a force

Accuracy and precision

The words accuracy and precision are often confused with each other. You need to understand what the two terms mean and how they relate to science investigations.

A useful way to think about accurate and precise is to think about trying to hit a target with several arrows. Each of the four images in Figure 0.11 shows whether the strikes are accurate and/or precise.

Faults in equipment can cause a lack in accuracy. For example, a tape measure that has been stretched would have larger intervals in the measurements than it should have. So, a measurement of 4.2 m could actually be 4.4 m, no matter how many times you measured this. Using equipment in the wrong way can also cause a lack of accuracy, for example not resetting a balance to zero before measuring the mass.

You get precise results when using the smallest increment on a piece of measuring equipment. For example, a ruler marked in cm and mm can measure to the nearest half an interval, such as 0.5 mm. If you only record results to the nearest cm then you are not recording as precisely as possible.

When using a measuring cylinder to measure volume, use the smallest measuring cylinder available that can contain the full volume required. For example, you might need to measure 20 cm³ of water for an experiment. You could choose to use one of these measuring cylinders: 10 cm³, 25 cm³, 50 cm³ or 100 cm³. Which should you use? Although the 10 cm³ measuring cylinder is the most precise, it will not hold 20 cm³ of water, so the 25 cm³ measuring cylinder is the most suitable to use.

KEY WORDS

accuracy: a measurement result is described as accurate if it is close to the true value

precision: quantitative – how close the measured values of a quantity are to each other; qualitative – descriptions or observations that closely match the characteristics being recorded

increment: (of a measuring instrument) the smallest interval on the scale

---

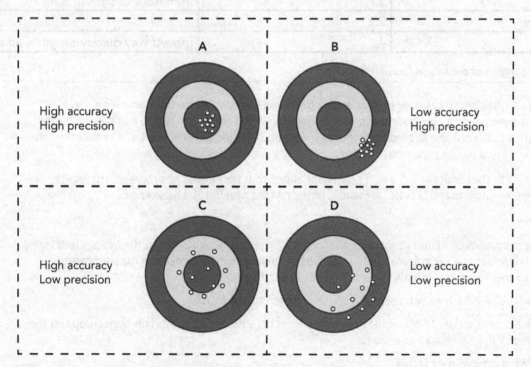

High accuracy
High precision — A

Low accuracy
High precision — B

High accuracy
Low precision — C

Low accuracy
Low precision — D

Figure 0.11: Four target boards showing different combinations of accuracy and precision.

Precise observations

When describing qualitative observations such as colour, you need to be as clear as possible so the results are also precise. For example, a liquid in a test-tube might be yellow. If it is transparent (clear), so that you can see through the yellow liquid, you should add this. You need to state 'clear yellow solution' as this is different to an 'opaque yellow solution'. In the same way, you can describe pure water as a 'clear, colourless liquid' – if you do not state that the liquid is colourless then 'clear' could describe a coloured clear liquid.

Planning experiments and investigations

Hypotheses

You may confuse a prediction with a hypothesis. A prediction is a best 'guess' at what you think may happen in an investigation. For example, in an investigation into the length of the day and the maximum air temperature recorded on that day, you might predict that as the length of the day increases the maximum air temperature also increases.

WORKED EXAMPLE 0.1

A student collected the following set of results from an investigation into lengths of organisms found in a rock pool. They used a 30 cm ruler marked to the nearest mm to measure their lengths. They also recorded some notes about their measurements. The results are shown in Table 0.9.

Organism	Length / cm	Notes
shrimp	3	ignored antennae
crab	5.7	from front to back of shell
anemone	2.2	
fish	4	moved very quickly, length is an estimate

Table 0.9: Lengths of organisms found in a rock pool.

The result for the shrimp has only been recorded to the nearest cm. We do not know if this was carelessly measured, or if the student saw that it was exactly 3.0 cm. If the length has been recorded to the nearest mm, then this should be shown in the result by writing '3.0' to make clear that the result has been measured to this precision.

Compare this to the result for the fish. The student stated that they could not measure the length precisely, so we know that this is not measured to the nearest mm but the nearest cm.

Now you try

1   Use a ruler marked in mm to measure the length of a pencil. Record this to the nearest half mm. Use a different ruler (e.g. from another student or the teacher) to repeat this measurement. Are the measurements exactly the same? What does this show?

2   What type of data have you used to record the length of the pencil?

3   A teacher asks a class to count the number of birds on a beach. Each student then compares their results to other students in the class.

   a   What type of data is this?

   b   Why might the results be different for each member of the class?

   c   How could you make the results more accurate?

A hypothesis is based on prior knowledge or observations and should link the variable that is being changed to the variable that is being measured. For example, in Chapter 1 you will learn about the link between the Moon and the tides. A hypothesis should therefore link the change we measure (difference in height between high tide and low tide) to the change we decide to make measurements on (the observed shape of the Moon). So, we could suggest a hypothesis as shown below:

The difference in height between high tide and low tide depends on the observed shape of the Moon.

In general, we can write a hypothesis as:

The dependent variable depends on the independent variable.

As you can see, we need to understand and identify the dependent variable and independent variable to be able to make a hypothesis.

In this hypothesis, the dependent variable is the difference in height between high and low tides. The independent variable is the observed shape of the Moon.

KEY WORDS

variable: a factor in an investigation that can be changed, or that changes as a result of changes we make in an investigation

moon: a natural satellite of a planet

dependent variable: the variable we measure in an investigation

independent variable: the variable that is being changed in an investigation

Variables

Variables are factors in an investigation that can be changed, or that change as a result of changes we make in an investigation. We need to think about three types of variables.

Independent variable

The independent variable is the factor that we investigate – we try to find if changing this variable will have an effect on another variable that we measure.

We must choose a suitable range of values for the independent variable. The range must cover enough change so that we can clearly see any impact of changing the independent variable. We can divide this range of values into smaller changes at regular intervals.

KEY WORDS

range: the upper and lower values for the independent variable

interval: the gap between separate values for the independent variable

Dependent variable

The dependent variable is the factor that we measure to see if it changes (due to the independent variable changing). If the dependent variable changes, there is likely to be a link with the independent variable. If the dependent variable does not change then there is unlikely to be a link with the independent variable. We can then review the hypothesis and investigate other variables instead.

Standardised variables

Standardised variables are all the other factors in an investigation that might affect the dependent variable. To make the investigation valid, we must try to keep all these other factors constant, so that they do not affect the dependent variable and alter the results.

A control experiment is a trial that all the other trials are compared against, in which you try to remove the independent variable and fix the values for the standardised variables. For example, if trying to investigate the effect of light on production of bubbles of gas, we would fix the other standardised variables such as temperature, salinity, volume of water, etc., and measure how much, if any, gas is produced without any light.

KEY WORD

valid: a valid experiment is well designed, so that it successfully measures the relationship you intend to measure, for example keeping all other variables constant as much as possible

salinity: a measure of the quantity of dissolved salts in ocean water; represented by parts per thousand (ppt)

Replicates

Replicates are experimental trials held under the same conditions. It is useful to repeat experiments to obtain many results:

- Replicates are checks on results. Similar results in two or more replicates suggest that an experiment has been done accurately. This allows you to identify **anomalous results**.

- Replicates allow you to calculate an average (or mean) result. To find the mean, you can add up the values for similar replicates and divide the total by the number of replicates added together.

KEY WORDS

replicates: two or more trials of the same experiment, using the same materials and apparatus

anomalous results: results that do not fit the observed pattern or trend. When results have been repeated, an anomaly is a result that is significantly different from two or more similar values

WORKED EXAMPLE 0.2

Aquatic plants live in water. A student wants to investigate the rate of bubbles produced by an aquatic plant in light. They know that the plant uses light, so they decide to change the light intensity and see how this affects the rate of bubbles produced.

The student must develop a hypothesis to investigate. To do this they need to identify the independent and dependent variables:

Independent variable = the variable we are changing in the investigation (light intensity)

Dependent variable = the variable we are measuring in the investigation (rate of bubbles produced)

The student suggests this hypothesis:

The rate of bubbles produced depends on the light intensity.

To make the results of the investigation valid the student needs to control any other variables that could affect the results. They should think of any variables that could change and might affect the dependent variable, and plan to keep these constant. These might include:

- the amount of plant used (use approximately the same length of plant)
- the type of plant used (use the same type of plant)
- the size of the container (use the same size of beaker)
- the volume of water in the container (always use 200 cm³ water)
- the temperature of the water (place the beaker with the plant into a water bath set at 25 °C).

You might think of other variables that could be controlled. A good investigation identifies a range of standardised variables and describes how these will be kept constant to make the results valid. This also helps you to develop your method by making you think about how you are going to make the experiment as consistent as possible.

Now you try

1   A student notices that the number of different types of organism on a rocky shore seems to increase as you get closer to the sea.

   a   Identify the independent and dependent variables.

   b   Suggest a hypothesis that the student could investigate.

2   A student thinks that the mass of solid that dissolves in water increases as the water gets warmer.

   a   Identify the independent and dependent variables.

   b   Suggest a hypothesis that the student could investigate.

   c   Identify two standardised variables for this investigation, and suggest how these could be controlled.

Describing a method

In the 'Experimental techniques, apparatus and materials' section of this chapter, you looked at practical apparatus and methods used for investigations. When writing a method, you must organise your instructions in a clear and logical sequence. If you do this, then another student with similar experience could follow your instructions to carry out the experiment.

It is useful to plan the points you want to include. This gives you the important information you need to write a method. Think about these questions:

- What is the independent variable?

  - What range of values will you use? (It can be useful to state how you might identify a suitable range, such as with some trial experiments.)

  - What intervals will you use within your chosen range?

  - How will you set up your independent variable in your experiment and change the values in your chosen range and intervals?

- What is the dependent variable?

  - How will you measure this?

  - What will you measure it with?

  - When or how often will you measure it?

- What are the standardised variables?

  - What do you need to keep the same?

  - How will you try to keep these variables constant?

- How many replicates do you want to obtain?

  - How many repeats will you carry out of each trial?

  - What is the purpose of the repeats? (The purpose is to identify anomalous results and calculate mean results.)

As you become familiar with different experimental methods in this course, observe how the methods are written. It is helpful to use short bullet points, and to use a logical sequence of steps that are in the correct order.

Look back at Practical Task 0.3. This could have been written as:

Get some salt and sand and water and put it in a beaker. Give it a good stir. Pour the mixture through a filter funnel and let the water evaporate for a few days. Write down what each substance looks like.

If this method is followed exactly as described, you would finish with a wet sandy puddle on the desk that would need cleaning up before any water could evaporate. Compare this with the method written for Practical Task 0.3. This has a list of equipment and describes how each piece of equipment is used in a logical sequence. Each step is also clearly numbered, but bullet points are also good for writing methods. Notice also how a diagram can really help to show how to set up equipment – drawing simple diagrams can save you lots of time when trying to explain how to set up equipment.

Risks and safety precautions

When you have written a method, think about the risks involved in the experiment. Risks can be due to individual pieces of equipment or how you use equipment.

When you have identified any risks, describe how you might reduce these risks. For example, if you are using electrical equipment and water there is a risk of electrocution.

So, to reduce the risk you should keep water away from electrical devices and dry your hands before using electrical devices or switches.

Ethical considerations

Some investigations involve working with living organisms. This means you need to think about ethical considerations and how you treat the living organisms, as well as any risks to yourself from stings or pincers.

When describing a method involving living organisms, think about how you will handle the organisms. You might need to keep them at a suitable temperature, or avoid stepping on organisms on beaches.

WORKED EXAMPLE 0.3

In Worked Example 0.2, a student wanted to investigate the rate of bubbles produced by an aquatic plant in light. They identified the variables:

- Independent variable = light intensity
- Dependent variable = rate of bubbles produced.

The student suggests a suitable hypothesis:

The rate of bubbles produced depends on the light intensity.

They also identified some standardised variables and how to keep these constant:

- the amount of plant used (use approximately the same length of plant)
- the type of plant used (use the same type of plant)
- the size of the container (use the same size beaker)
- the volume of water in the container (always use 200 cm³ water)
- the temperature of the water (place the beaker with the plant into a water bath set at 25 °C).

To produce a method, we must think about how we can change the light intensity and how we can measure the rate of bubbles produced.

The light intensity could be changed by changing the amount of energy going to the lamp, such as using a dimmer switch, but most lamps have simple on and off switches. Instead, we can move the lamp to different distances from the aquatic plant. The further away the lamp is, the less light the plant will receive. We could carry out some trial experiments to check how far away the light can be while the aquatic plant still produces a few bubbles – this would help to identify a suitable range of values for the independent variable. This distance might be 50 cm. If we divide 50 cm into five equal intervals of 10 cm, this gives us the values for changing the light intensity (lamp at 10 cm, 20 cm, 30 cm, 40 cm and 50 cm from the plant).

We could try and count the number of bubbles produced by the aquatic plant. But bubbles might be produced too quickly to count, and the size of the bubbles might change. A better method is to collect the gas produced and measure the volume after a fixed period of time, such as 2 minutes.

Use the techniques you are familiar with to choose the most suitable equipment and techniques to carry out this experiment. To collect and measure the volume of gas produced we could use an upside down (inverted) measuring cylinder filled with water. Trying to explain this in a method can be difficult, so draw a simple labelled diagram instead:

CONTINUED

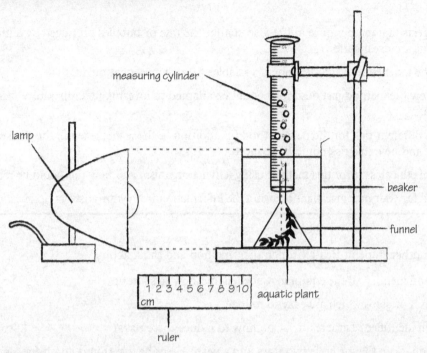

Figure 0.12: A diagram to show apparatus to investigate light intensity and rate of bubbles produced.

Now describe the steps needed to complete the investigation in a logical series of bullet points:

- Set up the equipment as shown in the diagram.

- Place the lamp at 10 cm from the beaker. Measure the volume of gas in the measuring cylinder, then start the timer.

- Record the volume of gas in the measuring cylinder after 2 minutes, 4 minutes and 6 minutes to obtain replicate results.

- Move the lamp to 20 cm from the beaker. Refill the measuring cylinder with water. Measure the volume of gas in the measuring cylinder, then start the timer.

- Record the volume of gas in the measuring cylinder after 2 minutes, 4 minutes and 6 minutes to obtain replicate results.

- Repeat at 30 cm, 40 cm and 50 cm.

Finally, we should identify any risks in the method and how these risks could be reduced.

Risks might include:

- Risk of electrocution from touching the lamp with wet hands. Dry your hands before touching the lamp.

- Risk of slipping on spilled water from filling the measuring cylinder to the top. Wipe up any spills immediately.

- Risk of glass measuring cylinder falling over and breaking. Clamp the measuring cylinder in place to avoid it falling and breaking.

CONTINUED

Now you try

1   A student suggests that temperature might also change the rate of bubbles produced by aquatic plants and plans an investigation.

    a   Identify the independent and dependent variables for this investigation.

    b   Suggest how the method just described could be adapted to investigate temperature instead of light intensity.

    c   Identify a different risk for the new method (in addition to those identified in the worked example), and how this risk could be reduced.

    d   Identify an ethical issue for this method using a living organism and how this could be reduced.

2   Write a method for your new investigation using the information from your answers to Question 1.

Peer assessment

Give feedback to another student. Read through their method and think about:

- Does the method identify all the equipment needed and how to set it up?

- Are there a series of steps which are easy to follow?

- Have risks been identified? Is there advice on how to reduce these risks?

Provide written feedback in the form of 'two stars and a wish': describe two things about the work that you liked and give one suggestion for improvement: 'It could be even better if…'.

Reflection

Think about your work when planning and writing out a method:

- How easy was it to put the method into a logical sequence of steps?

- Did you think of all the equipment you would need?

- Did a diagram help to explain how to set up the apparatus?

What could make it easier to plan writing a method next time? Try to think about writing methods when you read other experimental methods.

Recording results

When carrying out investigations you should record your results in a table of results. Tables help you to organise the data you collect so that it is easy to read and understand.

- Use ruled columns and rows and a border around your table to contain all the data.

- The first column should contain the independent variable. Write a heading to clearly identify the variable and the units (if it has any units).

- The other columns should be spaces to record your results from the dependent variable. If you are taking replicate readings there should be a column for each replicate, and an extra column for the mean result from the replicates.

- Make sure these columns have headings (and units if appropriate) as well.

When recording results in the table:

- Do not write the units with the values – the units are only needed in the heading for each column.

- Write results clearly – numbers such as 1 and 7 can be confused if not written carefully.

- Record to the maximum precision available. If a volume can be recorded to 0.1 cm³, and the value is exactly 3 cm³, record this as 3.0 cm³ to show that this is a precise reading.

- Ignore anomalous results when you calculate a mean. It is helpful to circle anomalous results to identify them.

- When calculating mean results use the same precision as the individual results.

WORKED EXAMPLE 0.4

In Worked Example 0.3, the results collected are not the final results. This is an example of how data collected during an experiment can sometimes need further processing.

The independent variable is the light intensity, which we changed by changing the distance of the lamp from the plant. This is the first column in the results table.

The dependent variable is the volume of gas collected every two minutes. We planned to measure the volume of gas at 0 minutes, 2 minutes, 4 minutes and 6 minutes. This allows us to calculate the volume of gas for three replicates at the same distance.

Table 0.10 is an example of a table we could use to record these results, filled with some data collected during an experiment:

Distance of lamp from plant / cm	Volume of gas in measuring cylinder / cm³			
	0 minutes	2 minutes	4 minutes	6 minutes
10	0.7	3.2	5.8	8.5
20	0.0	2.8	4.6	6.4
30	1.2	2.3	3.3	4.3
40	2.7	3.2	3.6	4.2
50	0.3	0.5	0.7	0.9

Table 0.10: Results table to collect results during an experiment.

To produce the final results, we must carry out some simple calculations by subtracting the previous value.

e.g. at a distance of 10 cm: result for 2 minutes = $3.2 - 0.7 = 2.5$ cm³

result for 4 minutes = $5.8 - 3.2 = 2.6$ cm³

result for 6 minutes = $8.5 - 5.8 = 2.7$ cm³

$$\text{mean} = \frac{2.5 + 2.6 + 2.7}{3} = 2.6 \text{ cm}^3$$

These calculated results are shown in Table 0.11 below, which has an extra column for the mean.

Distance of lamp from plant / cm	Volume of gas in measuring cylinder / cm³			
	2 minutes	4 minutes	6 minutes	mean
10	2.5	2.6	2.7	2.6
20	(2.8)	1.8	1.8	1.8
30	1.1	1.0	1.0	1.0
40	0.5	0.4	0.6	0.5
50	0.2	0.2	0.2	0.2

Table 0.11: Results table to collect results during an experiment.

The result for 20 cm at 2 minutes has been circled as an anomaly because this value of 2.8 cm³ is significantly different from the two other values at 20 cm of 1.8 cm³. We must therefore ignore this value when calculating the mean.

Now you try

1 A student investigates the hypothesis:

The number of organisms of each type depends on the distance from the sea at low tide.

They collect the following data:

2 m: anemone ×5, starfish ×3, crab ×6

4 m: anemone ×8, starfish ×1, crab ×8

6 m: anemone ×4, crab ×3, limpet ×9

8 m: limpet ×12, barnacle ×63

10 m: limpet ×3, barnacle ×72

a Identify the independent and dependent variables for this investigation.

b Draw a results table to present the data shown above. Add the data to your results table.

c Identify an ethical issue for this investigation and explain how this could be reduced.

d Identify the different types of data shown in these results.

2 Table 0.12 shows a set of data collected for an investigation into the effect of light intensity on the rate of production of bubbles of gas.

Distance of lamp from plant / cm	Volume of gas in measuring cylinder / cm³			
	0 minutes	3 minutes	6 minutes	9 minutes
15	0.3	3.5	6.6	9.8
30	0.9	2.8	4.9	6.9
45	0.5	1.8	4.5	4.5
60	0.2	0.8	1.3	2.0
75	1.0	1.1	1.2	1.3

Table 0.12: Results table for investigation into aquatic plant producing gas for different light intensities.

CONTINUED

a   Produce a results table to record the replicates and mean results from this data.

b   Complete the results for the replicates in the table.

c   Identify any anomalous results by circling them on your table.

d   Calculate the mean result for each distance.

Making and recording observations, measurements and estimates

Understanding scales

It is important to read scales correctly to ensure that results are both accurate and precise. One of the most common mistakes when making measurements is misunderstanding the scale and the value of each smaller interval on the scale.

Figure 0.13 shows a 100 cm³ measuring cylinder.

The first important point when measuring the volume of liquids is to read to the bottom of the meniscus.

Many people will look at this and state the volume is 71 cm³, but this is not correct. To identify the volume, we need to understand the scale. The values are marked in multiples of 10 cm³. Between each 10 cm³ mark there are five intervals (four smaller unlabelled lines dividing five intervals). To calculate the value of each interval we must divide the total change across these intervals (10 cm³) by the number of intervals (5). This tells us that each small interval is 2 cm³, so we can read the full scale as shown in Figure 0.14.

Whenever you are reading a value from a scale you must check how many intervals are between the values shown. Divide the difference between the two values by the number of intervals.

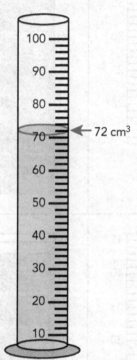

Figure 0.13: Scale on a 100 cm³ measuring cylinder.

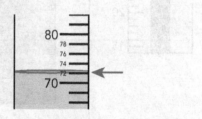

Figure 0.14: Understanding the scale on a 100 cm³ measuring cylinder. We can now see that the volume in this measuring cylinder is actually 72 cm³.

WORKED EXAMPLE 0.5

A student working on the aquatic plant investigation in the previous worked examples made the observations shown in Table 0.13, which extends over the next two pages.

Temperature / °C	Volume of gas in measuring cylinder / cm³			
	0 minutes	2 minutes	4 minutes	6 minutes

Temperature / °C	Volume of gas in measuring cylinder / cm³			
	0 minutes	2 minutes	4 minutes	6 minutes

CONTINUED

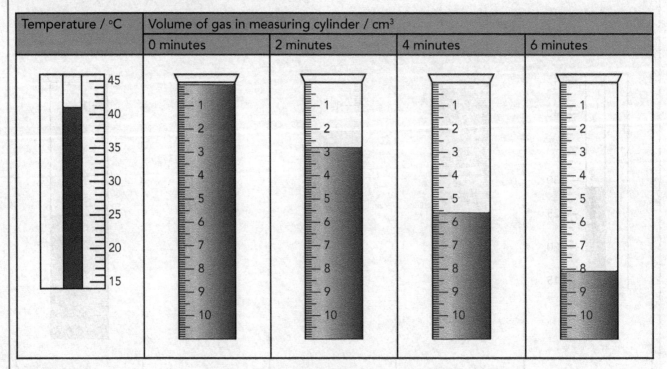

Temperature / °C	Volume of gas in measuring cylinder / cm³			
	0 minutes	2 minutes	4 minutes	6 minutes

Table 0.13: Observations in an experiment into effect of temperature on rate of production of gas.

The student read the results for the first set of replicates shown in the table and started to complete Table 0.14 below.

Temperature / °C	Volume of gas in measuring cylinder / cm³			
	0 minutes	2 minutes	4 minutes	6 minutes
21	0.2	1.0	1.8	2.7

Table 0.14: Results for an experiment into effect of temperature on rate of production of gas.

Now you try

1   Complete a copy of Table 0.14 using the information in Table 0.13.

    a   Produce a results table to record the replicates and mean results from this data.

    b   Complete the replicates in the table.

    c   Identify any anomalous results by circling them on your table.

    d   Calculate the mean result for each temperature.

Biological drawings

Sometimes you will need to draw diagrams of organisms. These could be from real organisms or from photographs.

You should:

- Make good use of the space provided – your diagram should use well over half of the space. But do not try to make your diagram too big or you might squash the diagram at one side. You may also need some space to add labels to your diagram.

- Draw an outline of the main shape first.

- Add features in proportion to the overall size – estimate the distance along the main shape, using quarters or thirds, to roughly keep everything the correct size.

- Add details that look important, such as eyes, and fins.

- Anything that repeats a lot, such as scales on fish, do not need to be drawn.

- Do not shade or colour your drawing.

- If asked to add labels – use a ruler and pencil to draw a line to the feature, and make sure the line ends on the feature. Add the name of the feature in the space at the other end of the line, away from the diagram.

WORKED EXAMPLE 0.6

A student is asked to make a large drawing of the fish shown in Figure 0.15.

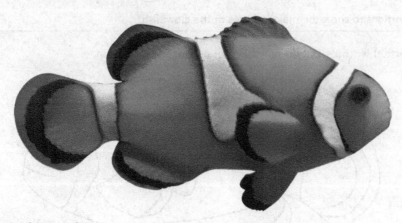

Figure 0.15: Photograph of a clownfish.

The first step is to draw a large outline of the fish:

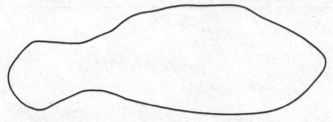

Figure 0.16: Outline of the clownfish.

Then start to add the main features of the fish, such as fins, taking note of how long the main body is and the relative proportions:

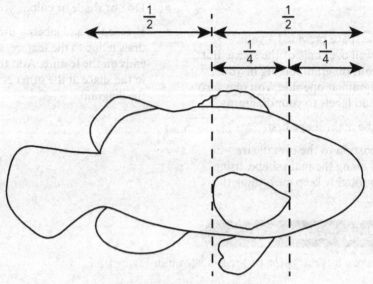

Figure 0.17: Use proportions to show the main features of the clownfish.

Finally, add any important features, but do not shade or colour your diagram:

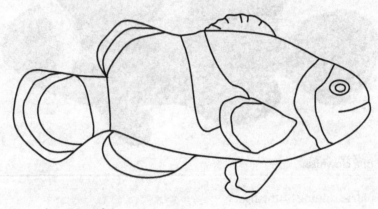

Figure 0.18: Finished drawing of the clownfish.

CONTINUED

Now you try

1   Make a large drawing of the shark shown in Figure 0.19.

Figure 0.19: A shark.

2   Make a large drawing of the turtle shown in Figure 0.20.

Figure 0.20: A turtle.

Peer assessment

Give feedback to another student. Look at their drawing and think about:

- Does the drawing take up over half of the space?
- Does the diagram show the main features?
- Are the sizes approximately similar to the photo?

Provide written feedback in the form of 'two stars and a wish': describe two things about the work
that you liked and give one suggestion for improvement: 'It could be even better if…'.

Interpreting and evaluating experimental observations and data

You need to be able to present and understand data from investigations in the form of graphs. The evaluation of data means looking at a set of data and identifying if results produce a consistent pattern or trend, or if any results stand out as anomalous.

Representing data graphically

There are four types of graphical representation of data you need to understand: bar charts, histograms, line graphs and pie charts.

Bar charts

We use a bar chart when there is no direct link between the values for the independent variable. For example, we might count the numbers of different types of organism. The type of organism is a qualitative variable, and there is no numerical link between each type of organism. For example, there is no numerical link between a crab and a starfish.

To show the data in a bar chart we place the categoric variable on the x-axis, with spaces between each bar to show there is no link between the bars. We then plot the number of each type of organism up the y-axis.

The bars in a bar chart must all be an equal width and have equal spaces between each bar.

Histograms

A histogram is like a bar chart but is for a continuous independent variable.

For example, a set of data shows the lengths of fish caught. Each fish will have a different length to all the other fish, and very few fish will have the same length. By plotting length on the x-axis, we can create equal groups of length such as:

- 0 to less than 10 cm
- 10 to less than 20 cm
- 20 to less than 30 cm
- 30 to less than 40 cm
- 40 to less than 50 cm.

We then count the number of fish in each group and plot a graph, which looks similar to a bar chart. The difference here is that the bars on a histogram must touch each other – the length of the fish is a continuous variable so each bar represents the number of fish *between* each of the lengths represented by the bar.

Line graphs

When plotting a line graph the independent variable must go on the x-axis, and the dependent variable on the y-axis. The only exception to this is when plotting changes related to depth in the ocean – the depth can then be on the y-axis with 0 starting at the top to better represent changes in deeper water.

When plotting the points use small crosses (x) or small dots in circles (⊙) to clearly identify the points. Use a sharp pencil so the points are precise – plots must be accurate to within half a small square so if the point plotted is wider than half a small square it will be incorrect.

When all the points are plotted join them with ruled lines. Or if there is a clear trend, draw a line of best fit – this ignores anomalous points that do not fit the trend. A line of best fit may be a straight line (Figure 0.21a) or could be a curve (Figure 0.21b). Instructions will often tell you if you need to draw a line of best fit or join points with straight lines – make sure you check for these instructions.

KEY WORDS

trend: a general pattern in data showing an increase, decrease or remaining constant, when smaller changes are ignored

bar chart: a graph showing the relationship between a categoric variable and a quantitative variable

histogram: a graph showing the frequency of a continuous variable

line graph: a graph showing the relationship between two quantitative variables

pie chart: a chart showing the proportions of different parts making up the total

categoric variable: a variable that has limited values or discrete groups

line of best fit: a line drawn on a graph to show the general trend in the data plotted

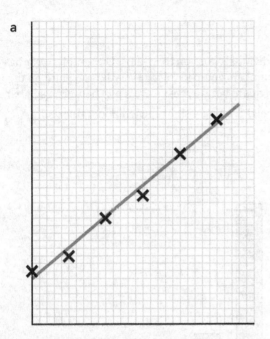 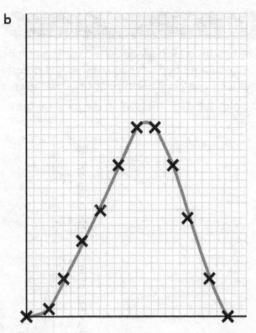

Figure 0.21: a A straight line of best fit; **b** a curved line of best fit.

Pie charts

A pie chart shows information about proportions. It is often used to show qualitative data.

You are unlikely to have to draw a pie chart for this subject, but you should understand what pie charts show.

For any graph, it is important to use the space available – the scales on axes on line graphs, bar charts and histograms should extend over half of the space available in both directions (if not, you should consider doubling the scale).

Numerical scales must also be regular, so the intervals on the scale are all equal values.

Try to use scales that are easy to plot and read – good intervals on graph paper using grids of 10×10 squares are usually in increments such as 1, 2, 5 or 10. This makes it easier to read the values of smaller squares. Avoid using intervals of 3, 6 or 7 as these make plotting and reading graphs very difficult.

WORKED EXAMPLE 0.7

A student is provided with the data shown in Table 0.15 about organisms in an aquarium and asked to draw an appropriate graph to show the data.

Type of organism	Number of individuals in aquarium
starfish	2
seahorse	5
shrimp	18
crab	3

Table 0.15: Number of each type of organism in an aquarium.

The first step is to identify the independent variable. In this example this is a categoric variable, the type of organism. The best graph to plot is therefore a bar chart.

The type of organism must go on the x-axis. The number of individuals goes on the y-axis. Our graph paper has a grid of 5 large squares by 5 large squares, so it is easiest if the numbers go up in '5' for every large square on the y-axis. For the x-axis we can place one type of organism in each large square but we must leave a gap between each bar.

Finally, we plot the data carefully so the bars are the correct height, using a sharp pencil and a ruler.

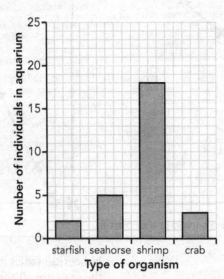

Figure 0.22: A bar chart for results shown in Table 0.15.

This data could also be represented as a pie chart, shown in Figure 0.23.

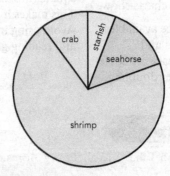

Figure 0.23: A pie chart for results shown in Table 0.15.

The length of each shrimp was recorded in Table 0.16.

Length of shrimp / cm	Number of shrimp
0 to less than 1	8
1 to less than 2	5
2 to less than 3	3
3 to less than 4	2

Table 0.16: Length of shrimp in aquarium.

CONTINUED

In this data the independent variable is a continuous measurement, divided into groups of equal length. This is best represented as a histogram.

On the same size graph paper as before we now plot length of shrimp on the x-axis (with each large square representing 1 cm) and the number of shrimp on the y-axis (with each large square representing 2 shrimp). The bars must touch each other so each bar is a full large square wide. Again, we plot the bars carefully with a ruler and a sharp pencil.

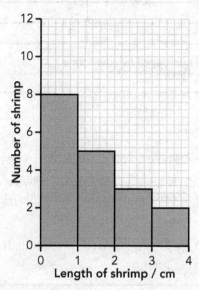

Figure 0.24: A histogram for results shown in Table 0.16.

Now you try

1 Plot a histogram of the data shown in Table 0.17.

Width of crab / cm	Number of crabs
0 to less than 2 cm	12
2 to less than 4 cm	6
4 to less than 6 cm	2
6 to less than 8 cm	3
8 to less than 10 cm	1

Table 0.17: Lengths of crabs found on a rocky shore.

CONTINUED

2   Plot a line graph of the data shown in Table 0.18. Join each point on your graph with a straight line.

Year	Estimated number of fish / thousands
2000	10
2005	15
2010	18
2015	7
2020	3

Table 0.18: Changes in the estimated number of fish over time.

Self assessment

Look at your line graph from Question 2:

*   Does the area containing plotted points take up over half of the space on your graph?

*   Do both scales have regular intervals? (Is there an equal space between each of the years shown? Is there an equal distance on the *y*-axis between the values for 1, 2, 3, 4 all the way to 18?)

*   Have you labelled both axes?

*   Are the points plotted carefully with small thin crosses or precise small dots in circles?

*   Have you joined each plot with a ruled line?

Trends, patterns and conclusions

When looking at data we have collected, or data provided to us about investigations, we need to be able to identify if there are trends or patterns, and if there is a correlation between the independent variable and dependent variable.

A positive correlation is shown when an increase in the independent variable occurs at the same time as an increase in the dependent variable. Examples of positive correlations are shown in Figure 0.25.

KEY WORD

correlation: a pattern between two variables; this *may* be due to a causal link between them but a correlation is not proof of cause

A negative correlation is shown when an increase in the independent variable occurs at the same time as a decrease in the dependent variable. Examples of negative correlations are shown in in Figure 0.26.

No correlation is shown when an increase in the independent variable does not directly affect the dependent variable. Examples of results with no correlations are shown in in Figure 0.27.

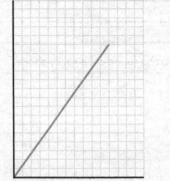 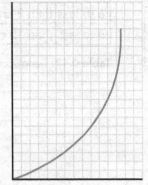

Figure 0.25: Examples of positive correlations.

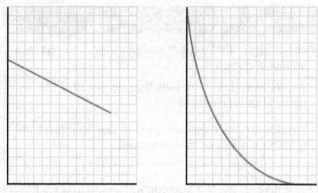

Figure 0.26: Examples of negative correlations.

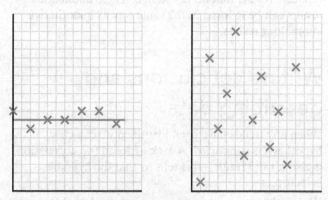

Figure 0.27: Examples of no correlation.

Sometimes a correlation (positive or negative) can show a direct link between the two variables. For example, doubling the independent variable results in doubling (or halving) the dependent variable. This type of correlation can be described as **directly proportional** or **inversely proportional**.

> ## KEY WORDS
>
> **directly proportional:** a positive correlation when the ratio between the independent and dependant variables is constant, for example, doubling the independent variable also doubles the dependent variable
>
> **inversely proportional:** a negative correlation when the ratio between the independent and dependant variables is constant, for example, doubling the independent variable halves the dependent variable

Data shown in line graphs can show variation over time, particularly when data is collected from habitats, such as fishing data on catches. The data shown in Figure 0.28 shows changes in the global catch of bluefin tuna from 1960 to 2020.

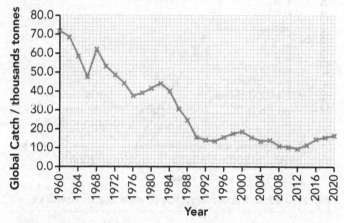

Figure 0.28: Line graph showing changes in global bluefin tuna catch.

It is important to look for an overall trend – in Figure 0.28 the catch has decreased overall from 1960 to 2020. Each year there are small variations, but overall, we can see a decrease in the number of fish caught. Once an overall trend has been identified, try to look for changes in the trend – here the steepest decrease is between 1960 and 1990, with more gradual increases and decreases between 1990 and 2020.

Intercepts and gradients

When analysing data, it can be useful to calculate when a plotted line might meet an axis. This point is called an **intercept**. This can be calculated by extending a line from your graph (**extrapolation**) until it reaches the axis. You can then read the value at which the line intercepts this axis. An example is shown in Figure 0.29.

> ## KEY WORDS
>
> **intercept:** the value on an axis when a line meets the axis
>
> **extrapolation:** extending a line on a line graph beyond the range of data collected

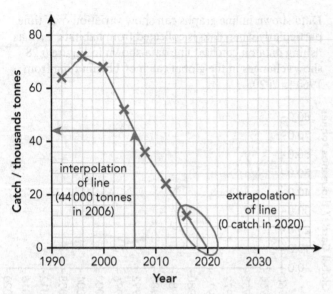

Figure 0.29: Extrapolating a line to estimate an intercept.

It can also be useful to use lines on graphs to estimate values between plotted data (interpolation).

Evaluation of data and observations

You learnt in the 'Planning experiments and investigations' section of this chapter about planning to repeat readings in investigations to identify anomalous results. Look out for anomalous results in data – these may be in tables of results, or in data plotted on graphs. Anomalous results can be ignored when identifying trends. But when writing conclusions you should identify anomalous points and suggest reasons for anomalies occurring. This will help to identify results to discuss in the next section on evaluating methods. It may be possible that these anomalies are due to human errors such as reading the wrong value or recording a measurement too late. If you think these may be a cause of error, you should try to repeat these measurements at the time and replace the anomalous result.

Qualitative results can also contain anomalous results – when observations are repeated you may identify replicate results that do not match. These anomalous results can be ignored in the same way as quantitative anomalous results.

Writing conclusions and describing data

When any trends have been identified we can check if the hypothesis is supported. A lack of trend (no correlation) is also a valid result – this tells us that the hypothesis is incorrect.

We can then write a conclusion about the data. Make sure you answer the following questions in a conclusion:

- What is the overall trend?

- Is the trend directly proportional or inversely proportional?

- Are there any variations in the trend? Does the gradient change?

- Did you record any anomalous results? (What did you do about these?)

- Does the data support the hypothesis or prediction? (If either has been given.)

- What does your conclusion mean? (Can you explain what you have found out?)

- Quote relevant data from the graph to support your conclusion.

SKILLS TIP 0.12

To calculate the gradient of a straight line on a graph:

1   Select two points on the line that are at least half of the line on the graph apart.

2   Draw a right-angle triangle between the two points.

CONTINUED

3   Calculate the gradient using the vertical and horizontal sides of the triangle: gradient $= \dfrac{y_1}{x_1}$

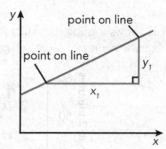

Figure 0.30: How to calculate the gradient from a graph.

WORKED EXAMPLE 0.8

Figure 0.31 shows the change in temperature with increasing depth of water.

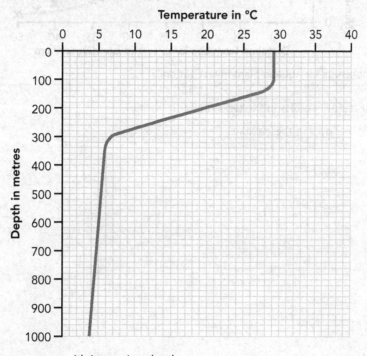

Figure 0.31: Changes in temperature with increasing depth.

Describe the pattern in the data shown in Figure 0.31.

CONTINUED

The overall trend is a decrease in temperature as depth increases. However, the change is not a constant decrease. The temperature remains fairly constant for the first 100 metres, then temperature decreases rapidly from about 130 m to 300 m. After 300 m the decrease in temperature is much more gradual.

Now you try

1   Figure 0.32 shows a graph of results for an investigation into the effect of moving a lamp away from an aquatic plant on volume of gas produced by the plant.

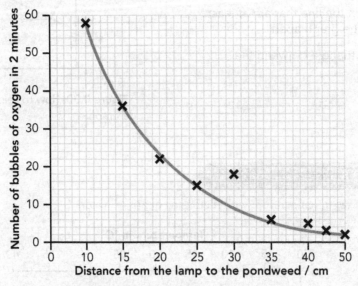

Figure 0.32: Graph of results for aquatic plant investigation.

a   Identify any anomalous results in the data plotted.

b   Describe the trend shown in these results.

2   Figure 0.33 shows a graph of the solubility of two chemicals from 0 to 100 °C.

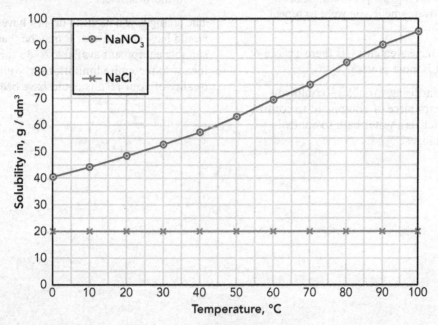

Figure 0.33: Graph of solubility of two chemicals at different temperatures.

a   Describe the change in solubility for NaCl.

b   Describe the change in solubility for NaNO₃.

Evaluating methods and suggesting possible improvements

Evaluating methods and techniques

It is important to avoid stating 'human mistakes' as sources of errors – this type of mistake should be recognised and corrected during an investigation. Evaluations should focus on the methods used and equipment selected.

Identifying sources of error

Sources of error are unavoidable limitations in the design of the experiment:

- Uncertainty in measurements – a lack of accuracy or precision in the measuring equipment used.

- Difficulty standardising variables – some standardised variables may be difficult to keep constant. Any small changes in the standardised variables may also affect the results.

- Difficulty measuring the dependent variable – this is particularly difficult if recording results at a fixed time, or if you have to use your judgement about when a colour change happens, for example.

Suggesting improvements

When you have identified where results could have gone wrong you should suggest practical ideas on how these could be overcome if you were to repeat the investigation:

- Uncertainty in measurements – is there a piece of equipment that is more precise?

- Difficulty standardising variables – could you have used an extra piece of equipment to control this variable, such as a water bath to control temperature changes?

- Difficulty measuring the dependent variable – could you use a digital probe to record changes over time, such as a temperature sensor instead of a thermometer?

The changes you identify do not have to be changes you would have carried out. It may be that you do not have suitable equipment available to do this. The important idea is to recognise limitations in your data and how the quality of your results could have been improved.

WORKED EXAMPLE 0.9

A student investigated the effect of light intensity on the rate of gas production in an aquatic plant. They carried out the following method.

- Set up the equipment as shown in the diagram:

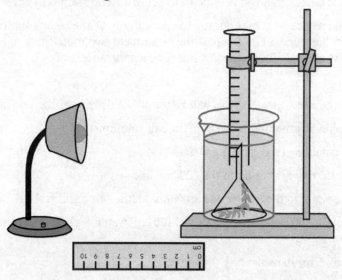

Figure 0.34: Equipment for investigating effect of light intensity on rate of gas production in a plant.

- Place a lamp 10 cm from the beaker, switch on and wait 2 minutes.
- Start a stopwatch and time 2 minutes.
- Record the volume of gas collected after 2 minutes in a results table.
- Repeat with the lamp at different distances from the beaker: 20 cm, 30 cm.

The results are shown in Table 0.19.

Distance from beaker / cm	Volume of gas produced / cm³
10	9
20	3
30	1

Table 0.19: Results for investigation into effect of moving a lamp further from an aquatic plant.

In this investigation the student has used a 100 cm³ measuring cylinder, but the largest volume recorded was only 9 cm³. A more appropriate measuring cylinder would have been a 10 cm³ measuring cylinder as the results can be recorded more precisely with a smaller measuring cylinder. This would allow the results to be recorded to 0.1 cm³ or 0.2 cm³ instead.

The student has also not checked how much gas was in the measuring cylinder at the start of the 2 minutes for each distance. It is likely that some gas will have been produced before they started the stopwatch so this will affect the results.

The lamp may have produced heat and warmed the beaker containing the plant, and this could have affected the results. To overcome this, they could have placed the beaker in a larger container of water to maintain a more constant temperature for the plant.

CONTINUED

The student has only measured the volume of gas at three distances. This might be because so little gas was produced at 30 cm, but they should have collected more results at distances between those collected such as 15 cm and 25 cm. This would have provided five different values, which would allow students to identify if there is a clear trend. It is difficult to prove a trend from only three values.

Finally, there are no replicate results – there is no way to check if any of the results shown are anomalous. To improve this, the student could repeat the experiment two more times at each distance to identify anomalous results and calculate a mean value for each distance.

Now you try

1 A student investigated the effect of salinity of salt water on the density of the salt water.

They carried out the following method to prepare the salt solutions:

- Use an electronic balance to measure 4 g of salt.

- Pour water into a 250 cm³ beaker up to the 100 cm³ line.

- Add the salt to the water in the beaker and stir until all the salt has dissolved.

- Repeat with 3 g salt in 100 cm³ water, 2 g salt in 100 cm³ water, 1 g salt in 100 cm³ water and no salt in 100 cm³ water.

a Identify a source of error in measuring the water.

b Identify a source of error in measuring the salt.

c Suggest improvements to the method for both these issues and explain why each will improve the accuracy of the investigation.

2 The student used the salt water samples prepared in Question 1 to investigate the density of each sample. They:

- Placed a 10 cm³ measuring cylinder on a balance and pressed the 'tare' button to zero the balance.

- Poured water from the 4 g salt water into the measuring cylinder up to the 10 cm³ line.

- Recorded the mass of salt water.

- Repeated this for each sample of salt water.

The results are shown in Table 0.20.

Mass of salt in 100 cm³ water / g	Mass of 10 cm³ of salt water sample / g	Density of salt water sample / g cm⁻³
4	10.7	1.07
3	10.6	1.06
2	10.6	1.06
1	10.2	1.02
0	10.0	1.00

Table 0.20: Results for investigation into density of salt water samples.

a Identify an anomalous result in the data shown in Table 0.20.

b The student repeats the reading for the anomalous result and obtains the same value as the result in the table. Use your answers to Question 1 to suggest why.

SUMMARY

The scientific process is a sequence of stages to develop a hypothesis, design a method, collect data, analyse the data and evaluate the investigation.
Data can be quantitative (numerical) or qualitative (non-numerical observations).
You need to choose suitable apparatus to collect valid, precise and accurate data.
You also need to choose a suitable method to investigate a hypothesis.
When planning investigations, it is important to identify the independent, dependent and standardised variables.
It is also important to communicate a method in simple, easy-to-follow steps.
You need to record observations in tables with columns and rows, identifying the independent and dependent variables (and their units).
You should complete results legibly and precisely in results tables.
Data should be presented in a suitable form. You need to choose from a bar chart, histogram or line graph. A line of best fit can be drawn on a line graph where there is a clear trend.
Trends can be interpreted to describe positive or negative relationships between the independent and dependent variables.
Data and methods can be evaluated to identify possible sources of error and how these could be reduced.

EXAM-STYLE QUESTIONS

1   A student plans to investigate the density of salt water samples.

   a   Describe the equipment needed and a suitable method to prepare
       five different samples of salt water at different salinities.   [4]

   b   The student carries out an investigation into the density of the
       samples by measuring the mass of exactly 20 cm³ of each sample
       of salt water. Draw a results table to record the results.   [3]

   c   The student calculated the density of a 20 cm³ water sample to
       be 1.04 g cm⁻³.

   Use the formula: $density = \dfrac{mass}{volume}$ to calculate the mass of this
   sample of salt water.   [1]

   [Total: 8]

COMMAND WORDS

describe: state the points of a topic / give characteristics and main features

calculate: work out from given facts, figures or information

CONTINUED

2   A student investigated the pH of a sample of water as carbon dioxide
    is bubbled into the water. They used a pH probe to measure the pH
    and repeated each measurement three times. They collected the
    results shown in Table 0.21.

Time / min	pH			
	run 1	run 2	run 3	mean
0	8.3	8.3	8.3	8.3
2	8.2	8.1	8.1	8.1
4	8.0	8.0	8.1	8.0
6	7.8	7.8	7.9	7.8
8	8.0	7.5	7.7	
10	7.5	7.4	7.5	7.5

Table 0.21: Results for investigation into effect of carbon dioxide in
water on pH.

a   Identify the anomalous result for time = 8 minutes.   [1]
b   Calculate the mean result for time = 8 minutes.   [1]
c   Plot a graph of the mean pH against time. Draw a line of best fit. [4]
d   State a conclusion for the results shown in Table 0.21.   [1]

                                                            [Total: 7]

3   Sketch a large diagram of the crab shown in Figure 1.
    Label a pincer on your diagram.   [Total: 4]

Figure 1

4   Outline a method for an investigation into the hypothesis:

    The number of starfish on a shore depends on the distance from the sea.

    In your outline describe:
    • the equipment you would use
    • how you would use this equipment
    • the independent and dependent variables
    • safety and ethical precautions you would take.   [Total: 6]

COMMAND WORDS

identify: name /
select / recognise

state: express in
clear terms

sketch: make a
simple freehand
drawing showing the
key features, taking
care over proportions

> Chapter 1
The Earth and its oceans

IN THIS CHAPTER YOU WILL:

- describe the motion of the Earth, the Moon and the Sun relative to each other and state what keeps them in regular motion

- describe the internal structure of the Earth and explain how this structure creates features that shape our oceans

- identify the five oceans and describe how water flows around and between them

- describe and explain the regular changes in tides

- describe tsunamis and rip currents and explain how they form.

MARINE SCIENCE IN CONTEXT

Do migrating turtles have a compass?

Year by year, sea turtles around the world return to the beaches they hatched on to lay their eggs (Figure 1.1). How do they know how to get there? Scientists have known for a long time that turtles, like many other animals, find their way using the invisible lines of the Earth's magnetic field. Turtles contain a magnetic material called magnetite in their heads, and scientists think they use this as an internal compass to find their way using the Earth's magnetic field. But how are the turtles able to find their way to the exact beach where they hatched?

Figure 1.1: Olive ridley sea turtles returning to a beach in Costa Rica.

We now know that each coastline has its own unique magnetic field based on the rocks and the shape of the coast. This helps the turtles, who remember and use this magnetic field to find their way home. However, this magnetic field is not as fixed and permanent as we might think.

The internal structure of the Earth offers clues to changes that have taken place through time. The Earth's magnetic field is created by the Earth's core, and this magnetic field has changed throughout the history of the Earth. Some of these changes in the magnetic field have been measured. The changes in the magnetic field affect the location of turtle nesting sites along beaches.

Discussion questions

1 If the Earth acts as a big magnet, what might be happening to the magnetic material inside the Earth to cause the magnetic field to change direction?

2 What might be the advantages to turtles of returning to the same beach to lay their eggs?

1.1 Structure of the Earth

The Earth is one of eight planets orbiting the Sun in the Solar System (Figure 1.2). The Sun is the largest object in the Solar System and it has the greatest gravitational pull (gravity) on other objects, particularly planets, in the Solar System. Gravitational pull keeps the Earth in orbit around the Sun. The Earth's position as the third planet from the Sun helps to create the ideal temperatures for life to exist on the Earth.

As the Earth orbits the Sun, the Earth is also spinning on its axis every 24 hours (one day).

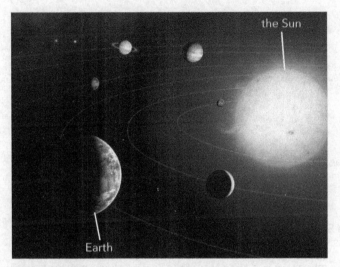

Figure 1.2: The Sun and the eight planets we now know orbit the Sun.

Figure 1.3 shows how the Earth spins on its axis at an angle of 23.5 degrees, so for most of the year there is unequal exposure to light and heat from the Sun on the surface of the Earth. In Figure 1.3 you can see that the Southern Hemisphere is exposed to more heat and light than the Northern Hemisphere during summer in the Southern Hemisphere.

The intensity of the Sun is greatest near to the Equator and between the Tropics of Cancer and Capricorn. The more intense heating in these regions continues throughout the year. In Figure 1.3 the Sun is directly over the Tropic of Capricorn in the Southern Hemisphere, causing this part of the Earth to experience the most intense light.

KEY WORDS

Solar System*: eight planets and their moons in orbit around the Sun

gravity / gravitational pull: the force that exists between any two objects with mass

orbit: the path of an object as it moves around a larger object

axis*: the imaginary line between the Earth's North Pole and South Pole

hemisphere*: half of a sphere; the Earth can be considered to be made of two hemispheres divided by the Equator

Equator: an imaginary line drawn round the Earth, halfway between the North Pole and the South Pole

tropics / tropical zones: the region between the Tropic of Cancer and the Tropic of Capricorn, between which the Sun moves directly overhead during a year

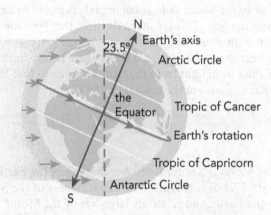

Figure 1.3: How the Earth's axis is tilted at 23.5° causing uneven heating in the Northern and Southern hemispheres.

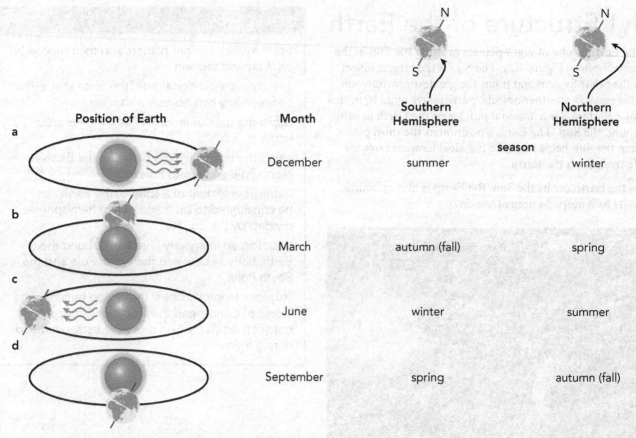

Figure 1.4: How the Earth experiences seasons as it orbits the Sun.

Position of Earth	Month	Southern Hemisphere season	Northern Hemisphere season
a	December	summer	winter
b	March	autumn (fall)	spring
c	June	winter	summer
d	September	spring	autumn (fall)

Light from the Sun only reaches the southern limit of the Arctic Circle, resulting in no light on any of the Earth's land or ocean north of this line. The Antarctic Circle, near to the South Pole, is completely exposed to light from the Sun. This results in daylight that lasts for weeks or months, but the light intensity is very low compared to near the equator. At the poles, there is very limited heating from light from the Sun. This means that the polar regions are the coldest on the Earth.

The Moon is a natural **satellite** that orbits the Earth every 27.5 days (Figure 1.5). The closeness of the Moon to the Earth, and relatively large size of the Moon compared to the Earth, causes a strong gravitational pull between them. This keeps the Moon in orbit around the Earth. This gravitational pull between the Earth and the Moon also has a large effect on the water in seas and oceans, causing tides (see Section 1.4).

The Earth takes $365\frac{1}{4}$ days to complete one full orbit of the Sun. As the Earth moves around the Sun, the Earth's axis continues to point in the same direction. This causes the Northern Hemisphere and the Southern Hemisphere to experience seasons because the number of hours of daylight changes during the year. Longer days, by which we mean longer periods of daylight, and greater exposure to more energy from the Sun, cause more warming of the Earth's surface in summer months. Shorter days, with less exposure to energy from the Sun, cause cooler weather in winter months. You can see this in Figure 1.4.

KEY WORDS

satellite: any object that orbits a planet

Figure 1.5: The Earth and Moon with the Sun in the distance.

ACTIVITY 1.1

Modelling day and night

You will need:

- a lamp
- a globe of the Earth.

For this whole-class activity, use a lamp to represent the Sun. This activity will work best in a darkened room.

- If you have a globe, use that to represent the Earth (Figure 1.6).

- You could use an orange with a pencil sticking through it instead, but make sure that the pencil is at an angle (around 23.5°) to the vertical.

Figure 1.6: Modelling changes each day, month and year.

CONTINUED

- Begin by turning the 'Earth' anticlockwise on its axis, assuming you are looking downward over the North Pole. This demonstrates why we experience day and night.

- Move the 'Earth' slowly around the 'Sun' in a large circle; this models a complete year. Rotate the 'Earth' on its axis at different positions in its journey round the 'Sun'; this models day / night at different positions around the Sun.

- Observe how the light reaches the North Pole or South Pole only when that pole is pointing towards the Sun.

- Investigate the difference in the length of the day in both hemispheres as the Earth moves around the Sun.

- Discuss how the length of day changes near to the poles.

- Discuss the intensity of light near the poles compared with the intensity of light near the equator.

The Earth is a rocky planet, but the rock is only solid at and near to the surface. Figure 1.7 shows a cross-section of the Earth, showing how the solid rocks at the surface form a thin layer called the crust. The crust beneath the ocean has a greater density and varies in thickness from 3 to 10 km. Continental crust has a lower density and usually varies in thickness from 35 to 40 km, though continental crust can be as much as 100 km in thickness.

Beneath the crust is a much thicker layer (the mantle), which is made of viscous molten rock called magma.

KEY WORDS

crust: outermost solid layer of the Earth

mantle: the region of the Earth found between the crust and the core

viscous: describes a liquid that flows slowly

magma: hot semi-liquid rock found below or within the crust

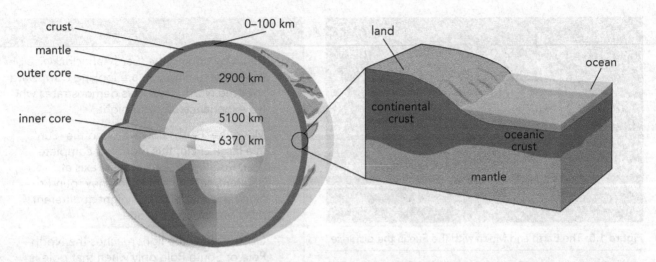

Figure 1.7: Cross-section of Earth showing relative depths of crust, including oceanic and continental, mantle and core.

Beneath the mantle is the core, made almost entirely of metal, particularly iron. The core is solid in the centre and molten around this.

An important effect of the iron in the Earth's core is that this creates a magnetic field around the Earth (Figure 1.8). We use the Earth's magnetic field for navigation. A compass uses a magnet that can freely rotate to align with the Earth's magnetic field and point to the magnetic North Pole. The Earth's magnetic field is important in helping some species to navigate during migration, as we saw at the beginning of the chapter.

KEY WORDS

core: the very hot, dense centre of the Earth

iron: a metallic element with magnetic properties

species: organisms that are able to breed and produce fertile offspring

navigate: the process of plotting a course from one place to another

migration: movement of animals from one region to another, usually in response to changes in the seasons

Questions

1 Name the force that keeps the Earth in orbit around the Sun.

2 Draw a cross-section of the Earth and label the layers found inside.

3 What produces the magnetic field around the Earth?

Figure 1.8: Earth's magnetic field.

1.2 Plate tectonics

Volcanoes and major earthquakes only occur in some regions of the Earth, and these regions often form patterns around the Earth (Figure 1.9).

It was only in the 1960s that the theory of plate tectonics was developed to help explain the distribution of earthquakes and volcanoes, and why these features exist.

In Section 1.1 we saw that the Earth's structure consisted of a core, surrounded by semi-molten rock called the mantle, covered with a relatively thin solid layer of rock called the crust that floats on top of the mantle.

Tectonic plate theory describes how radioactive decay of atoms in the Earth's core heats the mantle, creating convection currents in the mantle (Figure 1.10).

The convection currents create tension in the crust as the mantle moves in different directions beneath the crust, causing the crust to break into large pieces called tectonic plates (Figure 1.11).

> ## KEY WORDS
>
> theory of plate tectonics: a theory developed in the 1960s that helps explain the formation of some of the important features on the Earth's surface and how the continents move
>
> convection current: the transfer of thermal energy (heat energy) by the motion of a fluid
>
> tectonic plates: large sections of crust

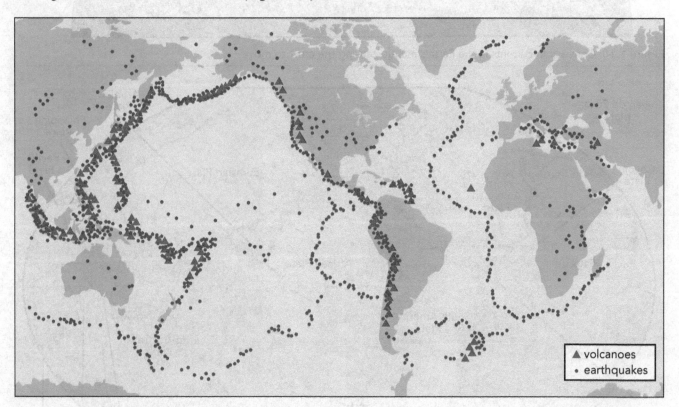

Figure 1.9: Earthquakes and volcanoes around the Earth.

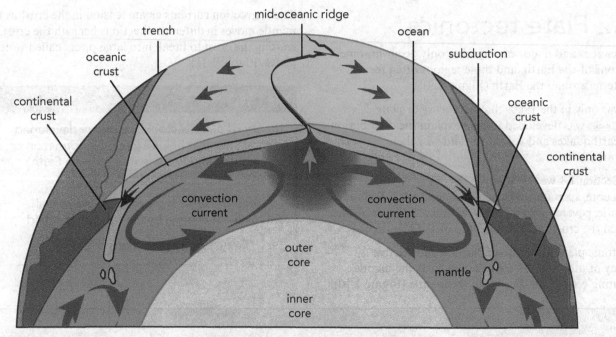

Figure 1.10: Convection currents in the Earth's mantle causing the crust to move.

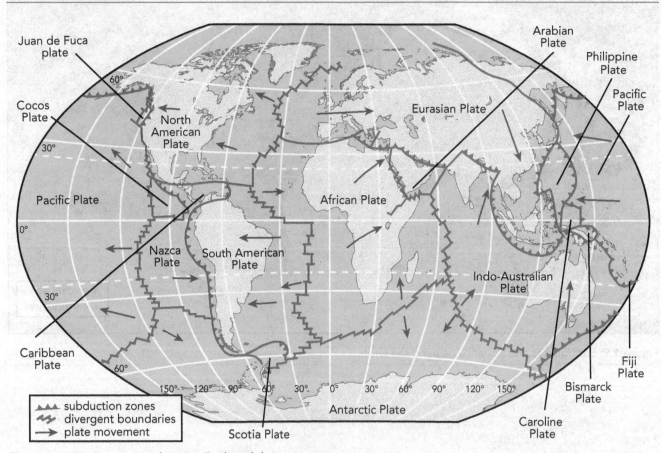

Figure 1.11: Main tectonic plates on Earth and their movement.

ACTIVITY 1.2

Modelling convection currents

> **You will need:**
>
> - a tripod and gauze
> - a Bunsen burner
> - a glass beaker
> - water
> - coffee granules.

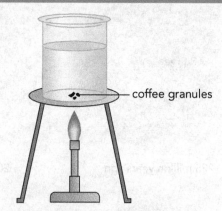

Figure 1.12: Equipment to demonstrate convection currents.

Use the equipment shown in Figure 1.12 to see convection currents occur. If you do not have this equipment, you could use a different container of water (e.g. a saucepan) over a different heat source (e.g. a cooker hob). Any soluble solid with a dark colour can be used to show the convection currents.

> **Safety:** take care when heating and when using flames – hot liquids and equipment can cause burns. Follow all safety instructions from your teacher.

When you heat the water, observe the direction in which the colour from the granules moves, both in the water and at the surface. What happens if you add small floating objects to the surface in the middle of the water? Compare what you have seen with what you have learned about convection currents in the Earth's mantle. Discuss what you observe with the rest of the class.

Self-assessment

How well did you complete this activity? Rate your work according to the following scheme for each of the points listed:

🙂 if you did it really well

😐 if you made a good attempt at it and partly succeeded

☹ if you did not try to do it or did not succeed.

- I set up the equipment correctly.
- I created a convection current and observed this using the coloured substance.
- I carried out the activity safely.

The theory of plate tectonics describes how this movement of tectonic plates has occurred over hundreds of millions of years. Using computer models, we can trace the movements of the plates back in time. Figure 1.13 shows how all the continents were once joined to form a giant supercontinent called Pangea. As you can see from the diagrams in Figure 1.13, most of the continents have slowly drifted apart from each other over time.

KEY WORDS

supercontinent: a large landmass thought to have broken up into several of the current continents

Pangea*: a large landmass thought to have broken up to create all the current continents

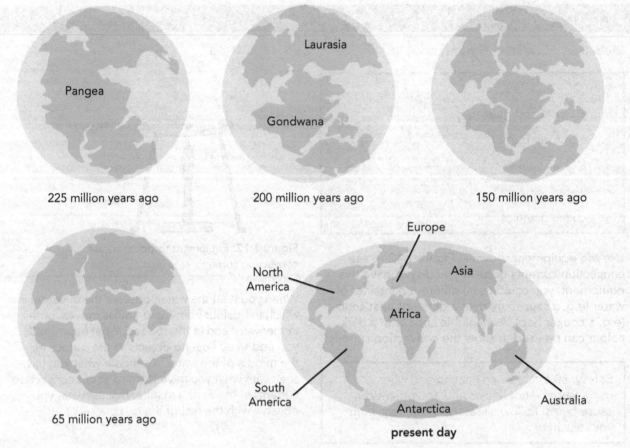

Figure 1.13: How the continents have moved over time.

Plate boundaries

Where two tectonic plates meet, one of three types of plate boundary can occur:

- **divergent plate boundaries** – plates move away from each other
- **convergent plate boundaries** – plates move towards each other
- **transform plate boundaries** – plates slide against each other.

KEY WORDS

divergent plate boundary: two tectonic plates move apart, forming new land between them

convergent plate boundary: two tectonic plates move towards each other

transform plate boundary*: two tectonic plates try to slide past each other

Divergent plate boundaries

When two tectonic plates move away from each other, a gap is created between the two plates. As the layer beneath the crust is molten, this causes magma from the mantle to rise and fill the gap. The molten rock is called **lava** once it gets to the upper surface of the crust. The lava cools when it is exposed to cool air or water above it, and solidifies to produce new solid rock.

The movement of the tectonic plates is not smooth and constant. The plates often move suddenly, causing **earthquakes**, and can suddenly release molten lava to the surface, which cools to form new rock. As a result, the new rock forms uneven mountain ranges either side of

KEY WORDS

lava*: molten rock that erupts from the Earth's crust

earthquake: a sudden shaking of the ground, usually caused when two plates suddenly slip against each other

the divergent plate boundary as the plates slowly move apart over time.

Most divergent boundaries occur in the oceans between continents. Figure 1.14 shows the Mid-Atlantic Ridge, which runs from Iceland in the North Atlantic, down the Atlantic Ocean to the Southern Ocean near Antarctica. This forms one of the longest mountain ranges in the world. Most of this mountain range is underwater, though some parts break above the ocean to form Iceland and other islands in the Atlantic, including the Azores, which is a group of volcanic islands in the Atlantic.

Figure 1.14: The Mid-Atlantic Ridge.

Features associated with divergent plate boundaries include:

- earthquakes, due to sudden movements of the tectonic plates

- volcanoes, both underwater and on land, formed as the plates move apart, allowing magma to rise up and escape as lava

- mid-ocean ridges, which are extensive mountain ranges formed deep in the ocean that extend for hundreds of miles either side of the parting plates

hydrothermal vents, formed where cold seawater seeps into cracks (or faults) in the sea floor and is superheated by the magma beneath, allowing minerals to dissolve in the water. The hot water is forced back into the sea, where it rapidly cools. The dissolved minerals solidify and create a chimney-like structure, a hydrothermal vent.

Convergent plate boundaries

When two tectonic plates move towards each other, the plates collide. What happens at the boundary depends on what type of crust is colliding.

volcanic islands: islands formed when volcanic eruptions result in the formation of an island or group of islands

volcanoes: part of the Earth's crust from which lava erupts

mid-ocean ridge*: mountain ranges formed deep in the ocean that extend for hundreds of miles either side of the parting plates

hydrothermal vent*: cold ocean water seeps into the Earth's crust and is superheated by underlying magma; this heated water is forced through vents (gaps) in the ocean floor and as it cools dissolved minerals solidify and form a chimney-like structure

minerals: nutrients that are needed by living organisms; examples include calcium and iron

subduction*: the downwards movement of one plate beneath another

If both sections of crust converging are continental crust, this results in fold mountains. While fold mountains are not directly linked to the oceans, they do provide evidence supporting the theory of plate tectonics. The Himalayan mountain range is an example of fold mountains created by the convergence of the Indo-Australian Plate into the Eurasian Plate. Fossils of sea creatures can be found on mountains in the Himalaya, such as the shell shown in Figure 1.15. These fossils support the idea of plate movement and uplifting of land over time as the Himalaya are far too high to ever have been covered by ocean in their current position.

Figure 1.15: Fossilised shell found on a mountain.

If a section of continental crust converges with a section of oceanic crust, the denser oceanic crust undergoes subduction beneath the continental crust (Figure 1.16).

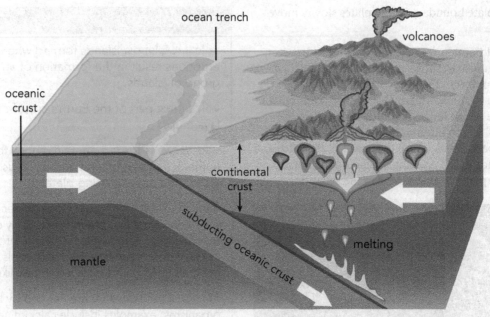

Figure 1.16: Subduction of oceanic crust at a convergent boundary with continental crust.

Features associated with convergent plate boundaries include:

- earthquakes, due to sudden movements of the tectonic plates

- tsunamis, caused by sudden violent earthquakes

- volcanoes on land formed as the plates converge, causing the oceanic crust to subduct and melt allowing magma to rise through the continental crust and escape as lava

- ocean trenches, which are deep underwater valleys running along the plate boundary; the Mariana Trench is the deepest part of the world's oceans, and is found between Japan and Papua New Guinea.

KEY WORDS

tsunami: a fast-moving wave with a long wavelength, created by ocean floor displacement or landslide

melt: the change of a solid into a liquid; during this process heat is taken in from the surroundings

ocean trench: a deep underwater valley formed when oceanic crust slides below continental crust

---

Transform plate boundaries

When two tectonic plates slide against each other, the movement of the plates is not smooth and constant. The plates build up tension until the forces pushing on them become so great that they slip suddenly, causing earthquakes. These earthquakes are less likely than earthquakes along convergent boundaries to cause a tsunami. This is because the movement of the plates does not usually cause a large displacement of seawater.

Most transform boundaries beneath the ocean occur near to mid-ocean ridges linking sections of divergent plates (Figure 1.17).

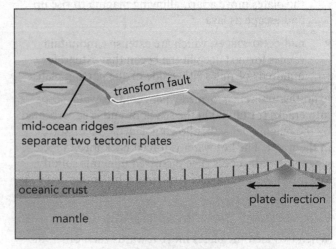

Figure 1.17: Transform fault beneath the ocean.

The features most associated with transform plate boundaries are earthquakes, due to sudden movements of the tectonic plates.

Tsunamis

Tsunamis occur when an extremely large volume of seawater is displaced, such as when two plates move suddenly. Figure 1.18 shows how a tsunami can be created by plate movements at a convergent boundary.

When a tsunami forms, the wave travels very quickly through deep ocean – this can be up to 800 km per hour, allowing tsunamis to cross oceans in less than a day. A tsunami wave may be as little as a few cm high in the middle of the ocean, but the wavelength (the distance between the tops of two successive waves) can be over 500 km long. As a tsunami wave nears the coast on the continental shelf, the ocean is much less deep. This causes the wave to increase in height as the wavelength decreases. The shallower depth also slows down the wave, causing the wave to gain even more height. As a tsunami wave reaches

the coast it may slow to as little as 30 km per hour, but the wave can be as high as 30 m, resulting in the wave flooding the coast and spreading as far as 16 km inland.

Tsunamis can also be caused by other events that displace huge volumes of seawater, such as a huge landslide underwater, a powerful volcanic eruption, or the impact of a large meteorite hitting an ocean. Whichever way they form, a tsunami wave always travels in the same way.

When a tsunami occurs, a huge amount of energy is transferred through the moving water in the tsunami wave. This energy moves rocks and sediments on the sea

> **KEY WORDS**
>
> **continental shelf:** part of the continental plate extending from the coast/shore in shallow waters with little or no slope
>
> **sediments:** small fragments of rock, such as gravel, sand and silt

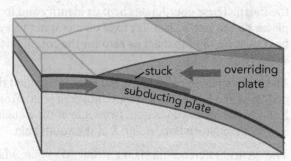

a   The continental plate gets stuck over the subducting oceanic plate.

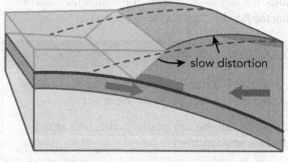

b   The continental plate distorts as tension continues to build.

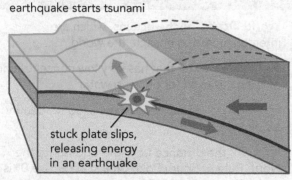

c   The plates suddenly slip, causing an earthquake and displacing a huge volume of water in the ocean above.

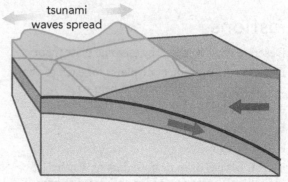

d   The displaced water sinks back down and spreads, creating a tsunami.

Figure 1.18: How earthquakes at convergent boundaries can cause a tsunami.

floor, destroying habitats and organisms on the seabed. The tsunami off the coast of Japan in March 2011 moved ocean sediments and deposited them over other habitats as huge sea-floor sand dunes.

Coral reefs act as natural breakwaters and coastal defences against tidal action and tsunamis. These important marine ecosystems face the full force of tsunamis and can suffer great damage, taking many years to recover from a tsunami. Other important marine habitats affected by tsunamis include coastal seagrass beds and mangrove forests.

Due to the great height of tsunami waves and the large amount of energy they transfer, tsunamis can do great damage to human communities along coastlines. The speed with which a tsunami wave floods a shore gives very little time for people to evacuate. A tsunami in the Indian Ocean on 26 December 2004 killed over 200 000 people in 14 countries around the Indian Ocean.

In addition to loss of life, the impact on coastal economies can be devastating, with fishing boats and gear destroyed and tourism disrupted. Farmland may be flooded with salt water, leading to the loss of crops and difficulties in farming the flooded land for many years after the tsunami.

KEY WORDS

breakwater*: a barrier which reduces the energy in waves before waves reach the coast

ecosystem: all the organisms in the area along with their environment

tourism: recreational visits to an area that brings money into local economies

Questions

4   Describe what is meant by tectonic plate theory.

5   Describe the movement of plates for each of these boundaries, using diagrams to help you:

   a   convergent

   b   divergent

   c   transform.

6   State the types of plate boundary at which the following features occur, and describe how they form:

   a   volcanoes

   b   earthquakes.

7   What is a tsunami? How does a tsunami form?

1.3 Oceans and seas

Oceans and seas cover 71% of the Earth's surface, with areas of land only covering 29%. The oceans are interconnected to encircle the Earth as a World Ocean – while water flows between the oceans and seas through currents. This is described in detail in Section 1.4.

Most of the water on the Earth (97%) is found in oceans and seas as salt water, with just 3% of the world's water as freshwater.

Oceans separate most of the continents and are generally much deeper than seas. Seas are smaller areas of water. Seas are sometimes found within oceans, such as the Bering Sea in the Pacific Ocean. Seas are often partially enclosed by land. The Mediterranean Sea is almost entirely enclosed by land, except for a very narrow strait past Gibraltar (south of Spain) to the Atlantic Ocean. The Earth's five oceans and many of the seas are shown in Figure 1.19. The Pacific Ocean is the largest ocean, with an area of over 160 million km^2 and a volume of 660 million km^3.

We use a system of coordinates to form a grid enclosing the Earth. These coordinates help us identify and locate places on the Earth. Just like axes on a graph, this system has reference lines that act as zero for the coordinate scales (Figure 1.20).

The horizontal reference line is the Equator, around the middle of the Earth. As you move north or south from the Equator the latitude increases, from zero at the Equator to 90° N at the North Pole, or 90° S at the South Pole.

The vertical reference line is the Prime Meridian, which runs from the North Pole to the South Pole through the

KEY WORDS

World Ocean: all the oceans, which are interconnected to encircle the world

freshwater: water that has very low concentrations of salts; it is used for drinking water

coordinates: a pair of numbers used to identify a point

latitude: the distance from the Equator to the North Pole or South Pole, on a scale where 0° is at the Equator and 90° is at the pole

Prime Meridian*: a line from the North Pole to the South Pole through the Royal Observatory in Greenwich, England

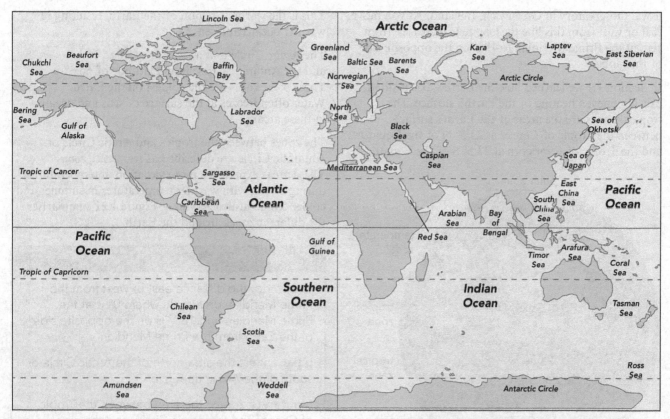

Figure 1.19: Earth's oceans and seas.

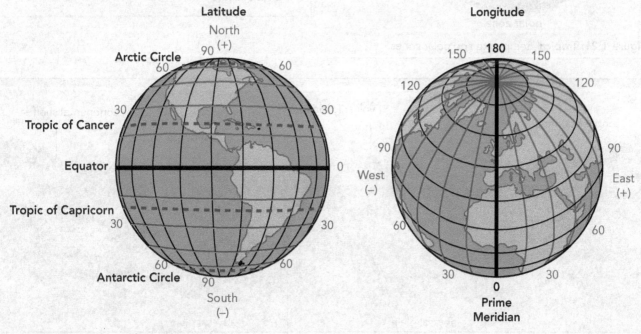

Figure 1.20: Latitude and longitude.

Royal Observatory in Greenwich, England. As you move east or west from this line the longitude increases, from zero at the Prime Meridian to 180° on the opposite side of the globe.

In Section 1.1 we learned how the Earth's axis is tilted, causing uneven heating of the Earth's surface. The tropical zones are the areas of the Earth's surface between the Tropic of Cancer at 23.5° N of the Equator, and the Tropic of Capricorn at 23.5° S of the Equator.

This is the warmest region of the Earth, resulting in warmer oceans and seas.

The Arctic Circle is at a latitude of 66.5° N and the Antarctic Circle is at a latitude of 66.5° S. These polar zones are the coldest on the Earth. Water often freezes at the surface of seas and oceans in these areas.

The zones between the tropics and Arctic Circle or Antarctic Circle are described as temperate zones. These areas experience more variation in temperatures during a year, with warmer temperatures in summer and colder temperatures in winter. Figure 1.21 summarises the different zones around the Earth.

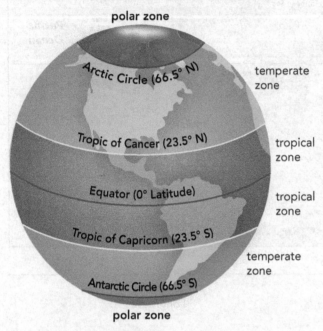

Figure 1.21: Tropical, temperate and polar zones.

KEY WORDS

longitude: the distance east or west from the Prime Meridian on a scale where 0° is at the Prime Meridian and 180° is on the opposite side of the Earth from the Prime Meridian

polar zones: the area north of the Arctic Circle or south of the Antarctic Circle

temperate zones: the area between the Tropic of Cancer and the Arctic Circle, and the area between the Tropic of Capricorn and the Antarctic Circle

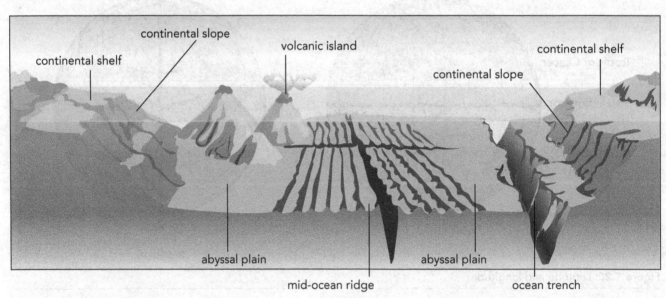

Figure 1.22: Geomorphology of the oceans.

In Section 1.2 we learned how the movement of tectonic plates has shaped the Earth, including the oceans, and how movements of plates create different features in and around the oceans. This link between geological processes and the physical features of the Earth's surface (both on land and below the seas and oceans) is referred to as geomorphology.

Figure 1.22 shows a simple cross-section of the ocean which illustrates some of the key features that shape the ocean floor. You can see a summary of each of these features and how they form in Table 1.1.

Feature	Description	How feature forms
continental shelf	part of the continental plate extending from the coast/shore in shallow waters with little or no slope; generally no more than 100–200 m deep	Continental crust that is below sea level: the sea covering it is often shallow due to sediments accumulating following erosion from the coast.
continental slope	the steeper slope from the continental shelf to near the abyssal plain, the edge of continental crust, where this meets oceanic crust	Oceanic crust is much thinner than the continental crust, causing steep slopes as the thickness of crust and the depth of ocean changes.
mid-ocean ridge	underwater mountain ranges found either side of diverging tectonic plates	Sea floor spreading causes tectonic plates to move apart. As magma rises to fill the gap this magma cools and solidifies. New rock is formed, creating ridges in the form of vast mountain ranges under the ocean.
abyssal plain	generally flat ocean floor usually at depths of 3000–6000 m	Sea floor spreading causes tectonic plates to move apart. The peaks of ridges created by new rock gradually erode and the gaps fill with sediment to create large flat areas.
ocean trench	very long deep depressions in the ocean floor; an example is the Mariana Trench, which is the deepest point in the oceans, with a maximum depth of about 11 000 m	Ocean trenches occur at convergent plate boundaries where oceanic crust is subducted beneath continental crust, creating a deep trench along the plate boundary.
volcanic islands	volcanoes that continued to erupt to break above sea level and create islands	Volcanic activity causes lava to erupt and solidify, gradually adding more height until they create islands above sea level.

Table 1.1: Summary of geomorphological features found in oceans.

KEY WORDS

erosion: the wearing away of rock along the coastline

geomorphology: the study of the physical features of the surface of the Earth and their relation to its geological structures and processes

continental slope: the steeper slope from the continental shelf to near the abyssal plain

abyssal plain: the generally flat ocean floor, usually at depths of 3000–6000 m

Questions

8   Figure 1.23 shows a photograph of the Earth taken from space.

Figure 1.23: The Earth seen from space.

a   The Arctic Ocean, at the top of the image, is mostly covered in ice. Explain why.

b   Which ocean is shown in the middle of the photo?

9   Why is it difficult to describe where one ocean ends and another starts?

10 Which ocean is:

a   the deepest

b   the largest?

11 Explain the differences between a mid-ocean ridge and an ocean trench.

1.4 Tides and currents

Tides

Throughout history, humans have observed the regular rising and falling of sea level along the coastline. The first record of a suggested explanation was given by the Greek astronomer, Pytheas, who sailed to the British Isles in about 325 BC and observed that the **tides** experienced round Britain were greater than in his native Greece. He noticed that the tides matched the movement of the Moon around the Earth, and also that the height of the tides depended on the **phase of the Moon**.

> **KEY WORDS**
>
> **tides:** the rising and falling of the sea in regular cycles, caused by the gravitational attraction between the Earth, the Moon and the Sun
>
> **phases of the Moon*:** the changes in the observed shape of the Moon caused by changes in the proportion of the visible surface of the Moon

We learned in Section 1.1 how gravity keeps the Earth in orbit around the Sun, and also keeps the Moon in orbit around the Earth. The gravitational force of the Moon pulls water in the oceans towards the Moon. Water is a liquid and able to flow, unlike solid land. This creates a bulge in the oceans on the side of the Earth nearest to the Moon. The centrifugal force caused by the Earth spinning also creates a slightly smaller bulge in oceans on the opposite side of the Earth from the Moon (Figure 1.24).

The bulge of water in the oceans caused by the gravitational pull of the Moon on the Earth moves around the oceans as the Earth rotates once on its axis every 24 hours. This causes the height of the sea level at any location on the Earth to rise and fall as it moves into and out of these bulges. It is this regular rising and falling of sea level each day that we call the tides. The time between each high tide and following low tide is actually a little over six hours due to the Moon slowly orbiting around the Earth. This adds about 25 minutes to each change in tide, or a total of 12 hours 50 minutes between each high tide.

But why does the height of the tides change during each month? The answer is that the Sun also has a gravitational pull on the water in the oceans. Although the Sun is much larger than the Moon, the gravitational pull of the Sun on the oceans is much less than the gravitational pull from the Moon. This is due to the distance between the Sun and the Earth being much greater than the distance between the Moon and the Earth. The Sun therefore causes a second set of bulges in the ocean. These are much smaller than the bulges caused by the Moon, but they do increase or decrease the height of the tides as the Moon orbits the Earth during each month.

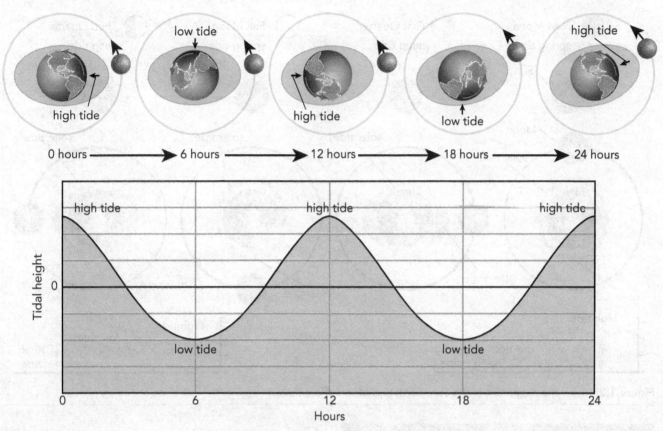

Figure 1.24: How the Moon causes tides each day.

When the Moon, the Earth and the Sun are lined up with each other in a straight line, the gravitational forces of the Moon and the Sun combine to create higher high tides and lower low tides. These are called spring tides. The spring tides are greatest when the Moon is between the Sun and the Earth, with the gravitational pull of both the Sun and the Moon acting in the same direction. When the Sun and the Moon are on opposite sides of the Earth the tides are still spring tides, but not quite as high or low.

When the Moon, the Earth and the Sun are at right angles to each other, the gravitational pull of the Moon and the Sun on the Earth are in different directions. This causes lower high tides and higher low tides. These are called neap tides. These effects are shown in Figure 1.25.

Two important terms relating to measuring tides are tidal range and tidal amplitude. The tidal range is the difference between the height of the sea at high tide, and the height at the following low tide. Tidal amplitude is exactly half of the tidal range. Spring tides are when the tidal range and tidal amplitude are greatest. These occur when the lunar tide (the bulge of water caused by gravitational attraction towards the Moon) adds to the

Solar tide (the bulge of water caused by gravitational attraction towards the Sun) to create the highest and lowest tides. Neap tides are when the tidal range and tidal amplitude are least. These occur when the lunar tide is separated from the Solar tide to create the lowest high tides and highest low tides.

KEY WORDS

spring tides: tides experienced during a new Moon and full Moon with higher high tides and lower low tides than usual

neap tides: tides experienced during the first and last quarters of the Moon with lower high tides and higher low tides than usual

tidal range*: difference in height between high tide and the following low tide

tidal amplitude: half the difference in height between high tide and the following low tide

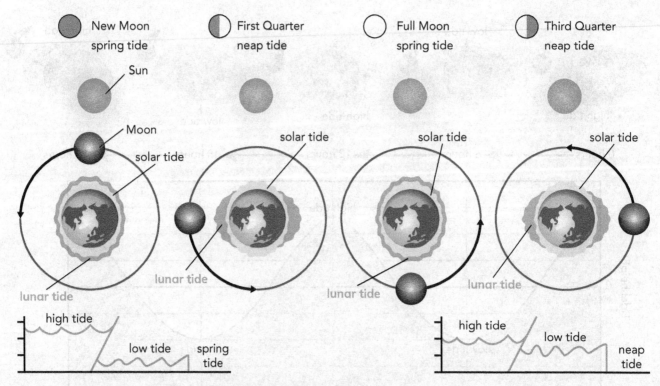

Figure 1.25: How the alignment of the Sun, Earth and Moon affect tides.

ACTIVITY 1.3

Measuring tidal amplitude

Look up some tide information for a location near to you. You can find this information by searching for 'tide times' on the internet. Identify the height of the next high tide and the following low tide. Calculate the difference between these two heights – this is the tidal range. To find the tidal amplitude, divide the tidal range by two.

Example:

The next high tide on the Maldives is 0.89 m

The following low tide is 0.15 m

The tidal range is 0.89 m – 0.15 m = 0.74 m

The tidal amplitude is 0.74 m ÷ 2 = 0.37 m

Calculate the tidal amplitude at the same location for the next two tides and compare this to the first value you calculated. Discuss why the tidal amplitude has increased or decreased.

Currents

An oceanic or sea **current** is a continuous flow of seawater in a particular direction. Currents at the surface are generally caused by the direction of **prevailing winds**. For example, at the Equator the prevailing winds blow from east to west. This movement of the air above the sea surface pushes water at the surface in the same direction as the wind, from east to west. Since the winds are often blowing in the same direction for much of the time this creates currents at the surface of the ocean, with the water moving in the same direction.

As these surface currents flow towards land, the direction of the current changes to move along the coast away from the Equator. This, combined with the spinning of the Earth on its axis, creates currents that flow in opposite directions in the Northern Hemisphere compared to

KEY WORDS

(sea or ocean) current: continuous flow of seawater in a particular direction

prevailing winds: the direction from which winds usually blow at a particular location

the Southern Hemisphere. In the Northern Hemisphere currents move in a clockwise direction. In the Southern Hemisphere currents move in an anticlockwise direction. Figure 1.26 shows the main surface currents in the oceans.

Surface currents circulating in the oceans form gyres in most of the oceans. These gyres, shown in Figure 1.27, circulate clockwise in the Northern Hemisphere (in the North Atlantic and North Pacific). Gyres circulate anticlockwise in the Southern Hemisphere (in the South Atlantic, South Pacific and Indian Ocean).

KEY WORD

gyre: a large system of rotating ocean currents

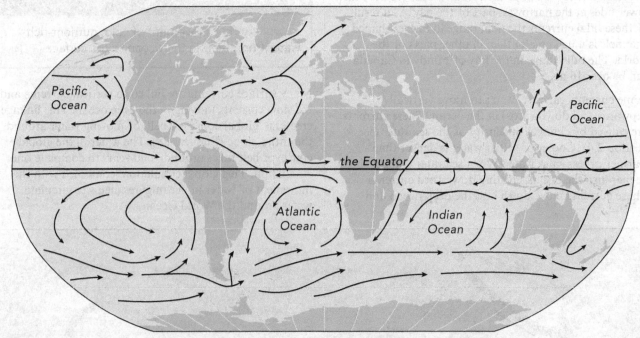

Figure 1.26: Major surface currents around the world.

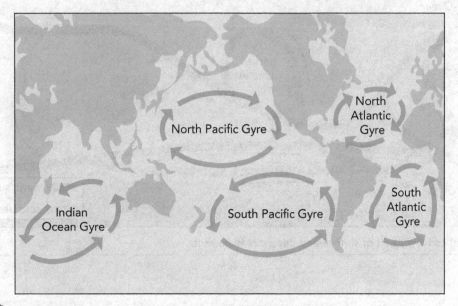

Figure 1.27: The five ocean gyres.

Tides can also cause currents, which reverse direction with each change in tide. You most often see tidal currents in areas where the coastline is funnel-shaped. As the sea level rises with a rising tide, the water moves up a narrowing funnel-shaped channel, creating strong currents. These currents also create much higher tides further up the enclosed channel. When the sea level starts to decrease again after high tide, the current reverses direction and flows out of the channel. This creates much lower tides at the narrowest part of the bay. As a result of these tidal currents the tidal range in funnel-shaped channels is much greater than in other parts of the world. The tidal range in the Bay of Fundy in Canada can be over 16 m.

Some currents cause seawater to move vertically (upwards and downwards) in the ocean. These currents are caused by changes in density of the seawater (see Section 2.4). Cooler or saltier water is denser than warmer or less salty water. When seawater cools it sinks deeper into the ocean, creating downward currents. These currents move down into the deep ocean and then flow along the ocean floor at much slower speeds than surface currents. Eventually, the currents are pushed up to the surface again, often many thousands of miles from where the water went down into the deep ocean. Winds can also cause water to move to the surface from the deep ocean. This is called an upwelling (see Section 2.6).

> **KEY WORD**
>
> **upwelling:** the movement of cold, nutrient-rich water from deep in the ocean to the surface

Many surface currents are linked to vertical currents and the slow currents moving in the deep ocean. This linkage creates a 'global conveyor belt' of moving water around the entire globe (Figure 1.28). The water in the global conveyor belt takes around 1000 years to complete one circulation. This global circulation, combined with the movement of water in ocean gyres, helps to circulate water around the World Ocean.

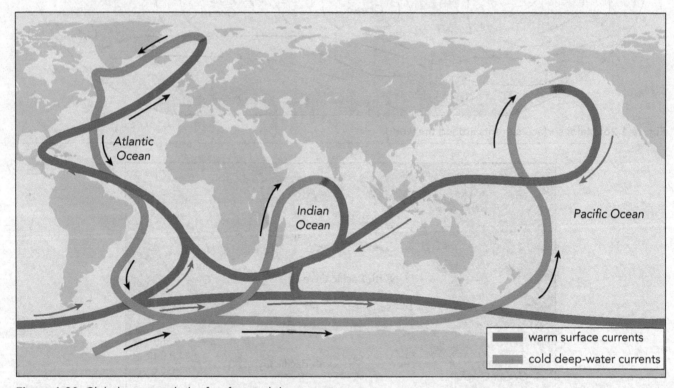

Figure 1.28: Global conveyor belt of surface and deep ocean currents.

Rip currents

A **rip current** (Figure 1.29) is a dangerous narrow current that can form on beaches; many people get into difficulties in these currents each year. Usually, when waves push water against a beach the water moves back to the ocean evenly across the width of the beach. This does not normally cause rip currents. Sometimes, sand or sediment in the sea near to the beach creates a sand bar. Waves moving water towards the beach flow over the bar easily. As water from the wave begins to flow back out to sea the water level over the sand bar falls, and water tries to get through where the sand bar is already lowest. Over time, the lower sections in the sand bar form gaps or channels. These channels get deeper as more water flows back to the ocean through them. This creates powerful rip currents flowing out to sea from the beach, and these rip currents can extend over 500 m into the ocean. Swimmers caught in rip currents are pulled far out to sea and then struggle to swim back to shore. Any swimmer who finds themselves in a rip current should remember that rip currents are very narrow. If swimmers try to swim at right angles to the current, they may escape the current and so be able then to swim back to the shore.

KEY WORD

rip current: a narrow powerful current moving from a beach out to the ocean

ACTIVITY 1.4

Danger – rip currents

Every year many swimmers get into trouble after being caught in rip currents. Working in a pair or small group, make a poster to warn swimmers at a beach. Your poster should clearly explain what rip currents are and describe how swimmers can escape from them.

Peer assessment

Rate the poster of another learner according to the following scheme for each of the points listed:

☺ if they did it really well

😐 if they made a good attempt at it and partly succeeded

☹ if they did not try to do it or did not succeed.

The poster should:

- identify what a rip current is

- describe the danger to swimmers caused by rip currents

- explain how to swim out of a rip current

- have a clear layout that is quick and easy to understand.

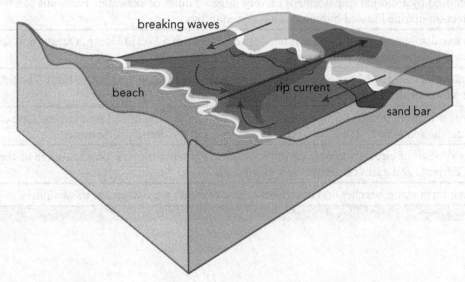

Figure 1.29: Formation of rip currents.

Measuring currents

Measurements of currents involve two separate pieces of information: speed and direction. We can measure the speed of currents in several ways. The simplest involves floating an object on the surface of a current and recording the time it takes to travel a known distance. This can be done with any floating object alongside a boat, using a compass to measure the direction the object moves in. Modern equipment often uses Global Positioning System (GPS) sensors to record speeds using locations and times. These devices may contain a compass to record the direction moved by the sensor in the current, although the direction can also be determined from the GPS data.

KEY WORD

Global Positioning System (GPS): a network of artificial satellites forming a navigation and location system

Questions

12 Describe the differences between spring tides and neap tides.

13 State what is meant by an ocean current.

14 State four factors that can cause ocean currents.

15 Compare the similarities and differences between tides, ocean currents and ocean gyres.

SUMMARY

The Earth is a planet and the Moon is a natural satellite of the Earth. Gravity keeps the Earth in orbit around the Sun, and the Moon in orbit around the Earth.

The Earth is a rocky planet, with a thin solid outer crust, and semi-molten mantle beneath. The planet has a core made mostly of iron, which creates a magnetic field around the Earth.

The Earth's crust is broken into large tectonic plates that float and slowly move around the Earth. This movement is caused by convection currents in the mantle.

The movement of tectonic plates caused giant supercontinents to break up and separate over hundreds of millions of years.

Tectonic plates move against each other in different directions, causing convergent, divergent and transform plate boundaries. These can cause earthquakes and create features that shape the Earth and oceans, including volcanoes, mid-ocean ridges and ocean trenches.

Tsunamis are caused by a sudden displacement of very large volumes of seawater. Tsunamis can have a devastating effect on marine life and human coastal communities.

The Earth has five distinct oceans which are interconnected to form a World Ocean. Oceans and seas contain most of the world's water and cover more than two thirds of the planet.

The gravitational effects of the Moon and the Sun on water in oceans and seas create tides. The tidal amplitude changes as the Moon orbits the Earth, causing spring tides and neap tides.

Oceanic currents are the continuous flow of seawater in a particular direction. These currents are caused by prevailing winds, the spinning of the Earth, tides and changes in the density of seawater.

Gyres are large systems of circular oceanic currents. There are five main gyres found in some of the largest oceans. Ocean currents and gyres circulate water around the World Ocean.

Rip currents can form along beaches and coastlines. These currents are dangerous to swimmers.

CASE STUDY PROJECT

Evidence for tectonic plate theory

Our understanding of plate tectonics has developed quite recently. It is only since the 1960s that we have begun to understand how plates move around the Earth. But what is the evidence to support the theory?

In 1912, the German scientist Alfred Wegener developed a theory called continental drift.

He noticed that fossilised remains of several species were found on different continents. He also saw that the coastlines of some continents appeared to fit together, and that the regions where fossils were found on each continent also matched, as shown in Figure 1.30. But the theory of continental drift was not accepted by most scientists for nearly 50 years as there was no explanation of how the plates were able to move.

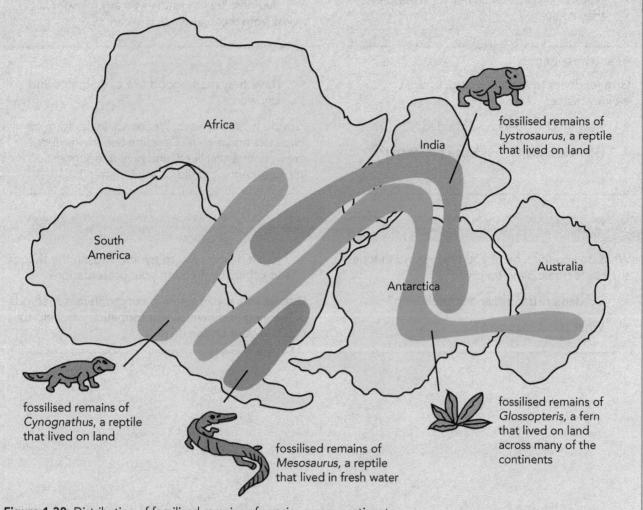

Figure 1.30: Distribution of fossilised remains of species across continents.

CONTINUED

In a pair or small group, produce a five-minute presentation to deliver to other learners in the class showing evidence to support tectonic plate theory.

Try to include a range of evidence, which could include:

- what you have learned about convection currents

- types of plate boundary and the features they create

- where fossilised remains have been found, and how this helps us to know that there used to be supercontinents in the past.

You could even research to see if the Earth's magnetic field has changed over time, and how this provides further evidence to support tectonic plate theory.

You should include diagrams to support your explanations. Try to include as many relevant key words from the chapter as you can.

Peer assessment

Give feedback to another group. Look at their evidence:

- How much evidence is included?

- How clearly is the evidence presented?

- Have they made good use of diagrams and key words?

Provide written or verbal feedback in the form of 'two stars and a wish'. Describe two things about the work that you liked, and give one suggestion for improvement: 'It could be even better if …'

REFLECTION

What do you think helps you understand theories such as tectonic plate theory?

- Do demonstrations and models help?

- What about diagrams?

- Has it helped you to try and explain the theory to others by creating your presentation?

Discuss with a partner how using different methods of learning and reviewing information can help to improve your understanding.

EXAM-STYLE QUESTIONS

1 The Moon orbits the Earth every 27.5 days.

a State the name of the force that keeps the Moon in orbit around the Earth. [1]

Figure 1

b Figure 1 shows the Moon at one point in its orbit around the Earth.

i Describe the alignment of the Moon with the Earth and the Sun causing the image shown in Figure 1. [1]

ii Explain how this alignment affects tidal amplitude. [2]

[Total: 4]

2 An earthquake occurs at a convergent plate boundary and creates a tsunami.

a Describe how an earthquake forms at a convergent plate boundary. [3]

b Describe a tsunami. [3]

c Explain how a tsunami is formed. [2]

d Describe the impacts of tsunamis on human coastal communities. [2]

[Total: 10]

3 Figure 2 shows some features on the ocean floor.

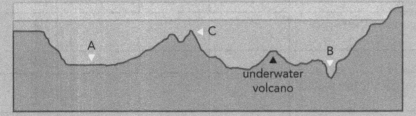

underwater volcano

Figure 2

a Identify features A, B and C. [3]

b Describe how the underwater volcano shown may one day form an island. [2]

[Total: 5]

4 The Atlantic Ocean contains two ocean gyres.
Describe how oceanic currents form to create ocean gyres. [Total: 5]

COMMAND WORD

state: express in clear terms

COMMAND WORDS

describe: state the points of a topic / give characteristics and main features

explain: set out purposes or reasons / make the relationships between things clear / say why and / or how and support with relevant evidence

COMMAND WORD

identify: name / select / recognise

SELF-EVALUATION CHECKLIST

After studying this chapter, think about how confident you are with the different topics. This will help you to see any gaps in your knowledge and help you to learn more effectively.

I can	Needs more work	Getting there	Confident to move on	See Section
describe the motion of the Earth relative to the Sun, and the Moon relative to the Earth				1.1
state the force that keeps the Earth and the Moon in their orbits				1.1
describe the layers and types of material that make up the structure of the Earth				1.1
state why the Earth has a magnetic field				1.1
explain what tectonic plates are, and outline tectonic plate theory and how supercontinents once existed				1.2
describe the three types of plate boundary				1.2
explain how plate boundaries give rise to earthquakes and volcanoes				1.2
describe how tsunamis form and outline their effects on marine ecosystems and human coastal communities				1.2
identify and describe the location of the Earth's oceans				1.3
describe the extent of the oceans and explain how they are interconnected				1.3
describe seas in comparison to oceans				1.3
describe and identify the geomorphology of the oceans				1.3
outline how the gravitational effects of the Sun and the Moon cause tides				1.4
describe how to measure tidal amplitude				1.4
describe ocean currents, and how to measure their speed and direction				1.4
state reasons why ocean currents form				1.4
describe gyres and identify the locations of the five main oceanic gyres				1.4
state how water circulates in the World Ocean				1.4
describe how rip currents form and why they are dangerous to swimmers				1.4

〉 Chapter 2

Seawater

IN THIS CHAPTER YOU WILL:

- describe and explain changes of state and diffusion using particle theory

- describe the water cycle and relate the water cycle to changes in state

- describe and investigate the pH of solutions

- describe the composition of seawater

- describe and explain how solubility affects the salinity of the oceans and the concentration of dissolved gases in the oceans

- explain the salinity of different bodies of water in terms of the water cycle and Earth processes

- describe and explain changes in density in seawater caused by temperature and salinity differences

- describe how physical and chemical conditions in water change with increasing depth

- describe how upwelling occurs and discuss the formation and local effects of El Niño.

GETTING STARTED

Particle theory helps us to explain how matter behaves.

- Here are five statements about the three physical states of matter: solids, liquids and gases. Which statements relate to each of these states of matter? Some statements can apply to more than one state.

  - The substance has a fixed shape in any container.

  - The substance takes the shape of the container it is in.

  - The substance has a fixed volume.

  - The substance can be compressed into a smaller space.

  - The substance can flow.

- If all substances are made of particles, can you explain any of the five statements using the idea of particles?

Be ready to share your ideas.

MARINE SCIENCE IN CONTEXT

A pioneering diver

Dr Sylvia Earle (born 1935) is a scientist who studies the oceans and an explorer from the United States. Her work includes the development of modern self-contained underwater breathing apparatus (SCUBA) gear and the development of deep-sea submersibles. At the age of 16, before the creation of SCUBA equipment, she attempted her first dive using a diving helmet. In 1979 she set the world record for the deepest untethered dive using SCUBA equipment, reaching a depth of 381 m. She achieved this by using an armoured diving suit while attached to the front of a small submersible vessel to reach the sea floor. When on the sea floor, she detached herself from the vessel and explored the sea floor for more than two hours. No one has repeated or exceeded this achievement in the past 42 years.

SCUBA diving equipment allows divers to stay below the surface of the sea for much longer periods of time (Figure 2.1). It consists of a tank containing compressed air and a regulator that reduces the pressure of the air from the tanks before the diver breathes this in. Reducing the pressure in this way reduces the risk of damage to the diver.

Figure 2.1: Dr. Sylvia Earle next to a small submarine.

CONTINUED

A few years after her deep dive, Sylvia Earle helped to design a submersible called *Deep Rover*, a submarine vehicle capable of reaching depths of 914 m.

These developments enabled other scientists to build on her work and create diving equipment capable of reaching even greater depths.

Discussion questions

1   What challenges do you think Dr Sylvia Earle had to overcome to set the world record for the deepest untethered dive?

2   Suggest why it is important that scientists record exactly how they carry out their investigations when they record and publish their findings.

2.1 The water cycle

Particle theory

All materials are made up of tiny particles called **atoms**. We can think of atoms as tiny balls or spheres. These atoms can form larger particles called **molecules** and other larger structures (Figure 2.2).

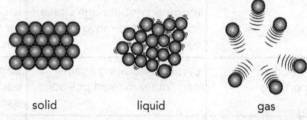

solid   liquid   gas

Figure 2.3: The arrangement and motion of particles in solids, liquids and gases.

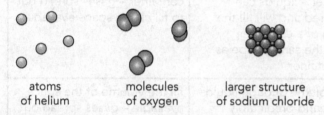

atoms   molecules   larger structure
of helium   of oxygen   of sodium chloride

Figure 2.2: Arrangement of particles as separate atoms, molecules and larger structures.

Particle theory is the idea that we can describe all materials as a collection of very many tiny particles that are constantly moving. The more energy the particles have, the more they move relative to each other. An increase in the energy of a substance causes all the particles to move faster, so the particles have more **kinetic energy**. As a material is heated, the particles gain more kinetic energy and move faster, and the temperature of the material increases. The temperature of a material is measured in degrees Celsius (°C) – this is a measure of the kinetic energy of the particles in the material.

Materials exist in three different **physical states**: solid, liquid and gas. Figure 2.3 shows how the particles are moving in each state. Table 2.1 compares the properties of each state of matter.

KEY WORDS

atom*: the smallest particle of a substance that can take part in a chemical reaction

molecule: a group of atoms held together by sharing electrons between atoms in the molecule

particle theory: a theory which describes the bulk properties of the different states of matter in terms of the movement of particles (atoms or molecules) – the theory explains what happens during changes in physical state

kinetic energy: the energy possessed by objects or particles due to movement

physical state*: solid, liquid and gas are the three states of matter in which any substance can exist, depending on the conditions of temperature and pressure

Physical state	Solid	Liquid	Gas
arrangement of particles	particles closely packed together; not enough space for particles to move past each other	particles closely packed together; just enough space for particles to move past each other	particles far apart from each other; lots of space for particles to move past each other
motion of particles	particles vibrating against each other in fixed positions	particles vibrating against each other and flowing past each other	particles moving fast, colliding with each other
shape of material	fixed shape; particles are in a fixed position so the material keeps its shape	takes the shape of the container – liquids can be poured and will fill the bottom of a container, having the same shape as the container	takes the shape of the container – gases spread out to fill all the space available
volume of material	fixed volume (though solids can expand predictably when heated) cannot be compressed as particles are already very close together	fixed volume (though liquids can expand predictably when heated) cannot be compressed easily as particles are too close together	fill the volume of the space available – gases spread out in larger volumes can be compressed into smaller volumes as there are large spaces between the particles

Table 2.1: Properties of solids, liquids and gases.

When a solid is heated, the particles gain more kinetic energy and move faster, as shown in Figure 2.4. These faster vibrations cause solids to expand slightly, so the solid takes up more space, and this reduces the density of the solid. Density is explained in more detail in Section 2.4.

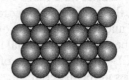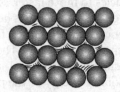

Figure 2.4: Atoms vibrating in a solid at two temperatures.

When the particles in a solid have enough energy, their vibrations create enough space between the particles so that the particles can move past each other. This is when a solid melts to form a liquid. The temperature at which this happens is called the melting point. While a substance is melting the temperature stops increasing. The energy transferred to separate the particles enough to move past each other is called the latent heat energy – the particles gain latent heat during melting. The levelling off of temperature that occurs as a solid is melting gives many materials a well-defined melting point (for example, pure water melts at 0 °C). When all the solid has melted, the particles then begin to move faster again as they gain more kinetic energy. The temperature of the liquid then begins to rise (Figure 2.5).

When a liquid is heated, the temperature continues to rise as the particles gain more kinetic energy. The temperature represents the average kinetic energy

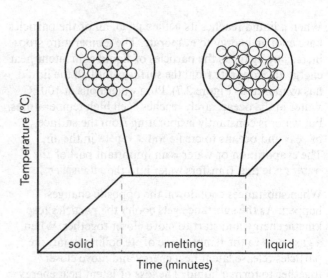

Figure 2.5: Change in the arrangement of particles in a solid melting into a liquid over time.

of all the particles in a substance, and some of the liquid particles have more energy than others. Particles at the surface of the liquid with more kinetic energy may have enough energy to completely escape from the liquid – this is called evaporation. Evaporation explains why water escapes from the surface of liquids that are not boiling, such as from seas or oceans or rock pools (Figure 2.6). Evaporation also explains why wet surfaces dry out. The warmer a liquid is the faster the rate of evaporation.

KEY WORDS

melting point: the temperature at which a solid turns into a liquid; it has the same value as the freezing point

latent heat energy*: energy absorbed or released by a substance during a change in its physical state

Figure 2.6: During hot weather water evaporates rapidly from a rock pool.

When a liquid reaches its **boiling point**, all of the particles have enough energy to evaporate. The temperature stops increasing again as the particles of liquid gain latent heat energy to evaporate from the surface, until all the liquid has evaporated (Figure 2.7). Pure water boils at 100 °C. Water in the ocean rarely reaches such high temperatures, but water is constantly evaporating from the surface of seas and oceans to create **water vapour** in the air. The evaporation of water is an important part of the **water cycle** that transfers water into the **atmosphere**.

When substances cool down, the opposite changes happen. As the substance gets cooler the particles lose kinetic energy and start to move closer together. When a gas cools to the temperature of its boiling point, the particles release latent heat energy and move closer together to form a liquid. The loss of latent heat energy causes the temperature to remain constant until all the gas has turned to a liquid. This change in state is called condensation.

When a liquid cools, the temperature will drop as the particles lose kinetic energy. When the liquid reaches the melting point, the particles release latent heat energy and **freeze** (or solidify). The melting point of a substance is the same temperature that a liquid becomes a solid. When all the liquid has become solid the temperature can begin to fall again. These changes in state are summarised in Figure 2.7.

> **KEY WORDS**
>
> **boiling point***: the temperature at which a liquid boils
>
> **water vapour***: gaseous water in the air that has evaporated
>
> **water cycle**: the cycle of processes by which water circulates between the Earth's oceans, atmosphere, and land; it involves precipitation, drainage and run-off into streams and rivers, and return to the atmosphere by evaporation
>
> **atmosphere**: layer of gases surrounding the surface of the Earth
>
> **freeze**: the change of a liquid into a solid; during this process heat is given out to the surroundings

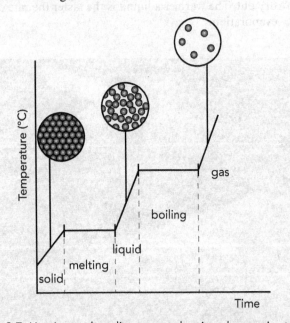 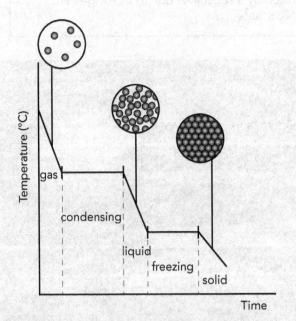

Figure 2.7: Heating and cooling curves showing changes in state and the arrangement of particles at each state.

Modelling changes in state

In a pair or small group, plan how a group of people can help to explain the movement of the particles in solids, liquids and gases. Think about:

- How would the people be arranged to represent the particles in a solid?

- How could you represent the movement of the particles?

- What would change as the solid melts to become a liquid?

- What would change as the liquid boils to become a gas?

Your plan should answer the following questions:

1   Why does it take time for a solid to melt, and for a liquid to boil?

2   Different substances also have different melting and boiling points. Suggest why this is.

3   Why is it that you can feel a liquid cooling your skin when it evaporates from your hand?

After you have answered these questions, share your ideas with the rest of the class.

Peer assessment

Give feedback to another group. Look at their plan and think about:

- How does the model help to explain particle theory?

- How clear is the explanation?

- Have they made good use of the model to support their explanation?

Provide written feedback in the form of 'two stars and a wish': describe two things about the work that you liked, and give one suggestion for improvement: 'It could be even better if…'. Alternatively, you could say what you think about their model, based on the questions above. This type of feedback is called verbal feedback.

After all the groups have shared their ideas, agree on one or more plans to use as a class.

Diffusion

We can use particle theory to help explain how different substances mix with each other. Particles in liquids and gases are able to move, so when other substances are added to a liquid or a gas, their particles can mix together.

When a soluble solid is placed into a liquid (such as water), the liquid particles allow the solid particles to mix (dissolve) with them. This process is called dissolving (Figure 2.8). The solid particles are in a high concentration where the liquid meets the solid. These solid particles slowly move further from the solid, mixing more with the liquid they are dissolving in. This is called diffusion.

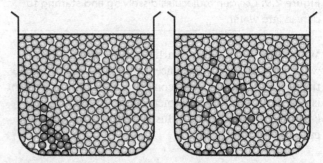

Figure 2.8: Particles in a solid dissolving and diffusing into water.

soluble: the description of a substance that dissolves in a particular solvent

diffusion: the random movement of particles (or molecules) from an area of higher concentration to an area of lower concentration (down a concentration gradient); it is a passive process, not requiring the input of energy

At the surface of a liquid, gases can also dissolve into the liquid. Oxygen and carbon dioxide both dissolve in water. These gases will dissolve into the water from the surface, and then diffuse further down into the water (Figure 2.9).

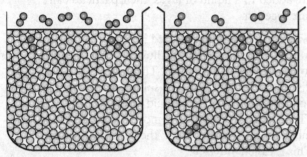

Figure 2.9: Oxygen molecules dissolving and starting to diffuse into water.

When diffusion happens, particles move from a region where they are in a high concentration to a region where the particles are in a lower concentration. This movement is due to the random movement of the particles. This can also be described as diffusing down a concentration gradient (Figure 2.10).

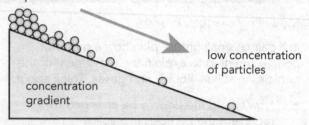

high concentration of particles

low concentration of particles

concentration gradient

Figure 2.10: This diagram shows how we can use the analogy of a slope to think about a concentration gradient. We can imagine particles moving down the slope, from a high concentration to a low concentration.

Questions

1 a Sketch the arrangement of particles in a solid, a liquid and a gas.

   b Describe the motion of particles in a solid, a liquid and a gas.

2 a State the name of the unit used to measure temperature.

   b What does the temperature of a substance measure?

PRACTICAL TASK 2.1

Investigating the effect of ice melting on sea level

Figure 2.11: Floating iceberg in the sea and land-based ice on mountains in Greenland.

Introduction

Ice can either form on land or in the sea (Figure 2.11). In this investigation you will try to find out if the place where ice melts has an impact on sea levels. You will compare ice melting on land to the melting of floating ice. You will use models to represent land and the sea.

You will need:

- two identical, clear containers (at least 10 cm width or diameter)

- modelling clay or play dough, or small rocks (enough to create a 3–5 cm high surface that half fills each container)

- a tray of ice cubes

- cold water

- a ruler

- a marker (to write on the side of the containers).

CONTINUED

Safety: Follow all laboratory safety rules. Clear up any water or ice spills immediately to avoid the risk of people slipping.

Method

1   Press equal amounts of clay (or place small rocks) into one side of each container, as shown in Figure 2.12. The clay or rocks represent the land.

2   In one of the containers, place as many ice cubes as you can in contact with the 'land'. This represents land-based ice.

3   In the other container, add the same number of ice cubes into the space next to the 'land'. This ice represents sea ice.

4   Add water to the container with 'sea ice' until all the ice floats and none is touching the bottom of the container.

5   Add water to the other container until the level of water is similar to the level in the 'sea ice' container. Take care not to knock any ice from the 'land' into the water.

6   Use a marker to record the starting height of the water in each container.

7   Allow the ice in each container to melt. Record the height of the water in each container at regular intervals in a copy of the results table (Table 2.2). You should try to obtain at least five measurements, including 'zero' for the first measurement when no ice has melted.

8   Use the measurements to draw a line graph of the change in height against time.

Results

Time (minutes)	Land ice Difference in height (mm)	Sea ice Difference in height (mm)
0	0	0

Table 2.2: Height of water as ice melts on land and in the sea.

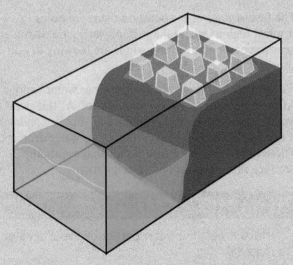
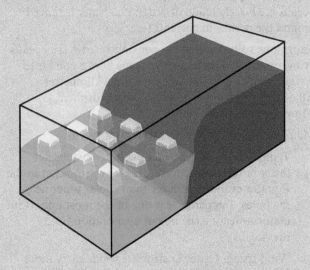

Figure 2.12: Diagram of setup for Practical Task 2.1.

CONTINUED

Questions

1 Describe the difference in the heights of water in the two containers after the ice melted.

2 Explain why the results show this difference.

3 Describe how your results represent what happens to melting glaciers and melting sea ice.

4 Explain which of these will have a greater impact on global sea levels:

- melting glaciers in mountains and in ice sheets on Antarctica
- melting sea ice in the Arctic.

This Practical task links to Skills tip 0.2.

Self-assessment

How well did you complete this practical task? Rate your work according to the following scheme for each of the points listed:

☺ if you did it really well

😐 if you made a good attempt at it and partly succeeded

☹ if you did not try to do it or did not succeed.

- I made the two containers as fair as possible, using the same area and depth of 'land' and arranged this 'land' in the same shape for both containers.
- I used the same amount of ice in both containers.
- I made sure the ice was all placed on 'land' in one container, and all in the water in the other container.
- I measured the heights of the water to within 1 mm.

The water cycle

Changes in state, as explained by particle theory, are important in understanding the water cycle. Seas and oceans are largely made of water, and water is moved around the oceans in currents (see Section 1.4).

Enormous volumes of water constantly leave the oceans by evaporation. The seas and oceans have a combined surface area of over 360 million square kilometres. All of this surface is exposed to the atmosphere, allowing water to evaporate.

Many factors affect how fast water evaporates.

- Temperature. We learned how water evaporates faster at warmer temperatures, so warm water at the Equator evaporates faster than cooler water near the poles. Temperature is one of the most important factors affecting the rate of evaporation from the oceans.

- Wind speed. Faster or stronger winds carry more energy, and the air particles can transfer this energy to water particles at the surface of the ocean. This is why puddles of water will evaporate very quickly on dry windy days, and why shallow rock pools can evaporate when it is windy.

- Humidity. Humidity is a measure of the proportion of water vapour in the air. Very humid air already contains a lot of water vapour, so there is less capacity for water to evaporate into the air.

The fastest rates of evaporation therefore occur in tropical regions where the surface waters are warm, and near to coasts when strong winds are blowing dry air off shore (from the land to the sea).

As water evaporates it rises in the air as water vapour. After some time, the rising air will cool. At this point the water vapour condenses. When water vapour condenses it releases latent heat energy and forms water droplets. These water droplets create clouds that eventually produce rain, snow or hail (precipitation).

KEY WORDS

surface area*: the outer part or exposed area of a material

humidity*: the proportion of water vapour in the air

precipitation: water that falls from the atmosphere to the Earth's surface as rain, sleet, snow or hail

Much of the precipitation will fall directly back into seas and oceans. However, some clouds will move over land and water from these clouds will fall onto the land. The water droplets might soak into the ground or flow above ground as **surface run-off**.

> ### KEY WORD
>
> **surface run-off:** water flowing over land to return to rivers and oceans (can occur on natural surfaces such as rocks, soil and vegetation, or artificial surfaces such as roads and buildings)

Some of this water evaporates back into the atmosphere from the land, or from areas of freshwater, such as lakes. Much of the water that falls on land will eventually flow into rivers and back into seas and oceans. This process is summarised in Figure 2.13.

Questions

3 Describe diffusion in terms of particles. Include the random movement of particles in your answer.

4 Explain the following terms, referring to arrangement of particles and energy changes:

   a evaporation

   b condensation

   c freezing

   d melting.

5 Compare how ice melting on land affects sea levels compared to the melting of ice floating on water.

6 a Sketch an outline of the water cycle that includes these terms: evaporation, condensation, precipitation and surface run-off.

   b Describe factors that affect the rate of evaporation of water from the oceans.

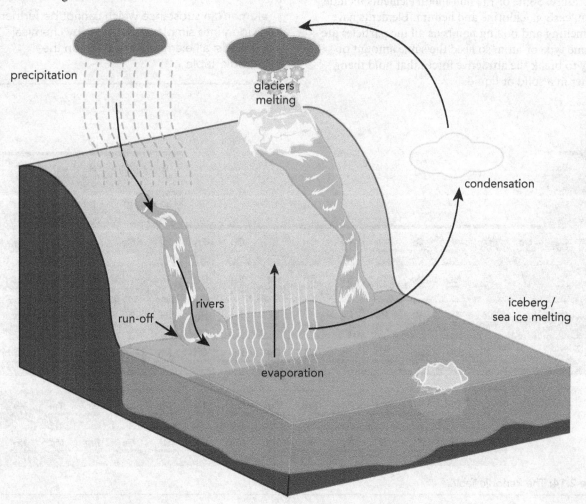

Figure 2.13: Processes in the water cycle.

2.2 pH and salinity

Elements, compounds and mixtures

We can group, or classify, all materials into three types depending on the combination of particles they are made from. These three types are elements, compounds and mixtures.

An **element** is a substance containing particles that are all the same type of atom. All the different elements are listed in the Periodic Table of Elements, shown in Figure 2.14. However, it is not necessary to learn the details of these elements.

Most of the elements are metals (such as iron, sodium and calcium), and most elements are solids at room temperature. Some of the non-metal elements include oxygen, carbon, chlorine and helium. Elements have fixed melting and boiling points as all the particles are the same type of atom so need the same amount of energy to break the attractive forces that hold them together in a solid or liquid.

Elements can be individual atoms with very weak attractions to other atoms of the same element, such as helium. Some elements, such as oxygen and chlorine, consist of molecules – groups of atoms of the same element. There are strong attractions to each atom within the molecule but very weak attractions to atoms in other molecules. Elements can also consist of large crystals with many atoms of the same element strongly attracted to each other in a giant structure, such as iron, sodium, calcium and carbon. Different elements and their structures are shown in Figure 2.15.

Oxygen is an element and it contains pairs of oxygen atoms held strongly together, forming oxygen molecules, O_2. Each molecule of oxygen has a very weak attraction to other oxygen molecules, resulting in oxygen being a gas at room temperature.

> ### KEY WORD
>
> **element:** a substance which cannot be further divided into simpler substances by chemical methods; all elements are listed on the Periodic Table

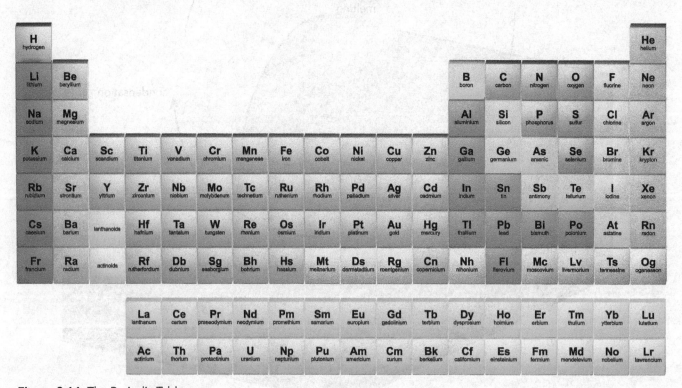

Figure 2.14: The Periodic Table.

A **compound** is a substance containing particles made from two or more different types of atom (two or more elements) in a fixed ratio. Like elements, compounds have fixed melting and boiling points as their particles are in a regular arrangement, and need the same amount of energy to break the attractive forces that hold them together in a solid or liquid.

Compounds must contain at least two atoms of different elements. Compounds can consist of molecules with a fixed number of atoms of each element, such as water (H_2O), carbon dioxide (CO_2) and glucose ($C_6H_{12}O_6$). Compounds can also have structures which are larger

than simple molecules, with a fixed ratio of atoms of each element, such as sodium chloride (NaCl) and calcium carbonate ($CaCO_3$). The formula of a compound tells us the ratio of each element in the compound. These examples are shown in Figure 2.16.

> ## KEY WORD
>
> **compound:** a substance formed by the chemical combination of two or more elements in fixed proportions

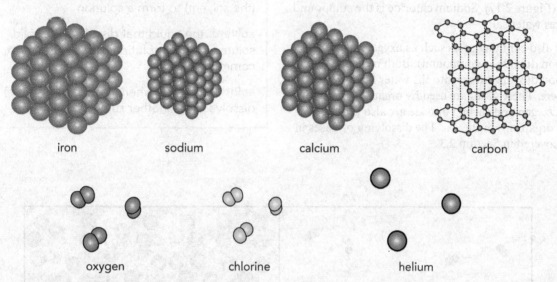

iron   sodium   calcium   carbon

oxygen   chlorine   helium

Figure 2.15: The arrangement of particles in the elements iron, sodium, calcium, carbon, oxygen, chlorine and helium.

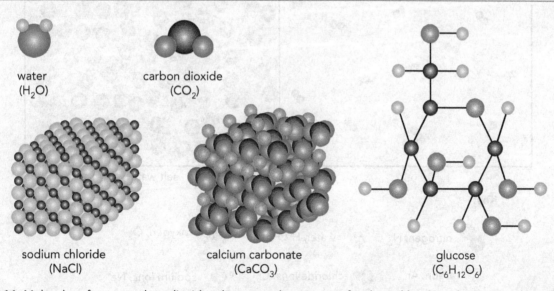

water
(H_2O)

carbon dioxide
(CO_2)

sodium chloride
(NaCl)

calcium carbonate
($CaCO_3$)

glucose
($C_6H_{12}O_6$)

Figure 2.16: Molecules of water, carbon dioxide, glucose, and structures of sodium chloride and calcium carbonate.

A mixture is a substance containing different types of particles. A mixture must contain different elements. But, unlike a compound, the substances in a mixture are not in a fixed ratio. Air is an example of a mixture as it contains the gases nitrogen, oxygen and many other gases (Figure 2.17). The proportion of each gas in the air can change – the air we breathe in contains more oxygen than the air we breathe out because some of the oxygen is removed from the air in our lungs.

Seawater is another example of a mixture. Seawater mostly contains the compound water, but seawater also contains other substances, such as the compound sodium chloride (Figure 2.17). Sodium chloride is the compound that makes water salty.

Seawater also contains gases such as oxygen (an element) and carbon dioxide (a compound). Both oxygen and carbon dioxide diffuse into the water from the atmosphere. These gases are used by organisms living in the sea. Oxygen and carbon dioxide are also produced by living organisms in the sea. The dissolving of gases in water is covered in Section 2.3.

Dissolving

When a solid substance dissolves in a liquid substance, a mixture is formed containing both substances.

- The solid that dissolves is called a solute.
- The liquid that does the dissolving is called a solvent.
- The mixture is called a solution.

KEY WORDS

solute: a substance that dissolves in a liquid (the solvent) to form a solution

solvent: the liquid that dissolves the solid solute to form a solution; water is the most common solvent

solution: formed when a substance (solute) dissolves into another substance (solvent)

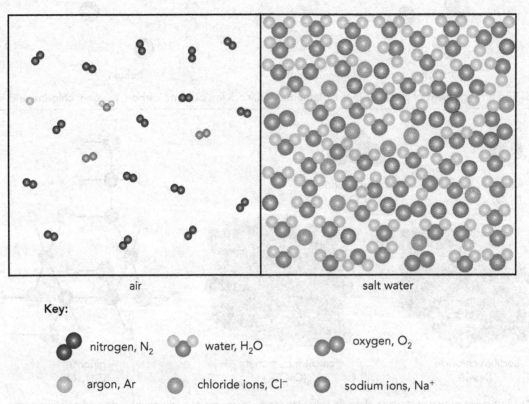

air   salt water

Key:

nitrogen, N_2 water, H_2O oxygen, O_2

argon, Ar   chloride ions, Cl^- sodium ions, Na^+

Figure 2.17: Particles in air and salt water.

A solid that dissolves well is described as soluble. A solid that does not dissolve is described as insoluble.

Salts are compounds that are made of ions. These ions are attracted to each other, forming a large crystalline structure. Some salts, such as sodium chloride and magnesium sulfate, are soluble in water. Other salts, such as calcium carbonate, are insoluble in water.

KEY WORDS

insoluble: the description of a substance that does not dissolve in a particular solvent

salts: ionic compounds that can be made by the neutralisation of an acid with an alkali

ions*: charged particles made from an atom or group of atoms

PRACTICAL TASK 2.2

Investigating the effect of temperature on the solubility of a solute in water

Introduction

This practical task investigates the solubility of a salt at different temperatures in water. The salt you will use is called ammonium chloride. You will dilute a concentrated solution of ammonium chloride to different concentrations. Then you will record the temperature at which the salt begins to recrystallise as it cools.

You will need:

- a boiling tube
- a boiling tube rack
- two 250 cm^3 beakers
- a stirring thermometer (−10 °C to 110 °C) (or a stirring rod and a thermometer)
- a 10 cm^3 measuring cylinder
- a dropping pipette
- a boiling tube holder
- 3.0 g ammonium chloride solid
- an electronic balance
- ice
- hot water.

Safety: Follow all laboratory safety rules.
Ammonium chloride is harmful if swallowed and is an irritant to the eyes.
Take care stirring with the thermometer.
Your teacher may advise you to use a stirring rod instead to ensure the solution heats and cools uniformly.
Take care with hot water as this can burn.
Wear eye protection.
Some types of glass may break when you heat or cool them quickly. Check with your teacher about clearing up broken glass.

Method

1. Set up a hot water bath in one of the beakers and an ice bath in the other beaker.

2. Weigh out 3.0 g of ammonium chloride and add this to the boiling tube.

3. Add 5.0 cm^3 of water to the boiling tube and warm the boiling tube and contents in the hot water bath until all the solid dissolves (Figure 2.18).

4. Transfer the boiling tube to the ice bath and stir with the thermometer (or stirring rod).

5. When crystals start to form, note the temperature in a copy of Table 2.3.

6. Add another 1.0 cm^3 of water to the boiling tube and warm the contents again in the hot water bath until all the solid dissolves.

CONTINUED

7   Transfer the boiling tube to the ice bath and stir with the thermometer (or stirring rod).

8   When crystals start to form, note the new temperature in a copy of Table 2.3.

9   Repeat steps 6–8 until a total of 12 cm³ of water has been used.

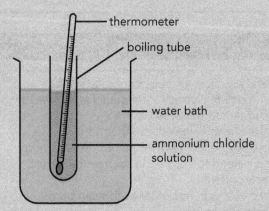

Figure 2.18: Diagram of setup for Practical Task 2.2.

Results

Volume of water (cm³)	Concentration (g / dm³)	Temperature at which crystals appear (°C)
5.0	600	
6.0	500	
7.0	429	

Volume of water (cm³)	Concentration (g / dm³)	Temperature at which crystals appear (°C)
8.0	375	
9.0	333	
10.0	300	
11.0	273	
12.0	250	

Table 2.3: The temperature at which crystals appear as the concentration of ammonium chloride decreases.

Questions

1   Plot a line graph of your results, with concentration on the x-axis and temperature at which crystals appear on the y-axis. Do not forget to label the axes and include the correct units. Draw a suitable line of best fit for the results you plot.

2   Describe the pattern in your results. What conclusion can you make from your results?

3   Are there any anomalies in your data? If you are not sure, is it easy to draw a line of best fit for your results? Are there any points that are further from the general trend?

> This Practical task links to Skills tips 0.1, 0.7 and 0.8.

Self-assessment

How well did you complete this practical task? Rate your work according to the following scheme for each of the points listed:

🙂   if you did it really well

😐   if you made a good attempt at it and partly succeeded

☹   if you did not try to do it or did not succeed.

• I measured all of the masses using a balance that measures to at least 1 decimal place.

• I did not write the units again next to the values in the results table.

• I labelled both axes on the graph to show what the data represents and included the units.

• I plotted the points for the line graph with small distinct crosses or marks that identified the point to within 1 mm.

• I drew a line of best fit to show the trend of the points plotted.

Salinity of seawater

We use the term salinity to describe the concentration of dissolved salts in water. Salinity is measured in parts per thousand (ppt). One litre of pure water has a mass of 1000 g. To calculate the mass of salt in seawater, convert the salinity in ppt into grams of salt. Seawater has an average salinity of approximately 35 ppt, so one litre of average seawater contains approximately 35 g of dissolved salts. Most of this is sodium chloride, but other salts are also present, such as magnesium sulfate.

The salinity of any sample of seawater varies, depending on several factors. Many of these factors are to do with the water cycle. These factors are summarised in Table 2.4.

Figure 2.19: Part of the shore along the Dead Sea – the salinity is so high that salt crystallises along the shore line.

Factor	Impact on salinity
erosion of rocks on land	Rocks contain many minerals and salts and some of these salts are soluble in water. As rain falls on rocks, the salts dissolve in the rainwater and are carried away in the water.
run-off	Most water falling on land as precipitation eventually finds its way into streams and rivers that flow into seas and oceans. This run-off carries dissolved substances, such as salts from rocks, into the sea. The concentration of these dissolved salts is very low compared to concentrations in seawater. Areas of sea near to the mouths of rivers have lower salinity due to the flow of freshwater into the sea at these points.
precipitation	Precipitation directly over the sea adds freshwater to the sea. Precipitation has no dissolved salts. This creates seawater with a lower salinity. Precipitation falling on land makes its way to the ocean in rivers which have very low salinity, as described above for run-off.
evaporation	Evaporation causes water to leave the surface of the sea, leaving dissolved salts behind in the seawater. This creates seawater with a higher salinity. Evaporation happens faster where surface water temperatures are warmer, the air is drier (less humid), or the wind speed is faster.
temperature	Higher temperatures cause faster evaporation of water from the surface of the sea. As water evaporates from the sea it leaves the salt behind. This creates seawater with a higher salinity. This is important in hot areas with smaller enclosed seas, such as the Red Sea and the Dead Sea (Figure 2.19). In these seas, salinity is very high.
melting of ice sheets and glaciers	Ice sheets and glaciers are stores of frozen freshwater on land. The melting of ice sheets and glaciers releases freshwater, which can flow into seas. This fresh water reduces the salinity of the seas.

Table 2.4: Factors affecting salinity of seawater.

Figure 2.20: An estuary forms where a river enters the ocean.

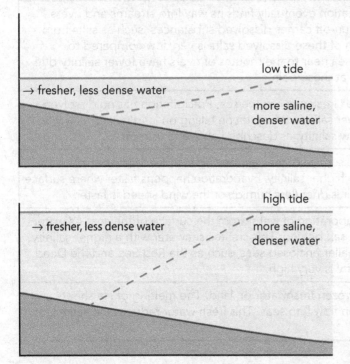

Figure 2.21: Low and high tides in an estuary and the impact on salinity in the estuary.

Sometimes a large river meets the ocean in a partly enclosed tidal area called an estuary (Figure 2.20). As the tides change, the salinity of the water in the estuary can change (Figure 2.21). The constant changes in salinity make life very difficult for organisms that live in the water in estuaries.

Figure 2.22: The Pacific Ocean.

The Pacific Ocean is the largest ocean on Earth (Figure 2.22).

The average salinity in the Pacific Ocean is 35 ppt.

However, salinity varies around the Pacific, particularly close to estuaries that release freshwater into the Pacific. Water flows freely between the Pacific Ocean and the Southern Ocean. Water also flows between the Pacific Ocean and the Arctic Ocean (see Figure 1.19 in Chapter 1).

The Red Sea is a small body of water between Africa and Asia (Figure 2.23). The Red Sea is almost entirely enclosed by land and is at a latitude that results in warm temperatures all year round. This means that there is a high level of evaporation from the surface of the Red Sea. There is also very little precipitation and run-off to replace the evaporated water. As a result, the Red Sea has higher than average salinity, ranging from 36 ppt in the south (where seawater can flow into and out of the neighbouring Gulf of Aden and the Indian Ocean) to 40 ppt in the north.

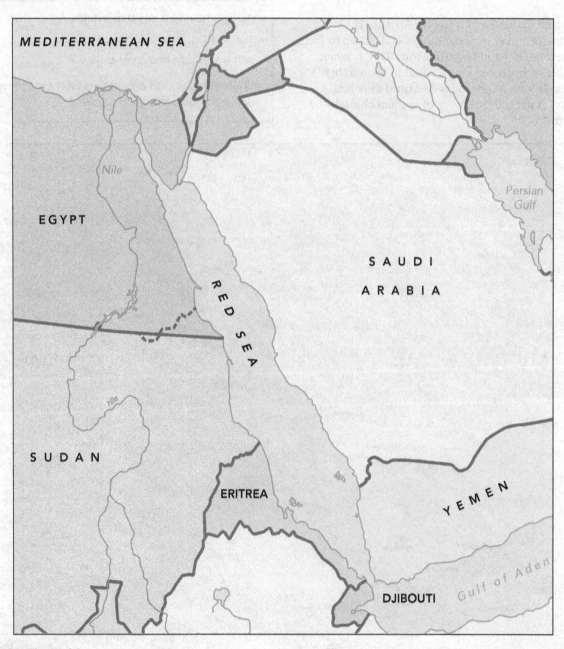

Figure 2.23: The Red Sea.

The Baltic Sea is another enclosed area of sea in Northern Europe (Figure 2.24). The Baltic Sea is surrounded by land. The climate of the Baltic Sea has low temperatures and much precipitation. This results in run-off of freshwater into the Baltic Sea. The fresh water reduces the salinity of the surface water to 3–9 ppt.

pH

Water is a compound and it has the formula H_2O. A very small number of water molecules split up to form hydrogen ions (H^+) and hydroxide ions (OH^-). When the number of hydrogen ions is equal to the number of hydroxide ions, a solution is described as neutral. Pure water is neutral. Solutions of sodium chloride are also neutral.

Some substances dissolve in water to produce a solution that is acidic. Other substances dissolve in water to produce a solution that is alkaline. Acids are solutions with more hydrogen ions than hydroxide ions. Examples of acids include hydrochloric acid (HCl). Alkalis are solutions with more hydroxide ions than

KEY WORDS

neutral: having a pH that equals 7

acidic: a solution containing H^+ ions in water; such a solution has a pH below 7

alkaline: a solution containing OH^- ions in water; such a solution has a pH above 7

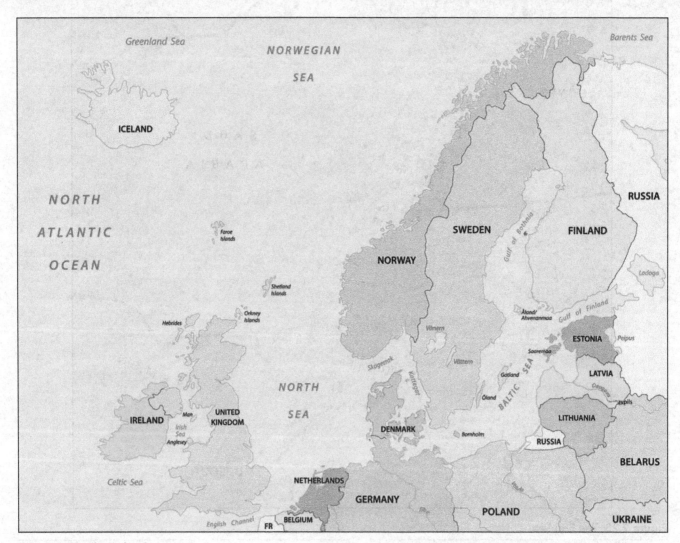

Figure 2.24: The Baltic Sea.

hydrogen ions. Examples of hydroxides include sodium hydroxide (NaOH).

We can measure if a solution is neutral, acidic or alkaline using the **pH scale**. This scale measures the concentration of hydrogen ions in a solution. A neutral solution has a pH of 7. Any solution with a pH lower than 7 is acidic. A solution with a pH greater than 7 is alkaline. We can measure the pH of a solution using universal indicator (Figure 2.25).

KEY WORD

pH scale: a scale running from 0 to 14, used for expressing the acidity or alkalinity of a solution; a neutral solution has a pH of 7

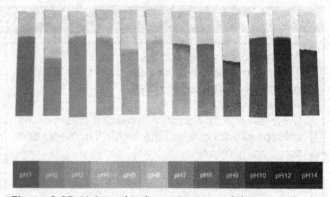

Figure 2.25: Universal indicator paper and the pH scale; the different colours indicate that a solution being tested has a certain pH.

Seawater has a pH of approximately 8.1, so is slightly alkaline. This is because there are large quantities of calcium carbonate on the seabed. Although calcium carbonate is insoluble in water, the carbonate ions react with water to produce hydrogencarbonate ions and hydroxide ions. The hydroxide ions increase the pH above 7 to make seawater weakly alkaline.

PRACTICAL TASK 2.3

Investigating the pH of seawater, freshwater and rainwater, using universal indicator

Introduction

The pH of a substance is a measure of how many hydrogen ions, H^+, a substance contains. A neutral substance contains an equal number of hydrogen ions and hydroxide ions. Solutions with more hydrogen ions are acids, and solutions with more hydroxide ions are alkalis.

We can use universal indicator to find the approximate pH of a solution. Universal indicator comes as a solution, which we can add directly to the solution being investigated, or as paper strips, which we can dip into the solution.

You will need:

- 1 mol / dm³ hydrochloric acid (up to 5 cm³ per group)

- 1 mol / dm³ sodium hydroxide solution (up to 5 cm³ per group)

- universal indicator solution or paper with corresponding colour pH chart

- six test-tubes

- a test-tube rack

- distilled water (up to 5 cm³ per group for testing, plus extra for rinsing test-tubes)

- seawater (up to 5 cm³ per group)

- freshwater (up to 5 cm³ per group)

- rainwater (up to 5 cm³ per group)

- dropping pipettes or glass rods (if using universal indicator paper).

CONTINUED

Safety: Follow all laboratory safety rules.
1 mol / dm³ sodium hydroxide is corrosive and particularly dangerous to eyes.
You must wear eye protection.
Universal indicator solution – check the risks of the solution provided. Many are highly flammable and some are harmful.
Check with your teacher about any potential risks for the seawater.

Method

Two methods are shown to allow for the use of universal indicator as either solution or paper (Figure 2.26). You do not need to carry out both methods.

Universal indicator solution

1   Pour an approximately 1 cm depth of 1 mol / dm³ hydrochloric acid into a test-tube.

2   Test the solution with a few drops of universal indicator solution. In a copy of Table 2.5, note the resulting colour of the indicator and the corresponding pH from the colour chart.

3   Repeat steps 1 and 2 with the following: 1 mol / dm³ sodium hydroxide solution, distilled water, seawater, freshwater and rainwater.

Universal indicator paper

1   Collect approximately 1 cm³ of 1 mol / dm³ hydrochloric acid in a test-tube.

2   Use a dropping pipette or a glass rod to transfer a drop of the hydrochloric acid to a piece of universal indicator paper. In a copy of Table 2.5, note the resulting colour of the indicator and the corresponding pH from the colour chart.

3   Repeat steps 1 and 2 with the following: 1 mol / dm³ sodium hydroxide solution, distilled water, seawater, freshwater and rainwater.

This Practical task links to Skills tips 0.1 and 0.3.

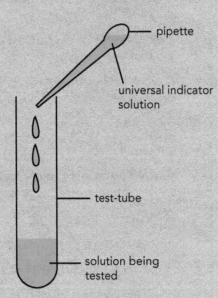

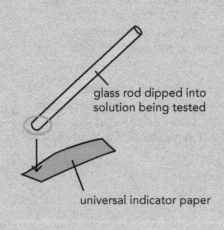

Figure 2.26: Using universal indicator solution or paper.

CONTINUED

Results

Sample	Colour of universal indicator	pH
1 mol / dm³ hydrochloric acid		
1 mol / dm³ sodium hydroxide		
distilled water		
seawater		
freshwater		
rainwater		

Table 2.5: Investigating the pH of seawater, freshwater and rainwater.

Challenge

If you have a pH meter, use this to obtain pH readings of the solutions tested. Compare the precision of your results using a pH meter to the readings using universal indicator.

Questions

1 Suggest reasons why the pH results varied for the samples of water tested.

2 What do you think might affect pH in oceans?

3 How could you check the accuracy of your results?

PRACTICAL TASK 2.4

Investigating the effect on pH of adding carbon dioxide to seawater

Introduction

- Carbon dioxide concentrations are increasing in the atmosphere as humans burn more fossil fuels. This investigation looks at the effect that increasing the concentration of carbon dioxide in the ocean has on the pH of seawater.

You will need:

- seawater
- a beaker or cup
- a straw
- universal indicator solution
- a stopwatch or timer.

Safety: Follow all laboratory safety rules. You must wear eye protection.

> Universal indicator solution – check the risks of the solution provided. Many are highly flammable and some are harmful.
> Take care not to suck the solution in to your mouth – only blow through the straws.

Method

1 Half fill the beaker with seawater.

2 Add a few drops of universal indicator, just enough to give a visible colour in the seawater.

3 Record the colour of the universal indicator solution. Use the colour chart to record the pH.

4 Start a stopwatch or timer and gently blow through the straw into the seawater (Figure 2.27). Take care not to splash the liquid on your face.

5 Keep blowing gently for 1 minute, taking your mouth off the straw to take breaths between blowing into the solution.

6 After 1 minute, record the colour of the universal indicator solution and the pH in a copy of Table 2.6.

CONTINUED

7   Repeat steps 5 and 6 until you have blown into the seawater for 5 minutes.

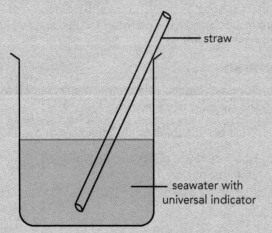

Figure 2.27: Diagram of setup for Practical Task 2.4.

Results

Time / minutes	Colour of universal indicator	pH
0		
1		
2		
3		

Time / minutes	Colour of universal indicator	pH
4		
5		

Table 2.6

Questions

1   What happens to the pH of seawater as the concentration of carbon dioxide increases?

2   What gases are present in the air we breathe out?

3   How could the experiment be adapted to show that it is carbon dioxide that is causing the change in pH?

4   What could we use instead of universal indicator to make the pH readings more precise?

KEY WORD

fossil fuels: energy-rich fuels that are extracted from underground; they were produced from plants and protoctists that lived millions of years ago

This Practical task links to Skills tip 0.1.

Questions

7   Match each of the following substances to the type of substance:

Substance	Type of substance
seawater	element
oxygen	compound
calcium carbonate	mixture

8   Describe the change in pH of seawater when carbon dioxide is added to the seawater.

9   Explain why the Baltic Sea has a much lower salinity than the Red Sea.

10 Freshwater enters estuaries to meet salt water. Use your knowledge about tides to explain why the salinity of the water in an estuary will change during each tidal cycle (just over 24 hours).

2.3 Dissolved gases

It is not just solids that can dissolve in water; gases can too. Most organisms that live in seas or oceans need to obtain oxygen or carbon dioxide from the water. Gases, such as oxygen and carbon dioxide from the atmosphere, dissolve in water in a process called atmospheric dissolution. Oxygen and carbon dioxide have much lower solubilities in water than salts, as shown in Table 2.7.

Substance	Solubility (g / dm³)
sodium chloride, NaCl	357
oxygen, O_2	0.04
carbon dioxide, CO_2	1.50

Table 2.7: Relative solubility in water of sodium chloride, oxygen and carbon dioxide.

The solubility of oxygen in water is very low. However, there is quite a lot of oxygen in the air (about 20% of the air is oxygen). This means that oxygen does diffuse into seawater and dissolve in seawater. Table 2.8 shows that there is a very low concentration of carbon dioxide in the atmosphere. Carbon dioxide makes up only 0.04% of the atmosphere but carbon dioxide is more soluble in water than oxygen.

The two gases making up most of the atmosphere are nitrogen and oxygen. However, in the ocean the dissolved gases have very different proportions. These are summarised in Table 2.8.

Gas	Atmosphere	Surface ocean	Total ocean
nitrogen, N_2	78%	48%	11%
oxygen, O_2	21%	36%	6%
carbon dioxide, CO_2	0.04%	15%	83%

Table 2.8: Proportion of gases in the atmosphere and dissolved in oceans.

When the temperature of water increases, the particles gain more kinetic energy and move faster. Dissolved gases near to the surface of the water will begin to diffuse out of solution faster than molecules of gas diffusing into the solution. So warm temperatures reduce the concentration of dissolved gas in solution. You can see this in Figure 2.28 – the higher the temperature the lower the concentration of dissolved gases in the water.

It is important to remember that this trend is the opposite to the effect of increasing temperatures on the dissolving of solids.

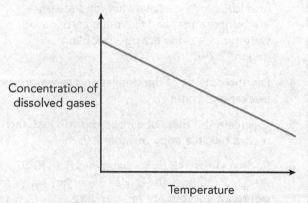

Figure 2.28: The effect of increasing water temperature on the concentration of dissolved gases.

PRACTICAL TASK 2.5

Investigating the effect of temperature on gas solubility

Introduction

Carbonated water is a solution of carbon dioxide in water. The carbon dioxide is stored in the water at high pressure, maintaining a higher concentration of carbon dioxide than can normally dissolve in water. We can use carbonated water to investigate the effect of temperature on the solubility of carbon dioxide.

You will need:

- carbonated water at 4 °C
- five glass beakers
- ice
- hot water
- a large beaker or plastic tub (to use as a water bath)
- a thermometer
- an electronic balance.

CONTINUED

Safety: Follow all laboratory safety rules. Take care with water and wet hands around electrical equipment.
Clear up any water or ice spills immediately to avoid the risk of people slipping.

Method

1   Zero the balance before placing a beaker on the balance. Record the mass of the beaker.

2   Add approximately 100 g of carbonated water to the beaker. Record the mass of the beaker and the carbonated water.

3   Place the beaker in a water bath set at 0 °C (use lots of ice in some water and measure the temperature) and leave the carbonated water until it stops fizzing / bubbling (Figure 2.29).

4   Dry the outside of the beaker and re-weigh the beaker and water.

5   Calculate the mass of carbon dioxide lost and record this in a copy of Table 2.9.

6   Repeat steps 1–5 using water baths at 10 °C, 20 °C, 30 °C and 40 °C. Use ice or hot water to get to an appropriate temperature.

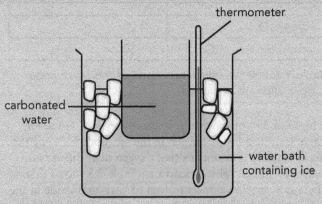

Figure 2.29: Diagram of setup for Practical Task 2.5.

Questions

1   Describe what happens to the mass of carbon dioxide lost as the temperature increases.

2   Explain what this means for the concentration of dissolved carbon dioxide at different temperatures.

3   How could the accuracy of your results be checked?

This Practical task links to Skills tips 0.1 and 0.7.

Results

Temperature (°C)	Mass of beaker (g)	Mass of beaker plus carbonated water (start) (g)	Mass of beaker plus carbonated water (finish) (g)	Mass of carbon dioxide lost (g)
0				
10				
20				
30				
40				

Table 2.9: Investigating the loss of carbon dioxide at different temperatures.

2.4 Density

Manipulating mathematical formulae

Sometimes we need to carry out simple calculations using a formula, for example calculating density and calculating magnification for microscopes (Chapter 3). It is useful to be able to rearrange a formula to calculate any of the values the formula uses. We can do this using a triangle.

The formula for density is given as:

$$\text{density} = \frac{\text{mass}}{\text{volume}}$$

As mass is placed above volume in the formula, mass goes at the top of the triangle. The bottom of the triangle contains both the other values: density and volume:

mass = density × volume illustrated as a triangle

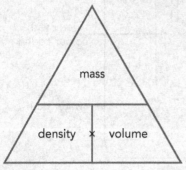

Figure 2.30: Mass = density × volume illustrated as a triangle.

If you are given any two of the values in the equation you can use the triangle to calculate the unknown third value.

To calculate volume:

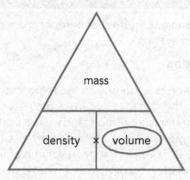

Figure 2.31: Calculating volume.

You divide the mass by density.

To calculate mass:

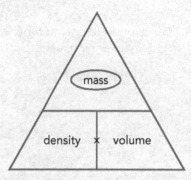

Figure 2.32: Calculating mass.

You must multiply density by volume.

Density is a measure of the mass of an object relative to the volume of the object. Density is measured using the formula:

$$\text{density} = \frac{\text{mass}}{\text{volume}}$$

Density has an important role in seas and oceans as it affects the properties of seawater. Seawater will rise or sink, depending on its density, and this creates currents. Changes in the density of water are particularly affected by:

- changes in temperature of the water
- changes in salinity of the water.

PRACTICAL TASK 2.6

Investigating the effect of temperature on the density of water

Introduction

Water changes in density as the temperature changes. The changes in density are very small and difficult to measure using standard lab equipment. For example, for 100 g of pure water a temperature rise of 40 °C gives a change in volume of less than 1 cm³. This investigation uses a narrow glass tube to help you see and measure the changes in volume as the temperature changes.

You will need:

- a boiling tube
- a rubber bung to fit boiling tube, with a hole containing a thin glass tube
- a marker to write on glass
- a ruler
- ice
- hot water
- a large beaker or plastic tub (to use as a water bath)
- a thermometer
- distilled water stored in the fridge at 4 °C.

Safety: Follow all laboratory safety rules. Clear up any water or ice spills immediately to avoid the risk of people slipping.

Method

1   Almost fill a boiling tube with cold distilled water. Add a few drops of dye or indicator to give the water a visible colour (this is to help make the results easier to see). Shake well to mix the colour with the water.

2   Fit the rubber bung containing a thin glass tube to the boiling tube – take care to make sure there is no air trapped in the boiling tube (Figure 2.33).

3   Place the beaker in a water bath at 10 °C (use ice in some water) and leave until the coloured water stops moving in the glass tube. Make a copy of Table 2.10 and mark the height of the coloured water; this is the zero mark.

4   Repeat step 3 using water baths at 20 °C, 30 °C, 40 °C and 50 °C. Use ice or hot water to get to an appropriate temperature. Measure the difference in height of the coloured water for each temperature compared with the mark made in step 3.

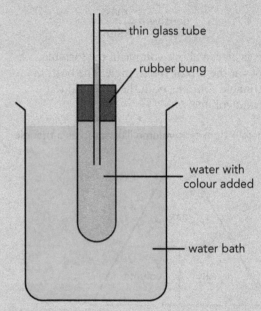

Figure 2.33: Diagram of setup for Practical Task 2.6.

Results

Temperature (°C)	Change in height of water from 10 °C (mm)
10	0
20	
30	
40	
50	

Table 2.10: Change in height of water as temperature increases.

CONTINUED

Questions

1 Describe the change in the volume of water as the temperature increases.

2 Explain how this change in volume relates to the change in density of water as the temperature increases.

3 How could you improve the accuracy of your results?

4 Using what you have learned from this experiment, suggest what your results could mean if global ocean temperatures increase.

This Practical task links to Skills tip 0.1.

PRACTICAL TASK 2.7

Investigating the effect of salinity on the density of water

Introduction

Ocean water has an average salinity of 35 ppt. The salinity of seawater can vary from less than 10 ppt to as high as 280 ppt in the Dead Sea. In this investigation you will use accurate measurements of the mass and volume of samples of water of different salinities to calculate the density.

You will need:

- an accurate electronic balance (capable of measuring to 0.1 g)
- a 10 cm³ syringe
- a 50 cm³ or 100 cm³ beaker
- 100 cm³ of 50 ppt salt water.

Safety: Follow all laboratory safety rules.
Take care with water and wet hands around electrical equipment.
Clear up any water spills immediately to avoid the risk of people slipping.

Method

1 Use the syringe to measure exactly 10 cm³ of 50 ppt salt water.

2 Place the beaker on to the balance and zero the balance.

3 Carefully add all of the salt water from the syringe into the beaker.

4 Record the mass of the 10 cm³ sample of 50 ppt salt water in a copy of Table 2.11.

5 Repeat steps 1–4 two more times to give you three results for 50 ppt salt water.

6 Use the syringe to measure exactly 8 cm³ of 50 ppt salt water.

7 Carefully add exactly 2 cm³ of distilled water to the same syringe, giving a total volume of exactly 10 cm³ (this is now 40 ppt salt water).

8 Place the beaker on to the balance and zero the balance.

9 Carefully add all of the salt water from the syringe into the beaker.

10 Record the mass of the 10 cm³ sample of 40 ppt salt water in your results table.

11 Repeat steps 6–10 two more times to give you three results for 40 ppt salt water.

12 Repeat steps 6–11 for:

- 30 ppt (6 cm³ of 50 ppt salt water and 4 cm³ of distilled water)
- 20 ppt (4 cm³ of 50 ppt salt water and 6 cm³ of distilled water)
- 10 ppt (2 cm³ of 50 ppt salt water and 8 cm³ of distilled water)
- 0 ppt (10 cm³ of distilled water only).

CONTINUED

Results

Volume of 50 ppt salt water used (cm³)	Volume of distilled water used (cm³)	Salinity of 10 cm³ of water produced (ppt)	Mass of water sample (g)				Density of water sample (g / cm³)
			Test 1	Test 2	Test 3	Mean	
10	0	50					
8	2	40					
6	4	30					
4	6	20					
2	8	10					
0	10	0					

Table 2.11: Change in density of seawater as salinity decreases.

Questions

1   Draw a line graph of your results with 'salinity' on the x-axis and 'density of the water sample' on the y-axis.

2   Describe the change in the density of water as the salinity increases.

3   In this investigation you have repeated the measurements and calculated averages. How could the precision of your results be improved?

> This Practical task links to Skills tips 0.1 and 0.7.

Self-assessment

How well did you complete this practical task? Rate your work according to the following scheme for each of the points listed:

☺   if you did it really well

😐   if you made a good attempt at it and partly succeeded

☹   if you did not try to do it or did not succeed.

- I recorded all of the masses to at least 1 decimal place, including those with results that were whole numbers (for example,10.0 g).

- I did not write the units again next to the values in the results table.

- I labelled both axes on the graph to show what the data represents and included the units.

- I plotted the points for the line graph with small distinct crosses or marks that identified the point to within 1 mm.

- I drew a line of best fit to show the trend of the points plotted.

Denser water contains more particles in the same volume of water. This could be because:

- the particles are cooler and closer together

- the water contains more dissolved solute particles between the water molecules.

Water that is denser than surrounding water will sink and be replaced by water with a lower density. This movement of water can create convection currents – the denser water sinks deeper in the ocean and less dense water floats and rises towards the surface of the ocean. You will have seen convection by doing Activity 1.2 in Chapter 1.

As cooler water is more dense than warmer water, the cooler water sinks in the ocean. In warmer regions of the Earth, seawater at the ocean's surface is heated more than surface seawater in cooler regions. So tropical areas have a warm layer of surface seawater with a lower density. The changes in temperature with increasing depth are explained further in Section 2.5.

Questions

11 State the formula relating density, mass and volume.

12 Describe the effect of increasing temperature on the solubility of gases in water.

13 Use particle theory to explain why the density of water decreases as temperature increases.

14 Explain, using the term density, why colder water generally lies beneath warmer water in the oceans.

2.5 Effects of increasing depth

As you move deeper in the ocean so physical conditions in the water change. Many of these changes can be explained by particle theory. Some changes are caused by the increasing distance from the surface of the ocean.

When describing depth of water be very careful with your wording – try to use words such as 'deeper' or 'shallower' instead of 'higher' or 'lower'. A statement such as 'higher depths' is confusing because a high value is deeper, but a low value could mean that something is higher up in the ocean. When we describe an 'increasing depth' we mean moving deeper into the ocean.

There are five important conditions that change with depth:

- **light penetration**
- temperature
- pressure
- salinity
- dissolved oxygen.

The general impact of changing depth on these factors is summarised in Figure 2.34.

> KEY WORD
>
> **light penetration:** the depth light is able to reach in a body of water

Light penetration

Light from the Sun travels through space and the Earth's atmosphere. Light then reaches the surface of an ocean and enters the seawater. As it passes through seawater, the light is absorbed by water molecules, transferring light energy into heat energy. This results in the light intensity reducing as depth increases.

Depth	Light penetration	Temperature	Pressure	Salinity	Dissolved oxygen
surface ↓ increasing depth	surface ↑ increasing light intensity	surface ↑ increasing temperature	surface ↓ increasing pressure	surface ↓ increasing salinity	surface ↕ increasing oxygen content

Figure 2.34: Changes in conditions as depth increases.

Almost all the light is absorbed in the upper 200 m of the ocean, referred to as the sunlight zone. This is the region where there is sufficient light intensity for photosynthesis to occur, supporting food chains (see Chapter 4).

In ideal conditions with very clear water, some light can penetrate to as far as 1000 m depth. This is called the twilight zone. Organisms in this zone have enough light to see.

No light is able to penetrate below 1000 m and this is called the midnight zone. In this zone there is permanent darkness and many animals are transparent or colourless. Some animals are bioluminescent (Figure 2.35). Figure 2.36 shows the ocean zones.

KEY WORDS

sunlight zone: the upper layer of the ocean, generally the top 200 m, where there is sufficient light for photosynthesis to occur; also known as the epipelagic zone

twilight zone: the layer of ocean below the sunlight zone where there is some light but not enough for photosynthesis to occur; typically extends from 200 m to 1000 m; also known as the mesopelagic zone

midnight zone: the deepest layer of ocean where no light can penetrate

bioluminescent: the biochemical release of light by living organisms

Figure 2.35: Bioluminescent firefly squid.

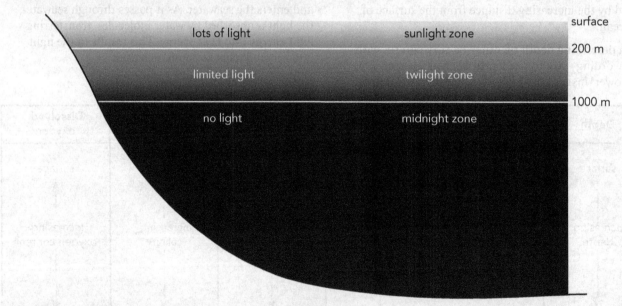

Figure 2.36: Zones in the ocean and relative penetration of light.

PRACTICAL TASK 2.8

Investigating light penetration through water using a Secchi disc

Introduction

A Secchi disc is a black and white disc with a weight attached to make the disc sink when it is lowered into water (Figures 2.37 and 2.38). The disc is also attached to a line or tape measure to record depth. This investigation can be used to measure the depth of light penetration by recording the depth at which you no longer see the Secchi disc. You can buy Secchi discs or make your own using a white plastic lid painted black on two of the quadrants.

You will need:

- a Secchi disc attached to a line / cord with marked measurements or attached to a tape measure

- access to a suitable body of water to record measurements.

Safety: Follow all safety rules and guidance from your teacher.
Take care around deep water to avoid falling in.

Figure 2.37: Using a Secchi disc from a boat.

Method

1 Lower the Secchi disc into the water until it just disappears. Record the depth of water on a copy of Table 2.12.

2 Continue to lower the disc for at least 1 metre more. Then slowly raise the disc until you can just see it. Record the depth of water.

3 Calculate the mean of the two readings to find the depth light penetrates to.

4 If possible, repeat these readings at different times of the year and compare your results.

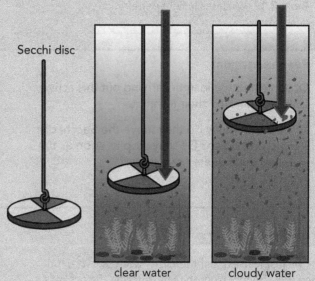

Secchi disc

clear water   cloudy water

Figure 2.38: Using a Secchi disc to investigate light penetration.

CONTINUED

Results

Date of readings	Depth at which disc disappears (m)	Depth at which disc reappears (m)	Mean depth at which disc cannot be seen (m)

Table 2.12: Changes in light penetration on different dates.

Questions

1 Compare your results with the results of another student. Discuss how similar the results are and any possible reasons for any differences.

2 Suggest reasons why the results may change during a year.

3 Suggest how the method could be improved to make results more reliable. You could consider equipment that might not be available to you.

Peer assessment

Observe another learner carrying out this activity. Give feedback on their technique:

- How carefully do they move the Secchi disc up and down? Do they stop as soon as the disc disappears / reappears?

- Are they consistent with how they measure the depth of the disc?

- Are the results recorded accurately and precisely?

Provide verbal feedback on these points to the other learner.

Temperature

As we just learned, light intensity decreases as depth increases. Energy from the Sun entering the ocean is transferred into heat energy in the water molecules, and it is water nearest the ocean's surface that is heated the most.

In colder regions of the Earth the heating effect may be very little, and any heat gained by the water is quickly transferred to the cold atmosphere above. However, in tropical regions the surface water can become very warm, with temperatures exceeding 30 °C near the Equator in the western Pacific Ocean.

As depth increases, the temperature of seawater decreases. This is mainly due to less light reaching deeper waters, so less heat is transferred to seawater at depth. We also know that warmer water is less dense than colder water – so warm water floats above colder denser water, reducing the mixing that occurs between these layers. This creates a rapid change in temperature with increasing depth, called a thermocline. Figure 2.39 shows the temperature gradients in polar, temperate and tropical regions.

KEY WORDS

thermocline*: the zone between two layers of water with different temperatures; where the temperature rapidly decreases as depth increases

temperature gradients*: changes in temperature as ocean depth increases; polar regions have more gradual changes in temperature with increasing depth compared to tropical regions

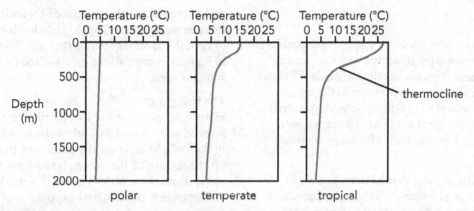

Figure 2.39: Temperature gradients in polar, temperate and tropical regions.

ACTIVITY 2.2

Modelling temperature gradients in water

In this activity you will model the formation of temperature gradients in water by adding colour to hot and cold water to help you see the layers of warmer and cooler water. This can be carried out in small groups or as a class demonstration.

You will need:

- cold water, e.g. stored in a fridge (up to 50 cm³ per group)

- blue and yellow food colours (any two contrasting colours can be used)

- two 100 cm³ beakers

- a dropping pipette and a stirrer

- hot water, e.g. from a hot tap (not boiling water, up to 50 cm³ per group).

Safety: Follow all laboratory safety rules. Take care with water and wet hands around electrical equipment.
Clear up any water spills immediately to avoid the risk of people slipping.
Take care if you are using hot water from a kettle, as both steam and hot water can cause burns. Beakers containing hot water can also quickly get very hot.

Method

1 Add a small volume of blue food colouring to about 50 cm³ of cold water in the first beaker to give the water a distinct colour. Mix well by stirring the water.

2 In a second beaker, add a small volume of a yellow food colouring to about 50 cm³ of hot water to give a distinct colour. Mix well by stirring the water.

3 Make sure the cold water has stopped swirling in the first beaker.

4 Use a dropping pipette to transfer 1–2 cm³ of coloured hot water (take care) into the cold water: insert the tip of the pipette into the middle of the cold water, then gently release the hot water into the coloured cold water. Observe what happens to the coloured hot water.

5 Repeat this process until you have transferred 15–20 cm³ of hot water.

6 Sketch a diagram to show any layers that have formed. Label the layers clearly to identify which is hot water and which is cold water. Show where some mixing has taken place. Note, however, that it is sometimes hard to see where mixing has occurred.

Pressure

Molecules of water have mass. As you move deeper into the ocean, the total weight of all the water molecules above you increases. This pushes the molecules of water closer together, increasing the pressure in the water. Pressure can be measured in atmospheres. 1 atmosphere is the pressure of the air at sea level. The pressure in water increases by 1 atmosphere with every 10 m of additional depth.

Organisms that live at great depths must be able to withstand very high pressures. Whales must breathe in air at the surface but dive to depths of over 2000 m where pressures exceed 200 atmospheres. A Cuvier's beaked whale has been tagged and recorded diving to a depth of 2992 m (Figure 2.40). This is the deepest recorded dive by any mammal.

Figure 2.40: Cuvier's beaked whale.

Dissolved oxygen

We learned earlier that oxygen is not very soluble in water, with only 0.04 g of oxygen able to dissolve in 1 dm³ of water at 25 °C. At the ocean's surface, oxygen can diffuse freely into seawater because the atmosphere contains 21% oxygen. This means that there is a significant concentration of oxygen in surface waters.

Oxygen is made by producers, which are organisms that perform photosynthesis to obtain their nutrition. A byproduct of photosynthesis is the release of oxygen,

and in the oceans this oxygen dissolves in seawater. Oxygen made by producers raises levels of dissolved oxygen in the sunlight zone (the top 200 m). This results in higher concentrations of dissolved oxygen in the sunlight zone.

The twilight zone is below the sunlight zone. Here light levels are too low for photosynthesis to occur so producers do not live below the sunlight zone. Also, in the twilight zone the distance from the atmosphere (at the surface of the ocean) is too great for diffusion to occur. Both these factors result in a sudden drop in the concentration of dissolved oxygen.

In the twilight zone there is an increase in bacteria that break down the detritus (called marine snow in the oceans) falling from the sunlight zone. These bacteria use oxygen to carry out respiration, which further reduces oxygen levels. The level of oxygen drops to a minimum, the oxygen minimum layer, at a depth of 200–1000 m.

KEY WORDS

producer: an organism that makes its own organic nutrients; generally using energy from sunlight, through the process called photosynthesis

detritus: solid remains and waste from living organisms

marine snow: particles of organic material that fall from surface waters to the deeper ocean

respiration: the chemical reactions in cells that break down nutrient molecules and release energy for metabolism

oxygen minimum layer*: the layer within the ocean where the concentration of dissolved oxygen is at its lowest; typically found in the twilight zone

Below the oxygen minimum layer, the concentration of dissolved oxygen rises and then remains fairly constant. This is because most of the detritus has been broken down, resulting in few bacteria. The change in concentration with depth is shown in Figure 2.41.

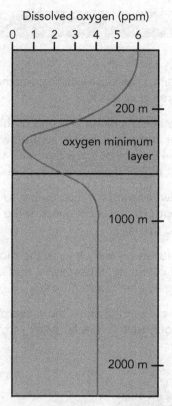

Figure 2.41: Change in oxygen concentration with depth.

2.6 Upwelling

An upwelling (see Section 1.4) is the movement of cold, nutrient-rich water from the deep ocean to the surface. Upwellings can occur when deep ocean currents are deflected (or bent) by the shape of the seabed.

Upwellings can also be caused by winds. When the wind blows away from the coast, the water at the surface of the ocean is pushed away from the land. This draws up cooler water from deeper in the ocean to replace the surface water. Figure 2.42 shows how this happens.

The cold water from deep in the ocean usually contains many dissolved mineral nutrients, which are taken in and used by producers to help them grow and multiply. This increases productivity in the food chain, with producers providing organic nutrients for animals.

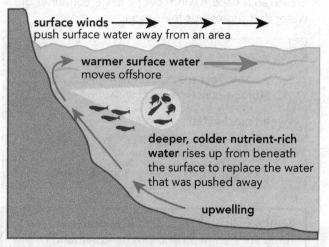

Figure 2.42: The process of upwelling.

KEY WORDS

nutrients: chemicals that provide what is needed for organisms to grow, repair damaged cells or tissues, release energy or for their metabolism

productivity: the rate of production of new biomass, usually through photosynthesis; biomass refers to any cells and tissues produced by organisms as they grow

food chain: a diagram showing the flow of energy from one organism to the next, beginning with a producer

ACTIVITY 2.3

Modelling an upwelling

In this activity you will work as a group to model the formation of an upwelling. You will use a fan to create an 'offshore wind' over a large container of water that represents the ocean.

You will need:

- a large clear plastic container, such as a storage container
- an electric fan
- water
- food colouring or water-soluble colour.

Safety: Follow all laboratory safety rules. Take care with water and wet hands around electrical equipment. Clear up any water spills immediately to avoid the risk of people slipping.

Method

1 Add water to the large plastic container so it is about three-quarters full.

2 Place the electric fan at one end of the container and angle the fan so it blows air across the surface of the water (raise the plastic container higher if necessary) (Figure 2.43).

3 Add a few drops of food colouring to the water on the bottom of the container at the end closest to the fan.

4 Switch the fan on and observe the movement of the food colouring. If necessary, add extra food colouring as the colour moves.

5 Sketch a diagram to show the movement of the food colouring in the water as air moves over the water.

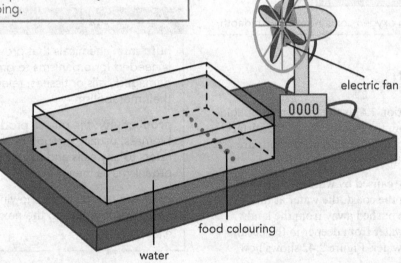

electric fan

food colouring

water

Figure 2.43: Diagram of setup for Activity 2.3.

REFLECTION

Some people find using a model as in Activity 2.3 helps them to understand.

- Did this model help you to understand how upwelling works?

- How do you think the design of the model could be improved to represent the land and ocean even better?

El Niño

El Niño is a weather event that occurs irregularly every two to seven years and involves changes in the weather patterns in the eastern Pacific Ocean. Further changes in weather patterns across wide areas of the Earth then follow, as well as more localised impacts on growth and reproduction in food chains in the ocean, which also impact on fisheries.

> ### KEY WORD
>
> **El Niño:** a warm current that develops off the coast of Ecuador, usually in December, which can cause widespread death within local food chains

Normal conditions

In the eastern Pacific Ocean, off the coast of Peru, equatorial trade winds usually blow from east to west. These trade winds push water away from the coast of South America in the Pacific. Usually, the trade winds create a persistent upwelling, cooling the surface waters and bringing up nutrients to the surface waters off the coast of South America. These normal conditions are shown in Figure 2.44.

This nutrient-rich water creates highly productive food chains, with many small fish including anchovies (Figure 2.45) and sardines. The large populations of these small fish support many large marine animals and birds, as well as a large fishing industry.

Figure 2.45: Blue sharks feeding on anchovies.

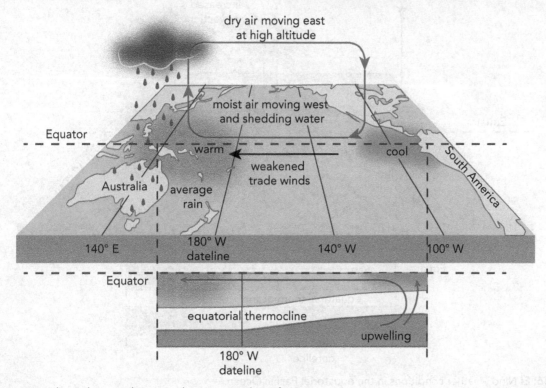

Figure 2.44: Normal weather conditions in the equatorial Pacific Ocean.

El Niño conditions

El Niño is caused by a change in the trade winds (blowing from the coast out to the ocean near to the Equator) that normally cause the upwelling. If the trade winds weaken or start blowing towards the coast of South America, the upwelling stops. This prevents cool, nutrient-rich water rising to the surface of the ocean in the East Pacific. These conditions are shown in Figure 2.46.

El Niño results in two local impacts in the waters off South America:

- The surface temperature rises, due to warm water not being replaced by cooler water from deep in the ocean.

- The concentration of nutrients in the surface waters reduces, so there are fewer producer organisms in surface waters; this means that there is much less productivity in the ocean in that area.

As the concentration of nutrients decreases, this reduces the rate of growth and reproduction of producers in the ocean. In turn, this reduces the availability of food for animals that eat producers, causing a fall in their populations. This reduces the populations all along the food chains in that area. Many predators are forced to migrate to other areas to find food during El Niño events.

Another impact of El Niño is the change in weather patterns around the Pacific Ocean. Under normal conditions the surface ocean water near to Australia and Asia is warm, resulting in moist air rising into the atmosphere so that rain falls over Australia and Asia. Cool air off the coast of South America causes low amounts of rainfall along the coast of South America.

During an El Niño event, the warm water is pushed away from Australia and Asia, into the Pacific and towards South America. This reverses the weather patterns, causing less rain in Australia and Asia and more rain in South America. You can see these changes in Figures 2.44 and 2.46.

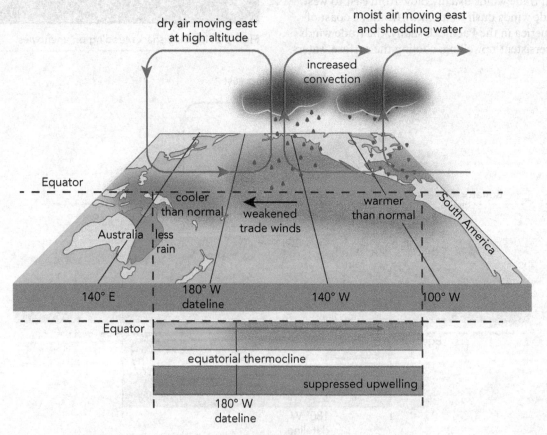

Figure 2.46: El Niño weather conditions in the equatorial Pacific Ocean.

Questions

15 State how each of the following conditions varies (increases or decreases) in deeper water:

  a light penetration

  b pressure

  c temperature

  d salinity

  e dissolved oxygen.

16 State what a Secchi disc is used for and describe how to use it.

17 a Describe what is meant by an 'upwelling'.

  b Explain what happens during an El Niño event. Include references to the wind and the impact of this on upwelling, and how changes in the upwelling affect the surface waters off the coast of South America.

SUMMARY

Particle theory describes the arrangement and movement of particles in solids, liquids and gases.

Particle theory explains the properties of the three states of matter, changes between these states, and how diffusion occurs.

Temperature is a measure of the kinetic energy of the particles in a substance and is measured in °C.

The water cycle is caused by changes in state for water.

Elements, compounds and mixtures describe the composition of different types of particles in substances.

Some substances dissolve in water to form solutions; we can describe these solutions as neutral, acidic or alkaline.

pH is a measure of the strength of acids and alkalis.

Salinity is a measure of the concentration of dissolved salts in water, in parts per thousand (ppt).

Environmental factors cause changes in salinity, linked to the water cycle and Earth processes.

The concentration of gases in the atmosphere differs from the composition of dissolved gases in the ocean, due to different solubilities of the gases and biological processes in the ocean.

Density is a measure of the volume occupied by a mass of substance.

The density of water depends on both the temperature and salinity of the water.

Changes in the density of seawater cause layers to form in the ocean and create convection currents in the ocean.

Surface currents driven by winds can cause the upwelling of cold, nutrient-rich water from the deep ocean to the surface.

When upwellings stop due to changes in surface winds this can create El Niño, which has many impacts locally and around the world.

CASE STUDY PROJECT

Seas and oceans

Figure 2.47: A whale diving in the southern ocean off the coast of Antarctica.

Work in a pair or small group to research a sea or ocean. Prepare a poster to share the information you find with the rest of the class. Use what you have learned in both Chapters 1 and 2 to help you complete your project.

Present information about the sea or ocean including:

- name of the sea or ocean, and its location; the caption for Figure 2.47, for example, states the name of an ocean and its location

- information about the depth

- any features such as trenches or mid-ocean ridges

- information about important currents in the sea or ocean, including any upwellings or other vertical movement of water caused by changes in water density

- how the water cycle affects the salinity and temperatures in the sea or ocean

- an interesting fact relating to discoveries in the sea or ocean.

EXAM-STYLE QUESTIONS

1 a Complete Table 1 to **describe** the changes in particle arrangement and energy that occur when water evaporates and condenses. **[4]**

	Changes in arrangement of particles	Changes in energy in particles
evaporating		
condensing		

Table 1

> **COMMAND WORD**
>
> **describe:** state the points of a topic / give characteristics and main features

b Table 2 shows data about the movement of water through the water cycle.

Water movement (thousands of km³ per year)			
	Ocean	Land	Total
precipitation	369	116	
evaporation	411	74	

Table 2

Complete Table 2 and **compare** the totals for world precipitation and world evaporation. **[2]**

c Describe factors that affect the rate of evaporation of water from the oceans. **[3]**

[Total: 9]

> **COMMAND WORD**
>
> **compare:** identify / comment on similarities and / or differences

CONTINUED

2 During low tide a storm reduces the tide height to lower than the forecast tide height, due to the winds pushing seawater away from the estuary.

Describe and explain how the salinity of the water in the estuary during this storm at low tide would compare to normal salinity. [4]

[Total: 4]

3 A student is provided with potassium chloride crystals and water.

a Describe how the student could investigate the solubility of potassium chloride at different temperatures. Include suitable safety precautions. [4]

b State what equipment would be needed to carry out the investigation described in part a. [3]

c State the most suitable type of graph to present the results. Describe the trend you would expect the graph to show. [2]

[Total: 9]

4 Figure 1 shows the change of temperature with increasing depth in a tropical region, a temperate region and a polar region.

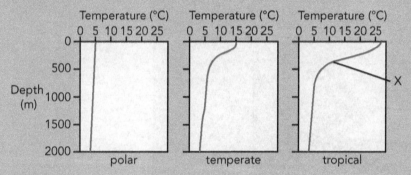

Figure 1

a State the name for the region of water where the temperature changes rapidly with depth, marked X on Figure 1. [1]

b Describe how the temperature changes in tropical waters and in polar waters. [3]

c Describe and explain how the density of water in tropical waters will change with increasing depth. [2]

[Total: 6]

5 Complete Table 3 to describe and explain the change in conditions with increasing depth in the ocean. [4]

	Light penetration	Pressure	Salinity
change as depth increases (get deeper)			
explanation			

Table 3

[Total: 4]

6   Figure 2 shows the Pacific coast of South America in a normal year and in an El Niño year.

Normal year

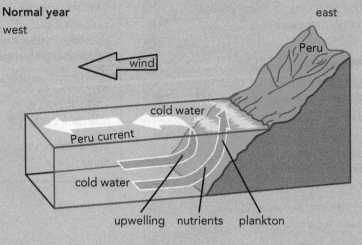

El Niño year

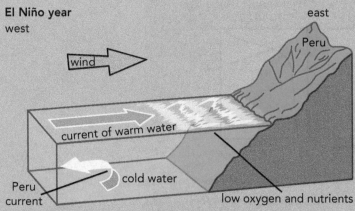

Figure 2

a   Use the diagrams to help complete the passage.

In a normal year _____ water upwells off the coast of Peru in South America. This water is rich in _____. In an El Niño year the upwelling stops and a _____ current replaces the cold current.   [3]

b   Use the diagrams to describe why upwelling occurs, and why the upwelling stops in an El Niño year.   [2]

[Total: 5]

SELF-EVALUATION CHECKLIST

I can	Needs more work	Getting there	Confident to move on	See Section
describe and explain the properties of solids, liquids and gases using particle theory				2.1
state the units for temperature and use energy changes to explain changes in state				2.1
use particle theory to investigate and explain diffusion				2.1
describe and interpret the water cycle				2.1
use and explain the terms element, compound and mixture				2.2
use pH to investigate and describe solutions that are acidic, neutral or alkaline				2.2
describe the salinity of seawater in terms of ppt and explain salinity in terms of dissolved salts				2.2
compare and explain the salinity in different bodies of water including estuaries, seas and oceans				2.2
compare and explain the concentration of dissolved gases with the concentration of gases in the atmosphere				2.3
investigate the effect of temperature on dissolved gases and explain the results				2.3
recall, manipulate and use the formula to calculate density				2.4
investigate the effects of temperature and salinity on the density of water				2.4
explain the formation of layers and convection currents in the ocean caused by changes in density of water				2.4
state and describe how physical and chemical conditions change with increasing depth in the ocean				2.5
investigate the light penetration through water using a Secchi disc				2.5
describe an upwelling and how winds lead to their formation				2.6
outline the formation and local effects of El Niño				2.6

> Chapter 3

Marine organisms

IN THIS CHAPTER YOU WILL:

- describe the main features of animal, plant and bacterial cells

- understand the differences between sexual and asexual reproduction

- describe how marine organisms are classified using the binomial system

- describe the three domains used in classification and the main Eukarya kingdoms

- identify the major classification groups for marine animals

- use practical techniques to observe and classify organisms

- identify the major classification groups of marine plants and protoctists

- describe the life cycles of leatherback turtles and coral polyps

- explain the importance of migration of marine organisms.

This chapter is all about developing your knowledge of the structure of organisms, how we group them and how some of their life cycles help them to survive. To find out how much you know before you begin the chapter, try the following activities.

- Draw an animal cell and a plant cell. Label as many structures as possible. Compare your diagram with other learners.

- Write down one marine example for each of the following: mammal, bird, reptile, fish, crustacean, mollusc, plant and seaweed. Compare your list with those completed by other learners.

- Look at the seaweed shown in Figure 3.1. Draw a diagram of this seaweed. By the side of your diagram, write down the many ways that the seaweed is adapted to survive. Share your diagram and your ideas with other learners.

Figure 3.1: Seaweed floating close to the surface of the water.

MARINE SCIENCE IN CONTEXT

Kelp forests: the rainforests of the ocean

Many people know that rainforests are important ecological areas and are habitats for many different plants and animals. They also know that rainforests help to remove carbon dioxide from the atmosphere and that we need to do all that we can to preserve them. But there is an equally important ecosystem hidden from view under the waters around coastlines. Kelp forests are just as rich in life and just as important as rainforests. A typical kelp forest, as shown in Figure 3.2, contains giant kelp that can stretch up to 80 m from the seabed. Kelp is not a plant but a type of seaweed. Like other seaweeds, kelp uses sunlight to photosynthesise and make its own food. Kelp is the food for many species and it brings energy into the ecosystem. Because kelp is so efficient at photosynthesis, it can provide food for a wide range of organisms.

Kelp forests provide a habitat for animals from many different groups. Mammals, such as sea otters and seals, swim around the forest looking for food.

Sea turtles are found in kelp forests and many fish species use the kelp as a food source and a safe place to breed. Invertebrates, such as crustaceans and sea urchins, also live in kelp forests.

Figure 3.2: An area of kelp forest that has a rich diversity of life.

CONTINUED

One animal species that harms kelp forests is the purple sea urchin, shown in Figure 3.3. Purple sea urchins can totally destroy a kelp forest if their numbers get out of control. Fortunately, these sea urchins are a favourite food of sea otters. As long as there are plenty of sea otters, the purple sea urchin population does not become too big.

Kelp forests also help birds to survive. Seagulls and terns often live near the kelp forests, diving down to catch fish that live there.

Kelp is also very important to humans. Like rainforests above ground, kelp forests remove carbon dioxide gas and so help to reduce climate change (see Section 6.8). Kelp is highly nutritious and has many vitamins and minerals so it is an important food source for humans. We also use kelp to make a substance called alginate, which is used in making ice cream and toothpaste. There are even plans to develop kelp farms to grow kelp as a sustainable biofuel.

Kelp forests are one of the most important ecological areas of our planet. We need to save kelp forests as much as we need to save rainforests.

Discussion questions

1   Why do you think kelp forests are such important areas for different species of animals?

2   In your opinion, how can we benefit from preserving kelp forests?

Figure 3.3: Purple sea urchins feeding on kelp.

3.1 Cell structure and function

Cells are the basic building blocks of life. All marine organisms, both single celled and multicellular, are made of cells. Animal cells and plant cells are made of many smaller structures, called organelles. Some of these organelles are found in both animal cells and plant cells, and some organelles are only found in plant cells.

Animal cells

Figure 3.4a shows a diagram of a generalised animal cell. Animals are made up of a wide range of different, highly specialised cell types. Each type of cell has adaptations for its role. However, there are certain structures that are found in all animal cells.

*   Cell membrane – this is the outer boundary of a cell. It controls the movement of substances into and out of the cell.

KEY WORDS

animals: multicellular organisms; animal cells have nuclei but do not contain chloroplasts, cell walls or permanent vacuoles; examples include fish, mammals, reptiles and insects.

plants: multicellular organisms; plant cells contain nuclei, chloroplasts and permanent vacuoles and are surrounded by cells walls; examples include seagrasses

KEY WORD

cell membrane: the outer boundary of the cytoplasm of cells; it controls the movement of substances in and out of cells

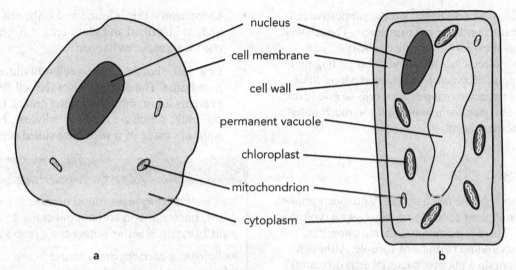

Figure 3.4: a Generalised animal cell structure; **b** Generalised plant cell structure.

- **Nucleus** – this organelle contains the genetic material of a cell in the form of the molecule, DNA. The DNA is arranged into chromosomes that are surrounded by a nuclear membrane. The nucleus controls the overall activity of a cell.

- **Mitochondria** – these organelles have an outer membrane that surrounds an inner membrane. The inner membrane is folded to give it a large surface area. Mitochondria are where **aerobic respiration** takes place inside cells. Any cells that have a high respiration rate will have many mitochondria.

- **Cytoplasm** – this is the liquid part of the cell contained within the cell membrane. It is the part of the cell where chemical reactions occur, such as protein synthesis.

Plant cells

Typical plant cells, as shown in Figure 3.4b, contain most of the structures found in animal cells, along with a few extra ones. These extra structures include:

- **Chloroplasts** – these are green organelles found within the cytoplasm of plant cells. Chloroplasts have two outer membranes and an inner set of membranes that contain chemicals such as **chlorophyll** to absorb light energy. Chloroplasts use light energy to perform photosynthesis, a process that produces glucose.

- **Large permanent vacuole** – most plant cells contain a large permanent vacuole inside the cytoplasm. A vacuole consists of a membrane surrounding a watery solution known as sap. Vacuoles have a range of functions, including the storage of water, salts, toxins and coloured chemicals called pigments.

KEY WORDS

nucleus: large cell structure that contains chromosomes made from DNA; it controls cell activities

mitochondria: cell organelles that perform aerobic respiration

aerobic respiration: the release of energy from glucose, using oxygen, by cells

cytoplasm: the substance that makes up most of the cell volume around the organelles; it is the site of chemical reactions such as protein synthesis (making proteins)

KEY WORDS

chloroplasts: organelles that perform photosynthesis; they are found in plant cells and some algal cells

chlorophyll: the green chemical found inside chloroplasts; it absorbs light energy for photosynthesis

large permanent vacuole: a large structure found in plant cells that consists of a membrane surrounding fluid called sap; it stores water and other substances

- Cell wall – plant cells have a strong, supportive cell wall that surrounds the cell membrane. The cell wall is made of a carbohydrate called cellulose. Each cellulose molecule has thousands of repeating units of a sugar called glucose, arranged in a long chain. Cellulose molecules wrap around cells to give them strength and stop them bursting if too much water enters the cytoplasm.

- Cytoplasm – this is found inside the cell membrane and, as in animal and plant cells, it is where chemical reactions happen.

- Cell wall – bacteria have a cell wall outside the cell membrane. The cell wall gives the cell strength and prevents it bursting when water enters. Unlike plant cell walls, which are made of cellulose, bacterial cell walls are made of a substance called peptidoglycan.

Bacterial cells

The cells of bacteria are much simpler, and much smaller, than animal and plant cells. Figure 3.7 shows a typical bacterial cell. There is no nucleus, no mitochondria, no chloroplasts and no permanent vacuole. Although they do not contain a nucleus, bacterial cells do contain genetic material in the form of DNA in the cytoplasm.

The structures that are found in bacterial cells include:

- Cell membrane – this controls the movement of substances into and out of the cell.

KEY WORDS

cell wall: strong layer found around the outside of plant, bacterial and some algal cells; it prevents cells bursting if water enters the cytoplasm

cellulose: a carbohydrate found in the cell walls of plants and some algae

bacteria: a group of single-celled organisms that do not have nuclei; bacteria are different from organisms in the Archaea group (see Section 3.3)

ACTIVITY 3.1

Identifying cell structures in images

In this activity, you are going to identify some of the features of cells and then discuss your findings with another learner.

1   Figure 3.5 is a photograph of some blood cells from a salmon. Unlike human red blood cells, the red blood cells of fish contain a nucleus. Identify the structures labelled X, Y and Z.

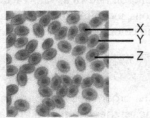

Figure 3.5: Photograph of salmon blood cells as seen through a light microscope. Red blood cells in fish possess a nucleus.

2   Figure 3.6 is a photograph, as seen through a light microscope, of leaf cells from a piece of pondweed. Identify the structures labelled P and Q.

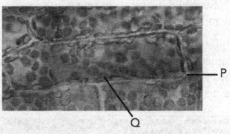

Figure 3.6: Cells from the leaf of Canadian pond weed, *Elodea*.

Peer assessment

Now compare your answers with another learner. Discuss how the two types of cell are adapted for their functions of:

- transporting oxygen around the body
- photosynthesis.

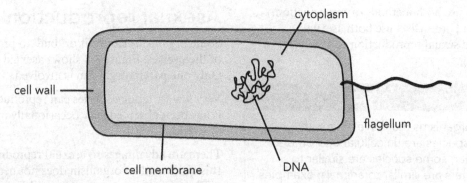

cytoplasm

cell wall

flagellum

cell membrane

DNA

Figure 3.7: Generalised bacterial cell.

ACTIVITY 3.2

The differences between animal, plant and bacterial cells

Working with other learners, draw a table to compare the structures found in animal cells, plant cells and bacterial cells. You will need a large piece of paper. The table headings should be: 'Cell structure', 'Animal cell', 'Plant cell' and 'Bacterial cell'.

One learner should write down the name of one organelle in the structure column and then tick the type of cells where this organelle is found. (Remember: an organelle is a structure found inside a cell.) The second learner then checks the table and corrects it if necessary. The second leaner then adds a second structure, adds ticks to the table, and passes the paper on. Keep going until no one can add any other organelles to the 'Cell structure' column.

Questions

1   Give the functions of the nucleus, mitochondria, chloroplasts, permanent vacuole and cell membrane.

2   List the organelles that are only found in plant cells.

3   Table 3.1 shows the number of mitochondria found in three different types of cell and gives the volume of the three cells.

Cell type	Number of mitochondria in one cell	Volume of cell (µm³)	Density of mitochondria (mitochondria per µm³)
muscle	3000	800	3.75
skin	100	400	
sperm	75	100	

Table 3.1: Mitochondria in different cell types.

a   Calculate the density of mitochondria in skin cells and sperm cells.

b   Explain why it is better to compare the density of mitochondria rather than the number of mitochondria per cell.

c   Suggest a reason for the differences in the density of mitochondria in the different types of cells.

3.2 Reproduction

All organisms produce offspring by reproduction. There are two methods of reproduction: **asexual reproduction** and **sexual reproduction**. Some organisms use only one of these methods.

KEY WORDS

asexual reproduction: a single organism producing exact copies of itself

sexual reproduction: organisms producing male and female sex cells, which fuse to produce offspring with characteristics from both parents

Other organisms use both methods of reproduction. Marine plants and protoctists use both asexual reproduction and sexual reproduction to produce offspring.

> ### KEY WORD
>
> protoctists: organisms that have cells with nuclei; some species are unicellular and others are multicellular; some species are similar to plants and others are similar to animals; examples include seaweeds (such as kelp) and other algae

Asexual reproduction

Some organisms can split or 'bud' to produce copies of themselves. Figure 3.8 shows asexual reproduction. Only one parent organism is involved.

Very few vertebrate species can reproduce asexually but it has been observed very occasionally in some species of shark.

There are advantages to asexual reproduction. It is quick and an organism does not need to find a different organism to reproduce with. Because asexual

Fission

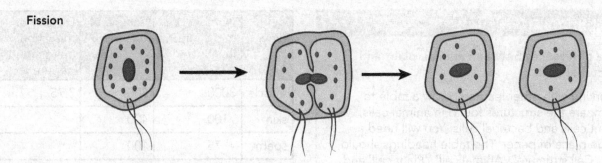

Figure 3.8: Asexual reproduction.

In asexual reproduction, the offspring are all identical to each other and the parent. There are several methods of asexual reproduction, and these are shown in Figure 3.8 and Figure 3.9.

- Fission: single-celled organisms, such as dinoflagellates (see Section 3.5), will often split into two identical daughter cells.

- Budding: coral polyps and sea anemones can develop a small bud on the side of their bodies that develops into a new polyp. Eventually, the new polyp separates completely to form a new organism.

- Fragmentation: parts of some species of coral and echinoderms (such as starfish) sometimes break away and develop into new, identical, copies of the parent organism.

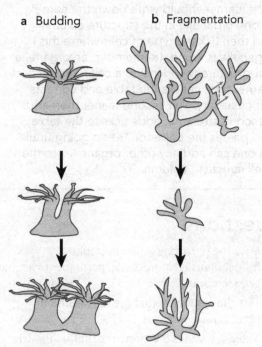

Figure 3.9: a Coral polyps reproducing by budding. A second polyp devlops from the first polyp and eventually separates. **b** Coral polyps reproducing by fragmentation. A piece of coral breaks away and grows into a new coral in another location.

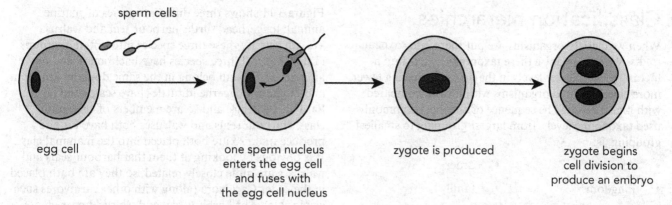

Figure 3.10: Fertilisation of a dolphin egg cell.

reproduction is quick, this means that one parent organism can rapidly reproduce to cover an area.

The disadvantage of asexual reproduction is that all the organisms are identical. This means they would all be destroyed if the environment changes, or if a new disease appears.

Sexual reproduction

Most organisms perform sexual reproduction. Organisms produce male sex cells (sperm) and female sex cells (eggs) and these cells fuse together during fertilisation to produce offspring. The offspring have characteristics of both parents. In sexual reproduction the fertilised egg is called a zygote. The zygote then begins to divide into more cells, forming an embryo. Figure 3.10 shows the fertilisation and development of a bottlenose dolphin. Fertilisation in marine animals can be external, taking place in the water, or internal, when the male introduces sperm into the female's body. Plants and protoctists reproduce sexually by producing sex cells such as pollen cells, egg cells or spores.

The main advantage of sexual reproduction is that it produces offspring with genetic variation. This means that if the environment changes or a new disease evolves, some organisms may have characteristics that help them survive.

The disadvantage of sexual reproduction is that it can be wasteful, as it may produce offspring with weaker genetic characteristics than their parents. Another disadvantage is that each organism has to find a partner and this is sometimes difficult.

3.3 Classification

Many different species of animals, plants and bacteria live in the marine world. To help to make sense of all this life we can put organisms into groups based on shared, common features. Classifying organisms into groups makes it easier for scientists all around the world to recognise those organisms by their internationally agreed scientific names.

We try to place organisms into groups according to how closely they are related. For example, mammals all have common features such as fur and making milk. Two species of mammal are more closely related to each other than to a species of fish. We use a classification system that organises organisms into groups according to their relatedness (how closely organisms are related to each other). Grouping organisms like this helps us to make sense of the variety of life on planet Earth.

Classification hierarchies

When we classify organisms, we put them into **taxonomic ranks**. We can organise these taxonomic ranks into a **hierarchy**, with lower levels in the hierarchy having fewer, more closely related organisms within them compared with higher levels. The sequence of the most commonly used taxonomic levels, from largest grouping to smallest grouping, is:

- domain
- kingdom
- phylum
- class
- order
- family
- genus
- species.

Figure 3.11 shows three different species of marine animal: loggerhead turtle, harbour seal and walrus. We can classify these three species into different groups (Table 3.2). All three species have backbones, and are animals, so they all belong in the same domain, kingdom and phylum. Loggerhead turtles have scales and lay hard-shelled eggs, and so are members of the reptile class. Harbour seals and walruses both have fur and produce milk, so are both placed into the mammal class. It is obvious by looking at them that harbour seals and walruses are quite closely related, so they are both placed in the order Carnivora (along with other carnivores such as big cats). The harbour seal and walrus, however, are placed into different families, orders, genera and species, due to the differences between them.

Figure 3.11: Three vertebrate species: **a** loggerhead turtle, **b** harbour seal and **c** walrus.

Taxonomic level	Loggerhead turtle	Harbour seal	Walrus
Domain	Eukarya	Eukarya	Eukarya
Kingdom	Animalia	Animalia	Animalia
Phylum	Chordata	Chordata	Chordata
Class	Reptilia	Mammalia	Mammalia
Order	Testudines	Carnivora	Carnivora
Family	Cheloniidae	Phocidae	Odobenidae
Genus	*Caretta*	*Phoca*	*Odobenus*
Species	*caretta*	*vitulina*	*rosmarus*

Table 3.2: Classifying loggerhead turtle, harbour seal and walrus.

KEY WORDS

taxonomic rank*: the different classification levels, such as kingdom or phylum

hierarchy: arrangement or placing of groups of organisms into smaller groups

domain: the highest taxonomic rank; the three domains are the Archaea, Eukarya and Bacteria

The binomial system

Every species of organism has a scientific name. Scientists have developed an internationally agreed naming system so that everyone understands exactly which organism is being described. Different languages will have different names for a great hammerhead shark, but the scientific name of *Sphyrna mokarran* is the same all over the world.

The scientific name of each organism is made up of the genus and the species. Because two words are used, we call this system of naming organisms the binomial system, which means 'two names'. There are rules that you need to follow when using scientific names.

- Scientific names (the genus and the species) are always written in italics when they are typed. When writing scientific names by hand, you should always underline the name.

- The genus always has a capital first letter.

- The species always has a lowercase first letter.

> **KEY WORD**
>
> **binomial system:** the system we use to give scientific names to organisms, referring to them by their genus and species; for example, *Carcharodon albimors* is the great white shark

Figure 3.12 shows how we write the scientific name for the orca by hand.

Genus starts with a capital letter.

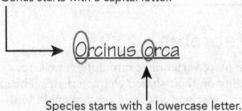

Species starts with a lowercase letter.

Figure 3.12: Use of the binomial system to give the scientific name of orcas. Note that the genus has a capital letter and the species has a lower case letter. The name should be underlined when written by hand.

Domains

The highest taxonomic rank is the domain.

We can classify all living things into three domains (Figure 3.13).

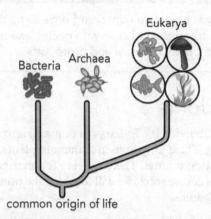

common origin of life

Figure 3.13: The three-domain classification system. The three domains are the Bacteria, Archaea and Eukarya. Note that the Archaea may be more closely related to Eukarya than they are to Bacteria.

The three domains are:

- Bacteria. These are the true bacteria. All organisms in this group are unicellular. Bacteria have peptidoglycan cell walls, and they have no nuclei, mitochondria or chloroplasts.

- Archaea. Organisms in this domain appear to be very similar to bacteria and were once placed into the same classification group. Archaea are unicellular and have cell walls. They lack most organelles, so have no nuclei, mitochondria or chloroplasts. Living members of Archaea are often extremophiles – organisms that can live in very extreme conditions, such as near hydrothermal vents. Some extremophile organisms in the Archaea domain can live at very high temperatures, very high salinities and very high acidities. Members of Archaea have several features that are different to bacteria, and they also share some characteristics with Eukarya.

> **KEY WORD**
>
> **Archaea:** a domain containing single-celled organisms similar in structure to bacteria; the Archaea may have more features in common with Eukarya than with Bacteria

- **Eukarya**. Organisms that have cells with nuclei are members of this domain. Plants, animals, fungi and protoctists are members of Eukarya.

KEY WORD

Eukarya: a domain containing organisms that are all composed of cells with nuclei; examples include plants, animals and protoctists

Kingdoms

We can subdivide the Eukarya (a domain) into four **kingdoms**. These kingdoms are: animals, plants, protoctists and fungi. There are very few marine fungi so, in this coursebook, we will focus on the other three kingdoms.

- Animals. There are many marine animals, all sharing certain common features. All animals are multicellular organisms. Animals have cells without chloroplasts or cell walls; they are able to move from place to place and usually have nervous coordination. Animals do not photosynthesise and so gain nutrients by eating. Animals store carbohydrate as glycogen, a substance that is made up of many glucose sugars joined together.

- Plants. All plants, like animals, are multicellular and usually have cells with chloroplasts and cell walls. Plants obtain their nutrients through the process of photosynthesis. Plants store carbohydrates as starch, a substance that is made up of many glucose sugars joined together.

- Protoctists. This group is always very difficult to define. Like other members of the Eukarya domain, they have cells with nuclei. Some protoctists have plant-like features, such as chloroplasts and cell walls, but others have animal cell features. Many protoctists are single celled, such as dinoflagellates and diatoms (see Section 3.5), but there are also multicellular protoctists, such as **kelp**. Seaweeds, although they look like plants, are actually protoctists. This is because seaweeds have a closer evolutionary relationship to other organisms in the protoctist kingdom.

KEY WORDS

kingdom: a domain can be divided into kingdoms; marine kingdoms include animals, plants and protoctists

kelp: large, multicellular organism that grows in coastal areas; it photosynthesises to produce glucose

Questions

4 *Chlorella vulgaris* is a protoctist. It is single celled, and the cells contain chloroplasts for photosynthesis. The cells also have nuclei and cell walls. Explain why *Chlorella vulgaris* is classified as a protoctist rather than a plant.

5 Give the domain, kingdom, genus and species of the grey reef shark, *Carcharhinus amblyrhynchos*.

3.4 The animal kingdom

We can divide the animal kingdom into **vertebrates**, animals with backbones, and **invertebrates**, animals without a backbone.

KEY WORDS

vertebrates: animals that have a vertebral column (backbone)

invertebrates: animals that do not have a backbone

Vertebrates

We can place vertebrates into different classes depending on their shared characteristics. The four classes of marine vertebrate are mammals, **birds**, **reptiles**, and **fish**. Figures 3.14, 3.15, 3.16 and 3.17 show examples of animals from each of these

KEY WORD

birds: animals that have skin covered by feathers, and lungs; the young develop inside hard-shelled eggs

Figure 3.14: Typical marine mammals include: **a** cetaceans, like this orca, **b** pinnipeds, like this seal, and **c** sirenians, like this manatee.

vertebrate classes. Amphibia are another class of vertebrate, but there are very few examples in the marine environment. Table 3.3 summarises some of the key features of the four main classes of marine vertebrate. We group the different classes of vertebrate according to their skin coverings, reproductive methods and **gas exchange structures**.

Mammals

- All mammals have fur or hair on their skin. Cetaceans such as whales, dolphins and porpoises lack hair over most of their body but still have hair in the form of eyelashes. Fur or hair is made of a protein called keratin.

- Mammals reproduce using **internal fertilisation**. They mate so that sperm is introduced into the female, and the young develop inside the mother until they are ready to be born.

- All mammals have lungs for taking in oxygen and getting rid of carbon dioxide.

Figure 3.14 shows three examples of marine mammals: cetaceans, which include dolphins and whales; pinnipeds, which include seals; and sirenians, which include manatees.

KEY WORDS

reptiles: animals that have skin covered with scales made from keratin and lungs; the young develop inside hard-shelled eggs

fish: animals that have skin covered with scales and gills; they reproduce using external fertilisation

gas exchange structure: organs or structures, such as lungs and gills, that exchange oxygen and carbon dioxide

internal fertilisation: the process by which fertilisation occurs inside a living organism

Figure 3.15: There are many species of bird that live in the marine environment. Some, like **a** the albatross, fly over the open sea; others, like **b** the oystercatcher, are shore birds that live in coastal areas.

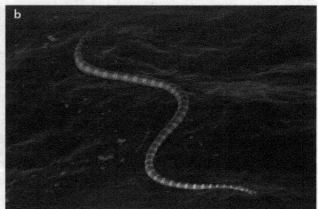

Figure 3.16: Marine reptiles include **a** sea turtles and **b** sea snakes.

Birds

- The skin of birds is covered by feathers. Like fur, feathers are made of keratin.

- Birds, like mammals, use internal fertilisation but the young do not develop inside the mother's body. Female birds lay hard-shelled eggs which are incubated. The parent birds sit on top of the eggs to keep them warm.

- Birds also use lungs for gas exchange.

There are many species of bird found in the marine environment, as shown in Figure 3.15. Many species, such as oystercatchers, live around the coasts and are called shore birds. Other species, such as albatrosses, fly further out to sea. Birds that spend a large portion of their life out at sea are called pelagic birds.

Reptiles

- The skin of reptiles is covered with scales. The scales are, unlike the scales of fish, made of keratin. Mammal fur, bird feathers and reptile scales are all made of keratin.

- Fertilisation of eggs by sperm is internal. As in birds, the female reptiles lay hard-shelled eggs, although the eggshells are softer than those of birds.

- Gas exchange is by lungs.

The main species of marine reptile are turtles but there are also sea snakes. Crocodiles are reptiles found in estuarine waters. Figure 3.16 shows two different reptile species found in the marine environment.

Fish

There are many different marine species of fish. The two main groups are the cartilaginous fish, which includes sharks and rays, and the bony fish, such as tuna. Both groups of fish, shown in Figure 3.17, have an endoskeleton but in cartilaginous fish the endoskeleton is more flexible. Bony fish have a skeleton hardened with calcium salts.

- The skin of most marine fish is covered with scales. Unlike the scales of reptiles, fish scales are not made of keratin.

- Fish reproduction almost always involves external fertilisation after sperm and eggs are released into the water. The fertilised eggs hatch in the water and few species of fish provide parental care.

- Gas exchange is through gills rather than lungs.

KEY WORDS

endoskeleton*: a skeleton that is found inside the body, such as the bones inside a whale

external fertilisation: the process by which fertilisation occurs outside the body

gills: gas exchange structures that are often used by marine organisms

Figure 3.17: Fish are the most numerous marine vertebrate organisms. The two major groups are **a** cartilaginous fish, such as sharks, and **b** bony fish, such as this tuna.

Vertebrate class	Skin covering	Reproductive method	Gas exchange structure	Examples
mammals	fur or hair made from keratin Some mammals, such as dolphins, have lost most of their fur but still have eyelashes.	Egg cells are fertilised internally by the male introducing sperm into the female's body. The offspring develop inside the mother's body until born.	lungs	cetaceans (whales and dolphins), pinnipeds (seals), sirenians (manatees)
birds	feathers made from keratin	Egg cells are fertilised internally by the male introducing sperm into the female's body. The fertilised eggs, which are hard-shelled, are laid, and offspring develop inside the eggs.	lungs	albatross, shore birds such as oystercatchers
reptiles	scales made from keratin	Egg cells are fertilised internally by the male introducing sperm into the female's body. The fertilised eggs, which are semi-hard-shelled, are laid, and offspring develop inside the eggs.	lungs	sea snakes, turtles
fish	scales, not made from keratin	Egg cells are released by females and are then fertilised in the water by sperm from the males. Fertilisation is external. Larval fish hatch from free-floating eggs and grow in the sea.	gills	shark, rays, tuna

Table 3.3: A summary of structures in different vertebrates.

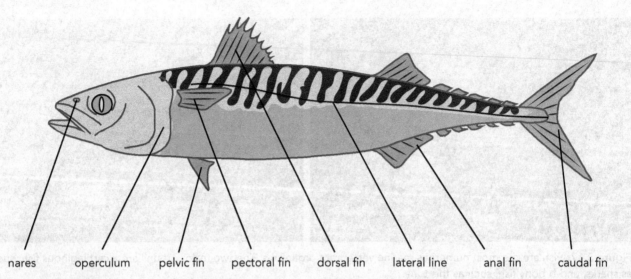

nares   operculum   pelvic fin   pectoral fin   dorsal fin   lateral line   anal fin   caudal fin

Figure 3.18: External features of a mackerel. Note the presence of the operculum, lateral line, fins and nares. Mackerel have a second dorsal fin. Scales are present on the body, but they are not clearly visible.

The external features of fish

Fish are the most common vertebrate group in the marine environment and they live in almost every part of every ocean. Fish, like all organisms, have many adaptations for survival. Some adaptations are found in just one or two species but other adaptations are common to all species of bony fish. Figure 3.18 shows the main external features of a mackerel.

Each of the labelled structures in Figure 3.18 has a particular function.

- **Operculum**. The operculum is a bony cover over the gills. As well as having a protective function, it also acts as a valve to prevent water flowing backwards over the gills. Cartilaginous fish do not have an operculum but have gill slits.

- **Scales**. Most bony fish are coated in scales. The scales reduce drag, which is the resistance to swimming forwards due to friction with the water. Scales protect the skin and also reduce water loss.

- **Fins**. Most fish have a range of different fins, each with their own function. Figure 3.19 shows the functions of the dorsal fins, pelvic fins, pectoral fins, anal fins and caudal fins.

- **Lateral line**. The lateral line is a sensory organ the runs down the length of the fish. It can detect vibrations in the water so that fish can sense danger or food.

- **Nares**. The nares are sensory organs that detect chemical scents in the water. Fish use their nares to find food, to find mates and to sense danger. Migratory fish, such as salmon, use nares to find the river that they were spawned in.

Functions of the fins

Each type of fin has a function in controlling movement of the fish. Different fins control roll, pitch and yaw, and provide forward thrust in the water. These movements in the water are shown in Figure 3.19.

- Roll is the spinning, turning movement of a fish around its central axis. It is mainly controlled by the dorsal fin and the anal fins.

- Pitch is the movement of the fish's head up and down in the water. A fish will move its head up and down depending on whether it wants to swim upwards or downwards. Pitch is controlled by the pectoral fins and pelvic fins.

- Yaw is sideways movement in the water from left to right. It is controlled by the pectoral fins and pelvic fins.

- Thrust is the force the pushes the fish forwards in the water. The caudal fin provides thrust. The pectoral fins are used as a brake to slow the fish down in the water.

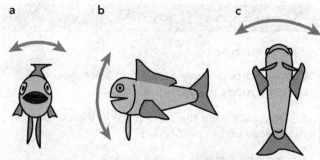

Figure 3.19: The fins are responsible for thrust and the control of movement in the water: **a** roll is the spinning movement around the axis of a fish that occurs when the fish moves forward, it is reduced by the dorsal and anal fins; **b** pitch is the up and down movement of the head and is controlled by the pectoral and pelvic fins; **c** yaw is the side to side movement of the fish and is controlled by the pectoral and pelvic fins.

KEY WORDS

roll: circular, rolling movement of the body of a fish as it moves forwards

pitch: the movement of the head of a fish up or down in the water

yaw: the side-to-side movement of the head of a fish

thrust: the forward force that pushes a fish through the water; the caudal fin gives thrust

Questions

6 Give the names of the external structures of a fish that:
   a protect gills
   b detect chemicals
   c prevent water loss.

7 Name the fins that are used to control:
   a roll
   b pitch
   c yaw.

ACTIVITY 3.3

Making a model of a fish

In a group or pair, make a model of a fish to show all the fins and their functions.

You could make your model with modelling clay, a wire frame covered with papier-mâché, polystyrene or any other suitable material. Alternatively, you could make a two-dimensional fish model from card with separate pieces of card for each fin.

Find a way to label each of the fins.

CONTINUED

Peer assessment

If several groups have each made a fish, you could compare models. Assess them for:

- accuracy – are the correct fins in the correct places and in proportion?

- art – how lifelike are the models?

How well did you complete the activity? Rate the models according to the following scheme for each of the points listed:

😊 if the model has fins in proportion and in the correct places, and the model is lifelike

😐 if the fins are mostly in proportion and in the correct places, and the model looks fairly lifelike

☹ if the fins are not in proportion and not in the correct places, and the model does not look at all like a real fish.

Invertebrates

Huge numbers of invertebrates live in the oceans and almost every invertebrate group has members there. Marine invertebrate groups include crustaceans, cnidaria, echinoderms, molluscs and annelids.

KEY WORDS

crustaceans: invertebrate animals that have segmented bodies, skeletons on the outside of the body, jointed limbs, compound eyes and two pairs of antennae; examples include crabs, lobsters, shrimp and barnacles

cnidaria: a group of invertebrate organisms that have radial symmetry, tentacles and stinging cells; examples include sea anemones and coral polyps

Crustaceans

Many crustaceans live in our oceans. Some crustaceans live in the upper, planktonic layers of the ocean, while others live on the seabed. Crustaceans can appear so different to each other that they may not look as if they belong to the same group. Figure 3.20 shows some crustaceans – it is difficult to believe that barnacles are closely related to crabs and lobsters.

Some features are, however, common to all crustaceans. These features, shown by the lobster in Figure 3.21, include:

- **Bilateral symmetry.** All crustaceans have bilateral symmetry. This means that you can draw a line through the middle of them and the two halves are reflections of each other.

- **Exoskeleton.** An exoskeleton is a hard, outer case. Vertebrate organisms have an endoskeleton that is on the inside of the body, but the skeleton of crustaceans is on the outside of the body. The exoskeleton helps crustaceans to move and also protects them from damage. The exoskeleton is made from a hard material called chitin.

- **Compound eyes.** The eyes of all crustaceans are very different from vertebrate eyes. Crustacean eyes are made of many small eyes that each form an image. This image is decoded by the brain of the crustacean.

KEY WORDS

bilateral symmetry: the body shape of organisms that can be divided along the body midline to make reflections (mirror images) of each other

exoskeleton: a hard, rigid covering on the outer surface of the body of many invertebrate animals such as crustaceans

compound eye: a type of eye that is divided into thousands of individual light receptor units

Figure 3.20: A range of different crustacean species: **a** flaming reef lobster, **b** spider crab, **c** microscopic copepods and **d** barnacles.

exoskeleton

antennae (lobsters have two pairs)

compound eye

jointed limbs

Figure 3.21: This lobster illustrates the main features of crustaceans.

- Two pairs of **antennae**. Many organisms have antennae that are sensory organs sticking out from their head. Crustacea, however, have two pairs rather than just one. Some species, such as lobsters, have long antennae that are easy to see. Others have much smaller ones.

- Abdominal segments with jointed legs. The abdomen of crustaceans is divided up into segments, many with a pair of jointed legs. The joints in the legs enable the crustaceans to move easily. Leg number varies from one species of crustacean to another – crabs and lobsters all have five pairs of legs.

Cnidaria

Cnidaria are a group of organisms with a simple structure. Some cnidaria float free in the oceans while others are attached to a **substrate**. Some jellyfish and sea gooseberries are free-floating cnidaria. Anemones and corals are cnidaria that attach to substrates. Figure 3.22 shows different cnidarians, all with different specialisations.

All cnidaria share certain features, shown by the coral polyp in Figure 3.23:

- **Radial symmetry**. Instead of the bilateral symmetry of vertebrates and crustacea, cnidaria have radial symmetry. They have a circular structure and their body can be divided equally around a central point.

- **Tentacles** with **stinging cells**. All cnidaria have tentacles that increase their surface area for gaseous exchange. The tentacles contain stinging

cells called nematocysts that are used to catch prey, or to protect the organism from predators. The tentacles are obvious on cnidaria like coral and sea anemones, and jellyfish also have tentacles. Many coral species take algae called **zooxanthellae** into their cells. These algae gain protection and minerals from the coral. In return, the coral gains sugars from the algae.

KEY WORDS

antennae: sensory organs that stick out from the head of an organism; crustaceans have two pairs of antennae

substrate: hard surface to which organisms can attach – rock is an example

radial symmetry: the shape of organisms, such as cnidaria, where the body can be divided equally around a central point

tentacles: long, slender, flexible organs that stick out from the body of an organism; used in feeding or gas exchange

stinging cells: cells that can inject a toxin into other organisms; they are used to catch food and to defend against predators (also called nematocysts)

zooxanthellae: a type of algae that lives inside coral polyps; the algae benefits the coral and the corals benefit the algae

 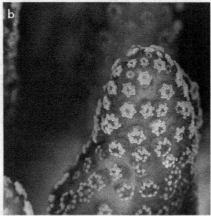 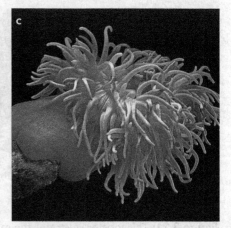

Figure 3.22: Different types of Cnidaria **a** purple striped jellyfish, **b** coral polyps and **c** sea anemone.

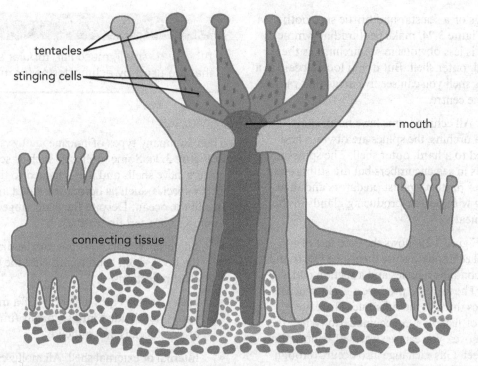

tentacles

stinging cells

mouth

connecting tissue

Figure 3.23: Structure of a coral polyp.

Echinoderms

Figure 3.24 shows a wide range of marine **echinoderms**, each with different adaptations. Most echinoderm species are free living, but a few, such as crinoids, attach to a substrate.

All echinoderms have these shared features:

- **Pentaradial symmetry.** All echinoderms have a basic structure with five points that radiate out from the centre.

 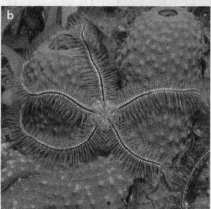 

Figure 3.24: Different groups of echinoderms: **a** sea star, **b** brittle star and **c** crinoid.

The five legs of a sea star and brittle star, both shown in Figure 3.24, make pentaradial symmetry obvious. It is less obvious in sea urchins, as these have a hard, outer shell. But if you look closely at a sea urchin's shell you can see five areas that radiate out from the centre.

- Spiny skin. All echinoderms have hard, spiny skin. In sea urchins, the spines are obvious and are attached to a hard, outer shell. The spines are less obvious in sea cucumbers but are still present. These spines protect against predators and may work along with poison-producing glands in the skin underneath.

- Tube feet. Figure 3.25 shows the tube feet of a starfish. All echinoderms use their tube feet to move. Each foot contains muscles and a suction pad at the end. The feet also produce a sticky mucus that attaches them to the substrate. There are thousands of feet on every echinoderm. When the organism moves, you can see waves of contractions along the feet. Gas exchange also occurs through the tube feet. The many tube feet on an echinoderm together provide a large surface area for gas exchange.

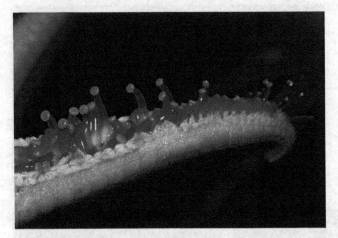

Figure 3.25: Tube feet of a starfish.

> **KEY WORD**
>
> **tube feet:** small, muscular, tubular structures that are used by echinoderms for moving around

Molluscs

There are many types of marine **molluscs**, as shown in Figure 3.26. Some molluscs, such as scallops and oysters, have shells and live attached to their substrate. Other species, such as octopuses, squid and sea slugs, live free in the ocean. Despite the wide range of forms, all molluscs have certain features:

- Bilateral symmetry. A line can be drawn along the body, from head to tail, and the two sides are clear reflections.

- **Unsegmented body.** The body of a mollusc is soft and is not divided into segments (unlike the bodies of crustaceans and annelids).

- Internal or external shell. All molluscs have some form of a shell. Oysters, clams and whelks have very obvious external shells. These shells protect the organisms from predators. Bivalves, such as oysters and clams, have two shells attached together that can be opened and closed by muscle contractions. When bivalve molluscs are feeding, reproducing or need gas exchange, the shells are open.

> **KEY WORDS**
>
> **molluscs:** group of invertebrate organisms that have bilateral symmetry, a shell and an unsegmented body; examples include squid, octopuses and scallops
>
> **unsegmented body:** a body that is not divided into segments; for example, molluscs and cnidarians have unsegmented bodies

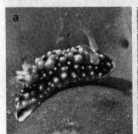    

Figure 3.26: Marine molluscs: **a** sea slug, **b** scallop, **c** squid, **d** harp snail and **e** octopus.

But the shells are quickly closed if there is danger. In species such as squid, octopuses and sea slugs, the internal shell is not obvious as it is found inside the body and may only be small. These internal shells stiffen the body and attach to muscles to allow movement. The internal shells of dead cuttlefish, shown in Figure 3.27, are often washed up on beaches.

Figure 3.27: Cuttlefish skeleton washed up on a beach.

Annelids

Over 20 000 different species of **annelid** live in the sand or silt of the seabed. Some species swim among the plankton and others can live in the heat of hydrothermal vents. Annelids have even been found 10 000 m below the ocean's surface at the Challenger Depth of the Marianas Trench, which is the deepest part of any ocean. Two annelid species are shown in Figure 3.28.

All annelids have several shared features that include:

- Bilateral symmetry.

- Segmented body. The body of annelids is segmented (divided up into individual sections). Almost every segment is identical although a few are specialised by having structures such as a mouth or anus.

- Soft body. Annelids do not have a hard, outer casing. Although the skin may be tough, the body is actually soft. This soft body means that they can easily burrow through sand and silt.

KEY WORDS

annelids: a group of invertebrate organisms that have bilateral symmetry, a segmented body and setae that stick out from segments; examples include lugworms and fan worms

segmented body: a body that is divided up into separate sections; annelids and crustaceans have segmented bodies

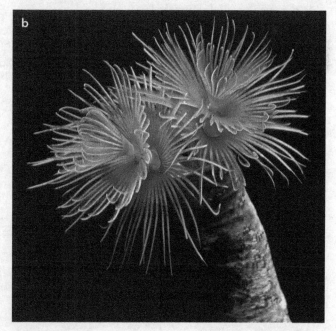

Figure 3.28: Different types of annelid: **a** bearded fireworm and **b** fanworm.

- **Setae.** Each body segment has tiny hairs called setae on its surface (Figure 3.29). In some species the hairs are not obvious. In other species the hairs can be very long and found on the top of projections of the body called parapodia. These parapodia help in gas exchange, protection from predators, movement and anchorage into burrows.

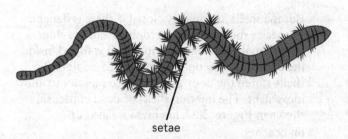

setae

Figure 3.29: Diagram of a lugworm showing setae and segmentation.

> **KEY WORD**
>
> **setae:** bristles or hairs that are present on the segments of annelids

Questions

8 Identify which phylum organisms with the following characteristics belong to:

a spiny skin, pentaradial symmetry, tube feet

b compound eyes, two pairs of antennae

c tentacles with stinging cells, radial symmetry

d soft body, bilateral symmetry, shell

e segmented body, setae.

9 Which classes of organism have:

a bilateral symmetry

b radial symmetry

c pentaradial symmetry?

Group	Shared features	Examples of organisms
crustacea	bilateral symmetry exoskeleton compound eyes two pairs of antennae abdominal segments with jointed legs	crabs, lobsters, barnacles
cnidaria	radial symmetry tentacles with stinging cells	corals, jellyfish, anemones
echinoderms	pentaradial symmetry spiny skin tube feet	sea urchins, sea cucumbers, starfish, brittlestars
molluscs	bilateral symmetry unsegmented body internal or external shell	squid, cuttlefish, octopuses, oysters, whelks, sea slugs
annelids	bilateral symmetry segmented soft body setae	lugworms, ragworm, tubeworms

Table 3.4: A summary of structural features of the invertebrate groups.

ACTIVITY 3.4

The variety of life

This is a group activity but you can do it in pairs or on your own, although it will take longer. Produce a small booklet with one example of an organism from each of the following groups: cnidarian, crustacean, annelid, mollusc and echinoderm. Choose organisms that are not in this coursebook. For each organism, try to include:

- a photo

- its scientific name

- where it lives

- what it eats

- the key features of its classification group

- any unusual adaptations.

The information on each group should fit on one page and each learner can choose one group.

Peer assessment

Share your booklet with people who are not marine scientists (these could be younger learners) to see if you have been able to communicate your research well. Ask them to assess your booklet on:

- how detailed the information is

- how easy it is to read.

Ask other people to rate your booklet according to the following scheme:

- ☺ if the booklet is very detailed and easy to read

- 😐 if the booklet has some detail but is not always clear

- ☹ if the booklet lacks detail and is difficult to understand.

PRACTICAL TASK 3.1

Identifying, comparing and drawing biological specimens

Introduction

You need to be able to identify what group an organism belongs to when shown a photograph. A photograph could be of a whole organism, part of an organism, or a group of cells as seen with a light microscope.

For this practical task you will look at real specimens. If you cannot use real specimens, you can also do this practical task using photographs.

You will need:

- a hand lens

- a dead fish, e.g. mackerel, from a fish seller, and other specimens that are available, such as shrimp or scallop (in shell)

- photographs of coral, starfish, lugworm, squid, scallop, lobster, crab

- a tray

- a lamp

- a sharp pencil

- an eraser

- blank paper.

Safety: Take care when handling the specimens as there may be sharp spines.
Wash your hands thoroughly after handling the specimens.
Gloves may be worn when handling the specimens.

CONTINUED

Method

1 Take the fish and lay it in the tray.

2 Identify the following features: scales, eyes, mouth, nares, fins (caudal, pectoral, pelvic, dorsal, anal), operculum and lateral line.

3 Use the hand lens to have a closer look at the scales, nares and operculum.

4 Make a large drawing of the fish on blank paper using the pencil, following these rules:

- Only use pencil – do not use ink.

- Do not have broken lines or sketchy lines; make sure that all the lines are clear and firm.

- Do not add shading.

- Make sure that the proportions are correct.

- Only draw what you can see.

- Do not try to draw every detail, for example, just draw a few scales; Figure 3.30 shows an example of how to draw a specimen.

5 Label the structures you have identified. Print the labels and use a ruler to draw straight lines.

6 Add notes to your diagram giving any observations that you have made; for example, is the upper surface of the fish darker than the lower surface?

Results and conclusions

- The results for this practical task are your diagrams and notes.

- Look at the fins and shape of the fish. Explain how the fish is adapted to survive in its habitat.

Challenge

- You need to be able to identify and draw examples of animals from any of the groups listed in this chapter. Try to draw examples of one from each of these groups: mammals, birds, reptiles, crustaceans, cnidaria, echinoderms, molluscs and annelids. Some of these you may obtain from a fish market but others you will need to draw from photographs. If you do look at living specimens, treat them in a way that does not cause them harm or distress and return them to their habitat when finished.

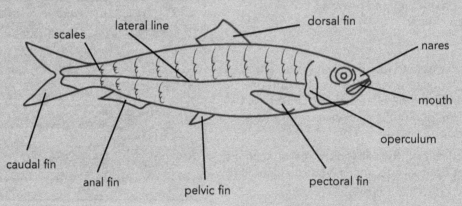

Figure 3.30: Student diagram of a fish.

CONTINUED

Questions

1   Look at Figure 3.31, which is a drawing of an annelid made by a student. Identify three mistakes that the student has made when making their drawing. Re-draw the diagram without the mistakes.

2   State which of the features present in the annelid would also be present in a crustacean.

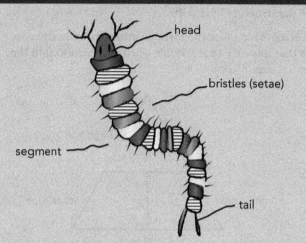

Figure 3.31: Student diagram of an annelid.

Self-assessment

Review your diagram and check that it follows all the drawing rules:

•   Are all the lines clear and unbroken?

•   Did you add any shading?

•   Is the diagram large enough?

Measurements and magnifications

You need to know how to determine the actual lengths of organisms and structures when looking at photographs and diagrams.

You can use different units when measuring the dimensions of a structure. The unit you choose should be the one most appropriate for the length. For example, you need to express the length of a fish in centimetres or millimetres, not kilometres. You need, therefore, to know how to convert between the different units of length:

•   1 centimetre (cm) is equal to 10 millimetres (mm).

•   1 millimetre (mm) is equal to 1000 micrometres (μm).

To convert a length that is given in centimetres to millimetres, we multiply by 10:

$$5 \text{ cm} = 5 \times 10 = 50 \text{ mm}$$

To convert from millimetres to centimetres we divide by 10.

To convert a length in millimetres to micrometres, we multiply by 1000:

$$75 \text{ mm} = 75 \times 1000 = 75\,000 \text{ μm}$$

To convert from micrometres to millimetres, we divide by 1000.

Magnifications and calculating actual lengths

We usually magnify diagrams and photographs of specimens and cells so that we can see details. You need to be able to:

•   calculate the magnification of diagrams

•   calculate the actual sizes of specimens when given the magnifications.

The formula for calculating magnification is:

$$\text{magnification} = \frac{\text{image size}}{\text{actual size}}$$

where 'image size' is the size of the diagram that you are given (measured with a ruler) and 'actual size' is the size of the structure in real life.

It is useful to place the formula into a formula triangle so that it is easy to rearrange when you need to find the actual size.

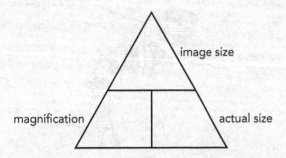

To understand how to calculate magnifications and actual lengths, it is best to work through examples.

Example calculation of magnification

• Look at the fish cells shown in Figure 3.32.

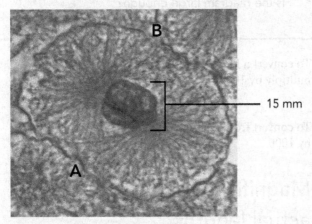

Figure 3.32: Fish cells showing a nucleus.

• Measure the maximum diameter of the nucleus, labelled X, with a ruler. In this case, it is 22.5 mm wide. This is the image size.

• The actual size of this nucleus is 6 μm.

• You now have to make sure that you have your image size and actual size in the same units. You can have both in micrometres or both in millimetres, but it is essential that both are in the same units. In this example, we will use micrometres for both, so we need to convert the image size to micrometres.

$$22.5 \text{ mm} = (22.5 \times 1000) \text{ μm}$$

• We can now use the formula to calculate the magnification.

$$\text{magnification} = \frac{\text{image size}}{\text{actual size}}$$

$$\text{so, magnification} = \frac{22\,500}{6} = \times 3750$$

Example calculation of actual size

To calculate the actual size of a specimen, we use the same formula but rearrange it so that the actual size is the subject of the equation.

$$\text{Actual size} = \frac{\text{image size}}{\text{magnification}}$$

• Look at the cells shown in Figure 3.32.

• We have calculated that the photograph has a magnification of ×3750

• Measure the length of the cell between A and B.

• Use the formula to calculate the actual length of the cell.

• $$\text{actual size} = \frac{\text{image size}}{\text{magnification}}$$

$$\text{so, actual size} = \frac{15}{3750} = 0.004 \text{ mm}$$

which equals 4 μm

Questions

10 Convert the following measurements:

    a 25 mm into μm

    b 500 cm into mm

    c 250 cm into μm

    d 50 μm into cm.

11 **a** An image of a cell has a width of 35 mm. The actual width of the cell is 250 μm. Calculate the magnification.

    b An annelid has an actual length of 15 cm. The length of the annelid in a photograph is 35 mm. Calculate the magnification of the photograph.

12 A student wants to calculate the area of a circular diatom skeleton. The radius of the skeleton on an image of a diatom is 25 mm. The magnification of the image was ×250. Calculate the actual area of the diatom skeleton.

$$\text{area of a circle} = \pi r^2$$

PRACTICAL TASK 3.2

Drawing and measuring cells

Introduction

You need to be able to draw cells as seen using a light microscope. You also need to be able to calculate magnifications and determine cell sizes.

You will need:

- a microscope and a light source
- microscope slides and coverslips
- scalpels or sharp knife
- a mounted needle
- forceps
- an onion, ideally a red onion
- iodine stain and dropper
- methylene blue stain
- a sterilised cotton bud
- tissue paper
- Canadian pond weed, *Elodea*
- disinfectant
- a pencil, paper and eraser
- gloves and eye protection.

Safety: Scalpels, forceps and mounted needles are sharp so be careful when using them. Iodine and methylene blue are both irritants, so use eye protection. You should use gloves when handling the methylene blue and if you get any on your skin, wash it off with lots of water.
Be careful when pressing the coverslip down onto the slide. Coverslips are made of very thin glass and can break.
Iodine should not be disposed of into drains as it is hazardous to the aquatic environment. Methylene blue is flammable if dissolved in ethanol so there should be no naked flames.

Method

Onion cells (Figure 3.33)

1 Peel the onion and slice it into two. Pull apart the layers and take a piece of the thin epidermis (skin) – this will be like a sheet that can be easily peeled away. If it is a red onion, try to get a piece that has some of the red coloured area.

2 Using the scalpel or a pair of scissors, cut a section of the epidermis to a size of about 1 cm × 1 cm. Place this onto the centre of a slide. Make sure that the epidermis is not folded. You can use the mounted needle and forceps to lay it flat.

3 Add a drop of iodine stain to the centre of the epidermis. If you have red onion, you may not need to use the iodine.

4 Carefully use a mounted needle to lay a coverslip over the top of the epidermis, as shown in Figure 3.33. Wrap a thick piece of tissue paper around the slide and coverslip and press down very gently to remove any air bubbles. Do not press too hard or you will break the coverslip.

5 Set up your microscope on the lowest power. Place the slide onto the stage and bring the image into focus. You can now change the lenses to view the cells under higher magnifications.

6 Make a large, labelled drawing of two or three of the onion cells. Label a nucleus, the cell wall and the cytoplasm.

7 Arrange the cells so that they fill the full diameter of the field of view. Count how many cells fit into the diameter of the field of view. Remove the slide and place a transparent ruler with millimetre divisions across the field. Use this to measure the diameter of the field of view. You can now calculate the mean length of one onion cell by dividing the length of the diameter by the number of onion cells that fit across the field of view. Add a scale bar, similar to the one shown in Figure 3.34, to your diagram to show the length of one cell.

CONTINUED

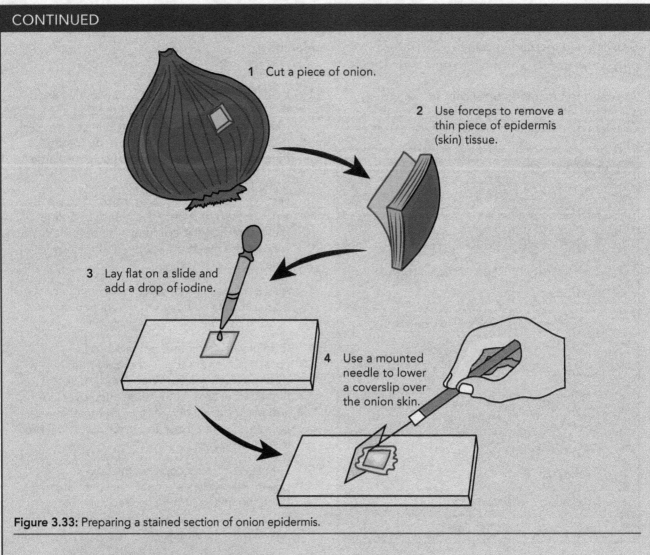

1 Cut a piece of onion.

2 Use forceps to remove a thin piece of epidermis (skin) tissue.

3 Lay flat on a slide and add a drop of iodine.

4 Use a mounted needle to lower a coverslip over the onion skin.

Figure 3.33: Preparing a stained section of onion epidermis.

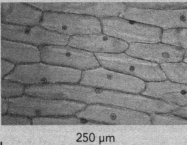

250 µm

Figure 3.34: Onion cells.

Cheek cells

1 Although you are not a marine organism, your cheek cells are a good example of animal cells.

2 Rub the sterile cotton bud around the inside of your cheek to remove a few cheek cells. Smear them onto a microscope slide.

3 Place a drop of methylene blue stain onto the cells. This should stain the cytoplasm pale blue and the nuclei dark blue.

4 Place a coverslip over the top of the stained cheek cells as you did with the onion cells. Wrap the slide in tissue paper and gently squeeze to remove excess stain and bubbles.

CONTINUED

5 Use the microscope to look at the cheek cells. They will be much harder to see than the onion cells, so do not give up if you cannot find them immediately. Cheek cells are smaller than onion cells so move to a higher magnification after finding them first on low power.

6 Draw one or two of the cheek cells, labelling a cell membrane, the nucleus and the cytoplasm.

Elodea cells

1 Take a small leaf from the pond weed and place it on the slide with a drop of water.

2 Place a coverslip over the top of the leaf.

3 Use the microscope to view the cells. You should see rectangular cells that contain green chloroplasts. If you are able to, draw two or three of the cells, labelling the chloroplasts and cell walls.

Results and conclusion

Your results will be your diagrams. Try to explain why each of the cell types is adapted in different ways. For example, why do the *Elodea* cells have many chloroplasts?

Challenge

Once you are confident with using microscopes, you can use them to look at all sorts of cells and structures. Try looking at some of the following: fish gills, diatoms and plankton. If you are working with a group of other people, you can all look at different organisms and structures and share your findings.

Questions

1 Draw a table to show which of these structures were present in each of the three cell types you looked at: nucleus, chloroplast, cell wall, cytoplasm and cell membrane. Remember that the *Elodea* (pond weed) cells will have nuclei, but they will not be visible without being stained.

2 Explain why you are not able to see mitochondria in any of the cells, even though they are present in all of them.

3 State which of the structures present in the onion cells would be present in a bacterial cell.

This Practical task links to Skills tips 0.1 and 0.10.

Self-assessment

Review your diagrams and decide how you could improve them.

• Are all the lines clear and unbroken?

• Did you add any shading?

• Is the diagram large enough?

3.5 Plant and protoctist kingdoms

Most of the producers in marine ecosystems are plants and protoctists. The true plants living in marine ecosystems are mainly species of seagrass. You might think that seaweeds are plants because they photosynthesise. Actually, seaweeds, along with single-celled algae, are members of the protoctist kingdom.

Seagrass

Many species of plant are adapted to live in coastal areas close to the sea but few live entirely under the water. One group of plants that has evolved to live in the marine environment is the seagrasses.

KEY WORD

seagrass: true plants that are found in the marine environment; they have adaptations for surviving underwater

Figure 3.35: Seagrass growing in the Mediterranean Sea.

There are many species of seagrass, including turtle grass and manatee grass, but all have similar characteristics. Similar to all flowering plants, seagrasses are multicellular, have cellulose cell walls and photosynthesise. Seagrasses grow in areas called beds, or meadows, as shown in Figure 3.35. Seagrass meadows are extremely important to ecosystems, providing functions that include:

- stabilising the seabed with their roots to prevent soil erosion
- bringing energy into food chains and providing food for many organisms
- releasing oxygen from photosynthesis for animals to use in respiration
- providing shelter for organisms
- providing nesting and nursery sites for many species of animals
- reducing the impact of waves and storms on coasts.

Living permanently underwater is difficult for true plants and seagrasses have evolved adaptations to survive. Some species spend their lives permanently underwater. Other species, such as seagrasses that live in estuaries, have periods of being submerged and periods of being exposed to the air. Figure 3.36 shows a diagram of a seagrass.

Seagrasses are adapted in many ways.

- Leaves. these are the organs of photosynthesis. Seagrasses have many leaves that point upwards to give a large surface for absorbing as much sunlight as possible. The leaf cells contain a large number of chloroplasts and have adaptations to prevent water being lost into saline seawater.

- Roots. these anchor seagrasses into the sediment of the seabed. Seagrasses have large root systems holding them in place so that they are not removed

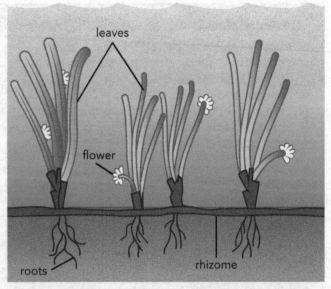

Figure 3.36: Structure of seagrass showing the leaves, rhizomes, flowers and roots.

by strong water currents. The roots also absorb nutrients such as nitrate ions from the sediment.

- Rhizomes. seagrass reproduce asexually using thick underground stems called rhizomes. These rhizomes are buried in the sediment and grow horizontally. Sediment is formed from insoluble materials that sink through the water column and settle on the seabed. New stems and leaves grow from rhizomes, allowing seagrass to spread across an area of seabed. The rhizomes also hold seagrass in the sediment and prevent erosion of the sediment.

- Flowers. seagrasses have flowers for sexual reproduction. Like all flowering plants, seagrasses produce pollen that is then transferred to other seagrass flowers where the pollen can fertilise egg cells. The pollen has a coat of protective mucus and is carried to other flowers by water currents. Scientists have recently found that some tiny crustaceans can transfer pollen from flower to flower, just as bees do with land plants.

KEY WORDS

nursery site: a habitat that is used for breeding or where the young live

rhizome: a swollen plant stem that may be buried under sediment; it provides stability and is used for asexual reproduction

Kelp

Seaweeds such as kelp are algae, not plants. They are members of the protoctist kingdom and have evolved independently of the plant kingdom. Some seaweeds can grow to nearly 100 m in height. Because they are large and multicellular, seaweeds are called **macroalgae**, which means 'large algae'.

Figure 3.37: A kelp forest.

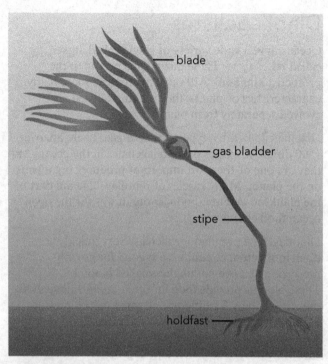

Figure 3.38: Structure of kelp showing the blade, stipe, gas bladders and holdfast.

Kelp are brown seaweeds. There are many different species of these brown seaweeds; most grow in underwater forests in shallow coastal areas, such as the kelp shown in Figure 3.37. Kelp are producers and a wide range of animals live in the kelp forests. Figure 3.38 shows the structure of a species of kelp and some of its adaptations.

Most species of kelp have these adaptations:

- Flat **blades** for photosynthesis. Because they are not true plants, the photosynthetic organs of kelp are called blades instead of leaves. The blades, however, have some features in common with leaves, such as chlorophyll and a large surface area to absorb as much light as possible.

- **Gas bladders** that provide buoyancy for the kelp blades. This means that the blades and stipe always float on the surface where most light is available for photosynthesis.

- A **stipe** that acts as a stem. This is a thickened, flexible structure that supports the blades. The flexibility means that kelp can bend in water currents and is not broken.

- A **holdfast** to anchor the kelp to the substrate. Kelp do not have true roots and do not obtain minerals from the sediment. Kelp anchors itself onto the rocky substrate using a holdfast, which stops the kelp floating off in water currents or during storms.

KEY WORDS

macroalgae: large, multicellular algae such as kelp

blade: the photosynthetic organ of kelp; it is similar to the leaf of a true plant

gas bladders: organs found in kelp and other seaweeds; they contain gases and are used for floatation

stipe: the stem of kelp that holds the blades upright in the water

holdfast: the part of kelp that anchors it to a substrate

Dinoflagellates

Oceans have a wide variety of single-celled algae called microalgae. These microalgae belong to the protoctist kingdom. Although microalgae share many characteristics of plants, they are single celled and evolved separately from plants.

Dinoflagellates are a type of microalgae. There are over 1500 different species of dinoflagellates in the oceans and they are one of the most important producer organisms on the planet. Many species of dinoflagellate are part of the plankton and are producer organisms for the open ocean food chains.

Dinoflagellate populations increase very quickly if environmental conditions are good for growth, producing massive populations called blooms. These blooms provide food for other organisms such as tiny crustaceans. The blooms of some species produce harmful algal blooms known as red tides. These red tides can poison animals. People can get sick if they eat shellfish which have fed on dinoflagellates.

Some species of dinoflagellate, such as those in Figure 3.39, glow when they are moved around. Bioluminescence is the term given for the production of light by living organisms.

Figure 3.39: Bioluminescent dinoflagellates.

Other dinoflagellate species, called zooxanthellae, live inside the cells of coral. The association between zooxanthellae and the coral is mutually beneficial, which means that both the zooxanthellae and the coral benefit. If coral has an environmental stress, such as becoming too warm, the coral may eject (throw out) the dinoflagellates. This causes the coral to lose colour and become 'bleached'.

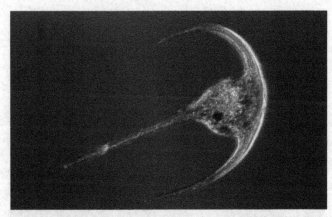

Figure 3.40: Dinoflagellate structure as seen through a microscope.

All dinoflagellate species, such as the example shown in Figure 3.40, have these shared characteristics:

- They are microscopic single-celled organisms. You can see a large algal bloom in the ocean because it contains millions of single-celled organisms. But to see an individual cell you would have to use a microscope.

- They have chloroplasts within their cells for photosynthesis.

- They have two flagella. These flagella are like tails and are used for locomotion.

Diatoms

Diatoms are also microalgae and belong in the protoctist kingdom.

KEY WORDS

microalgae: microscopic, single-celled algae that are part of the phytoplankton; examples include dinoflagellates and diatoms

dinoflagellates: microalgae that have chloroplasts, two flagella and cell walls

flagella: microscopic tails attached to some animal cells and some protoctists; they are used for movement

diatoms: microalgae that have chloroplasts and delicate skeletons made from silica

Most species are single-celled but a few species produce 'ribbons' of cells that remain attached to each other when they reproduce by asexual reproduction. There are many marine species of diatom and most live in the plankton layer. Diatoms rely on photosynthesis for energy. When environmental conditions are good, diatoms produce huge algal blooms. These blooms are consumed rapidly by primary consumers. As a primary producer, diatoms are important in ecosystems and for all life on Earth. The photosynthesis of diatoms produces about half of all the atmospheric oxygen on the planet.

Diatoms have these shared characteristics:

- They are microscopic, single-celled organisms.

- They have chloroplasts within their cells for photosynthesis.

- They all have external skeletons made from a substance called silica, which is similar to glass. These skeletons, shown in Figure 3.41, often have beautiful geometric patterns and each species has a different structure.

KEY WORD

silica: a glass-like substance used to produce the cells of diatoms

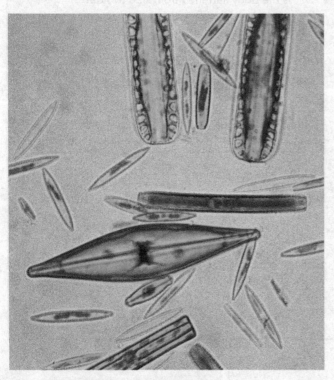

Figure 3.41: The silica skeletons of diatoms.

Group	Kingdom	Features
seagrass	plant	uses leaves for photosynthesis
		cells contain chloroplasts for photosynthesis
		uses roots to anchor into sediment and obtain minerals
		have underground stems called rhizomes that connect individual seagrass plants
		asexual reproduction using rhizomes
		sexual reproduction using flowers
kelp	protoctist	multicellular macroalgae
		have flat blades for photosynthesis
		often have gas bladders to float the blades
		have a stipe that supports the blades
		attaches to substrate with a holdfast
		cells contain chloroplasts for photosynthesis
dinoflagellates	protoctist	microscopic, single-celled microalgae
		cells contain chloroplasts for photosynthesis
		have two flagella for movement
diatoms	protoctist	microscopic, single-celled microalgae
		cells contain chloroplasts for photosynthesis
		cells have an intricate silica skeleton

Table 3.5: Summary of the features of marine producers.

PRACTICAL TASK 3.3

Making and using dichotomous keys

Introduction

A dichotomous key is useful for identifying organisms. This kind of key has a series of questions to which the answers are often 'yes' or 'no'. By answering these questions, the key will lead you to just one organism. The most frequently used dichotomous keys are 'nested keys'. Figure 3.42 shows a nested, dichotomous key used to identify insects and crustaceans on beaches. You need to be able to use and construct dichotomous keys.

You will need:

a range of six to ten different specimens; for example, a collection of shells with different shapes or a collection of different seaweeds. If you cannot collect marine examples, you can use leaves from trees or even different sweets.

Safety: If you are using biological material such as leaves, do not select anything that may cause an allergic reaction.

Method

1   Compare your specimens and think about ways in which you can divide them into two groups. For example, if you are using shells, you could start with whether there are two shells hinged together or one shell.

2   When you have asked your first question, divide up your specimens into the two groups. Then look carefully to identify more ways of separating these groups: for example, texture of shells, spiral patterns, colours and sizes. Keep careful records of all the questions.

3   Keep subdividing the groups until you find it is not possible to split up the shells into smaller groups.

4   Write down your full dichotomous key. Then test it with all the shells.

1   Does the animal withdraw into a shell?
   - Yes: **hermit crab**
   - No: go to question 2

2   Does the animal have three pairs of jointed legs?
   - Yes: go to question 3
   - No: go to question 4

3   Does the animal have three tail filaments?
   - Yes: **bristle tail**
   - No: **spring tail**

4   How many pairs of jointed legs does the animal have?
   - Five pairs: go to question 5
   - More than five pairs: go to question 6

5   Does the animal have a large abdomen and tail fan?
   - Yes: go to question 7
   - No: go to question 8

6   What is the body shape of the animal?
   - Flattened from side to side: **sandhopper**
   - Flattened from top to bottom: **sea slater**

7   Is the body flattened from side to side?
   - Yes: **prawn**
   - No: **shrimp**

8   What is the colour of the shell?
   - Green: **shore crab**
   - Red: **edible crab**

Figure 3.42: Example of a dichotomous key that can be used to identify insects and crustaceans found on a beach.

Results and conclusions

Swap your key with another learner and get them to test it.

Challenge

You can extend your key by adding more shells with different shapes or trying a different set of organisms, such as seaweeds.

CONTINUED

Questions

1 Use the dichotomous key in Figure 3.42 to identify the organisms in Figure 3.43.

2 Suggest why dichotomous keys are better to use when identifying unknown organisms compared with a series of identification photographs.

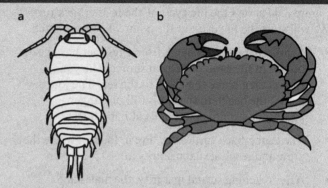

Figure 3.43: Diagrams of organisms to identify using the key: **a** Organism A; **b** Organism B.

Peer assessment

Work with other learners to compare different keys. Decide which key works best and discuss why this key is the most accurate and/or why it is the easiest to use.

Questions

13 State the differences between asexual and sexual reproduction.

14 Explain how the structure of seagrass is adapted to survive in marine ecosystems.

15 Explain the function of rhizomes in seagrasses and their importance in seagrass ecosystems.

3.6 Animal life cycles

An animal **life cycle** describes the series of stages that an organism passes through from its beginning to its sexually mature stage. Different animals have evolved different life cycles depending on their needs. Higher vertebrate animals, such as mammals, often have simple life cycles. For example, after an orca calf is born, it is cared for by its mother while it grows. The young animal eventually reaches sexual maturity (when it can breed) and the life cycle begins again. The orca has only one type of body form that grows and matures. An orca does not have separate stages that live in different environments.

However, many invertebrate species have much more complex life cycles. There are several **larvae** stages with each larva living in a different **habitat**. For example, corals produce larvae that live in the planktonic surface layers before settling on a substrate to form adult coral polyps.

We will look at the life cycles of two species. The leatherback turtle has a fairly simple life cycle, while the coral polyp has a more complex life cycle.

KEY WORDS

life cycle: the stages that an organism passes through from its beginning until it reaches sexual maturity

larvae: intermediate form of an organism that occurs before the organism reaches adulthood; they often have different diets and locations compared with adult organisms

habitat: the area where an organism lives and interacts with its environment and other organisms

Leatherback turtle

Figure 3.44 shows the life cycle of the leatherback turtle. We will start the life cycle at the point when eggs hatch.

- Leatherback turtles hatch from eggs that have been buried in the sand of coastal shores. The young turtles then make their way to the sea. The journey across the beach to the sea is full of danger – predatory seabirds hunt and eat baby turtles.

- The leatherback turtles now live in the sea, where they grow and reach sexual maturity after 15–25 years.

- After reaching sexual maturity, the males and females mate out at sea. Females mate and reproduce every 2–5 years. The males remain at sea and never return to land.

- After mating, the females return to the same sandy shore where they hatched. At night, they dig out sand with their rear flippers to make nests. Each female lays 65–115 eggs in the nest. She then covers the eggs with sand and returns to the ocean.

She repeats this in different places every 10 days so that not all the eggs are placed into one nest. In one breeding season, a female leatherback turtle may make 7–11 nests.

- The temperature of the sand affects the sexual development of the baby turtles. If the temperature is below 27.7 °C, the embryos develop as males. If the temperature is over 31.0 °C, all the embryos develop as females. At temperatures between these a mixture of male and female turtles is produced. The eggs incubate in the sand for 55–60 days. After hatching, the young turtles enter the ocean. Only about 1 in 1000 will reach adulthood. The life cycle then begins again.

Coral polyp

Coral reefs are built by tiny cnidarian organisms called coral polyps. A reef starts to form when a coral larva settles onto a surface.

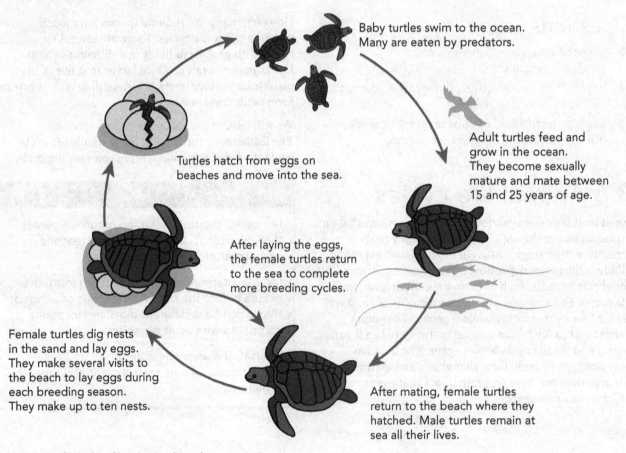

Baby turtles swim to the ocean. Many are eaten by predators.

Turtles hatch from eggs on beaches and move into the sea.

Adult turtles feed and grow in the ocean. They become sexually mature and mate between 15 and 25 years of age.

After laying the eggs, the female turtles return to the sea to complete more breeding cycles.

Female turtles dig nests in the sand and lay eggs. They make several visits to the beach to lay eggs during each breeding season. They make up to ten nests.

After mating, female turtles return to the beach where they hatched. Male turtles remain at sea all their lives.

Figure 3.44: Life cycle of leatherback turtle.

The larva changes into a polyp and then reproduces asexually to form hundreds of other identical polyps in a colony. The polyps form a limestone skeleton. It is these limestone skeletons that make the solid structure of the reef. Several colonies join together to form a reef. Figure 3.45 shows the life cycle of a typical coral polyp. We will start the life cycle at the point when coral polyps reproduce.

- Mature coral polyps release a massive number of sperm and egg cells into the water. This form of sexual reproduction is called broadcast spawning. We do not understand the way by which polyps time the release of the sperm and eggs cells but they are released at the same time meaning the release is synchronised. Maturation of the sex cells may be triggered by temperature and day length. The trigger to release the sex cells may be due to the cycles of the Moon and the time of sunset.

- The sperm fuse with the egg cells in the water and the fertilised eggs float towards the surface of the water. While floating upwards, the fertilised eggs hatch into larvae. The larvae, called planulae, are attracted to the light so they swim to the surface. They live in the surface water, where they feed on plankton and are distributed by currents. The distribution of larvae is important for organisms such as coral because, as adults, they are attached to a substrate and so cannot move. If larvae settle in different areas, there is less competition for resources.

- The length of time that the larvae spend in the plankton varies from species to species. It can range from a few days up to several months. After the larvae have grown, they fall to the seabed where they attach to a hard surface and change into coral polyps. The name given to the process while a larva is changing into a different form is metamorphosis.

- The coral polyps now undergo asexual reproduction by budding to produce more coral polyps. These polyps are genetically identical to the parent polyp. They eventually form a colony and produce the hard, limestone skeleton.

- The coral polyps grow and become sexually mature. When triggered by the environment, the adult polyps release sperm and egg cells. We do not understand the way by which polyps time the release of the sperm and eggs cells but they are released at the same time, meaning the release is synchronised.

KEY WORD

metamorphosis*: the change of a larva into a different form of larva or into an adult organism

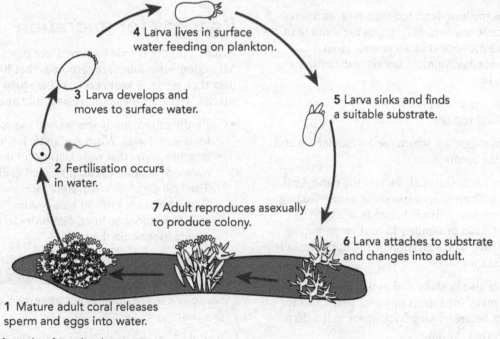

4 Larva lives in surface water feeding on plankton.

3 Larva develops and moves to surface water.

5 Larva sinks and finds a suitable substrate.

2 Fertilisation occurs in water.

7 Adult reproduces asexually to produce colony.

6 Larva attaches to substrate and changes into adult.

1 Mature adult coral releases sperm and eggs into water.

Figure 3.45: Life cycle of coral polyp.

ACTIVITY 3.5

Life cycles of marine organisms

Work as a group of four. Each person should pick one of the following marine organisms and find out about its life cycle. Make sure that people choose different organisms:

- any species of Pacific salmon

- giant clam

- any species of seahorse

- any species of barnacle.

Summarise the life cycle on a poster and explain how the different stages benefit the organism. Share your findings with other learners.

Peer assessment

Display the posters along a wall. Then take a walk along the wall and look at all the posters. Use post-it notes to add some helpful comments about each poster. Give positive feedback about what is good about the poster and some suggestions to make it even better.

Questions

16 Suggest why an increase in global temperature could affect loggerhead turtle reproduction.

17 Explain why it is an advantage to coral polyps to have a larval stage.

3.7 Migration

A migration is the long-term movement of an animal from one place to another. Migrations are more than just the routine movement of an animal around an area. The marine environment has three dimensions so migration can be:

- horizontal migration to different geographical regions

- or vertical migration, which means moving up and down in the ocean.

Migrations are often seasonal, such as the movement of tiger sharks. These sharks spend the winter feeding around the Caribbean islands before moving to the Mid-Atlantic Ocean in summer to feed on immature loggerhead turtles. The migration of the tiger sharks is over a long distance.

Migrations can also be daily and over a shorter distance. For example, many organisms move up to the surface waters at night before sinking back down to the deep, dark waters during the day.

KEY WORDS

horizontal migration: the movement of organisms from one geographical place to another geographical place

vertical migration: the movement of organisms between the sunlight zone and twilight zone of the oceans

Reasons for migration

Animals do not decide to move from one area to another. Migration behaviours are responses that have evolved over thousands of years because they help organisms to survive. Here are the main reasons that animals migrate.

- Finding food: many species will migrate because food is seasonal. When Antarctic ice melts in the summer, algae that were trapped in the ice are released. Small crustaceans called krill eat the algae. The krill population therefore increases rapidly. Blue whales eat krill, so blue whales migrate every year from more northerly latitudes to the Antarctic waters to feast on the krill.

KEY WORDS

seasonal: events that occur at certain times of the year

population: the number of organisms of the same species in a specific area at the same specific time

- Finding mates: due to the large sizes of the oceans, it can often be difficult for species to find mates. When European eels reach sexual maturity they migrate to the Sargasso Sea, an area of the western Atlantic Ocean, where they mate. They make this journey once in their life and die after mating. The young eels that are produced drift on sea currents back to the European waters. Grouping together in the same area makes it easier for eels to find a mate and increases the genetic diversity of the eel population.

- Spawning in a different habitat: Pacific salmon are spawned in rivers and streams. After hatching, the young salmon live and feed in these rivers for several years until they are old enough to migrate into the Pacific Ocean. Here, they grow and reach sexual maturity before migrating back to the river where they were spawned to breed.

- Avoiding predators: many animals live in the depths of the ocean during the day, where they are hidden from predators due to the lack of light. Every evening, these animals move upwards to the surface waters. At night they can feed in surface waters as their predators cannot see to hunt in the dark.

KEY WORDS

genetic diversity*: range of genetic variation in a population

predator: animal that hunts, catches and eats other animals

Vertical migrations

During the Second World War, naval ships used echo sounders to detect enemy submarines. These ships reported large masses underwater that appeared and disappeared. The large masses were in fact masses of living organisms that lived in deep water during the day and moved to surface waters at night, as shown in Figure 3.46. This daily vertical movement is the biggest migration of organisms on the planet. Many different species make this daily vertical migration between the sunlight zone of the upper waters and the deeper twilight zone where there is little light. Some organisms do a reverse vertical migration, moving downwards at night. Species making these vertical migrations include squid, plankton, fish and crustaceans such as shrimp. The main benefit of vertical migration is the avoidance of predators but it may also be to reduce damage caused by ultraviolet light.

Vertical migration is important for recycling energy and nutrients through the water column. Most of the deep ocean food chains gain energy and nutrients from faeces and dead material that continuously falls to the ocean floor as 'marine snow'. When organisms descend to the twilight zone during the day, their faeces fall to the seabed. This speeds up the transfer of energy and nutrients from the surface waters to the deeper parts of the ocean.

Horizontal migrations

Many species of animal migrate from one geographical area to another, and an example is the migration of blue whales in search of Antarctic krill. These geographical migrations are also called horizontal migrations.

Horizontal migrations are often seasonal and are important for breeding or to obtain food during different times of year. We will look at examples of horizontal migration in tuna, turtles and whales.

Tuna migration

Figure 3.47 shows the migration patterns of Pacific bluefin tuna.

Bluefin tuna spawn in areas of the western Pacific Ocean near to Japan and China. After about a year living and feeding in these areas, most tuna migrate across the entire Pacific Ocean to an area off the west coast of the US and Mexico. The tuna grow larger in these waters for another two years before returning to the spawning grounds. While swimming back to the western Pacific, the tuna become sexually mature and are ready to spawn. After spawning, some of the tuna return to the eastern Pacific.

The bluefin tuna migrate so that they can feed in waters rich in food, and so that all the tuna come together to breed in the same water. This makes it much more likely that breeding will be successful.

Loggerhead turtle migration

Female loggerhead turtles return to the beaches where they hatched to lay eggs. Radio tracking shows that loggerhead turtles hatching on beaches in Florida immediately begin a migratory journey that takes them to the eastern Atlantic Ocean, shown in Figure 3.48.

Figure 3.46: Vertical migration of organisms: **a** at night; **b** during the day.

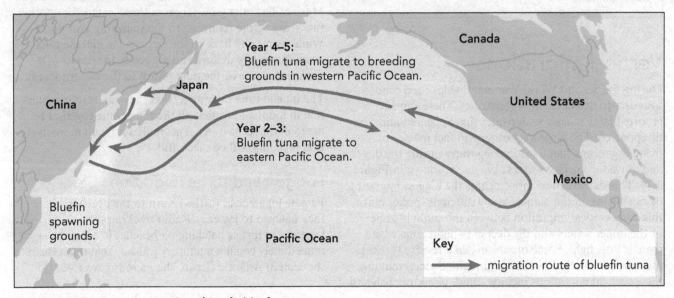

Figure 3.47: Horizontal migration of Pacific bluefin tuna.

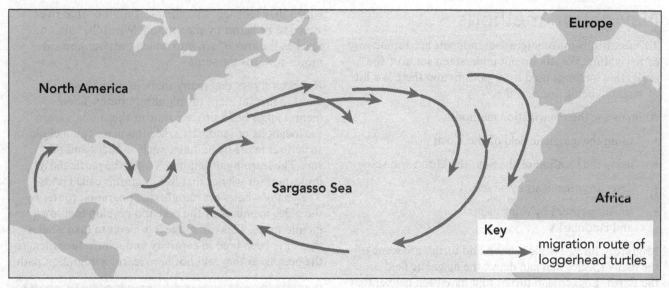

Figure 3.48: Horizontal migration of loggerhead turtles.

The turtles are moved by the current system of the North Atlantic Ocean that circles around the Sargasso Sea. Eventually, the turtles complete a circuit of the North Atlantic that returns them to Florida, where they breed. This single, round trip takes 6–12 years. Young turtles have few defences against predators and the migration takes them to the open ocean where there are fewer predators. Only one out of every 4000 turtles that hatch will survive to adulthood and successfully return to the beach where they hatched. Even in the open ocean, life for the young turtles is full of danger as sharks migrate to the mid-Atlantic to feast on them.

Whales

Many species of whale migrate to seasonal feeding grounds or to join up to breed. Research on humpback whales, usually using satellite tracking, shows that populations of humpback whales make massive annual migrations. Figure 3.49 shows the migration route of one population that spends the winter in coastal waters of the Pacific Ocean near Peru, Ecuador, and even goes as far north as Costa Rica. The whales migrate south during the spring to reach Antarctic waters in the summer where the melting ice causes a rapid increase in their food. As the ice melts, it releases microalgae which are food for crustaceans called krill. It is krill that are a major food source for the whales. The microalgae population increases rapidly as the ice melts. The krill population also increases, which provides rich feeding for the whales. During the summer, the whales build up the fat stores that are needed for their journey back to the winter breeding grounds. Their journey can be over 7000 km in length.

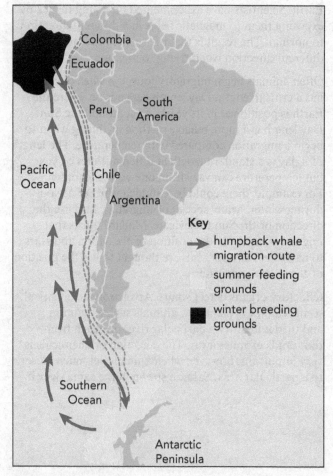

Figure 3.49: Horizontal migration of a population of humpback whales.

Navigation methods

To successfully make migrations, animals need some way of navigating. We still do not understand some of the navigation methods used by organisms and there is a lot of research being done on this.

Animals use these navigation methods:

- using the magnetic field of the Earth
- using the location of the Sun, the Moon and stars
- detecting chemicals by olfaction
- learning routes by using mental maps and landmarks.

Migratory birds, Pacific salmon and turtles are some of the many species that can detect the magnetic field of the Earth. Loggerhead turtles that have been deliberately moved to a different place can return to their migratory path by detecting the North and South Poles of the Earth. Scientists have experimented on young turtles by exposing them to magnetic fields in a different direction to normal. The result is that the turtles move in a different direction when trying to migrate.

Often animals begin migratory journeys when day length has a critical length. Day length depends on where the Earth is positioned in its yearly orbit around the Sun. Day length is a more reliable method of timing when to begin a migration compared with temperature. The length of a day is a standard length at different times of year but temperature can vary from one year to another. For example, there could be a sudden warmer period during winter. Many species of migratory bird use the direction of the Sun to navigate. Mallard ducks that migrate at night use the position of the Moon and stars to navigate. Harbour seals are thought to use the position of the stars to navigate.

Olfactory organs detect scents. Attractions to chemical scents cannot explain how animals such as salmon and turtles identify a particular river or beach from thousands of miles away. The detection of chemicals is very important, however, when animals get much closer to a particular area. Salmon spawn in the same river in which they hatched. The chemical scent of that river seems to be learnt by the salmon. When the salmon reaches the area of sea into which the river flows, it moves towards the scent.

Research shows that many shark and whale species develop mental maps of migration routes. These mental maps build up over time as the animals learn the locations of landmarks. Mental maps can include structures made by humans, such as buoys and oil rigs. The learning of landmarks may be particularly important for whales that live in groups called pods. The young whales are 'taught' the migration routes by the older members of the pod and develop their own mental maps. This can make it difficult to take whales that have been bred in captivity and reintroduce them to the oceans, as they will not have learnt a migration path.

KEY WORDS

navigation: the finding of direction so that animals can move from one place to another

olfaction: the detection of chemical scents

mental maps: memory maps of landmarks that animals learn when making migrations

buoy*: a floatation device, sometimes used to mark shipping lanes and the location of fishing gear

Questions

18 Explain why many species, such as squid, move to the surface waters at night and move down to the deep, twilight zone during the day.

19 Explain why humpback whales move to Antarctic waters during the summer months and return to more shallow waters in warmer areas during the winter months.

20 Suggest why large artificial structures, such as offshore wind turbines that have electrical power cables, could affect migratory animals.

SUMMARY

All animal cells contain a nucleus, cytoplasm, cell membrane and mitochondria.

All plant cells contain a nucleus, cytoplasm, cell membrane, cellulose cell wall, mitochondria and a large permanent vacuole. Most plant cells also contain chloroplasts.

Bacterial cells contain a cell wall, cytoplasm, and a cell membrane. They do not contain a nucleus, mitochondria or chloroplasts.

Marine organisms are classified into groups by shared features.

All species are given a scientific name using the binomial system. The name consists of the genus and the species.

The three largest classification groups are the domains. These are Bacteria, Archaea and Eukarya.

The main kingdoms of Eukarya found in the marine environment are animals, plants and protoctists.

The main vertebrate groups found in the marine environment are mammals, birds, reptiles and fish. They are classified according to skin covering, reproductive method and gas exchange method.

Examples of the main groups of marine vertebrates include mammals (cetaceans, pinnipeds and sirenians), birds (albatross, shore birds), reptiles (sea snakes, turtles) and fish (cartilaginous fish and bony fish).

Fish have external features that have specific functions. The operculum is a gill cover, scales provide protection, fins control stability in the water, the lateral line detects vibrations in the water, and the nares on the head detect chemicals.

The dorsal, pelvic, pectoral, anal and caudal fins of fish control pitch, roll, yaw and thrust.

There are many groups of marine invertebrates, including crustaceans, cnidaria, echinoderms, molluscs and annelids. These groups are classified according to features such as symmetry, eye structure, antennae, segmentation, tentacle structure, the possession of a shell and structures such as tube feet or jointed limbs.

A microscope or hand lens is used to view the detailed structures of biological specimens. Biological drawings must not be shaded, and must have firm, unbroken lines.

Units of measurement include centimetres, millimetres and micrometres. We can easily convert between these units by multiplying or dividing by the correct magnitude.

To calculate magnifications, we divide an image size by the actual size of a structure.

A dichotomous key is used to identify an unknown organism by answering a series of questions.

Asexual reproduction is where a single organism produces exact copies of itself. Sexual reproduction is where organisms produce male and female sex cells, which fuse to produce offspring with characteristics from both parents.

Seagrasses are one of the only true plants found in the marine environment. They have leaves for photosynthesis, roots to anchor in the sediment and obtain minerals, underground stems called rhizomes to reproduce asexually, and flowers to reproduce sexually.

Kelp is a protoctist macroalga. It has flat leaf-like blades for photosynthesis, gas bladders to float the blades in the water, a stipe that acts as a stem, and a holdfast to anchor the kelp to the seabed.

Dinoflagellates and diatoms are two major groups of single-celled microalgae. Both groups are part of the phytoplankton. They are important marine producers as they have chloroplasts for photosynthesis. Dinoflagellates have two flagella to move and diatoms have a skeleton made of silica.

CONTINUED

All organisms have a life cycle that describes the series of changes that occur from the beginning of their lives until they reproduce. Leatherback turtles have a life cycle that involves time spent at sea until the female lay eggs on beaches. Coral polyps have a complex life cycle with larval stages that are free living and adult stages that are attached to a substrate.

Migrations are movements of organisms from one area to another. Organisms may migrate for a range of reasons, such as to access feeding grounds, find mates, spawn and avoid predators. Vertical migration is the daily movement of organisms between the dark twilight zones and the sunlight zones of the ocean. Horizontal migration is the movement of organisms from one geographical location to another.

Organisms use a variety of methods to navigate during migrations. These include using the Earth's magnetic field, the locations of the Sun, the Moon and stars, detecting scents by olfaction and making mental maps. Most organisms probably use a mixture of navigation methods.

CASE STUDY PROJECT

Human impacts on animal life cycles

Humans are the dominant species on the planet. We affect all other organisms more than any other species. Our ever-increasing population and consumer demands are putting more and more pressure on the marine environment.

Pollution from fertilisers used on farmland causes toxic algal blooms that kill dolphins and manatees. Farming can also release toxic pesticides that harm marine animals, including young animals and larval stages. Thousands of ships transporting cargo may collide with migrating whales, killing them or causing severe injury. Tourist resorts have been developed and built on beaches that turtles once used for nesting (Figure 3.49). Dams placed across rivers block the migration of salmon up to their breeding grounds.

The release of greenhouse gases, such as carbon dioxide and methane, is leading to global warming (see Section 6.8). Many whale species use day length to time their migration to the melting Arctic and Antarctic ice. The melting ice releases phytoplankton that leads to a massive bloom of krill, the whales' favourite food. But global warming is changing the time when the ice melts so the blooms of krill may not coincide with the whale migrations. The temperature as turtle eggs develop determines whether male or female turtles are produced, so warmer temperatures could change the proportion of males and females.

KEY WORDS

fertilisers: chemical substances added to fields to increase crop growth; they contain mineral nutrients including nitrates, phosphates and magnesium

pesticides: chemicals that are used to kill pests such as sea lice

greenhouse gases: atmospheric gases that reflect radiation back to the Earth; examples include carbon dioxide, methane and water vapour

global warming: the long-term increase in temperature of the planet

Figure 3.49:

CONTINUED

Working in a small group with other learners, produce a webpage to advise people about the risk of human activities on loggerhead turtles and humpback whales. If you cannot produce a webpage, you could present the information as a leaflet.

You could include details about:

- the life cycle of loggerhead turtles, including the reasons for migration

- the migration of humpback whales, including the reasons for migration

- the impacts of human activity, including global warming, loss of beaches and boat collisions.

Peer assessment

Look at your webpage or leaflet with some other learners. Ask them to assess how informative your webpage or leaflet is. Ask other learners to say how much they learnt about the threats to organisms from human activity.

Produce a questionnaire to test their understanding of:

1   which activities affect the life cycle of other species

2   how the life cycles of other species are affected.

REFLECTION

Think about your own learning from this case study.

- How much accurate information did you include in your webpage or project?

- How could you have included more detailed information about the life cycles, and the effects of human activities on the organisms?

Ask the other learners who read your webpage or leaflet if they found it easy to understand and extract the key information. If they did not find this easy, think about how you could make it easier for them to read.

EXAM-STYLE QUESTIONS

1   *Chlamydomonas reinhardii* is an alga.

a   Complete the classification scheme in Table 1 for this alga.   [3]

Taxonomic level	This alga
	Eukarya
Kingdom	Protoctists
Genus	
Species	

Table 1

CONTINUED

b Figure 1 shows a diagram of an algal cell.

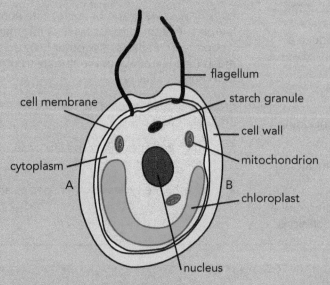

Figure 1

i **Give** two labelled structures, other than the flagellum, in Figure 1 that are not found in animal cells. [2]

ii **State** the function of the cell membrane. [1]

iii The actual width of the algal cell, measured between A and B, is 25 µm.

Calculate the magnification of the diagram. [3]

c A student noticed that the starch granule inside the algal cell decreased in size when it was placed into the dark for 24 hours.

Suggest an explanation for the reduction in size of the starch granule. [3]

[Total: 12]

2 The photograph in Figure 2 shows a red snapper.

Figure 2

COMMAND WORDS

give: produce an answer from a given source or recall / memory

state: express in clear terms

calculate: work out from given facts, figures or information

suggest: apply knowledge and understanding to situations where there are a range of valid responses in order to make proposals / put forward considerations

CONTINUED

a i Sketch a large diagram of the red snapper. Do not draw all the scales. [4]

 ii On your diagram, label the operculum, lateral line, pectoral fin, dorsal fin and caudal fin. [5]

b i Describe the function of the caudal fin. [1]

 ii Describe the functions of the pectoral fins. [3]

c Compare the skin covering and reproductive method of fish with those of birds. [3]

[Total: 16]

3 Marine organisms have evolved different life cycles and reproductive methods.

a Compare asexual and sexual reproduction. [3]

b Describe the life cycle of the leatherback turtle. [5]

c Coral life cycles have a larval stage. These larvae live in the plankton before settling on a substrate to form polyps.

 i Suggest why having a larval stage is an advantage for the coral. [3]

 ii Describe a laboratory experiment that could be carried out to investigate the effect of light or darkness on the settling of coral larvae onto a substrate. [5]

[Total: 16]

4 Figure 3 shows a diagram of a seagrass.

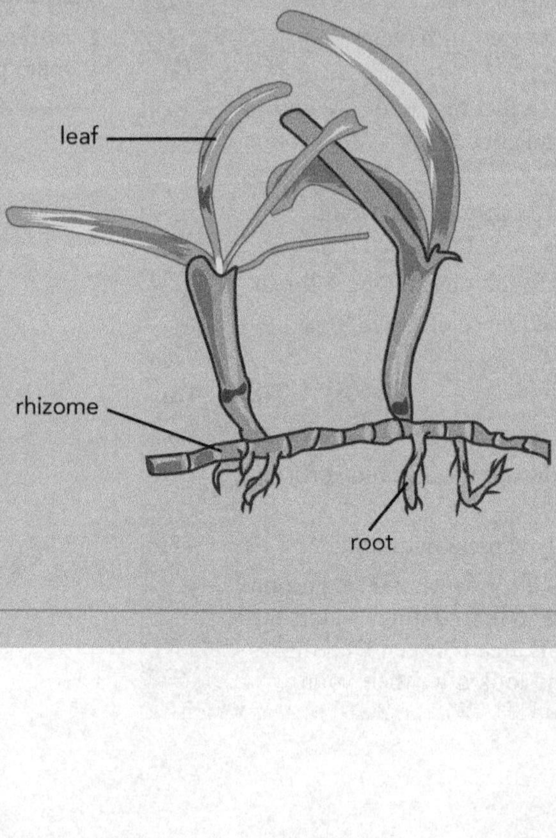

Figure 3

> **COMMAND WORDS**
>
> describe: state the points of a topic / give characteristics and main features
>
> compare: identify / comment on similarities and/or differences

CONTINUED

a i Give two functions of the seagrass roots. **[2]**

   ii Explain the function of the rhizome shown in Figure 3. **[3]**

b Scientists investigated the change in area of seabed covered by seagrass in a North American river estuary over a six-year period.

Table 2 shows the scientists' data.

Year	Area of seabed in estuary covered by seagrass (km^2)
2007	285
2008	275
2009	280
2010	285
2011	160
2012	105

Table 2: Area of estuary covered by seagrass between 2007 and 2012.

   i Plot a line graph of the area of seabed covered by seagrass from 2007 to 2012.

     Join your points with a ruler, using straight lines. **[5]**

   ii Outline the change in area of seabed covered with seagrass between 2007 and 2012. **[2]**

c Manatees are sirenian mammals that have a diet that is almost entirely made up of seagrass. An adult manatee can consume 9% of its own body mass each day.

   i Calculate the mass of seagrass that a 250 kg manatee would consume in one week if it ate 9% of its body mass each day. **[2]**

   ii Use Table 2 to explain why manatee populations are under threat. **[2]**

   iii Explain one other environmental consequence of the loss of seagrass. **[2]**

[Total: 18]

5 Migrations are the movements of organisms from one area to another.

a Some species of squid live in deep water during the day and vertically migrate to the sunlight zone at night.

Explain why these squid perform this daily vertical migration. **[2]**

b Between May and October every year, Pacific grey whales feed around the coast of Alaska. These whales then migrate to shallow waters near the coast of Mexico. The whales live in this area between December and April. During this time they breed and look after their young.

COMMAND WORD

explain: set out purposes or reasons / make the relationships between things evident / provide why and / or how and support with relevant evidence

---

COMMAND WORD

outline: set out main points

CONTINUED

i Suggest why the Pacific grey whales live in waters near Alaska between May and October. [3]

ii Suggest why the Pacific grey whales breed in the shallow waters around Mexico between December and April. [2]

iii Suggest two methods by which the grey whales navigate during their migration. [2]

[Total: 9]

SELF-EVALUATION CHECKLIST

After studying this chapter, think about how confident you are with the different topics. This will help you to see any gaps in your knowledge and help you to learn more effectively.

I can	Needs more work	Getting there	Confident to move on	See Section
describe and compare the structure of a plant cell with an animal cell				3.1
describe the structure of a bacterial cell				3.1
describe the structures and functions of organelles and structures shown in diagrams and images of plant, animal, and bacterial cells				3.1
describe what is meant by sexual and asexual reproduction				3.2
state that marine organisms can be classified into groups by the features that they share				3.3
describe the binomial system of naming species				3.3
describe the three domains used in classification and the main kingdoms of the Eukarya				3.3
describe the main characteristic features of the following groups of marine vertebrates: mammals, birds, reptiles and fish				3.4
identify and give the functions of the operculum, scales, fins, lateral line and nares of fish				3.4
describe the main characteristic features of the following groups of marine invertebrates: crustacea, cnidaria, echinoderms, molluscs and annelids				3.4
observe and draw biological specimens, using hand lenses, light microscopes or photographs				3.4

CONTINUED

I can	Needs more work	Getting there	Confident to move on	See Section
convert measurements between centimetres (cm), millimetres (mm) and micrometres (μm); be able to use the magnification formula to calculate magnifications and sizes of structures				3.4
make and use dichotomous keys				Practical Task 3.3
explain the differences between asexual and sexual reproduction				3.5
describe the main features of different groups of marine producer organisms including: plants (seagrasses), macroalgae (kelp), microalgae (dinoflagellates and diatoms)				3.5
describe the life cycles of coral polyps and leatherback turtles				3.6
explain the reasons for vertical and horizontal migrations of organisms				3.7
explain how organisms navigate when migrating				3.7

Chapter 4

Nutrients and energy

IN THIS CHAPTER YOU WILL:

- understand what is meant by a nutrient

- understand the functions of the different groups of nutrients needed by animals and plants

- learn how nutrients are recycled between organisms and the environment

- learn how energy is released from nutrient molecules by respiration, and how respiration is different from gas exchange

- learn how plants are able to produce glucose by the process of photosynthesis

- identify the different groups of marine organisms that can photosynthesise

- learn about the importance of producers in food chains

- understand how energy and biomass are transferred through food chains

- learn about the different types of consumer in food chains

- understand how to draw pyramids of number, biomass and energy.

GETTING STARTED

A healthy diet must contain these nutrient groups: proteins, carbohydrates, lipids, vitamins and minerals. Think about a meal that you could design with each of these nutrient groups.

- Make a spider diagram with the name of the meal in the centre of the page and a link to each of the nutrient groups.

- For each nutrient group, try to think of their functions and add them to the spider diagram.

Compare your spider diagram with those of other learners. Add any features that you missed to your own spider diagram.

Respiration is the release of energy from food. We need to release this energy for a variety of reasons.

- Write down a list of reasons why we need to release energy from our food.

MARINE SCIENCE IN CONTEXT

Fishing down the food chain

Fish is a highly nutritious food for humans but the global human population is growing fast. To satisfy this high demand for fish, fishing industries are taking more and more fish, from our oceans. They often target large fish such as tuna (Figure 4.1), as these species have the highest market value. A single bluefin tuna can sell for over US$2 million on the Tokyo fish markets.

Most of the large fish caught are predators at the top of food chains and are slow growing. These large fish take a long time to reach sexual maturity. When too many of these species are caught there will be fewer large fish in the oceans.

The fishing fleets then turn to the next stage of the food chain, the smaller species that the top predators eat, for example, cod and groupers. When few of these smaller species are left, even smaller fish species are taken by fishermen until their populations also reduce. Eventually, all that is left are species with little market demand, such as cnidarians like jellyfish and sea anemones.

The process of catching smaller and smaller species is known as 'fishing down the food chain' and it greatly damages marine environments. Once marine areas have lost most of their species it can take many, many years for these areas to recover. Conservation organisations say that individual government action

Figure 4.1: Tuna on sale at a market.

is not enough. They say that nations need to come together to prevent the loss of our marine species and stop 'fishing down the food chain'.

Discussion questions

1 Why do you think it will take a long time to recover the top predator species if a marine area loses most of its species?

2 Conservationists say that single governments cannot deal with the problem of fishing down the food chain. Why do you think that a single government cannot deal with the problem? How could this problem be solved?

4.1 Nutrients

A nutrient is any substance that is used by an organism for growth, repair or as a source of chemical energy. Examples of animal nutrients include **carbohydrates**, **proteins** and fats and minerals such as calcium and iron.

The gas carbon dioxide is a nutrient for plants. The plants use carbon dioxide during photosynthesis to make **sugars**.

KEY WORDS

carbohydrates: organic molecules containing carbon, hydrogen and oxygen; they are used as a source of energy in living organisms

proteins: organic molecules containing the elements carbon, hydrogen, oxygen and nitrogen; they are used for cell growth and repair in living organisms

sugars: simple carbohydrates, such as glucose, that provide living organisms with a source of immediate energy

---

Major nutrient groups and their functions

The major nutrient groups needed by animals in their diets include:

- proteins
- carbohydrates
- **lipids**, including fats and oils
- **vitamins**
- minerals.

Each of these groups has specific, essential functions for organisms.

Protein

Proteins are a major part of all organisms and Figure 4.2 shows the structure of protein molecules. A protein molecule is made up of many repeating units called amino acids. Animals, unlike plants, cannot make their own amino acids so need to obtain amino acids in their diet.

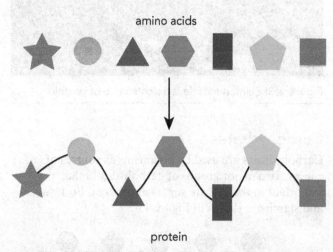

Figure 4.2: Structure of proteins showing how they are made up of repeating amino acids joined together.

Proteins are essential for living organisms for growth and repair and for the production of new cells. Muscle tissues have a large amount of protein. As fish have a high muscle content, they are a rich source of protein for many people (Figure 4.3). Protein can also act as an energy supply for living organisms, usually when body stores of carbohydrates and lipids are low.

KEY WORDS

lipids: organic molecules containing carbon, hydrogen and oxygen; they are used in living organisms for energy, insulation and are a source of fat-soluble vitamins

vitamins: nutrients that are required by living organisms; they are manufactured or produced by living organisms; examples include vitamin A and vitamin C

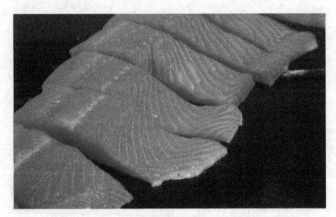

Figure 4.3: Salmon muscle is a rich source of protein.

Carbohydrates

Carbohydrates are used by organisms as sources of energy. Two major groups of carbohydrates that are important in the diet are sugars and starch. Both sugars and starch are shown in Figure 4.4.

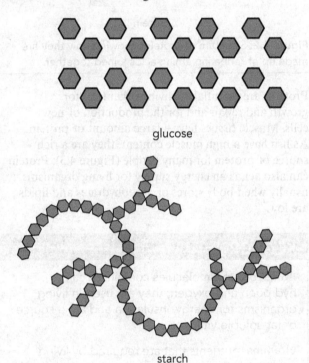

glucose

starch

Figure 4.4: Starch is a large carbohydrate made up of many glucose molecules joined together.

Sugars, such as glucose, are small molecules that taste sweet. When sugars are eaten, they are absorbed into the blood quickly. Sugars are used by the body for quick energy release.

Starch is a polysaccharide molecule made by plants and some protoctists. Animals do not make starch but they do have a very similar substance called glycogen. Starch is a large molecule made up of many molecules of glucose bonded together, as shown in Figure 4.4. Because starch molecules are large and compact, they make good long-term storage molecules inside plant and protoctist cells. Unlike glucose molecules, which are soluble and dissolve in water, starch molecules are insoluble and do not dissolve in water. This means that starch molecules do not diffuse out of cells. When sugar is dissolved in cell cytoplasm, it can affect the movement of water in and out of cells. However, because starch molecules are insoluble, they do not affect the movement of water in and out of cells.

Many marine organisms eat plants and protoctists, so they consume lots of starch. After starch has been eaten, it is digested into glucose, which is absorbed into the blood. The glucose is then used by body cells as an energy source.

KEY WORDS

starch: a complex carbohydrate made of many glucose sugar molecules joined together; it is used as a long-term energy storage molecule by plants and some protoctists

polysaccharide*: long chain of sugar molecules bonded together; examples are starch and cellulose

Lipids

Lipids are molecules that do not dissolve in water but do dissolve in alcohol. Two major groups of lipid are fats and oils. Both fats and oils have a range of functions in marine organisms:

*   Energy sources. Fats and oils are molecules that contain a lot of energy. They are 'energy dense', which means that a set mass of fat or oil contains more energy than the same mass of carbohydrate. Fats and oils make good long-term energy storage molecules. Many species of fish and marine mammal eat seasonal food that is only available at certain times of year. Fats and oils are very good energy storage molecules that can then be used by fish and mammals when food is scarce.

- **Insulation**. Fats and oils are poor thermal conductors so make very good insulating molecules. Cetaceans, such as the humpback whale shown in Figure 4.5, often live in very cold water. This means they are at risk of losing heat energy to the water. Whales do not have fur covering their skin. Instead, whales have a layer of thick fat called blubber under their skin to insulate them. The blubber also makes the whales more buoyant and is an excellent long-term energy store that help whales to make long migrations.

- Source of fat-soluble vitamins. Some vitamin molecules, such as vitamin A and vitamin D, are not soluble in water but are soluble in oil.

Figure 4.5: Humpback whales have thick layers of fat under the skin for insulation.

These vitamins are known as fat-soluble vitamins. Oily fish such as salmon contain a lot of omega-3 oils. Although omega-3 oils are not vitamins, they are essential oils in the human diet.

KEY WORD

insulation: a layer wrapped around a body that prevents heat loss; fur and feathers insulate the bodies of mammals and birds

Questions

1 Which nutrient groups are used for:
   a cell growth and repair
   b energy
   c insulation?

2 Explain why oil-rich fish have a high vitamin A content and a high vitamin D content.

3 Sea otters swim in surface waters and have fur which traps of a layer of insulating air. Whales can swim at great depths where the water pressure is high. Whales do not have fur on the surface of their skin but instead use blubber under the skin as insulation.

   Suggest why whales rely on a layer of blubber rather than fur for insulation.

PRACTICAL TASK 4.1

Investigating foods to test for starch, sugars, proteins and lipids

Introduction

We can test foods for the presence of different nutrient groups. You need to know how to test foods for starch, sugar, protein and lipid. This practical task will show you how to carry out these tests.

You will need:

- boiling tubes
- 100% ethanol
- Benedict's solution
- biuret solution
- iodine solution

- a hot water bath; this could be a beaker with hot water from a kettle
- a hot water bath; this could be a beaker with hot water from a kettle
- a thermometer
- starch powder
- protein, this could be powder such as casein, or liquid egg white
- glucose
- vegetable oil
- 10 cm^3 syringes or pipettes
- distilled water
- a spatula

CONTINUED

- a range of different foods, for example, fruit juice, potatoes, milk, cheese, bread, fish

- a pestle and mortar or alternative method of grinding up food

- eye protection.

Safety: 100% ethanol is highly flammable so no naked flames must be present when using ethanol. Hot water will burn so take care with the water bath. Benedict's solution, biuret solution, iodine solution and 100% ethanol are irritants so eye protection should be worn at all times. Any splashes on skin should be washed off with water.
Make sure that nobody has any allergies to any of the food substances.

Method

Starch test

1 Place a small amount of powdered starch into a boiling tube.

2 Add about 5 cm³ of distilled water to the starch and stir to dissolve.

3 Add a few drops of iodine solution.

4 Record the colour change.

Sugar test

1 Place a spatula full of glucose into a boiling tube.

2 Add about 5 cm³ of distilled water to the glucose and stir to dissolve.

3 Add an equal volume of Benedict's solution to the glucose solution.

4 Set up a water bath with a temperature of at least 70 °C.

5 Place the boiling tube containing the glucose and Benedict's solution into the water bath and leave for 10 minutes.

6 Record the colour change.

Protein test

1 Place some protein (either casein powder or liquid egg white) into a boiling tube.

2 If you are using casein, add about 5 cm³ of distilled water and stir to dissolve.

3 Add an equal volume of biuret solution to the boiling tube and mix.

4 Record the colour change.

Lipid test

1 Place a few drops of oil into a boiling tube.

2 Add about 5 cm³ of 100% ethanol to the oil and stir to dissolve.

3 Add about 25 cm³ of distilled water to the ethanol and oil and mix.

4 Record the colour change.

Nutrient test	Result of positive test
starch	Iodine solution changes from orange to black.
sugar	Benedict's solution changes from blue to red / orange / yellow.
protein	Biuret solution changes from blue to lilac / purple.
lipid	A milky, white emulsion is produced after water is added.

Table 4.1: Colour changes that occur with each nutrient test.

Testing other foods

1 Take a sample of one of the foods you are going to test and use the pestle and mortar to grind it up.

2 Dissolve some of the food in distilled water and test it for starch, glucose and protein.

3 Dissolve another sample of the food in 100% ethanol and test for lipid.

Results and conclusions

Draw a results table like the one shown in Table 4.2. Use your results to identify all the food groups present in the foods you tested.

CONTINUED

Food or nutrient	Result of test			
	Iodine	Benedict's	Biuret	Ethanol and water

Table 4.2: Results table for nutrient tests.

Processed food	Result of test			
	Iodine	Benedict's	Biuret	Ethanol and water
A	black	red	blue	colourless
B	orange	red	lilac	white
C	orange	blue	lilac	white

Table 4.3: Summary of results for nutrient tests.

Challenge

The sugar test used here is called a reducing sugar test and only tests for some types of sugar. Find out about the non-reducing sugar test that is used for a sugar called sucrose.

Questions

1   A student carried out nutrient tests on three processed sea food products. Their results are shown in Table 4.3.

State the nutrient groups that are present in each of the processed foods.

2   Explain why it is not possible to compare the amount of each nutrient in different foods when using these tests.

This Practical task links to Skills tips 0.1 and 0.3.

Self-assessment

Think about how you judged the colour changes. Is there any way that you could have made judging the colours more accurate?

Vitamins

Vitamins are molecules that are essential for the growth and activity of all organisms. Only small quantities of vitamins are needed, so we class vitamins as micronutrients. Plants and many protoctists make their own vitamins, but animals must consume vitamins in their diet. Sea foods are often a rich source of vitamins in the human diet. Many vitamins need to be present in the diets of all animals (Table 4.4).

KEY WORD

micronutrients: essential nutrients that are needed in small amounts

Vitamin	Function in animals
vitamin A	a lipid-soluble vitamin that is essential for good vision and healthy skin
vitamin B	water-soluble and essential for energy release by cells; there are many different types of B vitamins
vitamin C	a water-soluble vitamin that plays an essential role in maintaining healthy skin, teeth and blood vessels
vitamin D	a lipid-soluble vitamin that helps the body to absorb calcium to strengthen bones and teeth

Table 4.4: Functions of different vitamins in animals.

Minerals

Like vitamins, minerals (also called mineral salts) are classed as micronutrients. All living organisms need minerals for a range of body processes. Animals generally obtain mineral salts through their diets. Protoctists, such as kelp and dinoflagellates, absorb minerals from the surrounding water. Plants, such as seagrasses, use their root systems to absorb minerals from sediment. Nitrates, calcium salts and magnesium salts are all examples of minerals. Mineral salts contain elements which are needed by living organisms.

ACTIVITY 4.1

Saturated and unsaturated fatty acids

Working with another learner, find out about the chemical differences and physical differences between saturated and unsaturated fatty acids. Try to explain why many marine fish have a lot of unsaturated fatty acids. Then, on your own, write a paragraph to explain why eating oily fish is thought to be healthy.

Peer assessment

Swap your paragraphs and rate each other's paragraphs. Add any extra points that you think should be included.

Use the following scheme for rating:

☺ if they did it really well

😐 if they made a good attempt at it and partly succeeded

☹ if they did not try to do it or did not succeed.

KEY WORD

haemoglobin: protein that contains iron and is used to transport oxygen in blood

The functions of essential elements

Plants and photosynthetic protoctists obtain most of the elements they need from mineral salts. Animals obtain the elements they need from their food (see Table 4.5).

Carbon is the element found in all organic molecules, such as carbohydrates, proteins and lipids. Carbon is essential for life. There is a constant recycling of carbon between organisms and the environment. Plants and photosynthetic protoctists obtain carbon by taking in carbon dioxide gas. Animals obtain carbon from their food.

Like carbon, nitrogen is necessary for life. Without a source of nitrogen, organisms cannot grow. Proteins are made up of repeating units called amino acids. All amino acids contain the elements carbon, hydrogen, oxygen and nitrogen, and a few also contain sulfur. Plants and protoctists synthesise (make) their own amino acids and proteins, obtaining nitrogen as nitrate ions from the sediment or surrounding water. Animals obtain nitrogen from their food.

Magnesium is essential for all organisms but it is particularly important for plants and protoctists. Magnesium is needed to produce chlorophyll, so plants and protoctists cannot photosynthesise without magnesium.

Element	Function	Source
carbon	essential to make all organic molecules	plants and protoctists: carbon dioxide in air or water animals: diet
nitrogen	helps to make proteins	plants and protoctists: nitrate ions in soil, sediment and water animals: diet
magnesium	helps to make chlorophyll	plants and protoctists: magnesium ions in soil, sediment and water animals: diet
calcium	builds the shells of molluscs and skeleton of coral	plants and protoctists: calcium ions in soil, sediment and water animals: diet and surrounding water
iron	synthesis (making) of haemoglobin to transport oxygen	plants and protoctists: iron ions in soil, sediment and water animals: diet

Table 4.5: Some of the essential chemical elements and their functions.

Chlorophyll gives producers their green colour, as shown in Figure 4.6. Plants and protoctists obtain magnesium from sediment or surrounding water. Animals obtain magnesium from their food.

Calcium salts can be found dissolved in oceans and seas. Molluscs, such as mussels, extract the calcium ions from the water and use them to form shells of insoluble calcium carbonate. Some mollusc shells are shown in Figure 4.7. Some cnidarians, such as corals, use calcium to build skeletons of insoluble calcium carbonate. Coral reefs are formed from calcium carbonate being laid down in layers over many years. When corals are put under environmental stress, they eject (throw out) their zooxanthellae and the corals bleach. The white, bleached appearance of the corals shown in Figure 4.8 is due to the white of the calcium carbonate skeleton.

Iron is essential for making the protein molecule called haemoglobin, which transports oxygen around the body. In vertebrate animals, red blood cells are filled with haemoglobin molecules, which have a red colour. When blood passes through gas exchange organs, such as gills or lungs, the haemoglobin in the blood binds (joins) to oxygen molecules.

Figure 4.6: Seaweed being farmed in Bali; the green colour is due to the high concentration of chlorophyll.

Figure 4.7: Variety of mollusc shells composed of calcium carbonate.

Figure 4.8: Bleached coral that has expelled zooxanthellae. The white calcium carbonate skeleton is clearly visible.

When the blood reaches body tissues, such as muscles, the oxygen is released from the blood for respiration in the body tissues. Some invertebrates, such as the annelid lugworm, *Arenicola*, also have haemoglobin within their bodies to store oxygen. These lugworms, shown in Figure 4.9, live inside burrows on sandy beaches. At high tide, when covered with water, the haemoglobin binds to oxygen which is then stored. When the tide goes out and oxygen concentrations in the burrow become low, the stored oxygen is used by the lugworm.

Questions

4   Describe the functions of the following elements in living organisms:

   a   iron

   b   calcium

   c   magnesium.

5   Acidic water reacts with calcium carbonate, causing the calcium carbonate to dissolve. Explain why the acidification of seawater poses a threat to coral.

6   Fertiliser spread on farm land contains minerals such as nitrates and magnesium. Explain why fertiliser that is allowed to run off into the sea can cause algae populations to grow rapidly.

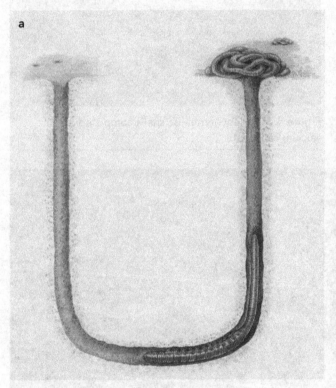

Figure 4.9: a The lugworm, *Arenicola*, shown in a burrow; **b** the appearance of casts of sand on a beach.

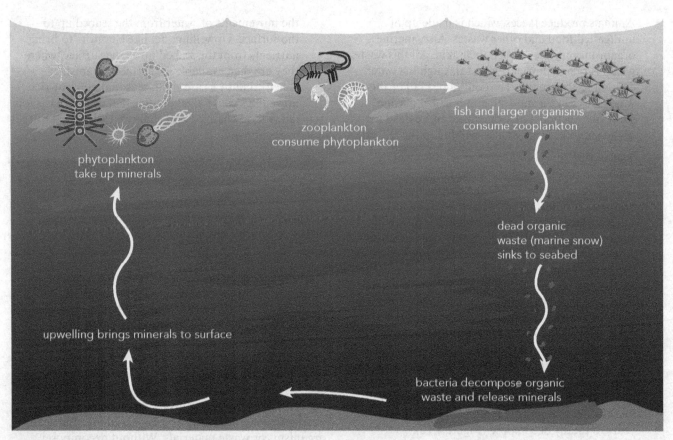

Figure 4.10: Summary of recycling of elements in marine ecosystems.

Recycling of nutrients through marine ecosystems

You learnt about elements in Chapter 2 and should know that there are a set number of elements on our planet. This means that every living organism is made up of atoms that have already passed through other organisms and also have been part of the environment. For example, some of the carbon atoms that we breathe out into the atmosphere as carbon dioxide will be taken up by seagrasses when they photosynthesise. The carbon atoms are then made into organic molecules, such as starch, inside the seagrass. If the seagrass is eaten by a manatee, the carbon will then become part of the manatee's body. Eventually, the carbon is released back into the atmosphere as carbon dioxide gas when the manatee breathes out. So, your body is made up of elements that have passed through many plants and animals, even dinosaurs, before becoming part of you.

All nutrients have slightly different recycling pathways. Figure 4.10 shows the general pathway through which all nutrients are recycled in marine ecosystems.

The general pathway has the following steps.

- Nutrients such as carbon (in the form of carbon dioxide) and nitrogen (in the form of nitrates) are taken up by producers. In open water ecosystems away from coastal areas, these producer organisms are usually photosynthetic dinoflagellates or diatoms that live at the surface. Seagrasses and macroalgae, such as kelp, are also producers that take up nutrients.

- The nutrients pass to **herbivore** animals that eat producers. The nutrients will then pass along food chains as predatory **carnivorous** animals eat other animals.

> ## KEY WORDS
>
> **herbivore:** animal that obtains energy by eating plants
>
> **carnivore:** animal that obtains energy by eating other animals

- Animals produce faeces, which is made up of undigested food and other wastes. Also, marine organisms may die or shed their skin. All this waste, which is rich in nutrients, sinks through the water column to the seabed. The continuous fall of this waste looks like a snowfall and is called marine snow (see Section 2.5). Sometimes entire dead organisms, like large whales, will fall to the seabed.

- The marine snow on the seabed is consumed by scavenger organisms that eat dead organisms and wastes. Much of the life on the deep seabed relies on the continuous fall of wastes from the surface waters. The arrival of a dead whale, as shown in Figure 4.11, can provide these scavenger organisms with enough food for several years. Large organisms, like hagfish and sleeper sharks, eat the soft muscle tissues and blubber of the whale. When the whale's body is reduced to mainly bones, invertebrates such as crabs, shrimp and annelid worms move in to feed. Eventually, bacteria consume the final remains so that nothing is left. Bacteria are decomposers and are very important in this recycling pathway. In the end, bacteria decompose everything and release nutrients such as nitrates and other mineral salts into the ocean depths. A whale can take up to 100 years to totally decompose (Figure 4.12).

- The water close to the seabed is rich in nutrients due to the constant decomposition of organic wastes. In Chapter 2, you learnt about upwellings – the movements of water from the seabed up to the surface. Upwellings act like elevators to bring nutrients from the seabed up to the surface, where they are then available for surface organisms. When conditions are right, seasonal nutrient-rich upwellings cause algal blooms that are the basis for many food chains. Food chains are discussed further in Section 4.4.

KEY WORD

decomposers: microorganisms that digest and breakdown dead organisms and organic waste; they often recycle nutrients in ecosystems

Decomposer bacteria are essential to the recycling of nutrients. Without these microscopic organisms we would not have life on our planet. When dead organisms and waste organic material sink to the seabed, the decomposer bacteria break these down. During this process of decay, the bacteria respire and release carbon dioxide gas. The bacteria also release nutrients such as magnesium, nitrates, calcium and iron into the oceans. Other living organisms can now take in these nutrients, which were previously locked into the dead organisms or waste materials. Without decomposer bacteria, the nutrient cycles would stop and life would not continue.

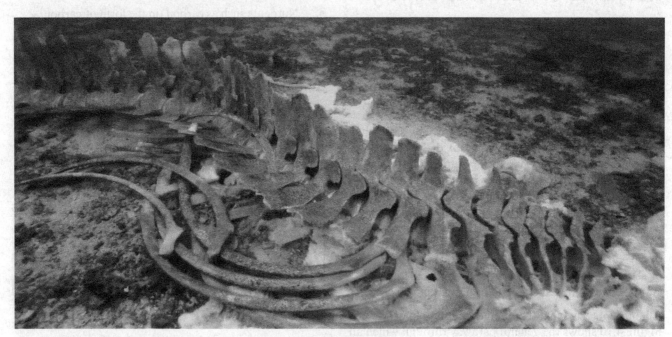

Figure 4.11: Skeleton of whale that has been decomposed on the seabed.

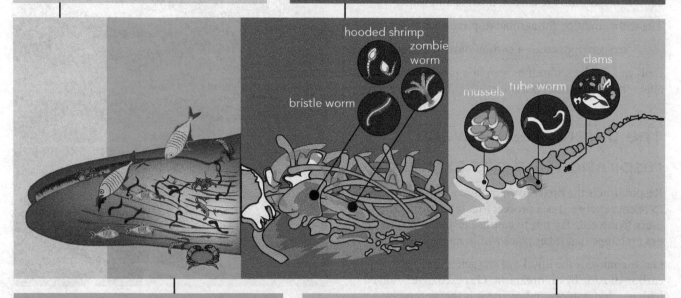

Dead whale sinks to seabed bringing food and energy for scavenger, detritivore and decomposer organisms. In reality all the stages overlap with each other, and decomposer bacteria are digesting dead tissues and recycling nutrients from the start.

Opportunistic stage:
smaller detritivore animals move in to consume the particles of flesh that are left. Annelid worms, small shrimp-like crustaceans and echinoderms strip away all the flesh leaving the bones. This stage can last for about two years. A food web develops as predator species begin to prey on species that consume the dead whale.

Scavenger stage:
large organisms such as hagfish, sleeper sharks and crabs move towards the dead whale. They consume large amounts of soft tissues such as muscles and blubber. This stage usually lasts for about two years.

Final decomposition:
when all the flesh has been consumed, only the bones remain. These bones are rich in minerals, fat and protein. Bacteria decompose the remains and recycle the minerals in the surrounding water. Some filter-feeding molluscs, annelids and crustaceans live around the remains eating tiny particles of tissue. The final stages of decomposition can last up to 100 years.

Figure 4.12: Sequence of events that occurs when a dead whale falls to the seabed.

Questions

7   Place the following statements about the recycling of nutrients into the correct order, starting with:

algae take up the nutrients from the surrounding water

A   nutrients move to the surface by upwelling

B   bacteria decompose the organic waste and make the nutrients available

C   waste organic material falls to the seabed as marine snow

D   nutrients are passed to animals

8   Explain why most life on the seabed depends upon organisms at the surface.

9   Use your knowledge of nutrient recycling to explain why harvesting too many fish from the ocean's surface could eventually reduce the growth of organisms at the surface.

4.2 Respiration

Energy is needed for life. We need energy to move, to breathe, to keep warm, to grow, to synthesise (make) molecules, and to transport substances in and out of cells. Respiration is the chemical process within every living cell that releases the energy from nutrient molecules in a usable form. The main nutrient molecule used in respiration is carbohydrate, but lipids and proteins can also be used.

Aerobic respiration

Aerobic respiration is the release of energy from glucose using oxygen. It takes place in mitochondria within cells. Those cells that use lots of energy, for example muscle cells, have many mitochondria. The waste products of aerobic respiration are carbon dioxide and water.

The word equation for aerobic respiration is:

oxygen + glucose → carbon dioxide + water

Cells can respire without oxygen in a process called anaerobic respiration, but this releases much less energy.

The differences between respiration and gas exchange

Respiration is the breakdown of glucose using oxygen to release energy. It is a process that takes place within every living cell. Try not to confuse respiration with the gas exchange that takes place within an organism.

Gas exchange is the uptake of oxygen and release of carbon dioxide by an organism. Gas exchange is linked with aerobic respiration because it is the method by which oxygen is obtained and waste carbon dioxide is removed. Gas exchange in plants and photosynthetic protoctists also means taking in carbon dioxide and releasing oxygen when photosynthesising.

Multicellular animals all have specialised gas exchange organs. Examples are the gills of fish, the lungs of mammals and the tentacles of cnidaria. All gas exchange organs in animals have certain features in common:

*   Large surface area to absorb lots of oxygen and release lots of carbon dioxide. The tentacles of the coral polyp and the fish gill filaments, shown in Figure 4.13, both have lots of parts sticking out to maximise the surface area.

*   Thin walls. The distance that the gases have to travel needs to be as small as possible so gas exchange organs have delicate, thin walls.

*   Good blood supply. Vertebrate organisms that transport gases around the body in the blood have gas exchange organs with a rich blood supply. An example is the gill of a fish.

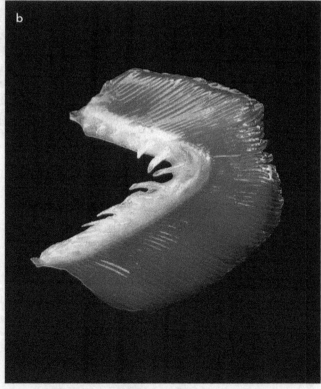

Figure 4.13: Gas exchange structures of **a** coral polyp and **b** fish.

ACTIVITY 4.2

Gas exchange

Find out how a bony fish moves water across its gills, and how the gills are adapted for gas exchange.

Draw diagrams to show the role of the mouth, operculum and gill structures. Put the diagrams on the wall as part of a display.

Peer assessment

Walk past all the diagrams and rate each of them. How accurate is the diagram? How informative is the diagram? Add some sticky notes with ratings and comments about how easy the information is to understand. Write on the sticky notes anything that could be added to the diagrams.

Rate the diagrams for accuracy, and how easy they are to understand, according to the following scheme:

☺ if they did it really well

☺ if they made a good attempt at it and partly succeeded

☹ if they did not try to do it or did not succeed.

PRACTICAL TASK 4.2

Investigating the release of energy by burning samples of food

Introduction

A calorimeter is a piece of equipment that is used to measure the energy stored within food substances. This investigation uses a simple calorimeter to compare the energy in different food items.

You will need:

- boiling tubes
- bosses, clamps and stands
- water
- a measuring cylinder, 50 cm^3
- a Bunsen burner or spirit burner
- a mounted needle
- eye protection
- two heatproof tiles
- a thermometer
- malted wheat cereal

- dry, stale bread (this can be lightly toasted bread)
- puffed starch snacks
- a balance.

Safety: Take care with the naked flames when using Bunsen burners or spirits burners.
Eye protection should be worn at all times.
Long hair must be tied back and loose clothing tucked away.
Check that nobody has any allergies to any of the food substances.

Method

1 Set up the apparatus as shown in Figure 4.14.

2 Use the measuring cylinder to place 20 cm^3 of water into the boiling tube.

3 Place the thermometer into the water and record the starting temperature, t_1.

CONTINUED

4   Weigh a malted wheat cereal biscuit and record the mass, m.

5   Place the cereal biscuit onto the end of the mounted needle.

6   Very carefully, use the Bunsen burner or spirit burner to ignite the cereal biscuit.

7   Quickly hold the burning cereal biscuit under the boiling tube so that it heats the water.

8   Record the maximum temperature, t_2, reached by the water.

9   Repeat the experiment using a piece of dry bread (approximately a 2 cm × 2 cm square) and a puffed starch snack.

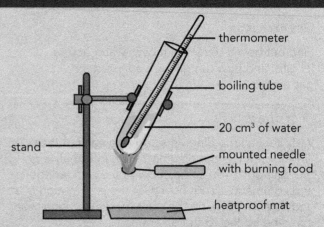

Figure 4.14: Diagram of apparatus to measure the energy content of food.

Results

- Make a copy of Table 4.6 and fill in your results.

- Calculate the change in temperature $(t_2 - t_1)$ and add it to your table.

- Calculate the energy content per gram for each of the foods using the following equation. Write the values in your table.

$$\text{energy (J / g)} = \frac{\text{mass of water (g)} \times \text{temperature change (°C)} \times 4.2}{\text{mass of food (g)}}$$

In this equation, 4.2 is the specific heat capacity of water, which is the energy required to raise the temperature of one gram of water by one degree Celsius.

Questions

1   Compare the energy in each of the foods that you have investigated.

2   Explain what the results show about the nutrient composition of the food. Remember that lipids have about twice as much energy per gram compared with carbohydrates.

3   Explain why it was better to calculate the energy per gram of food rather than simply the energy of each of the food samples used in the experiment.

Challenge

You could investigate other foods. When measuring the energy of substances such as oil and other lipids, remember that they cannot be held on a mounted needle. Always think about the risks when working

Food	Mass, m (g)	Initial water temperature, t_1 (°C)	Maximum water temperature, t_2 (°C)	Change in water temperature (°C)	Energy content (J / g)

Table 4.6: Results table to calculate energy content of food samples.

with any food substances. For example, many varieties of nut can cause severe allergic reactions. Also, some foods may contain oils that can easily catch fire.

This Practical task links to Skills tips 0.1 and 0.6.

REFLECTION

Look at the wrappers for your food items and note down the energy content that is stated on them. Compare this value with the value that you have calculated. The value on the wrapper is probably higher than your value. Why might the method you have used lead to inaccuracies? What could you do to make your value more accurate? Find out about other calorimeter designs and work out a more accurate method.

Questions

10 Give the word equation for aerobic respiration.

11 Suggest why mammals that migrate over long distances often store energy in the form of fat rather than carbohydrate.

12 Myoglobin is a protein found in the muscles of fast swimming fish species (such as tuna) and cetaceans that dive under water for long periods of time. Myoglobin, like haemoglobin, binds to oxygen. Suggest an explanation for myoglobin being in the muscles of tuna and cetaceans.

4.3 Photosynthesis

Photosynthesis may be the most important biological process on the planet. It is the process by which most of our atmospheric oxygen is produced and is also the process that takes in energy for most ecosystems on the planet. Without photosynthesis we would have no food or oxygen.

Producer organisms

Producers make their own organic nutrients, such as glucose, from inorganic chemicals. Glucose is then used by producers to make other nutrient molecules, such as starch, proteins and lipids. Most producers photosynthesise to make their nutrients. The energy source for photosynthesis is sunlight. The energy from sunlight is locked into nutrients made by producers in the form of chemical energy.

There are three groups of producer in the marine environment:

- plants, for example seagrasses
- protoctists, including single-celled microalgae such as dinoflagellates and diatoms, and macroalgae, such as kelp
- bacteria, known as **cyanobacteria**; these simple bacteria are similar in structure to the chloroplasts found in plants and protoctists.

KEY WORD

cyanobacteria: a type of bacteria that are producer organisms

The chemical process of photosynthesis

The word equation for photosynthesis is:

carbon dioxide + water → glucose + oxygen

Sometimes, we add chlorophyll and light energy to the equation, writing these words above and below the arrow, to show their importance:

carbon dioxide + water → glucose + oxygen

$$6CO_2 + 6H_2O \xrightarrow[chlorophyll]{light} C_6H_{12}O_6 + 6O_2$$

Carbon dioxide + Water → Glucose + Oxygen

You should notice that the equation for photosynthesis is the exact opposite of the equation for aerobic respiration. This is because photosynthesis involves taking light energy and using it to make glucose (and oxygen as a by product), while respiration releases that energy from glucose.

Unlike respiration, however, photosynthesis also needs chlorophyll and light.

Figure 4.15 shows a photograph of a cell from an aquatic plant. You can clearly see the green chloroplasts. Photosynthesis occurs inside the chloroplasts, which have membranes that contain a green chemical called chlorophyll. Chlorophyll absorbs the light energy so that it can be used to synthesise (make) glucose. It is the chlorophyll that gives plants and algae their green colour.

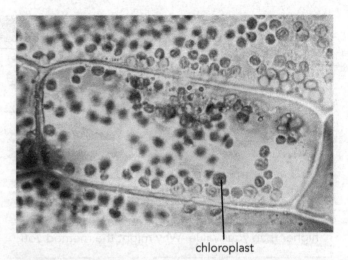

chloroplast

Figure 4.15: Photograph of cell from an aquatic plant showing chloroplasts.

PRACTICAL TASK 4.3

Investigating the effect of light intensity on the rate of photosynthesis in an aquatic plant or macroalga

Introduction

Light provides the energy for photosynthesis. This practical task investigates the effect of changing light intensity on the rate of photosynthesis of aquatic plants.

You will need:

- a boiling tube
- a large glass beaker, e.g. 250 cm³
- a paperclip
- scissors
- an aquatic plant such as *Elodea*
- 1% solution of sodium hydrogencarbonate
- a bench lamp
- a metre ruler
- a stopclock.

Safety: Take care and wear eye protection when using the lamp near water as the bulb can become hot and explode if splashed with cold water.

Method

1   Use the scissors to cut a section of the aquatic plant. You want to cut it so that you have an intact end and a cut end, as shown in Figure 4.16.

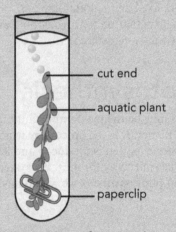

cut end

aquatic plant

paperclip

Figure 4.16: Diagram of aquatic plant in a boiling tube containing sodium hydrogencarbonate. Note that the cut end points upwards.

2   Put the paperclip onto the uncut end of the plant and put the plant into the boiling tube with the cut end pointing upwards. You may need to trim the end again so that the section of plant fits into the tube.

CONTINUED

3   Cover the plant with the sodium hydrogencarbonate solution.

4   Use the beaker to make a 20 °C water bath and place the boiling tube with the plant into the water bath.

5   Set up the apparatus as shown in Figure 4.17. Place the lamp 5 cm away from the boiling tube. Switch on the lamp and leave for about 5 minutes. Bubbles should begin to emerge from the cut end of the plant. If the plant is not producing bubbles, try cutting the end again.

6   Count the number of bubbles produced in a set time. The time you select should be appropriate to the rate that bubbles are being produced. If the rate is fast, you could count for two minutes. If the rate is slower, five minutes is more appropriate. Repeat this measurement two more times so that you get three readings.

7   Move the lamp so that it is 15 cm away from the boiling tube. Leave the plant for five minutes to adjust to the new light intensity and then count the number of bubbles produced in a set time. Repeat two more times.

8   Repeat step 7 at distances of 25 cm, 35 cm and 45 cm.

Results and conclusions

Draw a results table, as shown in the Table 4.7.

Distance of lamp (cm)	Number of bubbles produced in ... minutes			
	1	2	3	mean
5				
15				
25				
35				
45				

Table 4.7: Results table for investigating effect of light intensity on rate of photosynthesis.

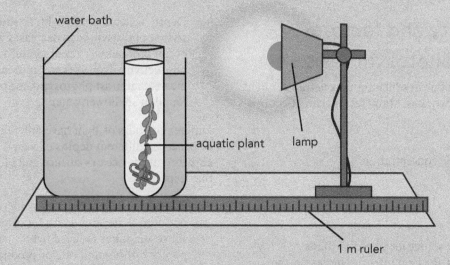

Figure 4.17: Diagram showing apparatus used to investigate the effect of light intensity on the photosynthesis rate of an aquatic plant.

CONTINUED

Calculate the mean number of bubbles produced at each distance. You should leave out any anomalous values when calculating the means.

Draw a graph of your results. You should follow these guidelines.

- Place the distance of the lamp on the horizontal axis and mean number of bubbles on the vertical axis.
- Choose linear scales for both axes that use at least half of your graph paper. Choose sensible increments, e.g. 5, 10 or 25.
- Label the axes with the headers from Table 4.7.
- Plot the mean number of bubbles produced for each distance.

- Use a ruler to join the points. Do not draw lines beyond the first and last points.

Challenge

You could try the experiment using pieces of macroalgae or other species of aquatic plant.

Questions

1 Describe the effect of increasing the distance of the lamp on the number of bubbles produced in the set time.
2 Explain the results of the experiment.
3 Explain why the plant was placed into a water bath.

This Practical task links to Skills tip 0.1.

KEY WORD

anomalous values: values that are very different from other results and do not fit the normal pattern

REFLECTION

Think about the design of this experiment. Suggest how you could make the results more accurate if you were to do the experiment again.

Productivity and factors affecting photosynthesis

Productivity is the rate at which producers transfer light energy into carbohydrates. Many factors can affect this rate, including:

- light intensity
- carbon dioxide concentration
- temperature
- mineral ions.

Light intensity

Light is the energy source for photosynthesis. This means that, if the light intensity increases, the rate of photosynthesis will increase. If the rate of photosynthesis increases, the rate of productivity also increases. In the marine world, light intensity is affected by latitude, depth and turbidity.

- Latitude. photosynthesis and productivity are greater in areas of ocean where the light intensity is greater or the periods of daylight are longer.

- Depth. water absorbs light, as shown in Figure 4.18, so that photosynthesis decreases with depth. Most ocean productivity occurs in the sunlight zone and productivity decreases as depth increases. This means that most photosynthetic organisms are found in shallower water.

Different colours of light have different wavelengths so penetrate different depths of water. Red light is absorbed at the ocean's surface and blue light penetrates the deepest.

- Turbidity. turbidity is a measure of the cloudiness of water. Water that has a lot of particles, such as silt or sand, has reduced light intensity. Therefore photosynthesis and rate of productivity decrease.

KEY WORD

turbidity*: cloudiness in water due to particles, which reduces the transmission of light

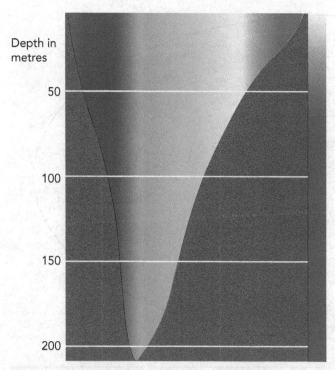

Figure 4.18: Penetration of light through the water.

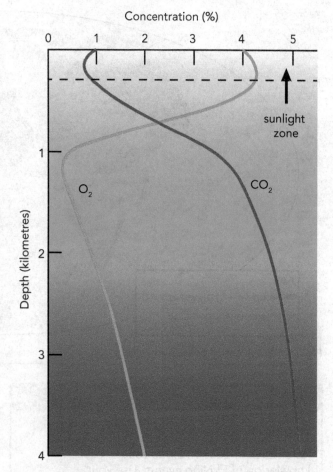

Figure 4.19: Changes in concentrations of oxygen and carbon dioxide with depth of ocean water.

Carbon dioxide concentration

Carbon dioxide is needed for photosynthesis, so low carbon dioxide levels in the water lead to low productivity. Figure 4.19 shows how carbon dioxide concentrations vary with depth. Photosynthesis rates are high in surface waters. However, many producers live near the surface, all competing with each other and using carbon dioxide to perform photosynthesis. This means that carbon dioxide levels in surface waters are low.

As depth increases, carbon dioxide levels increase due to the release of carbon dioxide from animal respiration. The change in concentration of oxygen with depth is an almost mirror image of the change in concentration of carbon dioxide with depth. At the ocean's surface, high rates of photosynthesis release lots of oxygen. But as depth increases, there is less photosynthesis and more animal respiration so the oxygen concentration decreases.

Temperature

Temperature affects all chemical reactions. The rate of photosynthesis will increase as temperature increases, so warmer areas of ocean have higher productivity.

Mineral ions

Productivity is affected by the concentration of mineral ions in the water, particularly the concentration of magnesium – this is because magnesium is needed to make chlorophyll. The concentration of nitrates also affects productivity. In the open ocean, most mineral ions result from upwellings of water from the seabed. Coastal upwellings are caused by surface winds moving surface water away from an area (see Chapter 2). This movement of surface water draws cold, nutrient-rich water from the seabed up to the surface. Figure 4.20 shows some areas of coastal upwelling. Some of these upwellings occur all year round, but others are seasonal. Upwellings cause high productivity. The nutrient-rich upwellings provide energy for all the food webs in that marine area.

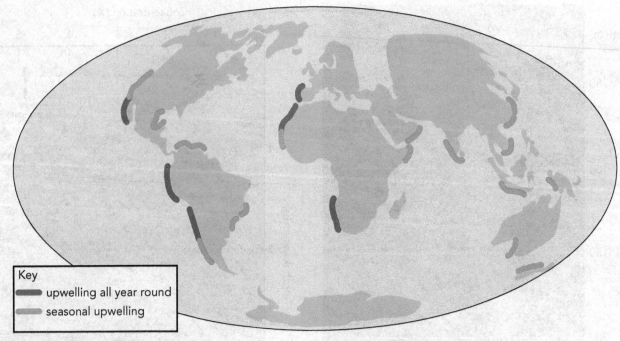

Figure 4.20: Areas of coastal upwelling.

ACTIVITY 4.3

Investigating the effect of El Niño

Refer back to Section 2.6 to refresh your knowledge of El Niño events. Use your knowledge of upwellings and photosynthesis to explain why El Niño causes a reduction in fish catches in the Pacific off the coast of South America. Write an information leaflet to explain to people fishing in South America why some years they will have lower catches due to El Niño. You should use very clear language and diagrams.

Peer assessment

Give your leaflet to another learner who does not study marine science. Ask them to read it and rate how easy it is to understand and how good the information is according to the following scheme:

☺ if you did it really well

😐 if you made a good attempt at it and partly succeeded

☹ if you did not try to do it or did not succeed.

Law of limiting factors

The law of limiting factors states that the rate of photosynthesis will be limited by the factor which is in the shortest supply. For example, this means that the rate of photosynthesis will be low if the light intensity is low, even though there may be plenty of minerals and carbon dioxide available and the seawater temperatures are warm.

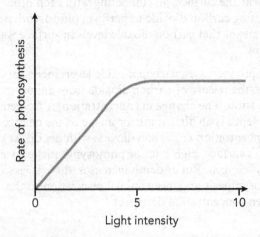

Figure 4.21: Effect of light intensity on rate of photosynthesis.

Figure 4.21 shows the effect of increasing light intensity on the rate of photosynthesis. At first, between 0 **arbitrary units** (a.u.) and 5 a.u. of light intensity, the rate of photosynthesis increases because light intensity is limiting the rate. But when the light intensity increases beyond 5 a.u., the rate of photosynthesis does not increase because another factor, perhaps the carbon dioxide concentration, is now limiting.

> **KEY WORD**
>
> **arbitrary units:** units that are relative to each other; for example, we can measure the mass of fish in arbitrary units where one arbitrary unit is the mass of one sardine

Questions

13 Give the word equation for photosynthesis.
14 Explain the role of chlorophyll in photosynthesis.
15 Explain why photosynthesis is limited in each of the following situations.
   a Warm tropical water with many animals and high turbidity due to silt.
   b Cold, clear Arctic water in the summer with many animals present.
   c Warm, clear water with many phytoplankton but few animals.
   d Coastal waters of South America during an El Niño event.

4.4 Feeding relationships

All living organisms are dependent on each other. Sunlight is the energy source for nearly all biological systems on the planet. Once energy enters an ecosystem through the producers, this energy is transferred from one organism to another, usually by feeding.

Food chains and food webs

We can represent feeding relationships between organisms by diagrams that show the transfer of energy. These diagrams are called food chains and **food webs**.

A food chain shows the transfer of energy from one organism to another within an ecosystem, starting with a producer (Figure 4.22). The arrows show the direction of energy transfer between the organisms. Consumer organisms are the organisms that gain their energy by feeding on other organisms.

The position that each organism occupies in the food chain is known as its **trophic level**. The names for each of the levels are shown in this general food chain:

producer → primary consumer (1°) → secondary consumer (2°) → tertiary consumer (3°)

In Figure 4.22, the phytoplankton is the producer, the zooplankton is the **primary consumer**, the small fish

> **KEY WORDS**
>
> **food web:** the interactions between all the food chains in an ecosystem
>
> **trophic level:** the position occupied by an organism in a food chain
>
> **primary consumer:** organism at the second trophic level of a food chain; a primary consumer obtains energy from eating producers

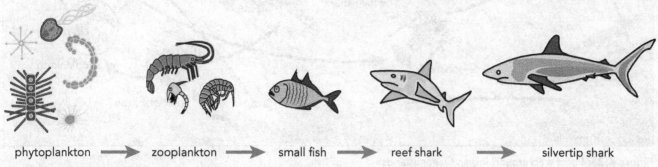

phytoplankton → zooplankton → small fish → reef shark → silvertip shark

Figure 4.22: Food chain from part of Indian Ocean ecosystem.

is the secondary consumer and the reef shark is the tertiary consumer. The number of trophic levels will vary between different food chains. In Figure 4.22, the silvertip shark is a quaternary consumer.

Consumers are also given names according to what they eat.

- Herbivores are animals that gain energy from only eating producers.

- Carnivores are animals that gain energy from only eating other animals.

- Omnivores are animals that gain energy from eating both plants and animals.

- Detritivores are animals that gain energy from eating dead or waste organic material.

- Predators are a type of carnivore that capture, kill and eat other animals; the other animals are prey.

In any ecosystem there is always more than one food chain. A food web shows all the food chains within an ecosystem and shows the inter-relationships between all

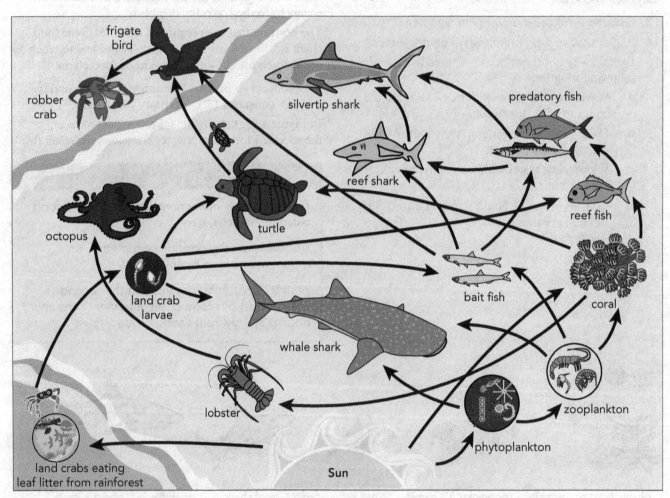

Figure 4.23: Food web around Indian Ocean islands.

the organisms. Figure 4.23 shows part of a marine food web for Christmas Island in the Indian Ocean.

An organism can belong to more than one food chain within the web. For example, the zooplankton in the Indian Ocean food web are consumed by three different organisms.

An organism can also occupy more than one trophic level in different food chains. The whale shark is both a primary consumer (because it eats phytoplankton) and a secondary consumer (because it eats zooplankton).

ACTIVITY 4.4

Constructing a food web

You need to be able to construct food chains and food webs. Read the following information about the interactions between organisms in a food web.

Information about the food web

Kelp is a protoctist producer that takes light energy from the Sun and converts it to chemical energy. Microalgae also grow on the kelp, using sunlight to photosynthesise. Small fish and sea urchins eat kelp and microalgae. The microalgae is also consumed by zooplankton and shrimps. The shrimps also eat zooplankton. Small fish eat the shrimps. Large predatory fish eat the small fish. The sea urchins and large fish are both eaten by sea otters.

Draw a food web based on this information. Your food web needs to be easy to follow, ideally with no arrows crossing.

Peer assessment

When you have completed your food web, give it to another learner and ask them to answer the following questions:

1 Name the organisms that consume kelp.

2 Give a food chain that has five organisms.

3 State the number of food chains in the food web.

If the other learner got all the questions correct, your food web is probably correct!

Questions

Use the food web in Figure 4.23 to answer these questions.

16 a List two primary consumers.

b List two secondary consumers.

c List two tertiary consumers.

17 Give the name of:

a an omnivore

b a carnivore.

18 Suggest what would happen to the turtle population if part of the rainforest on land was removed.

Pyramids of number, of biomass and of energy

We can represent the number of organisms, the biomass and the energy present in each trophic level of a food chain by drawing pyramid diagrams. The rules for drawing all the pyramids are the same:

- the width of each bar represents quantity
- the producers are always at the base of the pyramid.

Pyramids of number can have a range of different shapes, depending on the number and size of the organisms in each trophic level. Small organisms often have large populations compared with larger organisms. Figure 4.24 shows two pyramids of number, one for an open ocean food chain based upon phytoplankton and the other for a giant kelp forest. The open ocean food chain has a typical 'pyramid shape' with a wide base representing large numbers of microscopic phytoplankton. The kelp forest food chain has a narrower base as there are fewer individuals kelp plants compared with the more numerous sea urchins that feed on the kelp.

KEY WORDS

biomass: the mass of living matter; it is usually measured as dry mass

pyramid of number: a diagram that shows the number of organisms at each trophic level

Biomass is the dry mass of organic matter. It is a measure of the mass of organic molecules that have been synthesised (made) at each level of a food chain.

a open ocean

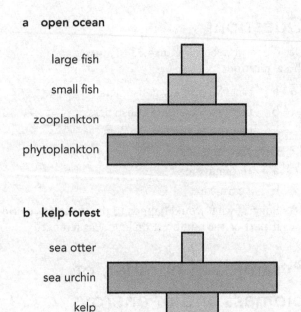

b kelp forest

Figure 4.24: Pyramid of numbers for **a** open ocean and **b** kelp forest.

We can measure biomass by drying samples of organisms to remove all their water before weighing them. Water content is variable and is not a measure of the organic material. Solid materials, such as the calcium carbonate skeletons of coral, are also not included when measuring biomass. The units of measurement for biomass are usually kilograms per square metre (kg/m^2) or kilograms per cubic metre (kg/m^3).

The shape of most **pyramids of biomass** is usually the same – broader at the base and narrower towards the top. Figure 4.25 shows a pyramid of biomass for a seagrass meadow that shows this shape. The pyramid narrows

KEY WORD

pyramid of biomass: a diagram that shows the biomass at each trophic level

towards the top because some biomass is lost from one trophic level to the next.

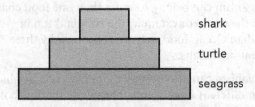

Figure 4.25: Pyramid of biomass for a seagrass meadow.

Biomass is lost from the food chain due to several reasons:

- Organic nutrients are used in respiration to release energy for body processes.

- Organisms use some organic material in respiration to provide energy for movement.

- Some organisms are lost to other food chains and are removed or harvested by humans.

- Some parts of organisms are not consumed, for example the roots and rhizomes of seagrass may not be eaten by turtles.

- After being consumed, some molecules are not digested; these molecules are then released as faeces, which is decomposed by bacteria.

- Some biomass is lost due to excretion and is not available for the next trophic level.

Occasionally, pyramids of biomass have different shapes. This is usually because the pyramid is a measure of the biomass at one particular time and populations in the food chain change rapidly. Figure 4.26 shows a pyramid of biomass for an open ocean ecosystem immediately after a phytoplankton bloom and a pyramid of biomass for the same food chain two weeks later. After two weeks, the biomass of phytoplankton has reduced as most has been consumed and the biomass has been passed up to the zooplankton.

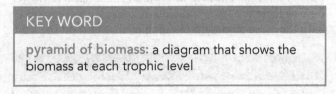

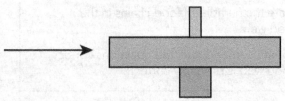

Figure 4.26: Pyramid of biomass for an open ocean ecosystem at two different times.

Pyramids of energy show how much energy is present at each trophic level of a food chain. These pyramids usually show the mean energy content over a period of one year. They are measured in kilojoules per square metre per year (kJ / m² / yr).

Pyramids of energy are always the same shape, becoming narrower from the base upwards, as shown in Figure 4.27. This means that not all the energy from each trophic level is passed to the next level. Food chains have a limited number of trophic levels because the energy in each level decreases along the food chain.

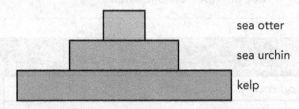

Figure 4.27: Pyramid of energy for a kelp forest.

The number of trophic levels varies from one food chain to another and depends on the efficiencies of energy transfer between levels. The number of trophic levels also depends on productivity from producers. Areas with low productivity have food chains with few trophic levels. Energy is lost in food chains for the same reasons as the loss of biomass:

- Organic nutrients are used in respiration to release energy for body processes.

- Organisms use some organic material in respiration to provide energy for movement.

- Some organisms are lost to other food chains and are removed or harvested by humans.

- Some parts of organisms are not consumed, for example the roots and rhizomes of seagrass may not be eaten by turtles.

- After being consumed, some molecules are not digested; these are then released as faeces which is decomposed by bacteria.

- Some energy is lost due to excretion and is not available for the next trophic level.

Decomposers are organisms that gain energy from breaking down organic material. Biomass lost from food chains (due to not being consumed, the organisms dying or not being digested) eventually passes to decomposer bacteria. These bacteria digest the dead material. The bacteria release the energy in this material by respiration and the nutrients are recycled into the seawater. Sediment on the seabed is full of decomposer bacteria that gain energy from marine snow.

Questions

19 Give three ways in which energy is lost from a food chain.

20 Figure 4.28 shows the energy fixed each year by three trophic levels of a marine food chain.

   a Calculate the percentage of energy that is transferred from the phytoplankton to the zooplankton and from the zooplankton to the shrimp.

   b Suggest why the percentage of energy transferred between the trophic levels is different.

21 Explain why food chains in areas with poor conditions for photosynthesis have fewer organisms at each trophic level and fewer trophic levels.

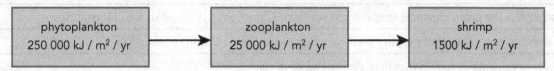

Figure 4.28: Flow of energy through an open ocean food chain.

ACTIVITY 4.5

Drawing ecological pyramids

Design a question for other learners. You need to ask them to draw a pyramid of numbers and a pyramid of energy for a food chain. Think about what you could ask them about the flow of energy along the food chain.

- Aim for a total of 7 or 8 marks divided up into separate questions.

- Each question should start with a command word such as draw, state, describe or explain. Command words are listed in the exam-style questions found at the end of each chapter.

- You will also need to write a mark scheme that clearly shows how each mark point is awarded – look at some of the exam-style questions to help you.

Peer assessment

When you have finished, give your question to another learner. Discuss how well your questions and mark scheme work. They can rate it according to the following scheme:

- ☺ if they worked really well
- 😐 if they worked well in parts
- ☹ if they did not work at all well.

SUMMARY

Nutrients are substances that are needed for growth, repair and energy.
Nutrients include gases such as carbon dioxide (which is used in photosynthesis), dissolved salts, such as nitrates, and organic compounds.
Major nutrient groups include proteins for cell growth and repair, carbohydrates for energy, lipids for energy and insulation, and micronutrients such as vitamins and minerals.
Marine organisms need essential elements with specific roles: nitrogen for proteins, carbon for organic compounds, magnesium for chlorophyll, calcium to make skeletons and shells, and iron for haemoglobin.
In marine ecosystems, nutrients are taken up by organisms and passed along food chains; these nutrients will sink to the seabed as waste, eventually being recycled by decomposer bacteria before being returned to the surface by upwelling.
Respiration is the release of energy from chemical nutrients and occurs in the mitochondria of living cells.
Aerobic respiration is the chemical breakdown of glucose using oxygen to produce carbon dioxide and water.
Photosynthesis is the synthesis (making) of glucose from carbon dioxide and water using energy from sunlight.
Chlorophyll is the green chemical that absorbs sunlight. Chlorophyll is found inside chloroplasts.
Producers are organisms that produce their own organic nutrients by photosynthesis.
Producer organisms include protoctists, plants and bacteria.
Productivity is the rate at which producers transfer energy into carbohydrates.
Local upwelling of nutrients, such as magnesium and nitrates, increases productivity due to phytoplankton growth.
Food chains and food webs show the transfer of energy through the organisms in an ecosystem.

CONTINUED

Producer organisms convert light energy into chemical energy; producers make this energy available to other organisms in food webs.
Consumers are organisms that get energy by feeding on other organisms; we class them as primary, secondary and tertiary consumers depending on their position in a food chain.
Consumers are classed as herbivores, carnivores, omnivores or detritivores, depending on their food source.
Biomass is the dry mass of living matter present in a trophic level.
A trophic level is the position of an organism in a food chain or food web.
Biomass and energy are lost along food chains due to respiration, movement, removal of organisms, excretion, undigested biomass and biomass that is not consumed.
Decomposer organisms break down dead organic material.
Pyramids of number show the number of organisms at each trophic level and can be different shapes.
Pyramids of biomass show the biomass of each trophic level and usually become narrower towards the top.
Pyramids of energy show the energy present in each trophic level and become narrower towards the top.
Predators are animals that catch and eat other animals; these other animals are prey.

CASE STUDY PROJECT

Is this the end for the orca?

Figure 4.29: Pod of orcas in the Arctic Ocean.

Figure 4.29 shows a pod of orcas. At first glance, populations of orcas seem to be fairly healthy and there are at least 50 000 orcas around the world. The real situation, however, may be somewhat more worrying. A recent scientific paper suggested that over half of the world's population of orcas could be lost within the next 30–50 years. The cause of this extinction is not hunting or habitat loss. Instead, the cause is an invisible, silent killer known as polychlorinated biphenyls (PCBs). These highly toxic chemicals (which were manufactured by humans) have been banned for many years yet are still being released into the oceans.

PCBs were used in electrical components, paints and plastics. But in the 1980s they were banned because they were found to be harmful to humans and the environment. However, PCBs continue to wash into the oceans from refuse.

Levels of PCBs build up in living organisms. PCBs are not broken down or excreted by living organisms because they are fat soluble.

KEY WORD

extinction: the loss of a species from the planet

CONTINUED

The concentration of PCBs increases along food chains so that top predators, such as orcas, get the highest concentrations. Because PCBs are fat soluble, they are transferred from mother to calf through milk. PCBs cause cancers, immune system damage and affect reproduction. Scientists have found that the PCB concentration in the bodies of orcas near industrial nations are up to 100 times the safe limit. Populations of orcas around the UK, Gibraltar, Japan, China and Brazil could become extinct in time. There is some hope, however, as orca populations in the less polluted waters of the Arctic have far less contamination with PCBs.

Imagine that you are advising a government on the threat of toxins on marine populations and humans.

Do some research about the threats posed by the build-up of toxins in the bodies of marine organisms.

- Work with another learner to produce a leaflet that explains the science behind the threat and gives advice on possible solutions.

- You could investigate two or three solutions and evaluate the benefits and costs of each solution.

KEY WORD

immune system: the system in the body that destroys infections

Peer assessment

When you have finished, give the leaflets to other learners and ask them to read the leaflets. Other learners can then evaluate your leaflet. You could also ask them questions about the pollution caused by toxins to see how effectively you explained the science.

EXAM-STYLE QUESTIONS

1   The nutrient contents of tilapia, mackerel and mussels are shown in Table 1.

Seafood species	Mass of nutrient per 100 g of fish (g)			Percentage of RDA for 16-year-old	
	Carbohydrate	Protein	Lipid	Calcium	Iron
tilapia	0.0	25.0	3.0	1	4
mackerel	0.0	18.7	13.9	15	8
mussels	3.0	21.9	1.7	4	24

Table 1

a   i   Identify which seafood species in Table 1 has the highest mass of protein. [1]

ii   Determine the mass of protein in 250 g of mackerel. [2]

iii   Explain which one of the seafood species in Table 1 has the most energy. [2]

iv   The recommended daily allowance (RDA) is the mass of a nutrient that is required in the diet of a human. The RDA of calcium for a 16-year-old is 1.3 g.

Calculate the mass of calcium in 100 g of mussels. [2]

COMMAND WORDS

identify: name / select / recognise

determine: establish an answer using the information available

explain: set out purposes or reasons / make the relationships between things evident / provide why and / or how and support with relevant evidence

calculate: work out from given facts, figures or information

CONTINUED

    v Tilapia are slow-swimming fish that do not travel long distances, mackerel are fast-swimming fish that travel long distances, and mussels are molluscs that remain attached to a substrate. Use this information and Table 1 to explain the differences in the mass of carbohydrate and mass of fat in these species. **[3]**

b Describe how the seafood species can be tested for the presence of protein. **[2]**

c Mackerel swim at the surface of the ocean. Describe how the nitrogen in the protein of the mackerel is made available to producers at the surface of the ocean. **[4]**

[Total: 16]

> **COMMAND WORD**
>
> **describe:** state the points of a topic / give characteristics and main features

2 A student investigated the effect of water temperature on the rate of opening of the operculum of a sea trout.

The sea trout was placed into a tank of water and the temperature of the water maintained at 5 °C. The number of times that the operculum opened in one minute was counted. This was repeated two more times and the mean number of opening times calculated. The student repeated this at other temperatures. The results are shown in Table 2.

Temperature of water (°C)	Mean number of times that operculum opened in one minute
5	6
10	8
15	11
17	13
20	14
25	14

Table 2

a **i** Describe how the student would calculate the mean number of times that the operculum opened in one minute. **[2]**

    ii Draw a line graph to show the mean number of times that the operculum opened in one minute at different temperatures. Join your points with ruled, straight lines. **[5]**

    iii Outline the effect of increasing temperature on the mean number of times that the operculum opened in one minute. **[2]**

b Give two variables that the student should have kept constant. **[2]**

c Opening the operculum allows water to flow over the gills for gas exchange to enable the process of aerobic respiration.

    i Complete the equation for aerobic respiration.

$$\text{glucose} + \underline{\hspace{2cm}} \rightarrow \underline{\hspace{2cm}} + \underline{\hspace{2cm}}$$ **[2]**

    ii Outline the differences between aerobic respiration and gas exchange. **[3]**

[Total: 16]

> **COMMAND WORDS**
>
> **outline:** set out the main points
>
> **give:** produce an answer from a given source or recall / memory

CONTINUED

3 Producers are organisms that make their own organic nutrients by photosynthesis. Macroalgae such as kelp are producers.

a i Kelp are protoctists. Give two other groups of producer organism other than protoctists. [2]

ii Complete the word equation for photosynthesis.

water + _____ → _____ + _____ [2]

iii State the name of the green pigment that absorbs light energy. [1]

b Figure 1 shows the effect of increasing carbon dioxide concentration on the rate of photosynthesis by a kelp in clear water, and the same kelp in water with sediment.

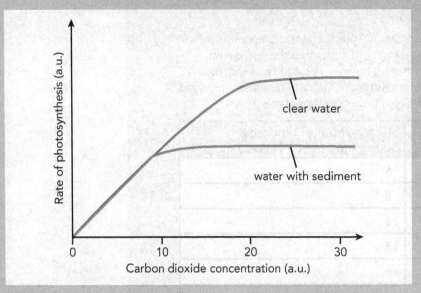

Figure 1

i Compare the effect of increasing carbon dioxide concentration on the rate of photosynthesis of the kelp in clear water with the rate of photosynthesis of the kelp in water with sediment. [2]

ii Explain the effect of increasing carbon dioxide concentration on the rate of photosynthesis of the kelp placed into water with sediment. [3]

iii Use the information in Figure 1 to suggest why dredging areas can result in reduced transfer of energy to secondary consumers. [3]

[Total: 13]

COMMAND WORD

state: express in clear terms

COMMAND WORD

compare: identify / comment on similarities and / or differences

4 Figure 2 shows a food web for an area of seagrass meadow.

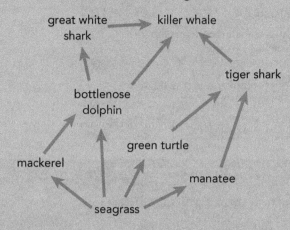

Figure 2

a Name the producer in the food web. [1]

b State what is meant by the term 'predator', giving an example from this food web. [3]

c Give the longest food chain in this food web. [1]

d Explain the importance of detritivores to food webs. [2]

[Total: 7]

5 Figure 3 shows the transfer of energy through a food chain.

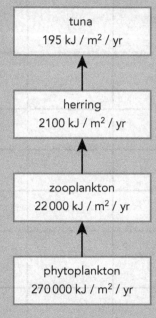

Figure 3

CONTINUED

a State why the energy flow is measured per square metre. [1]

b State which organism is the secondary consumer. [1]

c i Calculate the percentage of energy that is transferred from the zooplankton to the herring. Give your answer to two significant figures. [2]

 ii Explain why not all the energy in the phytoplankton is transferred to the tuna. [4]

[Total: 8]

SELF-EVALUATION CHECKLIST

After studying this chapter, think about how confident you are with the different topics. This will help you to see any gaps in your knowledge and help you to learn more effectively.

I can	Needs more work	Getting there	Confident to move on	See Section
describe nutrients as substances that are needed by living organisms for growth, repair and energy, including carbon dioxide gas, dissolved salts and organic compounds				4.1
describe and interpret nutrient tests for starch, sugars, proteins and lipids				4.1
describe the functions of proteins, carbohydrates, fats, vitamins, nitrogen, carbon, magnesium, calcium and iron				4.1
explain how nutrients cycle through marine ecosystems, including the role of decomposer bacteria				4.1
understand the process of aerobic respiration and know the word equation				4.2
describe the differences between aerobic respiration and gas exchange				4.2
describe how to investigate the release of energy from foods				4.2
understand the process of photosynthesis in converting light energy into chemical energy and know the word equation				4.3
understand the role of chlorophyll in photosynthesis				4.3

CONTINUED

I can	Needs more work	Getting there	Confident to move on	See Section
understand the role of different producer organisms, including plants, protoctists and bacteria, in food webs				4.3
describe how to investigate the effect of light intensity on the rate of photosynthesis of aquatic plants or macroalgae				4.3
outline the importance of upwellings in the productivity of organisms in coastal ecosystems				4.4
describe how energy flows through food chains and how it is lost due to respiration, movement, removal or harvesting and excretion				4.4
understand how to interpret and construct food chains				4.4
understand what is meant by the terms: trophic level, primary consumer, secondary consumer, tertiary consumer, herbivore, carnivore, omnivore, detritivore and predator				4.4
draw, describe and interpret pyramids of number, pyramids of biomass and pyramids of energy				4.4
describe decomposers as organisms that gain energy by breaking down dead or waste organic matter				4.4

Marine ecology

GETTING STARTED

Take a close look at the photograph of the rock pool ecosystem shown in Figure 5.1.

- Identify as many different organisms as you can. Use your knowledge of classification from Chapter 3 to suggest what groups they belong in.

- The rock pool is totally covered by water at high tide and then exposed to the air at low tide. Suggest what factors affect the organisms that live there and the challenges that these factors pose to life.

Figure 5.1: A typical rock pool ecosystem.

MARINE SCIENCE IN CONTEXT

Shrimp and rice farming and ecosystem loss

In 2021 the global human population was almost eight billion. This population brings a big demand for food. There is also a growing demand for work because people want to improve their living standards by working to make more money.

To meet the demands for food and work, many parts of the world have invested in shrimp farming and rice farming. Some of the products from this farming are kept within the area as food for local communities, but most products are exported to developed countries to raise money. Both shrimp farming and rice farming need to be done in the flooded coastal and estuarine areas of tropical regions.

Unfortunately, mangrove forests are the perfect location for these shrimp farms and rice farms. Mangrove forests around coastal areas have a huge variety of species. These forests stabilise the sediment in coastal areas, protecting them from storms and erosion. Mangrove forests are also breeding grounds for many species of fish. The trees in mangrove forests have adaptations that enable them to survive in flooded, coastal waters.

Scientists estimate that between 2000 and 2016, over 3400 km² of mangrove forest were lost and 62% of this loss was due to clearance for shrimp farms and rice farms. Figure 5.2 shows the remains of a mangrove forest in Java, Indonesia, that has been lost to shrimp farming and rice farming.

Figure 5.2: Area that has been converted from mangrove forest into shrimp and rice farms. The small strip of trees is all that remains of the mangrove forest.

CONTINUED

Over the last few years, the loss of mangroves has slowed but more needs to be done to protect them. Conservation programmes to replant mangrove forests have started. People in countries that import shrimps are also being taught about the effects of their demand for shrimp.

Discussion questions

1 Why do you think that many countries want to increase shrimp farming and rice farming?

2 In your opinion, why is the loss of the mangrove forests harmful to the environment and to coastal communities?

5.1 The components of ecosystems

Ecology is the study of how organisms interact with their environment and how different factors affect the numbers of individuals of different species.

The language of ecology

There are several key terms used in ecological studies that you need to understand.

A group of organisms that can breed together and produce fertile offspring is a classed as a species. For example, all bottlenose dolphins belong to the same species because they can breed together and produce offspring that can then go on to breed. Usually, organisms of the same species look very similar.

KEY WORD

fertile: organisms that are able to breed

It is not always easy, however, to decide if organisms belong to the same species. Sometimes males and females of the same species look very different, and sometimes two totally different species look like each other. Figure 5.3 shows a cleaner wrasse, *Labroides dimidiatus*, (a) and a false cleaner fish, *Aspidontus taeniatus*, (b).

Although they look similar, these two fish are separate species as they cannot breed and produce fertile offspring. The cleaner wrasse feeds by removing parasites, such as lice, from larger species of fish. As a result, most predatory fish do not eat the cleaner wrasse

Figure 5.3: Two fish species that look very similar. a The cleaner wrasse and b the false cleaner fish.

as the predatory fish are helped by them. The predators mistake the false cleaner fish for the cleaner wrasse and do not eat them. The false cleaner fish will, however, eat pieces of the fins of larger fish.

Sometimes different species do reproduce together, but these are rare occasions. A wholphin is a rare **hybrid** animal produced from the mating of a common bottlenose dolphin with a false killer whale (which is actually a different type of dolphin). Both these animals are shown in Figure 5.4. In 1985, a female wholphin called Kekaimalu was born. Kekaimalu was mated with a bottlenose dolphin and went on to give birth to three calves: one died after a few days, one lived to be nine, and the third, a female called Kawii Kai, was still alive in 2020 at the age of 16.

In biology, a population has a strict definition. A population is the number of organisms that belongs to a single species living in a specific area at the same time.

Figure 5.5 shows an area of tropical coral reef in the Red Sea near Egypt. The population of golden butterflyfish for this area is six.

Figure 5.4: Occasionally, two similar species can breed to produce an offspring, for example **a** false killer whale and **b** common bottlenose dolphin.

Figure 5.5: Part of coral reef ecosystem. The yellow fish are golden butterflyfish.

KEY WORDS

parasites: organisms that live and feed on other organisms, causing them harm

hybrid*: animal produced from the breeding of two different species; they are rarely fertile

The term community also has a biological definition. A community is the sum of all the populations of all the different species in a specific area at a certain time. In the coral reef shown in Figure 5.5, the community includes all the fish, the corals and all the other organisms that are present.

A habitat is the physical area that an organism lives in and where it interacts with its environment and other organisms. The habitat for the fish in Figure 5.5 is the coral reef area. A rock pool or an area of a sandy shore are other examples of habitats.

Do not confuse the habitat of an organism with its environment. A habitat is where organisms live. The environment is the external surroundings of an organism or population. The environment is the sum of all the factors that surround an organism and affect its life.

Two types of factor make up the environment of an organism: abiotic factors and biotic factors. Table 5.1 summarises some of the factors that may affect marine organisms.

KEY WORDS

community: all the organisms in an area at a specific time

environment: the abiotic and biotic factors that influence an organism in its habitat

abiotic factors: the non-living, physical and chemical factors that affect an organism in its environment

biotic factors: the living factors that affect an organism in its environment

Typical abiotic factors	Typical biotic factors
temperature, light intensity, carbon dioxide concentration, oxygen concentration, pressure, wind speed, humidity, salinity, mineral ion concentrations, current speed	predator number, food supply, disease, competition

Table 5.1: Summary of abiotic and biotic factors in ecosystems.

Abiotic factors are non-living, physical and chemical factors. Many abiotic factors can affect organisms in their habitats. These abiotic factors will vary from situation to situation and can include salinity, pressure, light intensity, acidity, exposure to the air, oxygen concentration, carbon dioxide concentration, current speed and wind speed. The abiotic factors affecting the coral reef shown in Figure 5.5 include the temperature, current speeds, light intensity and oxygen concentrations – along with many other factors.

Biotic factors are living factors that affect how fast populations of organisms grow. The four key biotic factors affecting organisms are food supply, disease, competition from other organisms, and predation.

- Food supply. A lack of nutrients prevents a population growing rapidly and an increase in nutrients will cause a population to increase. For example, a lack of phytoplankton reduces the population of zooplankton. But if the phytoplankton population increases, so will the zooplankton population as there is more food.

- Disease. A new disease reduces a population rapidly. Disease spread will be faster in dense populations as organisms live more closely to each other.

- Competition from other organisms. Population growth will slow if organisms are competing with each other. For example, if two species of barnacle live on the same rocky shore, one may outcompete the other for food and space.

- Predation. The presence of many predators slows the growth of a population. For example, if blue whales arrive in an area of ocean where there is a lot of krill, the population of krill will decrease as the whales consume them.

Population sizes can get larger and smaller due to changes in any of these factors. For example, because mackerel eat sardines, the populations of the mackerel and the sardines depend on each other. The populations change in the following way.

- When the population of mackerel is small, fewer sardines are eaten, so the sardine population increases.

- As the sardine population increases, there is more food for the mackerel and so the mackerel population increases.

- As the mackerel population increases, more sardines are eaten so the sardine population decreases.

- When the sardine population decreases, there is less food for the mackerel so the mackerel population begins to decrease.

This cycle keeps repeating and is called a predator–prey oscillation because the populations of both species move up and down. Figure 5.6 shows how the populations change.

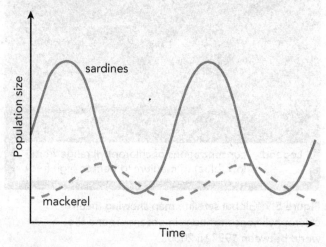

Figure 5.6: Graph to show how the populations of mackerel and sardines change in a predator-prey relationship.

Large organisms can even act as habitats for smaller ones. For example, barnacles and other crustaceans live on the surface of humpback whales. By living on the surface of the whales, the barnacles will be distributed all round the world.

ACTIVITY 5.1

Predator–prey oscillations

Do some research to find out some examples of predator–prey oscillations. Draw graphs to show how the populations of predator and prey change over time. Then use your graph to teach another learner about the oscillations.

Peer assessment

Ask another learner to review the quality of your graph and your explanation. They can rate both using the following scheme:

☺ if they worked really well and they understood the topic

😐 if they worked reasonably well and they partly understood the topic

☹ if they did not work well and did not succeed in helping them understand the topic.

An ecosystem is the community of organisms and their environment, all interacting together. To be called an ecosystem, the organisms do need to interact with each other and their environment. For example, an aquarium has a community and an environment, but it may not be an ecosystem unless there are interactions between the organisms and the environment. Rocky shores and coral reefs are marine ecosystems. Both have organisms that interact with each other through food webs and the organisms also interact with their environment. Figure 5.7 summarises the relationships between populations, communities, the environment and ecosystems.

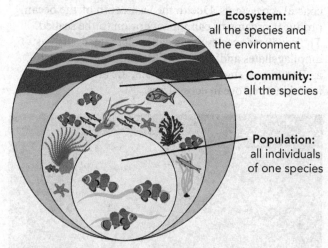

Figure 5.7: Summary of the relationships between populations, communities and ecosystems.

Questions

1 State the term for each of the following definitions:
   a all the organisms of every species in an area
   b all the individuals of one species in an area at one time
   c the abiotic and biotic factors that affect organisms.

2 Look again at Figure 5.5. What is the population of orange-face butterflyfish?

3 Why is it difficult to decide whether two organisms belong to the same species in the following situations:
   a two extinct fossil organisms?
   b species of bacteria that only reproduce asexually?

Marine ecosystems

We can divide marine ecosystems into two broad groups: open ocean ecosystems and coastal ecosystems. There are several sub-types of coastal ecosystems. Open ocean ecosystems are usually less affected by human influence as they are further away from our towns and cities.

Open ocean ecosystems

Open ocean ecosystems are areas of ocean located far away from the continental shelf or slope. These ecosystems have lower productivity compared with coastal ecosystems. Due to the vast depth of the ocean, producer organisms cannot anchor on to the seabed. The producer species are usually microalgae, such as dinoflagellates and diatoms. Floating seaweeds, such as *Sargassum*, shown in Figure 5.8, are also producers found in open ocean ecosystems.

Figure 5.8: *Sargassum*, a floating seaweed that is found in the open ocean.

There are fewer mineral ions in the open ocean. The source of mineral ions in the open ocean usually comes from upwellings, which may not be particularly strong and so may not bring up many minerals. If photosynthesis rates are low, not much energy is fixed into the ecosystem for higher trophic levels – so overall productivity is often low.

Figure 5.9 shows a map of mean chlorophyll in the oceans between 1997 and 2000. Higher chlorophyll levels are found in areas where there are more algae. The least chlorophyll, as measured by algal populations, is in the centre of the oceans. The most chlorophyll is along coasts.

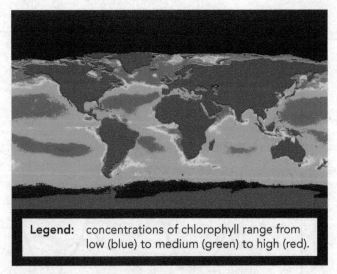

Legend: concentrations of chlorophyll range from low (blue) to medium (green) to high (red).

Figure 5.9: Global satellite map showing mean chlorophyll concentrations in oceans around the world between 1997 to 2000.

Because open ocean ecosystems are far from land, they are not as affected by human activities as coastal ecosystems. But this does not mean that they are safe from harm. Our oceans are filled with discarded fishing equipment, waste plastic, litter and dissolved toxins such as mercury. Fishing fleets constantly remove fish from more and more distant areas of ocean. Discarded litter and nets damage animals, such as the turtle shown in Figure 5.10.

Figure 5.10: Turtle trapped in discarded litter and netting.

KEY WORD

litter: waste materials, such as plastic bottles, that have been discarded

The environmental costs of Covid-19

The international reaction to Covid-19 in 2020 and 2021 caused an estimated release of over 1.5 billion face masks into the environment. Figure 5.11 shows a mask washed up on a beach. Massive quantities of single-use plastic gloves and overalls were also dumped into our oceans. All these plastic items circulate the world on ocean currents.

Figure 5.11: Discarded mask washed up onto a shore.

With a group of other learners, make a poster to evaluate the effects on marine life of using single-use plastics during the Covid-19 pandemic. You will need to discuss the positive and negative effects of how and why plastic equipment was used.

Peer assessment

Present your poster to other learners and ask them to review it. Do they think that it gives a balanced view? Do they feel that your poster helps them to understand the positive and negative effects?

Ask them to rate your work according to the following scheme:

☺ if they thought it worked really well

😐 if they thought it partly succeeded in delivering the message

☹ if they did not think that it worked very well.

Coastal ecosystems

Ecosystems along the continental shelf or slope are classed as coastal ecosystems. Most coastal areas are tidal, which means that shore areas may have periods covered by water and periods exposed to the air.

Humans often live near coastal areas and their activities can damage coastal ecosystems. Pollution from farming and industry often runs into the seas from rivers. Development of coastal resorts harms shores and affects populations of organisms, such as turtles that need sandy shores to nest in.

Types of coastal ecosystems include:

- wetlands
- muddy shores
- seagrass beds
- coral reefs
- rocky shores
- mangroves.
- sandy shores
- kelp forests

Productivity in coastal areas is much higher than productivity in open ocean ecosystems. Look back to Figure 5.9 to see the high levels of chlorophyll in coastal waters. The water around coasts is shallower compared with open ocean seawater, so producers, such as kelp and seagrass, can anchor to the seabed. These producers all contain chlorophyll. They also create rich habitats, nursery grounds and breeding grounds for other organisms.

Run-off from the land means that fertilisers and other soluble substances end up in the sea. Both run-off and sediments from rivers entering the sea increase the concentration of minerals and nutrients in seawater. This increase in nutrients helps producers grow. Figure 5.12 shows a mangrove forest at the point where a river enters the sea. The high levels of nutrients in the sediments washed down the river into the estuary help the trees to grow. Upwellings also occur close to coastal regions, bringing nutrient-rich water from ocean depths up to the surface.

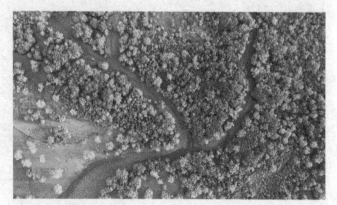

Figure 5.12: Mangrove trees growing in an estuary.

Questions

4 Outline which areas shown in Figure 5.9 have the highest levels of chlorophyll.

5 State why open ocean producers are often microalgae rather than macroalgae.

6 Explain why coastal ecosystems are more productive compared with open ocean ecosystems.

5.2 Investigating ecosystems

You need to be able to do ecological fieldwork investigations to assess ecosystems. You can apply these fieldwork methods to any type of ecosystem, but you may need to alter collection methods and measuring methods.

When doing a fieldwork investigation you should know how to:

- estimate population sizes and species richness
- investigate how the types of species change along a transect
- measure the profile of a shore or slope
- measure the particle profile of sand or sediment
- measure the moisture content of sand or sediment.

PRACTICAL TASK 5.1

Estimating population sizes and species richness of a shore

Introduction

It is usually impossible to count every single organism in an area, so we have to make an estimate by sampling. We can also estimate the species richness of an area, which is a measure of how many different species are present.

In this practical task you will learn how to estimate population sizes and the species richness of an area by sampling. Ideally, you will do this on a sandy or rocky shore, but you can try it on areas of grassland with plant species if there is no nearby shore.

Quadrats

Figure 5.13 shows a quadrat, which is a square frame. The size and design of the quadrat you might use will depend on what you are looking for. Most quadrats are a wire square of dimensions 0.5 m × 0.5 m, but quadrats can be of any size. Sometimes quadrats are open squares, called frame quadrats, but you could use a grid quadrat where the square is subdivided into smaller squares, as in Figure 5.13.

Figure 5.13: Quadrat on a beach.

KEY WORDS

sampling: fairly assessing a small number of a group or population

species richness: the number of different species in an area

quadrat: square frame that is used in ecological investigations to sample areas

CONTINUED

You can use quadrats to count the numbers of organisms, or measure the percentage of the quadrat that is filled with a particular species.

Counting numbers of organisms

Figure 5.14a shows a quadrat with several species inside. If we want to know the number of species X within the quadrat we can simply count them. However, we do need to think about what to do if organisms are touching the edges of the quadrat. The general rule is:

- Count any organism that is touching one vertical side or one horizontal side of the quadrat as being inside the quadrat.

- Do not count any organism that is touching the other vertical side or the other horizontal side.

So, for species X in Figure 5.14a, if we count those individuals that are touching the left side and the top, there is a total of 16 individuals.

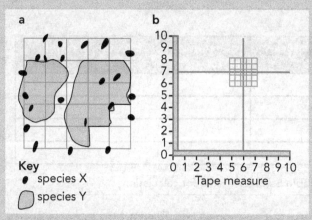

Figure 5.14: Sampling area using a quadrat: **a** placed over organisms and **b** placing the tape measures.

Measuring percentage cover

With some organisms, particularly producers, it is difficult to see where one organism ends and another starts. What we can do here is measure the percentage cover, again using a grid quadrat. If your grid quadrat has 100 squares, you can easily count the number of squares that contain the organism. Figure 5.14a shows a quadrat with 25 squares, so each square represents 4% of the total quadrat. Species Y in Figure 5.14a covers approximately 12 squares, so the percentage cover is 12 × 4 = 48%.

You will need:

- quadrats – ideally, both frame and grid quadrats of dimensions 0.5 m × 0.5 m

- two tape measures, at least 10 m length

- a clipboard

- ecological keys and field guides for identifying species

- a calculator or random number table.

Safety: It is really important to take care on any coastal areas. You should be aware of tide patterns so that you do not get cut off. You should be able to swim. Clothing needs to be appropriate, including waterproofs and protection from the Sun or from the cold. Footwear needs to have a sole that will grip rocks that may be covered with algae. Never work alone. If there are others around, they can help you if you get into difficulty. Take care when looking at species as some may be poisonous or dangerous. Take a whistle to alert others if you get into difficulties. If you dislodge any living organisms, make sure that you carefully return them to their original location.

Method

1   Draw a blank results table like Table 5.2. You should take this with you and secure it on your clipboard.

2   Lay out the tape measures as shown in Figure 5.14b into a 10 m × 10 m square.

3   Use your calculator, or a random number table, to generate 10 coordinates randomly. You will need one number for an x coordinate and one number for a y coordinate, for example 6, 7.

4   Walk along one tape measure until you find the x coordinate: for our example, this would be 6 m. Then walk at right angles until you reach the y coordinate: for our example, this would be 7 m.

5   Place the quadrat on the ground at this point, as shown in Figure 5.14b.

CONTINUED

Species	Number of organisms or percentage cover in each quadrat											
	1	2	3	4	5	6	7	8	9	10	Total	Mean

Table 5.2: Blank results table.

Species	Number of organisms or percentage cover in each quadrat											
	1	2	3	4	5	6	7	8	9	10	Total	Mean
limpet	2	6	5	3	2	0	0	2	1	2	23	2.3
kelp	12%	50%	0%	0%	14%	5%	0%	15%	3%	0%	99%	9.9%

Table 5.3: Results table for sampling on a shore.

6 Use your field guide to identify as many species as you can. Decide for each species whether to count individuals or estimate percentage cover. If there is something you are unsure about, take a photograph of the organism and identify it later.

7 Repeat this for your other sets of random coordinates.

Results and conclusions

- You will already have your results in your table.

- Add up the total number or total percentage cover of each species and add it to your table.

- Calculate the mean number or mean percentage cover by dividing the total by the number of quadrats, which in this case is 10.

- Table 5.3 shows an example of a results table that has been filled in. The limpets show the numbers of organisms counted in each quadrat and the kelp shows percentage cover.

- Make a copy of Table 5.4.

Species	Total number or percentage cover for 100 m²

Table 5.4: Blank table for calculations.

Now, calculate either the total number of a species in the 100 m² area, or the total area of the 100 m² covered by a species. Enter your data in the table. Table 5.5 shows an example of a partially completed table.

Total number in 100 m²

- Step 1: Calculate the mean number per square metre. We already have the mean number per quadrat. The size of the quadrat used was 0.25 m² so we just need to multiply our mean number per quadrat by four.
  e.g. mean number of limpets per square metre = 2.3 × 4 = 9.2 limpets per m²

CONTINUED

- Step 2: Calculate the total number in 100 m². We now need to multiple the value from Step 1 by the total area (100 m²). e.g. total number of limpets = 9.2 × 100 = 920 limpets in the whole area

Total area covered in 100 m²

- You will have calculated the mean percentage cover per quadrat. Because this is a percentage, it will be the same for the whole area. To calculate the area of the total area covered, we simply use the percentage of that area, e.g. total area covered by kelp = 9.9% of 100 = 9.9 m²

You can then use the same values to estimate how many of each species would be present in larger areas, or even on the whole shore.

Species	Total number or percentage cover for 100 m²
limpet	2.3 × 4 × 100 = 920
kelp	(9.9/100) × 100 = 9.9%

Table 5.5: Total number or percentage cover for 100 m².

- Calculate the species richness. This is the number of different species found in all of your quadrats.

Challenge

Try placing more quadrats and keep calculating means. If you recalculate the mean every time, this is called calculating a running mean. Eventually, you will find that the mean does not change a great deal each time another quadrat is added.

Self-assessment

Think carefully about this practical and answer the following questions.

1   Does using 10 quadrats give a result that represents the real number of organisms? Would it be better to use more or fewer quadrats? What would be the benefits of using more or fewer?

2   What have you assumed about how evenly your species were distributed in the area? Think about how your results would be different if your species were a very rare species. Think about what would happen if the distributions of species were not even all over the whole area.

3   Why was it important that you selected the coordinates randomly?

ACTIVITY 5.3

Estimating the number of letters on a page of a newspaper

This activity will help you to understand why we use more than one quadrat to improve accuracy.
You will need a page from a newspaper. You can work on your own or with another learner.

- Divide a page of a newspaper into 2 cm × 2 cm squares.

- Randomly select one square – try to come up with your own method of selection.

- Count the numbers of the following four letters within that square: e, q, r, p.

- Use your results to estimate the total number of each type of letter on the page.

- Randomly select another four squares and count the numbers of the same four letters.

- Use all your results to calculate the mean number of each letter per square. Use this to estimate the total number of each letter on the page.

CONTINUED

- Repeat, so that you have estimates based on: one square, five squares and ten squares.

- Now, count the total numbers of each of the four letters on the whole page and see how accurate your estimates were.

- Compare your findings with another learner.

- What does this exercise show you about the number of samples that you need to do to improve accuracy?

PRACTICAL TASK 5.2

Investigating how the distribution of species changes along a transect

Introduction

As well as finding out about the numbers of organisms, we might want to find out how the distribution of organisms changes along the shore. We can investigate changes both parallel to the coast and at right angles to the coast. It is also useful to see how abiotic factors, such as wind speed, light intensity and temperature, change along the shore. This practical task will explain how to use transects to observe how different organisms are distributed along a shore.

A transect is a line with specific intervals which we use as we measure the number of a species. A line transect is simply a rope or string laid across an area and we count all species that touch the rope. A belt transect involves placing a quadrat next to the rope, so a wider area is examined. Figure 5.15

shows some students investigating a transect up a shore from the low tide area to the high tide area. Taking samples at regular intervals is called systematic sampling.

You will need:

- quadrats – frame or grid

- a tape measure, 10 m long, or piece of string measured out into 1 m lengths

- identification keys and field guides

- a clipboard

- a thermometer.

Safety: It is really important to take care on any coastal areas. You should be aware of tide patterns so that you do not get cut off. You should be able to swim. Clothing needs to be appropriate, including waterproofs and protection from the Sun or from the cold. Footwear needs to have a sole that will grip rocks that may be covered with algae. Never work alone. If there are others around, they can help you if you get into difficulty. Take care when looking at species as some may be poisonous or dangerous. Take a whistle to alert others if you get into difficulties. If you dislodge any living organisms, make sure that you carefully return them to their original.

Figure 5.15: Students investigating a transect along a shore.

Method

1 Make a copy of Table 5.6 and fix it on your clipboard.

2 Choose an area of the shore that you want to investigate.

CONTINUED

Species or abiotic factor	Quadrat number									
	1	2	3	4	5	6	7	8	9	10

Table 5.6: Blank table to record results.

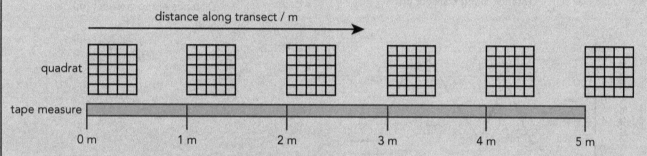

Figure 5.16: Placing quadrats at each point along the transect.

Species or abiotic factor	Quadrat number									
	1	2	3	4	5	6	7	8	9	10
limpet (number)	0	0	2	8	2	6	10	8	2	2
kelp (% cover)	0	0	10	20	25	60	80	60	80	100
temperature (°C)	8	6	8	8	10	10	12	10	8	10

Table 5.7: Results table for transect.

3 With another learner, stretch out the tape measure or string down the shore, in a direction towards the sea. Figure 5.16 shows how to make a transect.

4 Start at the end of the tape measure furthest away from the sea. Place the quadrat next to the tape measure and lay it on the ground. Count the number, or percentage, of each species. Then record the values in your table.

5 Place the thermometer in the centre of the quadrat. After two minutes, record the temperature. If you have other equipment available, you could measure other abiotic factors.

6 Move the quadrat to the 1 m point of the transect and repeat steps 4 and 5.

7 Continue to repeat steps 4 and 5 every 1 m until you reach the end of the tape measure.

Results and conclusions

- Table 5.7 shows a sample results table.

- To help understand your results, it is useful to have a series of graphs. These graphs will have a shared x-axis for the distance along the transect from the part of the shore that is furthest from the sea. You can have different y-axes, depending on the species or factor being investigated. Figure 5.17 shows three graphs like this, using the data in Table 5.7.

CONTINUED

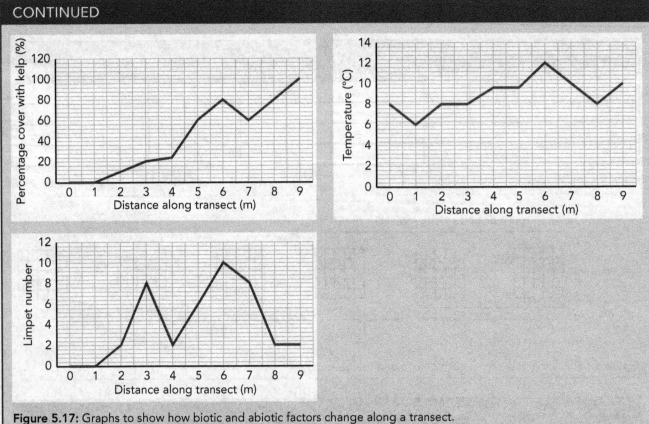

Figure 5.17: Graphs to show how biotic and abiotic factors change along a transect.

Challenge

Complete further transects along the shore and see if there is zonation in a different direction.

Peer assessment

1 Compare your results with those of another group of learners and discuss them. Are the results similar? Can you spot any patterns in the distributions of the species?

2 Are there any links between the species? For example, two different species may overlap as one species may depend on the other. Or species may not overlap because they compete with each other.

KEY WORD

zonation*: the distribution of the different species of a community into separate areas, which are created by variations in the environment

PRACTICAL TASK 5.3

Measuring the profile of a shore

Introduction

The profile of a shore is the angle of its slope into the sea. This practical task shows you how to measure a profile.

You will need:

- a tape measure or string, 10 m

- ranging poles: these are long poles that are about 2 m in height with 50 cm long red and white stripes, as shown in Figure 5.18b. They can be purchased, or made from wood such as bamboo

- a clinometer, these can be purchased or made (see below)

- a clipboard

- graph paper, protractor and ruler.

Making a clinometer

Figure 5.18a shows a basic clinometer. It is made from a protractor, a plumbline (piece of string with a weight, such as a bolt) and a drinking straw or hollow tube. You need to attach the straw or tube to the base of the protractor with tape. Then tape the plumbline to the centre of the protractor.

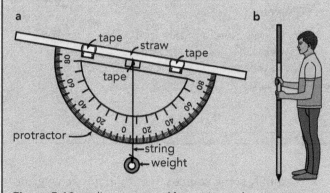

Figure 5.18: a clinometer and **b** ranging pole.

Safety: It is really important to take care on any coastal areas. You should be aware of tide patterns so that you do not get cut off. You should be able to swim. Clothing needs to be appropriate, including waterproofs and protection from the Sun or from the cold. Footwear needs to have a sole that will grip rocks that may be covered with algae. Never work alone. If there are others around they can help you if you get into difficulty. Take care when looking at species as some may be poisonous or dangerous. Take a whistle to alert others if you get into difficulties. If you dislodge any living organisms, make sure that you carefully return them to their original location.

Method

You will need to work with another learner to complete this practical task.

The shore may have a range of different profiles so you will need to measure the profile of each section.

1   Make a copy of Table 5.8 and fix it on your clipboard.

2   Lay the tape measure along the section of profile being measured.

3   Each person takes a ranging pole. One person stands at the lower point of the slope, nearest to the sea, and holds the ranging pole vertically with one end on the ground. The second person walks in a line along the direction of the tape measure until they reach the end of the profile being measured. Record the distance along the tape measure. The second person then places their pole vertically at this point.

CONTINUED

4   The person at the lower part of the profile holds the clinometer at one of the edges of a stripe of their ranging pole, as shown in Figure 5.19. They look through the tube of the clinometer, as if it were a telescope, rotating the clinometer up and down until it is lined up with the same section of the second person's pole. Record the angle of elevation shown by the clinometer.

5   Repeat this for each different section along the shore.

Results and conclusions

Section of beach	Angle of elevation shown by clinometer / °	Distance between poles / m
1		
2		
3		
4		
5		

Table 5.8: Results for beach profile.

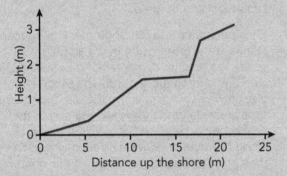

Figure 5.20: Diagram to show beach profile.

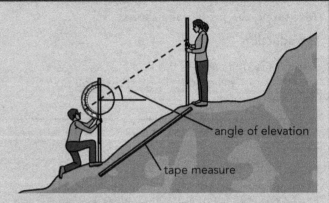

Figure 5.19: Measuring the profile of a slope.

- Figure 5.20 shows a way of displaying your results.

- On a piece of graph paper, make a scale on the horizontal axis that allows you to show the total distance along the shore profile you have measured.

- Starting at zero, use a protractor to measure the angle of elevation of your first section. Draw a line along this angle until you have reached the distance between the poles on the horizontal axis.

- Repeat this for each section of the beach until you have a complete profile, as in Figure 5.20.

Challenge

Try to complete a profile for the beach at 90° to the profile you already have. See if you can find a way of displaying it as a 3D profile of the shore.

Self-assessment

1   How accurate do you think your shore profile is?

2   Identify some sources of error in this activity and suggest how you could reduce them.

PRACTICAL TASK 5.4

Measuring the particle profile of sand or sediment

Introduction

The size and shape of sand or sediment particles varies along a shoreline. In this practical task, you will learn how to compare the sizes of particles from different areas of a sedimentary shore.

You will need:

- equipment for measuring lengths, such as callipers and rulers
- a tape measure or string, 20 m
- a balance
- a collection of sieves with mesh of different sizes
- specimen tubes or jars.

Safety: It is really important to take care on any coastal areas. You should be aware of tide patterns so that you do not get cut off. You should be able to swim. Clothing needs to be appropriate, including waterproofs and protection from the Sun or from the cold. Footwear needs to have a sole that will grip rocks that may be covered with algae. Never work alone. If there are others around they can help you if you get into difficulty. Take care when looking at species as some may be poisonous or dangerous. Take a whistle to alert others if you get into difficulties. If you dislodge any living organisms, make sure that you carefully return them to their original location.

Method

All shores have sand and sediment particles of different sizes. Some shores are composed of large pebbles, while other shores have sand or silt particles. This method will need to be adapted depending on the type of sediment on the shore. We can measure large particles, such as pebbles, with rulers and callipers, but small particles of sand or silt must be passed through mesh filters of different sizes.

For shores with large particles

1 Make a copy of Table 5.9 to record your results in. You will need a results table for each of the places where you take samples of particles.

2 Start at the top of the shore. Randomly select five particles or pebbles. Think of a method that you can use to choose the particles randomly.

3 Use the callipers or ruler to measure the maximum length, width and height of each particle. For this practical, we will class the longest of the three dimensions as the length, the middle one as the height, and the smallest one as the width. We can look at the three different dimensions because most particles will have irregular shapes. If it is not easy to measure all three dimensions, you can just measure the maximum length of the particle. Record your results in the table. Repeat for the other four particles.

4 Use the tape measure to repeat this at regular intervals, working down the shore towards the sea.

Distance from top of shore: ...... m			
Particle number	Maximum length of particle / mm	Maximum width of particle / mm	Maximum height of particle / mm
1			
2			
3			
4			
5			

Table 5.9: Results table to record lengths, widths and heights of particles along a shore.

CONTINUED

For shores with small particles

1. Start at the top of the shore. Put a sample of at least 150 g of sediment into a specimen bottle. Label the bottle with the distance from the top of the shore.

2. Use the tape measure to repeat your sampling at regular intervals down the shore.

3. Weigh out 100 g of one sample of sediment.

4. Pour the sediment through the sieve with the largest mesh and collect what passes through. Weigh the sediment that did not pass through. These sediment particles have a size that is bigger than the mesh size.

5. Pour the sediment that passed through the first sieve into the sieve with the next largest mesh. Weigh the sediment that does not pass through, recording its mass.

6. Repeat this with sieves with increasingly small mesh sizes.

7. Copy out Table 5.10 and record the mass of sediment that did not pass through each sieve. For example, sediment that does not pass through a sieve with a mesh size of 5 mm has a particle size greater than 5 mm. Sediment that passes through a sieve with a mesh size of 5 mm but does not pass through the 3 mm mesh has a size between 3 mm and 5 mm.

Results and conclusions

Large particles

Calculate the mean maximum lengths, mean maximum heights and mean maximum widths of particles from each area of the shore. Your original data is in the five versions of Table 5.9. Copy out and complete Table 5.11. Follow these steps to draw line graphs of your results:

- label the horizontal axis as 'Distance down shore (m)' and select a linear scale

- label the vertical axis as 'Mean maximum length of particles' and select a linear scale

- plot the mean maximum lengths of the particles and join the points with straight lines

- draw similar graphs for the mean maximum height and mean maximum width.

Small particles

For the small particles, use your results to draw a line graph to compare the mass of the different-sized particles at each area of the shore. Your data is in Table 5.10. Follow these steps:

- label the horizontal axis as 'Distance down shore (m)' and select a linear scale

- label the vertical axis as 'Mass of particle (g)' and select a linear scale

- plot the masses for the largest size of particle and join the points with straight lines

- plot the masses for the next largest size of particle and join the points with straight lines, using a different coloured line

- repeat for all the sizes of particle, each time using a different colour for each line

- add a key for each line.

Distance down the shore (m)	Mass of sediment that does not pass through sieve with different sized meshes (g)				
	> 5 mm	Greater than 3 mm and equal to or less than 5 mm	Greater than 1 mm and equal to or less than 3 mm	Greater than 0.1 mm and equal to or less than 1 mm	< 0.1 mm
0					
5					
10					

Table 5.10: Results table to show masses of different particle sizes in sediment.

CONTINUED

Distance down the shore	Mean maximum length of particles (mm)	Mean maximum width of particles (mm)	Mean maximum height of particles (mm)
1			
2			
3			
4			
5			

Table 5.11: Results table to show the mean maximum length, width and height of particles from different areas of shore.

Challenge

Investigate methods for estimating the shape and / or roundness of particles.

Self-assessment

1 Think about how you measured the larger particle sizes. Can you suggest why we choose the maximum height, length and width of irregular shaped particles?

2 Explain how would you expect particle size to change as you move up a shore away from the sea.

PRACTICAL TASK 5.5

Measuring the moisture content of sand or sediment

Introduction

Water content of sand or sediment is an important abiotic factor that affects organisms. In this practical task you will learn how to measure the water content of sand or sediment on a shore.

You will need:

- specimen bottles or jars
- a balance
- metal evaporating dishes or other metal lids
- an oven or other method of heating (if a Bunsen is used, do not overheat the sample and burn any organic material)
- eye protection.

Safety: It is really important to take care on any coastal areas. You should be aware of tide patterns so that you do not get cut off. You should be able to swim. Clothing needs to be appropriate, including waterproofs and protection from the Sun or from the cold. Footwear needs to have a sole that will grip rocks that may be covered with algae. Never work alone. If there are others around, they can help you if you get into difficulty. Take care when looking at species as some may be poisonous or dangerous. Take a whistle to alert others if you get into difficulties. If you dislodge any living organisms, make sure that you carefully return them to their original location. Take care when heating the samples. If samples are not covered when heated, particles of sand can become hot and jump around. Wear eye protection at all times. The evaporating dishes should be left to cool before touching.

CONTINUED

Method

1 Collect samples of substrate from different areas of the shore and place them into labelled specimen bottles or jars.

2 Use the balance to weigh out 100 g of sediment sample.

3 Place the sample into a metal evaporating dish.

4 Place the sample into an oven set at 105 °C for 5 hours.

5 When cool, re-weigh the sample.

Note that if you use a Bunsen burner, you should heat the sample gently so you do not burn any organic material. Keep stirring the mixture while heating. You will only need to heat it using this method for 5–10 minutes on a low flame.

Results and conclusions

Determine the percentage of water in the sample using the following steps.

Step 1: Calculate the mass of water.

mass of water = starting mass of sample − mass after heating

Step 2: Calculate the percentage of sample that is water.

$$\text{percentage water} = \frac{\text{mass of water}}{\text{starting mass}} \times 100$$

- Compare the percentage of water in samples from different areas of the shore.

Challenge

When you have measured the percentage water of your different samples, determine the particle profile of the samples using the method in Practical Task 5.4. Is there a correlation between particle size and water content?

Self-assessment

1 You used around 100 g of substrate for each of your samples. If you had used around 10 g, would this have affected your results?

2 Explain whether muddy or sandy substrates will dry out faster.

5.3 Open ocean ecosystems

We can divide the open ocean into vertical zones, as shown in Figure 5.21. Each zone has its own physical and chemical conditions and brings different challenges to the organisms that live there. All organisms have evolved adaptations for competing and surviving in each of the zones.

Pelagic and benthic zones

The entire column of open water is called the pelagic zone, shown in Figure 5.21. It stretches vertically from the surface of the ocean to the area close to the seabed. The pelagic zone stretches horizontally from just offshore out to the open sea.

We can divide the pelagic zone horizontally into:

- the neritic area, which lies above the continental plate

- oceanic zone, which is the area outside the continental plate.

KEY WORD

pelagic zone: the total volume of water in the ocean or sea that is not in contact with land

We can also divide the pelagic zone vertically into three main zones, shown in Figure 5.21: the sunlight zone, the twilight zone and the midnight zone. These were described in Chapter 2. Each of these three zones has different abiotic properties.

The seabed and the area just above the seabed is called the benthic zone.

> **KEY WORD**
>
> benthic zone: the seabed and the water directly above it

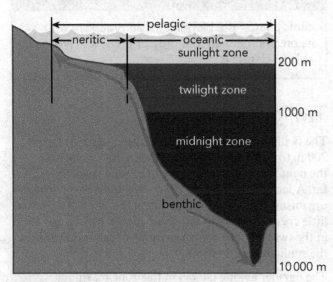

Figure 5.21: Zones of the open ocean.

Sunlight zone

The sunlight zone, also known as the epipelagic zone, lies just below the surface of the ocean and stretches downwards for about 200 m. The actual depth depends on the amount of sediment in the water because sediment affects light penetration. Most areas of ocean above the continental shelf do not reach a depth beyond the sunlight zone.

In the open ocean, the sunlight zone is the most productive of the vertical zones because nearly all photosynthesis takes place here. Most ocean life and most ocean food chains are located in the sunlight zone. Producers cannot anchor on to the seabed because the seabed is too far below them. Therefore most producers in the open ocean are free floating macroalgae, such as *Sargassum*, and microalgae, such as dinoflagellates and diatoms.

The abiotic factors in the sunlight zone are ideal for marine life.

- High light intensity means that photosynthesis rates are high, bringing energy into food chains. Wave action also helps carbon dioxide gas from the atmosphere to dissolve in the seawater, so there is plenty of carbon dioxide for photosynthesis.

- Oxygen levels are high due to the high rates of photosynthesis by producers. More oxygen means that animals can respire easily. Fast swimming fish, such as tuna, need lots of oxygen to maintain a high respiration rate.

- The pressure is relatively low. This means that organisms do not need adaptations to resist the higher pressures of deep waters.

- Temperatures are variable. Being close to the surface, the temperature varies according to seasons and weather conditions. Photosynthesis and respiration rates are both affected by temperature changes. In ocean areas with seasonal changes, microalgae usually only grow during warmer months. Some animals may migrate for food and to reach breeding grounds due to seasonal temperature changes.

- High biomass. Due to the high light intensity, there are many photosynthetic algae and plenty of energy for primary consumers and higher trophic levels. Food chains in the sunlight zone often have many trophic levels due to the large amount of light energy converted into chemical energy by the producers.

The sunlight zone is the vertical region where most open ocean life is found. Plankton, shown in Figure 5.22, is the floating mass of mainly microscopic organisms that drifts with the water currents. The plankton is made of two main parts: phytoplankton and zooplankton.

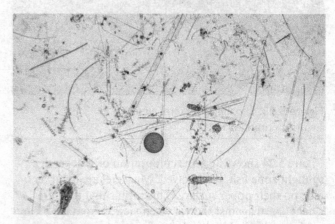

Figure 5.22: Marine plankton.

- Phytoplankton are the microscopic producer organisms at the base of most food chains in the sunlight zone. They include diatoms, dinoflagellates and cyanobacteria.

- Zooplankton are animals and are all consumers. Some zooplankton are herbivores, eating phytoplankton; some zooplankton are carnivores, eating other zooplankton; and some zooplankton are omnivorous, eating both phytoplankton and zooplankton.

Most organisms in the plankton are microscopic, such as the larvae of fish and larvae of invertebrates (cnidarians, molluscs and echinoderms, for example). However, some larger organisms, such as jellyfish, are also classified as zooplankton.

Plankton provides food for many predatory species of fish and invertebrates such as squid. Most consumers eat a wide variety of different species, not just one food type. There are complex food chains in the sunlight zone that end with large, top predators such as killer whales, swordfish and bluefin tuna. Competition among organisms is high and many fish species in the sunlight zone have evolved to become fast swimming. Predators must be fast to catch prey. As there is little shelter for prey to hide in, these prey species also have to be fast. Figure 5.23 shows shoaling behaviour of mackerel when approached by a predator.

Figure 5.23: Shoaling mackerel avoiding a swordfish predator.

Figure 5.24 shows how the colouration of mackerel, a sunlight zone fish, has evolved. Mackerel are a darker blue on their upper surface. This means that they are camouflaged against the sea when viewed from the air by predatory birds. Mackerel are silver underneath.

They blend in with the sunlight when viewed by predators in the waters below them.

Figure 5.24: Mackerel colouration showing darker upper surface and silver lower surface.

KEY WORD

camouflage: the blending of an organism with its environment so that prey or predators are less able to detect it

---

Twilight zone

The twilight zone, or mesopelagic zone, stretches from 200 m to 1000 m below the surface. Only about 1% of the light that hits the surface of the water penetrates this far. A lack of light means there are almost no producer organisms that stay permanently in this zone. As a result, little energy is brought into food chains. Most organisms in the twilight zone are carnivorous or move upwards to the sunlight zone to feed.

The harsher abiotic factors in this zone mean that organisms need special adaptations to survive.

- Light intensity is very low, and only blue light is present. Very few producers survive here so no energy is brought directly into the zone by photosynthesis. Food chains rely on feeding from dead organisms that have fallen from the sunlight zone.

- Oxygen levels are lower than in the sunlight zone but there is still enough oxygen for animals to respire.

- The temperature is colder than at the surface, but temperatures do not change much during a 24-hour period and do not change greatly over the seasons. This means that organisms are adapted to survive within a narrow range of temperatures.

- The pressure is higher than in the sunlight zone; a higher pressure means that organisms are at a risk of being crushed. Organisms are adapted so that they have high internal pressures inside their bodies. This helps them to resist the high water pressure.

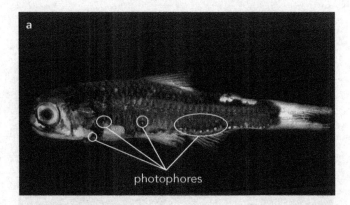

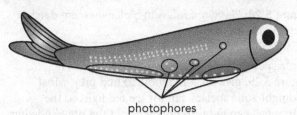

Figure 5.25: Deepsea lanternfish: **a** photograph showing bioluminescence and **b** diagram showing locations of bioluminescent organs.

Many animals living in the twilight zone make daily migrations up to the sunlight zone at night to feed, returning back to the twilight zone during the day. This daily migration means that these animals hide from predators during the day in the dark twilight zone. A wide range of species migrate to the sunlight zone at night, including zooplankton, crustaceans (such as copepods) and small fish.

Many twilight zone species have similar adaptations to species in the sunlight zone, such as eating a wide range of foods, being fast swimmers, and having a dark upper surface and shiny lower surface. However, a few species have unusual adaptations to help them survive.

- Deep sea lanternfish, shown in Figure 5.25, have special organs called photophores that luminesce. Some of the photophores are on the underside of the body so this bioluminescence helps to camouflage the fish from predators beneath them. Photophores on the head may be used for communication, to confuse predators or to light up the area. Lanternfish are very common fish and around 600 million live in the oceans. Every evening, they migrate to the surface waters to feed on plankton.

During the day they hide in the depths of the twilight zone. They are ecologically very important as they are a prey species for predatory species that live in the twilight zone. The lanternfish bring a source of energy from the surface to the twilight zone.

- The barreleye fish, shown in Figure 5.26, is an ambush predator. This fish has a transparent head and eyes that are directed upwards to detect the shapes of prey species above them. Barreleye fish do not migrate upwards but spend their lives in the twilight zone. Many fish in the twilight zone have oversized eyes to make the most of the little light that is present.

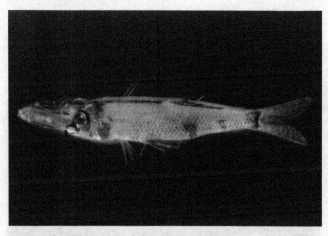

Figure 5.26: Barreleye fish with upward pointing eyes and transparent head tissues to detect prey above.

Midnight zone

The area of the ocean below 1000 m, where no light penetrates, is called the midnight zone. There is very little dissolved oxygen, little food, a high water pressure and it is very cold. Conditions in the midnight zone are very harsh and the only organisms that can survive there have special adaptations. There is little life in the midnight zone because of the difficult conditions.

- No light means that photosynthesis can not occur so there are no producers present. All midnight zone animals are predatory or detritivores. Because there are few living organisms in the midnight zone, animals have specialisations to help them catch prey. Some organisms lure (attract) prey so that it comes closer.

- Dissolved oxygen concentrations are very low. This, along with the lack of food, means that animals must have a very low respiration rate. They have a low energy lifestyle to reduce energy demand.

- Temperatures are very low but are stable. Most marine species are cold blooded and so have body temperatures that are the same as the water. Low body temperatures cause respiration rates to slow.

- The pressure from the massive volume of water above the midnight zone is very high. Few organisms can withstand this huge external pressure without being crushed.

Many of the species that do live at this depth look like something out of science fiction, with extraordinary adaptations. These adaptations help them to find prey in an area where food is sparse and a meal may not often swim past.

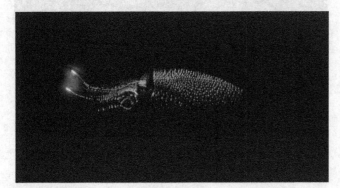

Figure 5.27: Bioluminescent squid swimming in the midnight zone.

Bioluminescence, the ability to produce light, is a common adaptation of deep sea organisms. It can be generated by bacteria that live within the organism or by cells in the organism. The deepest depths of the ocean are often lit up by flashing blue lights from squid, octopuses, shrimp and many fish species. Figure 5.27 shows a bioluminescent squid swimming in the water column. Bioluminescence has many functions in the deep including:

- attracting mates

- confusing predators

- attracting prey

- lighting up the area to find prey.

Flashlight fish, shown in Figure 5.28, have special bioluminescent organs under their eyes for lighting up the seabed to find food, possibly communicating with each other, and also confusing predators.

Figure 5.28: Flashlight fish with bioluminescent patches under the eyes.

Some species of deep-sea dragonfish, shown in Figure 5.29, give off a red glow to find prey. Most midnight zone species cannot see red light so the dragonfish can light up prey without the prey knowing that the dragonfish is near. The dragonfish also has sharp, backward facing teeth to help it to grab and hold prey.

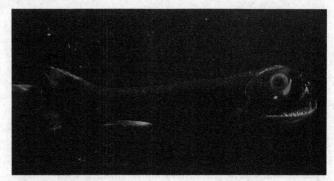

Figure 5.29: Deep sea dragonfish that emits red light to illuminate prey species.

The body colours of most midnight zone species are dark brown or black. These colours absorb light so that the organisms are not visible to the bioluminescent light from predators. Soft, gelatinous bodies are more able to withstand the high pressures of the deep sea compared with hard bodies.

There is very little food and oxygen in the midnight zone, so there is a need to conserve energy and have a low respiration rate. Most species are very slow moving, grow very slowly and have a very long life span – some of the fish can be over 100 years old.

Because there is little prey, the predatory species in the midnight zone need to make sure that they catch nearly every item of food that does arrive, or alternatively, they can lure the food towards them. Gulper eels and viperfish, both shown in Figure 5.30, have fang-like teeth that point backwards so that prey cannot escape. Gulper eels, also called pelican eels, have a stomach that can stretch to a massive volume to take large prey species.

The deep sea anglerfish, shown in Figure 5.31, is one of the best known fish in the midnight zone. There are many different species of anglerfish but nearly all have a modified dorsal fin which they wave over their mouth. The end of the dorsal fin often contains bioluminescent bacteria which glow, attracting other fish and squid. The mouth of the anglerfish, like many deep sea fish, is oversized with large teeth. This means that if prey does come near, it is very likely to be caught.

Figure 5.31: Deep sea angler fish with bioluminescent lure and large mouth to catch prey.

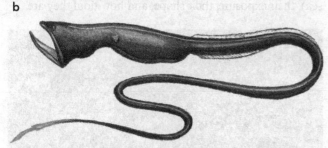

Figure 5.30: Feeding adaptations of deep sea fish: a viperfish with backward facing teeth and b pelican gulper eel with enlarged mouth and stomach.

ACTIVITY 5.4

Designing a deep-sea organism

Design an organism to live in the midnight zone. It will need to have adaptations to find food, avoid predators, find mates and cope with the low oxygen and high pressure of the deep sea. Draw a diagram of your deep-sea organism and annotate it to explain the adaptations.

Peer assessment

Ask another learner to assess your organism. Will it survive well in the deep ocean? Ask them to rate your organism according to this scheme:

- 😊 if they think it would survive well
- 😐 if they think it might survive but could have some problems
- ☹ if they do not think it would survive at all.

Benthic species

Benthic species are organisms that live on the seabed. They are not always deep-sea organisms as the seabed over areas of continental shelf may not be very far from the surface. Benthic species often have certain adaptations.

- Camouflage. Most species of organism need to either escape from predators or sneak up on prey. Many benthic species have body colourations that blend with the seabed, like the fantail sole shown in Figure 5.32a.

- Some can even change their colouration to match the seabed. Sometimes camouflage means burying inside the sediment, such as the stingray shown in Figure 5.32b.

- Dorsally flattened bodies. Many benthic fish, such as skates, rays and sole, have a flat body shape for lying on the seabed or burying themselves. When very young, a sole has an eye on each side of its head. But as the fish develops, one of the eyes moves its position so that both eyes eventually are on the same side of the body. The eyes can point upwards and protrude (stick out) from the sediment so that prey and predators are easily seen. The pectoral and pelvic fins are also elongated and flattened around the sides of the body; this is easy to see in the sole in Figure 5.32a.

- Adaptations of some invertebrates. Echinoderms such as starfish, shown in Figure 5.33, and sea urchins are common on the seabed. They attach to the seabed and move using tube feet on their lower (ventral surface).

Figure 5.33: Starfish living on the seabed.

Starfish and sea urchins are slow moving, so are easy prey for predatory species, but the hard, spiny skin on their upper surface reduces attacks from above.

Questions

7   Give two functions of bioluminescence.

8   Explain how anglerfish and gulper eels are adapted to live in the midnight zone.

9   Explain how the conditions in the midnight zone mean that most organisms do not move quickly, and grow slowly.

5.4 Rocky shores

Shores are the areas where the sea meets the land. Rocky shores, like the one shown in Figure 5.34, are areas of coast with solid rock formations. All rocky shores are slightly different in terms of their profile (or slope into the sea), their exposure, their shape, and how tidal they are.

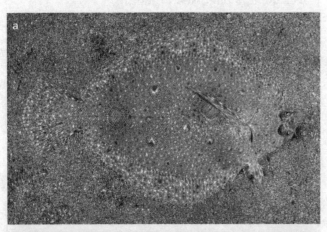

Figure 5.32: Benthic fish species that live on the surface of the seabed: **a** a fantail sole that is camouflaged with the sediment and **b** a sting ray that buries itself in sediment.

Figure 5.34: A typical rocky shore.

We can divide a rocky shore into three broad zones depending on exposure to sea. These are the supratidal zone, the intertidal zone and the subtidal zone. Each zone has different biotic and abiotic factors. The organisms living in each zone have adaptations for coping with these factors (Figure 5.35).

Environmental factors affecting organisms

When looking at the distribution of organisms across a rocky shore we need to think about abiotic and biotic factors.

Abiotic factors

- Exposure to air. Dehydration when exposed to the air is a problem for many marine organisms. Coastal areas are often very windy. Strong winds are very dehydrating, as they cause water to evaporate, and this also cools organisms down. Some organisms have evolved to cope with periods of time when they are submerged and periods of time when they are exposed to the air and wind.

- Wave action and tides. Strong waves and changing tides make it difficult for marine organisms to remain attached to a substrate.

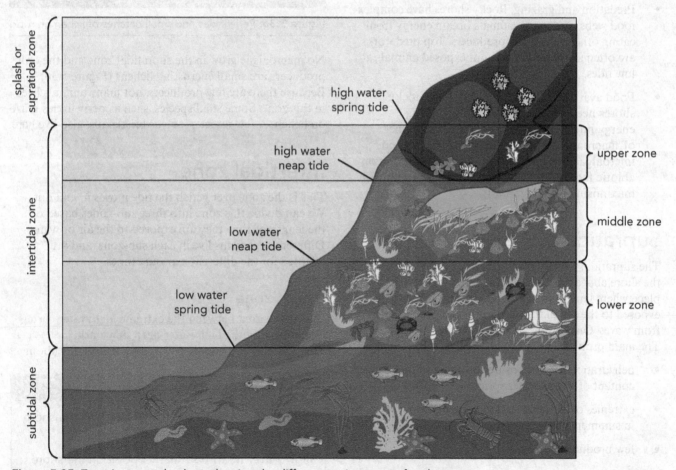

Figure 5.35: Zonation on rocky shore showing the different environment of each zone.

- Organisms on rocky shores that are exposed to waves need a way of firmly attaching themselves.

- Oxygen. Nearly all organisms need oxygen for respiration. Many marine organisms on rocky shores need to obtain oxygen from both the air and the water. Rock pools left behind at low tides can lack oxygen, particularly if the weather is hot.

- Air temperature. The air temperature varies in coastal areas, depending on the season and the weather. Organisms exposed to the air on rocky shores need to tolerate a wide range of air temperatures at different times of year.

- Water temperature. Although seawater temperature changes less than air temperature, seawater does not stay at the same temperature. Water in small rock pools left behind at low tides will have a greater variation in temperature than seawater in the ocean.

Biotic factors

- Predation and grazing. Rocky shores have complex food webs, and many animals obtain energy from eating other animals or producers. Top predators are often shore birds that hunt exposed animals at low tides.

- Food availability. Like all ecosystems, rocky shores need producer organisms to bring energy into the community. Different species of macroalgae (such as species of *Fucus*) and microalgae live in particular zones depending on abiotic factors. All the algae have adaptations for maximising photosynthesis.

Supratidal zone

The supratidal zone, shown in Figure 5.35, is the area of the shore above the highest tide level but below the place where land plants grow. Organisms here are exposed to the air all the time but get covered in spray from waves. Only rarely are organisms submerged. The main problems are:

- dehydration from exposure to wind and the high salt content of the seawater spray

- extremes of air temperature, ranging from very high in summer to very low in winter

- few producers live here.

Figure 5.36: Periwinkles and small patches of lichen on rock.

No macroalgae grow in the supratidal zone and the only producers are small encrusting lichens (Figure 5.36). Because there are few producers, not many animals live in this zone. Some snail species, such as periwinkles graze on lichen. A few insects, such as bristletails, also live here.

Intertidal zone

This is the zone over which the tide moves in and out. We can divide this zone into three sub-zones based on the length of time they are exposed to the air or water. Different organisms live in each sub-zone, and are adapted for the different exposure times.

Upper zone

This is the area between the extreme high water spring tide mark and the high water neap tide mark. The very top end is only covered by the sea for about

KEY WORDS
high water spring tide mark*: point on the shore reached by the highest spring tide
high water neap tide mark*: point on the shore reached by the highest neap tide

1% of a year. The lowest part is submerged for about 20% of a year. Organisms in this zone need to cope with:

- dehydration from long periods of time exposed to the air; organisms at the top end will spend most of their lives exposed to the air, only being submerged during the highest spring tides

- extremes of air temperature

- few producers

- tides and waves, which will dislodge unanchored organisms.

At the top of the upper zone, the only producers are lichens similar to those found in the supratidal zone. But as we descend the shore, there are a few species of macroalgae that can withstand drying out, such *Fucus spiralis* (Figure 5.37) and channel wrack. *Fucus spiralis* has several adaptations: thick, leathery fronds to resist dehydration when exposed to the air, air bladders to float when submerged, and a holdfast to attach itself to the rocks. It is important that the seaweeds can absorb sunlight for photosynthesis. The air bladders ensure that the seaweed fronds float in the surface waters where the light intensity is high.

Figure 5.37: *Fucus spiralis* showing large surface area of fronds and gas bladders.

The presence of more producers, such as seaweeds, means more consumer animals. In the lower areas of the upper zone, barnacles, shown in Figure 5.38, are permanently attached to rocks. Their strong attachment stops them being dislodged by waves. Barnacles can close their shells to prevent dehydration when out of the water. Limpets also live in the lower

areas. Limpets are molluscs with a muscular foot that attaches to rock and a single, hard shell that protects them from wave action and predators. When out of the water, a limpet clamps the shell firmly to the rocks. This prevents exposure to the air, so reducing water loss.

Figure 5.38: Barnacles and limpet on rock.

Middle zone

The middle intertidal zone stretches from the high water neap tide mark to the low water neap tide mark. Organisms at the top of this sub-zone spend 20% of the year covered by water while organisms in the lower part spend 80% of the year covered. Environmental conditions are usually less harsh than in the upper zone as less time is spent exposed to the air. Organisms here must cope with:

- strong wave action when the tides move in and out

- some dehydration due to exposure to the air

- more stable temperatures than in the upper zone, although there are some temperature changes

- more consumer organisms, both herbivores and carnivores

- high levels of competition between organisms

- reduced light intensity when submerged.

> **KEY WORD**
>
> **low water neap tide mark*:** point on the shore reached by the lowest neap tide

There are more species of macroalgae in the middle sub-zone, such as bladderwrack and the red and brown seaweeds. These seaweeds are less leathery than *Fucus spiralis*. Macroalgae living here are often larger than the macroalgae species higher up the shore and competition for light and space is much stronger. Bladderwrack (*Fucus vesiculosis*) has many air bladders to ensure that the fronds float upwards to absorb light when submerged. Red and brown seaweeds (Figure 5.39) have extra light-absorbing chemicals for photosynthesis as well as chlorophyll.

Figure 5.40: Sea anemones and starfish in a rockpool.

Figure 5.39: Brown and red seaweeds.

The larger number of producers means more food and shelter for primary consumers. Lots of limpets live here, along with other molluscs, such as topshells, that graze on seaweeds. Predators, such as dog whelks and shore crabs, live in pools and under rocks. These species prey on other molluscs and barnacles. Mussels are **filter feeders** and they attach themselves to rocks by strong threads. Like limpets, mussels have strong shells to protect them from predators. When exposed to the air, mussels close their shells to prevent water loss.

Sea anemones live in rock pools. These small cnidaria, shown Figure 5.40, prevent dehydration by bringing their tentacles back into their bodies when exposed to air. They often live beneath seaweeds because this helps to reduce evaporation.

Lower zone

The lowest sub-zone of the intertidal zone stretches from the low water neap tide mark to the **low water spring tide mark**. The upper parts are submerged for 80% of the year and the lower parts for 99%, only being exposed at the low tide during the spring tides.

Conditions for life are much more stable compared with the upper shore and include:

* stable temperatures as the area is mostly submerged

* greater depth of water

* little exposure to the air, so less risk of dehydration

* large numbers of producer organisms so that there are many complex food chains

* high competition between organisms

* less wave action compared with the middle zone

* reduced light intensity for producers when submerged.

The water here can be quite deep so less light passes through. Most of the producers are brown or red macroalgae, similar to those shown in Figure 5.39. As well as chlorophyll, these seaweeds have other chemical pigments that absorb light. Kelp grows here, attached by holdfasts to the rocks. Because there is such high productivity, there are many herbivorous molluscs, such as limpets and topshells. More carnivores, such as starfish, crabs and rock pool fish, also live here. There is a lot of decaying organic waste, which attracts detritivore organisms such as shrimps, prawns and filter-feeding sponges. Life becomes very competitive, and there is a rich range of species.

KEY WORDS

filter feeders*: organisms whose method of feeding involves extracting small particles from water

low water spring tide mark*: point on the shore reached by the lowest spring tide

Subtidal zone

The subtidal zone is really an extension of the lowest parts of the lower intertidal zone. There are many large, brown macroalgae such as kelp. High productivity means plenty of food chains with many trophic levels. Most marine animal groups are represented, including mammals such as seals and sea otters.

ACTIVITY 5.5

Rocky shore zonation

On a large piece of paper, draw a profile of a rocky shore showing all the different zones. Look back at Figure 5.35 if you need some help. Annotate your diagram with:

- the abiotic and biotic factors in each zone, including estimated air exposure times

- the types of organism found in each zone.

Share your diagram with another learner. Ask them to add other abiotic and biotic factors and other organisms in a different coloured ink.

Questions

10 Explain why few organisms are found in the supratidal zone of a rocky shore.

11 List differences between the abiotic factors in the upper zone of the intertidal zone and the lower zone of the intertidal zone.

12 Explain why competition between organisms is high in the lower areas of the intertidal zone.

5.5 Sedimentary shores

Sedimentary shores are coastal shores that are composed of particles of sediment. The formation of sedimentary shores is complex. It involves cycles of erosion of particles from rocks and soil and **deposition** of the particles. These particles come from the erosion of rocks in coastal areas, or can be washed into the sea from rivers. Sedimentary shores are constantly eroded and reformed by wave action and storms.

There are different types of sedimentary shores, including sandy shores and muddy shores. Sometimes,

plants can begin to root on muddy shores and stabilise the sediment. Wetlands are coastal areas that are always partly covered with seawater. Grasses and other flowering plants that grow on wetlands stabilise the sediment and create an area that forms a habitat for other species.

KEY WORDS

sedimentary shore: coastal shores that are composed of particles of sediment; the particles can range in size from silt to pebbles

deposition*: the settling and laying down of sediment or particles onto a landmass by water bodies

---

Zonation of sedimentary shores

Figure 5.41 shows the zones of a typical sandy or muddy shore. The zonation of organisms is less easy to see compared with rocky shores. However, there are three main zones, all with slightly different environmental conditions:

- supratidal zone

- intertidal zone

- subtidal zone.

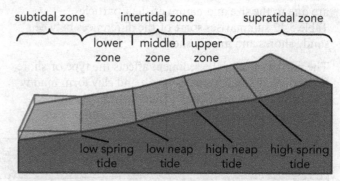

Figure 5.41: Zonation of sedimentary shores.

The supratidal zone is the area above the high water spring tide mark. Conditions for life are harsh as it is dry and exposed to the wind with few producer or consumer organisms.

We can divide the intertidal zones of sedimentary shores into three areas.

- The upper zone extends from the high water neap tide mark to the high water spring tide mark. The upper parts of this area spend less than 1% of the year under the sea while the lower parts spend around 20% of the year submerged.

- The middle zone extends from the low water neap tide mark to the high water neap tide mark. The upper parts of this area spend around 20% of the year under water and the lower parts spend around 80% of the year under water.

- The lower zone extends from the low water spring tide mark to the low water neap tide mark. The upper parts of this area spend around 80% of the year under water while the lower parts spend more than 99% of the year under water.

The subtidal zone is always covered by seawater. The conditions are similar to those in the lowest part of the intertidal zone.

Comparing sandy and muddy shores

There are many different types of sedimentary shore, including gravel, sand, silt and muddy shores. The differences between the different types of shore are due to the size and nature of their particles. Table 5.12 summarises some of the differences between sandy shores and muddy shores.

The particle size of the sediment affects the type of shore formed. Very small particles of silt and clay form muddy shores and larger particles of sand form sandy shores. The shapes of the particles are irregular with pits so

there is a large surface area on which organic material and bacteria can attach.

Sedimentation and erosion of sedimentary shores is affected by factors such as:

- coastline shape
- current speed
- organic material content of sediments.

> ### KEY WORD
>
> sedimentation: the settling of sand or silt particles onto a shore

Larger particles of sand need more energy to move, compared to smaller, lighter particles of silt and clay. Therefore, the upper areas of beaches have larger particles of sand compared to muddier areas further down the shore. Fine particles of sand and silt will erode more rapidly than larger, coarse sand particles. Muddy shores with a high organic material content, however, have a low erosion rate as the organic material 'glues' the clay or silt together.

When muddy shores become wet, they are stable due to organic substances gluing silt and clay particles together. Larger sand particles have less organic material so are bonded more loosely. Fine sands are very unstable as the particles are not bonded strongly, so they are easily moved by low-energy wave action. All sandy shores can be unstable, which means they are easily eroded by currents and waves.

The slope of shores is affected by the size of particles. Small particles of silt and clay stick together with few spaces between them. The particles are also bonded together by organic materials.

Factor	Type of shore		
	Coarse sand	Fine sand	Muddy
water turbulence	high	medium	low
particle size	> 2 mm	0.002 mm to 2 mm	< 0.002 mm
organic material	very low	medium	high
oxygen content	high	medium	low
water content	low	medium	high
speed of drying	fast	medium	slow
presence of microbes	low	medium	high

Table 5.12: Comparison of muddy and sandy shores.

This means that muddy shores are usually flatter, such as the typical mud flats shown in Figure 5.42. Sandy shores are often steep. Steeper slopes generally have larger particles of sand.

Figure 5.42: Mudflats, showing the shallow gradient due to the small particle size of silt.

Sandy shores are usually formed by water that has more **turbulence**. Muddy shores often form in more sheltered areas with less water turbulence. The high turbulence of sandy shores means that they are often unstable so it is difficult for organisms to stay attached. Muddy shores hold onto water better when exposed to the air, so they dry out less. A high water content helps the particles of clay or silt to stick together and reduces erosion by the wind. However, sand particles, particularly large ones, do not have much organic material attached. With little organic matter, the particles do not hold onto water, drying out easily when exposed.

Larger particles of sand do not bind together as much as clay or silt particles. This means that there are more air spaces and therefore more oxygen between particles on sandy beaches. Waterlogged muddy shores can lack oxygen and organisms that live in mud need special adaptations to survive.

> ## KEY WORD
>
> **turbulence***: the movement of water

Distribution of organisms on sandy shores

Although a sandy shore does not seem to have a wide variety of life, some organisms do live here; however, there is much less life than on a rocky shore. Because many organisms live buried in the sand, there is less obvious zonation of species than on rocky shores. Several abiotic and biotic factors affect life on sandy shores.

Abiotic factors

- Unstable substrate. Sand is constantly eroded and deposited by wave action. This makes it very difficult for any species to remain attached. There are few producer organisms, particularly macroalgae, as holdfasts cannot attach. The lack of producers means that food webs are quite simple. Little energy enters the community and there are few food sources.

- Air temperature. The supratidal zone and exposed areas of the intertidal zone are most affected by air temperature. Any organisms living here must cope with a wide range of temperatures. Air temperature is much more variable than water temperature. Areas lower down the shore that are submerged for longer have more stable temperatures.

- Exposure. The supratidal zone and exposed areas of the intertidal zone dehydrate easily. Sandy shores with large, coarse particles of sand retain less water than muddy shores or sandy shores with smaller particles. A lack of water can make it difficult for organisms to survive.

Biotic factors

- Predation. There are few areas of shelter on sandy shores so it is difficult for animals to avoid predators. Shore birds hunt for animals left behind on the shore at low tide. Many shore birds, such as the oystercatcher shown in Figure 5.43, have long beaks for pulling out organisms buried in the sand.

- Food availability. There are few producers for herbivores to eat. Many of the food chains begin with detritus-eating animals, such as lugworms, and filter-feeding molluscs, such as clams. Lugworms consume and digest bacteria, organic material and microalgae in the sand. Carnivores, such as annelid ragworms, prey on lugworms. Shore birds consume buried molluscs and crabs.

Figure 5.43: Oystercatcher hunting prey on sedimentary shore.

Adaptations of animals

All animals on sandy shores have **structural adaptations** and **behavioural adaptations** that enable them to survive the harsh conditions.

Figure 5.44 shows a photograph of a lugworm in a burrow on the beach. Lugworms live inside U-shaped burrows. They constantly **ingest** sand from one side of the burrow and digest the microorganisms that are inside it. They then push the waste sand out of the other side of the burrow to form a cast on the surface of the beach. Oxygen concentrations in the burrow can become low, especially when the tide is out. Lugworms contain haemoglobin, as mentioned in Chapter 4, to absorb any oxygen around them. At low tide, the water in the burrows has a low oxygen concentration so the haemoglobin releases oxygen to the cells of the lugworm for respiration. The bristle-like setae of lugworms on the sides of their bodies secure lugworms in their burrows and allow them to grip the sand when moving.

Figure 5.44: Lugworm in burrow on a sedimentary shore.

KEY WORDS

structural adaptations: physical structures of organisms that have evolved to enable them to survive

behavioural adaptations*: behaviours of organisms that have evolved to enable them to survive

ingest: the taking in of food or other material

Clams are bivalve molluscs that have a muscular foot for digging into the sand. Like all bivalves, they have two shells that they can open and close with muscles.

Figure 5.45 shows how a clam pushes its foot into the sand and anchors itself. The clam then uses its foot to pull the rest of its shell into the sand. Clams have a siphon, which is a tube for pulling in and pushing out water. The siphon sticks out from the surface of the sediment and is used for filter feeding and gas exchange.

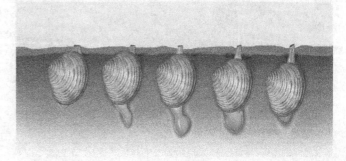

Figure 5.45: Clam burrowing into sediment.

Questions

13 Give two differences between sandy shores and muddy shores.

14 Describe how lugworms are adapted to live on sedimentary shores.

15 Explain why fewer organisms live on sandy shores compared with rocky shores.

5.6 Mangrove forests

Mangroves are trees that grow in the saline waters of coastal areas and estuaries. They form dense coastal forests in tropical and subtropical areas, as shown in Figure 5.46. Over 100 different species of tree grow in mangrove forests. True mangrove trees belong to a genus called *Rhizophora*. Mangrove forests form around sheltered coastal areas where mud and silt accumulate. As the trees grow, their root systems stabilise the substrate and encourage more trees to root there.

Mangrove forests are areas of great ecological importance:

- mangroves are habitats for thousands of different species

- mangrove forests form one of the most important carbon dioxide removers on Earth

- mangroves protect coastlines from erosion and storm damage.

Figure 5.46: Mangroves at coastal area.

Figure 5.47 shows where mangrove forests are found around the world. These forests are under great threat, however, from human development. Between 20% and 35% of mangroves on the planet have been lost since the early 1980s. The clearing of mangroves to make room for shrimp farms is the cause of about one quarter of all losses.

Structure of mangrove forests

Mangrove forests range from fully **terrestrial forests** to areas submerged by the ocean. Figure 5.48 shows the different zones in a mangrove forest. Different species of tree occupy different zones, depending on how well they are able to withstand salt.

- The terrestrial part of the forest (on land) is completely out of the water so the trees are rarely submerged. Trees growing here are the least salt tolerant type of mangrove but the soil still has high salinity. This part of the forest resembles inland rainforests.

- The intertidal zone is closer to the water. It has two subsections, depending on the time spent submerged. The middle zone is submerged during high tides but the substrate is uncovered at low tide. The coastal zone is submerged for longer and is only exposed during the lowest tides. The types of mangroves in each area are adapted for the conditions. Mangrove species in the middle zone have elongated **prop roots**. Mangroves in the coastal zones have aerial roots called **pneumatophores** that enable them to 'breathe' out of the water.

KEY WORDS

terrestrial forests: areas of forest that are fully on land

prop roots: adapted root system of mangroves with vertical roots that stick out from the stem and look like stilts

pneumatophores: adapted root structures of some mangroves that stick up from the soil and water; they are used for gas exchange

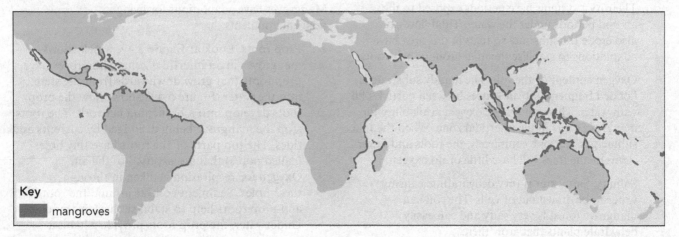

Key

■ mangroves

Figure 5.47: Global distribution of mangrove forests.

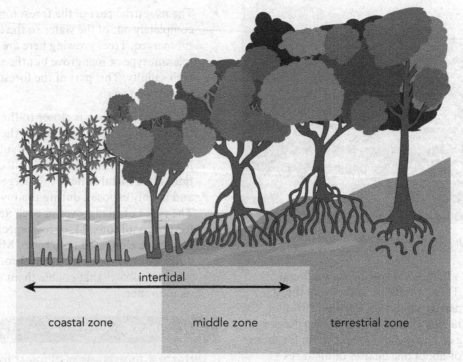

intertidal

coastal zone   middle zone   terrestrial zone

Figure 5.48: Zonation of a mangrove forest.

Adaptations of mangrove trees

Mangrove trees have to cope with many factors.

Abiotic factors in mangrove forests

- Tidal cycle. Trees in the intertidal zone have to cope with the tidal flow of salt water in and out. Their root systems have periods exposed to the air and periods under the water. Tidal flow can also erode the substrate so trees in this area have adaptations to stabilise the mud around their roots.

- Oxygen content of the soil. The muddy substrate is flooded frequently so air spaces between particles fill with water. This reduces the oxygen availability for mangrove roots in the intertidal zone. When the tide submerges the zone completely, the roots and lower stems of the trees will have little or no oxygen.

- Salinity. Salt water is very dehydrating, causing water to be drawn out of cells. The soil in a mangrove forest is very salty and can easily dehydrate plants that grow there.

- Temperature. The temperature of the substrate changes during the tidal cycle. When submerged, the temperature of the substrate is stable.

But when the substrate is exposed to the atmosphere, the temperature is much more variable. During a summer day, the temperature will become very high. However, at night in winter, the temperature will drop very low.

Specific adaptations of mangroves

Mangroves have adaptations for living in tidal environments.

- Prop roots. Look at Figure 5.49, which shows mangroves in an intertidal zone. Mangroves have prop roots that grow downwards from the stem into the water. Figure 5.49a shows how the prop roots develop into a branching network. The roots stop the mangrove being dislodged by currents and tides. The top parts of the roots have tiny holes (called pores) that are exposed to the air. Oxygen for respiration is taken in through these holes. Sediment collects around the roots and prop roots help to stabilise the substrate. Underwater, the prop roots provide a habitat for marine organisms where they can hide from large predators. Figure 5.50 shows how fish live in shoals around the prop roots.

a

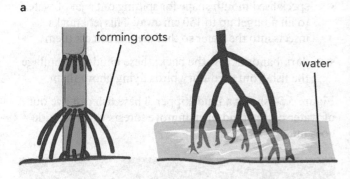

forming roots

water

b

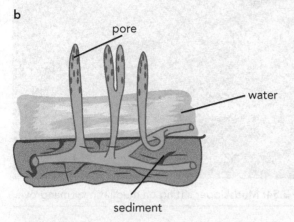

pore

water

sediment

Figure 5.49: Root adaptations of mangroves:
a development of prop roots and b Pneumatophores.

Figure 5.50: Fish swimming around prop roots.

- Pneumatophores. Mangroves in the coastal part of the intertidal zone spend long periods submerged. Pneumatophores, shown in Figure 5.49b and Figure 5.51, are vertical roots that point up out of the water like snorkels. Tiny holes in the pneumatophores take in oxygen, which is used for respiration.

Figure 5.51: Pneumatophores of mangroves in the intertidal zone.

- Salt secretion from leaves. Mangroves live in very salty places, so cannot avoid taking in too much salt through their roots. This extra salt needs to be removed. Mangroves can get rid of excess salt through their leaves. Figure 5.52 shows a mangrove leaf that is secreting salt.

Figure 5.52: Mangrove leaves showing secretion of white salt crystals.

Adaptations of organisms that live in mangrove forests

Mangrove forests have high productivity and are full of animal life. The trees photosynthesise so they bring in energy for the complex communities and provide nesting sites and habitats for many species. Like the trees, animals living here have adaptations to help them survive.

Banded archerfish and mudskippers are two species of fish found in mangroves.

Banded archerfish can live in freshwater, seawater and estuarine water. They often live in mangrove forests in river estuaries. These fish get their name from the stripes along their back and can spit a jet of water to knock insects into the water. Figure 5.53 shows a banded archerfish spitting a jet of water at an insect.

Figure 5.53: Banded archerfish spitting water to dislodge an insect.

Banded archerfish have several adaptations:

- large, moveable eyes that point forward to give them binocular vision; by seeing prey with both eyes, the fish can work out the distance easily

KEY WORD

binocular vision: having two eyes positioned on an organism so that objects can be seen by both eyes

- specialised mouth shape for spitting out a jet of water to hit a target up to 150 cm away. This jet knocks insects into the water so that the fish can eat them

- dark bands across the back; these bands camouflage the fish from predatory birds flying above them.

Figure 5.54 shows a mudskipper. These fish can live out of water on the mud of mangrove forests when the tide goes out.

Figure 5.54: Mudskipper sitting on mudflat near mangrove.

To survive both in and out of the water, mudskippers have several adaptations.

- Permeable skin. Permeable skin describes a skin which substances can pass through. The skin of the body, mouth and throat is thin. When the skin is moist, these fish can absorb oxygen through it. This means that, although mudskippers can survive on land, the skin needs to be kept moist.

- Enlarged gill chambers. Mudskippers trap water within their gill chambers when they move onto land. They absorb oxygen from this trapped water.

- Adapted pectoral and pelvic fins. The pectoral fins are located more under the body and function as limbs to help the fish 'skip' over the mud. The pelvic fins are located just behind the pectoral fins, adding strength. In some species the pelvic fins act like a suction pad to anchor the fish to the substrate. Figure 5.55 shows a mudskipper propelling itself into the air using its adapted fins.

- Eyes on top of head. When out of the water, mudskippers would be easy prey for predator species. Their eyes are large and located on the top of the head. This gives them all round vision to avoid predators.

Figure 5.55: Mudskipper jumping out of water.

Questions

16 Compare the abiotic conditions in the coastal and middle sections of a mangrove forest.

17 Explain how mudskippers are adapted to live on land for periods of time.

18 Explain how pneumatophores enable coastal mangroves to survive in muddy, submerged shores.

5.7 Tropical coral reefs

Tropical coral reefs are habitats for many different species. Generally, tropical reefs are found between 30°N and 30°S of the Equator and never below a depth of 50 m.

The structure of corals

Whole corals are animals made up of colonies of individual polyps. Figure 5.56 shows a Red Sea coral reef that has several different species of coral.

Figure 5.56: A coral reef ecosystem.

The shapes of coral vary enormously and different species of coral have different shapes. The environment also affects the shape of corals and sometimes very different looking structures may be made by the same species. The colours of corals vary, often depending on the type of microorganisms living inside the polyps. These microorganisms are photosynthetic dinoflagellates called zooxanthellae (see Chapter 4).

Structure of a typical coral polyp

A whole coral is made up of thousands of individual polyps embedded in a calcium carbonate skeleton. Figure 5.57 shows a close up of some coral polyps.

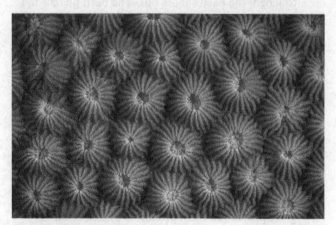

Figure 5.57: Coral polyps.

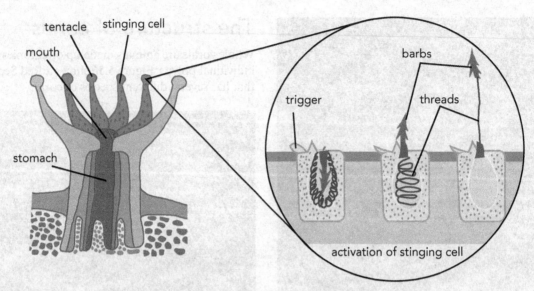

Figure 5.58: Generalised structure of a coral polyp showing the stinging cell mechanism.

Each species of coral polyp has its own specialisations, but there are some general structures that all coral polyps have. These are shown in Figure 5.58.

- Tentacles. All coral polyps are radially symmetrical with tentacles in a circle around a central mouth. The tentacles can be extended and brought back into the body. The tentacles are used for gas exchange and feeding. Specialised stinging cells called nematocytes lie along the surface of the tentacles. These cells are used to catch prey and protect against predators. The tentacles move food to the mouth of the polyp.

- Stinging cells. Figure 5.58 shows the action of a stinging cell. Inside the cells is a barb that is attached to a thread that lies coiled up like a spring. If the trigger on the side of the stinging cell is touched, the barb shoots out. The barb pierces the skin of prey or predator. The thread keeps the barb attached to the polyp.

- Mouth. The mouth lies at the centre of the polyp.

- Stomach. The stomach is a space in the centre of the polyp. Food is digested in here and the products absorbed by the polyp.

- Skeleton. Coral polyps produce a hard outer skeleton made from calcium carbonate. After the polyps have reproduced asexually to colonise a substrate, they produce a large communal structure. This structure forms the basis of a reef. The skeleton gives protection from predators and provides a stable substrate for the coral polyps.

The relationship between coral and zooxanthellae

The bright colours of most coral polyps are usually due to dinoflagellate microalgae. Figure 5.59 shows small, green zooxanthellae within a polyp.

Figure 5.59: Coral polyp with zooxanthellae.

The coral polyp and zooxanthellae have a **mutualistic relationship**. This means that the two organisms live together so that both organisms can benefit. The zooxanthellae photosynthesise, producing nutrients, and

KEY WORD

mutualistic relationship: ecological relationship between different species where both benefit

some of these nutrients are transferred to the coral polyp. In return, the zooxanthellae receive carbon dioxide and other minerals from the coral.

If corals undergo environmental stress, they often expel (get rid of) the zooxanthellae. Environmental stresses can be increases in water temperature or acidity. The corals become white due to their calcium carbonate skeleton and we say that the coral has become 'bleached'. If the corals recover, they will take in more zooxanthellae, which means that they can actually change colour.

Environmental factors that affect coral

Corals are affected by many abiotic and biotic factors. Because corals are very sensitive to changes in their environment, human activities can damage coral reefs.

Abiotic factors

- Temperature. The best temperature for growth of most corals is between 23 °C and 29 °C. There are a few cold water species of coral, but not many live below 18 °C. Only a few species can live in temperatures beyond 35 °C for short periods of time. High temperatures can result in bleaching. The rate of loss of coral reefs is accelerating due to global warming.

- Light intensity. Because corals are dependent on the zooxanthellae that live inside them, they need exposure to light for photosynthesis. Light intensity decreases with depth, so there are no corals below about 50 m.

- Clear water. The water around coral reefs is usually very clear and very low in nutrients. The nutrients in areas of coral reef are held within the organisms that live there and are recycled between the organisms very quickly. Sediment in the water would reduce light intensity, meaning that the zooxanthellae would not photosynthesise efficiently. The mineral content of water around coral reefs is often very low. This reduces algal growth, so there are few phytoplankton in the water to reduce the clarity. The nutrients are quickly transferred through food chains when animals consume other organisms. In areas where coral reefs are close to farmland, mineral runoff is damaging reefs as it encourages algal growth.

- Hard substrate. Coral polyp larvae must settle onto a hard substrate before metamorphosing into polyps. If there is too much sediment, there is nowhere for the larvae to settle. We can make artificial reefs by sinking objects such as old ships, cars and even old military tanks. Coral larvae attach rapidly to these artificial reefs and establish communities of organisms (Figure 5.60).

Figure 5.60: Coral growing on the wreck of USS Spiegel.

Biotic factors

Coral is consumed by animals and is an important part of food webs. If the primary consumer populations increase, however, coral can be damaged.

Figure 5.61 shows a parrotfish. These fish have specially adapted grinding teeth at the front of their mouths. They grind away at coral and then ingest it as food. The solid, calcium carbonate of the coral skeletons is indigestible and passes through the parrotfish in its faeces. Because it has been ground up, the waste coral skeletons are turned into sand. Just one parrotfish can produce over 90 kg of sand each year.

Figure 5.61: Parrotfish with teeth that are adapted for grinding coral.

The crown of thorns starfish, shown in Figure 5.62, is a natural predator of coral. In the correct numbers, these starfish are an important part of the coral ecosystem as they eat fast-growing coral. This gives slower-growing coral species a chance to compete. Occasionally, however, populations of these starfish increase very quickly and vast areas of coral are destroyed. Scientists estimate that the two main causes of coral reef destruction over the last 25 years have been storm damage and consumption by crown of thorns starfish. It is unclear what causes the starfish populations to suddenly increase. It may be due to the run off of nutrients from farms causing large numbers of algae to grow in the water. The larvae of starfish feed on the algae and so many starfish develop. Too much fishing of predator species, or the removal of natural predators, may also cause populations of the starfish to increase.

Figure 5.62: Crown of thorns starfish, a species of echinoderm that consumes coral.

The coral reef community

Coral reefs are areas of high species richness containing thousands of different species of organisms. There are complex food webs and communities that are all based on productivity of the zooxanthellae within the corals. Every species has its own ecological role in the ecosystem, from the cleaner fish that remove algae from the surface of the reefs to the sharks that keep coral-consuming organisms under control. Triggerfish, parrotfish and nudibranch molluscs are all species adapted for life on a coral reef.

Many species of triggerfish live around coral reefs. Their name comes from the adaptation of the dorsal fin into three spines, as seen in the triggerfish in Figure 5.63. These fish can lock the long, first spine into an upright position using the second, smaller spine. This makes it difficult for predators to eat the triggerfish. The spines are also useful for locking themselves into crevices in rock. When the third spine is pressed down, this unlocks the other two spines.

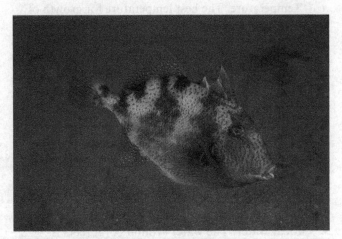

Figure 5.63: Trigger fish with modified dorsal fin.

Nudibranchs are also called sea slugs as they are molluscs that are related to snails; however, nudibranchs do not have shells. Their colouring is often very bright, as shown by the species in Figure 5.64, warning predators that they are poisonous. Species of nudibranch that eat toxic organisms, such as sponges, collect these toxins in their bodies.

Figure 5.64: Two species of nudibranch mollusc that are toxic to predators.

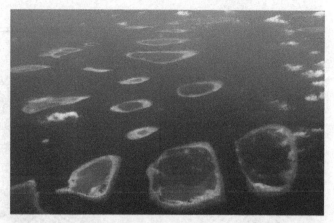

Figure 5.65: Coral atolls in the Maldives as seen from the air.

Two other geologists, Reginald Daly and James Dana, revised and developed his theories. They produced the Darwin–Daly–Dana model for coral atoll formation. Figure 5.66 shows the stages in coral atoll formation.

- Stage 1: An underwater volcano erupts and creates a volcanic island above the surface of the ocean.

- Stage 2: Coral begins to grow in water around the sides of the island creating a **fringing reef**. The volcanic island erodes from above and subsides (sinks) downwards.

- Stage 3: The island continues to erode and subside until a lagoon forms inside the circle of reef. The reef continues to grow and eventually forms a **barrier reef** around a central, shallow lagoon. This final structure is known as an atoll.

Although geologists think that tectonic plate movements may also play a role in atoll formation, the basic idea of the Darwin–Daly–Dana model is still accepted.

Parrotfish are also adpated for living on a coral reef. They have protruding, specialised grinding teeth to bite off pieces of coral reef. They release the sand from the ground-up coral reef in their faeces.

Coral atoll formation

An **atoll** is a ring of coral around a central shallow **lagoon** area (Figure 5.65).

Charles Darwin, in the nineteenth century, explained how he thought coral atolls formed. Darwin was a naturalist who took part in a global voyage of scientific discovery on the ship *HMS Beagle* between 1831 and 1836. He observed the effects of volcanic activity and other geological processes such as earthquakes. His observations of coral reefs made him realise that living creatures were able to build coral structures, and that land could sink due to subsidence. While on the voyage, he wrote his theory of coral reef formation. He published this in 1842, six years after his return.

KEY WORDS

atoll: a coral island that has formed around a central lagoon

lagoon*: area of shallow water separated by land from the sea or ocean

subsidence*: the sinking of land

fringing reef*: the coral reef that forms around the sides of a volcanic island

barrier reef: ridge of coral separated from land by a lagoon

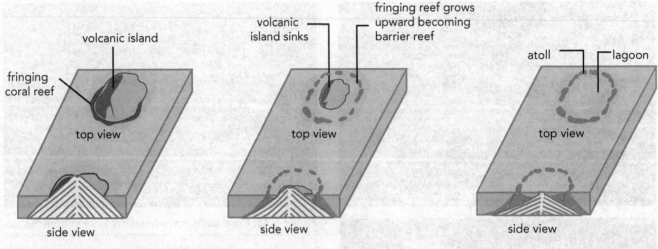

Figure 5.66: Stages in coral atoll formation.

Questions

19 Describe the adaptations of parrotfish.

20 Outline the stages that occur during atoll formation.

21 Explain how intensive agriculture could place coral reefs at risk.

ACTIVITY 5.6

Don't release your pets into the wild!

Do some research on the problems with lionfish in the Caribbean Sea. Find out:

* Why are the populations of lionfish so high?

* Where did the lionfish come from?

* Why are they now a problem?

* What could we do about the problem?

Summarise your findings on one large piece of paper. You can then display the poster so that other learners can see it.

SUMMARY

Species are organisms that can breed and produce fertile offspring.
A population is a group of organisms of the same species in a particular area.
A community is all the organisms present in an area.
A habitat is the physical location that an organism lives in and interacts with.
An ecosystem is the interaction between a community and the environment.
The environment is all the abiotic and biotic factors in an area.

CONTINUED

Populations of organisms are affected by biotic and abiotic factors.
Ecosystems can be investigated by using a range of practical techniques.
Open ocean ecosystems have different zones, each with different conditions, including pelagic, benthic, sunlight, twilight and midnight zones.
Different types of organism, all with specific adaptations, live in the sunlight, twilight and midnight zones.
Deep-sea species and benthic species have specific adaptations to enable them to survive.
Rocky shores are coastal areas with different zones, each with specific conditions.
Rocky shores have high species richness; organisms have adaptations to enable them to survive the different conditions in each of the zones.
Sedimentary shores are composed of unstable substrates that can be eroded and deposited by tidal movements.
Sandy shores and muddy shores have different features due to the sizes of the particles of sediment.
Sandy shores have different zones, each with slightly different conditions; organisms have adaptations to enable them to live in these zones.
Mangrove forests are ecosystems with high species richness and have high productivity.
Mangrove trees have adaptations such as prop roots and pneumatophores.
Animals that live in mangrove forests, such as mudskippers and archerfish, have adaptations.
Coral reefs are ecosystems with high species richness.
The general structure of a coral polyp includes a mouth, tentacles, stinging cells, stomach and skeleton.
Coral polyps contain mutualistic dinoflagellates called zooxanthellae.
Coral reef growth is affected by biotic factors, such as parrotfish and crown of thorns starfish, and abiotic factors.
Organisms that live in coral reefs, such as nudibranchs, parrotfish and triggerfish, have adaptations.
Coral atoll formation occurs in several stages, including volcanic eruption, fringing reef formation, subsidence and erosion of the island, and the creation of a barrier reef.

CASE STUDY PROJECT

Ecotourism holidays to coral reef ecosystems

Many people dream of going on holiday to coastal areas like the one shown in Figure 5.67. They want to see the beautiful coral reefs and enjoy the unspoilt natural world. Ecotourism is a type of tourism that aims to enable people to visit natural areas while minimising the environmental impact of visitors. The idea of ecotourism is to educate visitors about conservation, the natural world and the culture of the local people. Ecotourism also provides local people with useful income. You will learn more about ecotourism in Chapter 6.

KEY WORD

ecotourism: tourism that does not harm ecosystems; it aims to protect ecosystems and educate tourists about the environment and local cultures

CONTINUED

Figure 5.67: View of ecotourism in the Maldives.

This is what you need to do for this task.

- Select a coastal area where ecotourism occurs and do some research.

- Produce a tourism brochure to attract and inform people with no knowledge of the area about:

  - the ecosystem

  - the organisms that live in the ecosystem and how they are adapted – remember that you are trying to inform people and sell them a holiday, so make it interesting!

  - the local culture of the area

  - how the money they pay will be invested in the area

  - what has been done to make sure that their holiday will not damage the ecosystem.

  You could even produce an itinerary for them, for example, day one: diving on the reef to see rare turtle species, followed by a visit to a turtle conservation beach run by local volunteers.

- Your brochure could be a paper version or a webpage with links.

- You can work as a small team, with each learner completing a separate part of the brochure.

Peer assessment

To assess your brochure, let other learners, friends and relatives have a look and ask them to rate it. Ask them to provide written feedback in the form of 'two stars and a wish': describe two things about the work that they liked, and give one suggestion for improvement: 'It could be even better if …'.

REFLECTION

Think about how well your brochure was rated by other people.

- What could you have done better?

- Could you have found out more details about coral reef ecosystems?

- Was there an aspect that you did not cover?

- Was the language you used appropriate?

- Did you explain key terms to people?

EXAM-STYLE QUESTIONS

1 Table 1 shows the populations of anchovies and mackerel in an area of the Atlantic Ocean over a period of six years. Mackerel is a predator of anchovies.

Year	Anchovy population (thousand tonnes)	Mackerel population (thousand tonnes)
2010	3.5	1.5
2011	4.4	2.2
2012	3.1	2.8
2013	2.7	2.1
2014	3.4	1.6
2015	4.2	1.5

Table 1

a State what is meant by the term 'population'. [1]

b Calculate the mean rate of change of anchovy population between 2010 and 2013. Give your answer to two significant figures. [3]

c i Draw a line graph to show the populations of anchovy and mackerel between 2010 and 2015. [6]

   ii Describe the change in population of mackerel between 2010 and 2015. [2]

   iii Suggest an explanation for the changes in populations of anchovy and mackerel. [3]

[Total: 15]

2 The sunlight zone is the first 200 m of vertical open ocean. The twilight zone is the vertical area of water between 200 m and 1000 m.

a i Compare the abiotic factors of the sunlight zone with the abiotic factors of the twilight zone. [4]

   ii Explain why productivity is higher in the sunlight zone compared with the twilight zone. [3]

   iii Lanternfish live during the day in the twilight zone and move to the sunlight zone to feed on plankton at night. They are the main prey species of many species of fish that live permanently in the twilight zone. Evaluate the ecological importance of the lanternfish. [4]

b Bioluminescence is a common feature of deep-sea organisms. Give three functions of bioluminescence. [3]

[Total: 14]

3   Two students decided to measure the profile of a sandy shore. They measured two sections of the shore and collected the data shown in Table 2.

Section of the shore	Gradient of slope (°)	Distance between the students (m)
A to B	5	10
B to C	2	15

Table 2

a   i   Draw a profile of the beach from A to C.   [2]
    ii State how sediment grain size affects the gradient of a shore.   [1]

b   The students then investigated the distribution of two species of annelid worm on this sandy shore and a muddy shore.

Species A has haemoglobin. Species B does not have haemoglobin.

The students also investigated the mass of organic material, and mean diameter of sediment particles on each shore. Their results are shown in Table 3.

Shore	Mean number of annelids per square metre		Mass of organic material per 100 g sediment (g)	Mean diameter of sediment particles (mm)
	Species A	Species B		
Sandy	2	5	2.5	1.7000
Muddy	7	1	12.2	0.0004

Table 3

   i   Describe a method that the students could use to determine the mean number of annelid worms per square metre.   [4]
   ii   State the element that is needed to produce haemoglobin.   [1]
   iii Both species live in burrows under the surface of the shore. Use Table 3 to suggest explanations for the distribution of species A and species B on the two shores.   [5]

                                                                    [Total: 13]

4   In a mangrove forest, trees with pneumatophores were found close to the sea while trees with prop roots were found further inland.
    a   Explain the function of pneumatophores and prop roots.   [4]
    b   Explain how the tidal nature of mangrove swamps affects the distribution of the two types of tree.   [2]
    c   Suggest how global warming could lead to a change in the structure of mangrove forests.   [3]

CONTINUED

d Mudskippers live in mangrove forests. Explain how the adaptations of mudskippers enable them to survive in mangrove forests. [4]

[Total: 13]

5 The effect of heat stress on coral death was investigated.

a i Explain the structure of a coral polyp. [6]

ii Before the corals die, they often become bleached. This bleaching occurs because the coral polyps expel their zooxanthellae. Explain the relationship between the coral polyps and the zooxanthellae. [3]

b The scientists determined the threshold temperature at which bleaching would normally occur.

Heat stress was calculated using the following formula.

heat stress = number of weeks above threshold temperature × temperature in °C above the threshold

The results are shown in Figure 1.

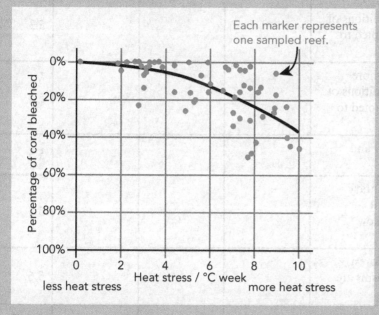

Figure 1

i A coral polyp spent three weeks at a temperature 0.7 °C above the threshold temperature.

Use the formula to calculate the heat stress this coral polyp was exposed to. [2]

ii Describe the effect of heat stress on survival of the coral. [2]

iii Use the information in Figure 1 to explain why global warming is a threat to coral ecosystems. [4]

[Total: 17]

SELF-EVALUATION CHECKLIST

After studying this chapter, think about how confident you are with the different topics. This will help you to see any gaps in your knowledge and help you to learn more effectively.

I can	Needs more work	Getting there	Confident to move on	See Section
confidently use terms such as species, population, community, habitat, environment, ecosystem				5.1
describe abiotic and biotic factors that can affect the growth of populations				5.1
explain why coastal ecosystems have higher productivity than open-ocean ecosystems				5.1
use a variety of practical techniques to investigate ecosystems				5.2
describe the zonal structure of open-ocean ecosystems; describe the different conditions of each zone and how organisms are adapted to live there				5.3
describe the zonal structure of rocky shore ecosystems; describe the different conditions of each zone, and how organisms are adapted to live there				5.4
explain the differences between muddy and sandy shores				5.5
describe the zonal structure of sedimentary shore ecosystems; describe the different conditions of each zone, and explain how organisms are adapted to live there				5.5
describe the structure of a mangrove forest, the abiotic conditions and how organisms are adapted to live there				5.6
explain the structure of corals, the general structure of coral polyps, and the role of zooxanthellae				5.7
explain how abiotic factors affect the growth of corals in oceans				5.7
describe how organisms such as triggerfish, parrotfish and nudibranchs are adapted to live in coral reefs				5.7
describe the Darwin–Dana–Daly theory of atoll formation				5.7

Chapter 6

Human influences on the marine environment

IN THIS CHAPTER YOU WILL:

- develop an overview of the importance of marine ecosystems to humans
- develop an overview of how some of our activities can affect marine ecosystems
- learn about the positive and negative effects of tourism on marine ecosystems
- learn how ecotourism can reduce the impact of tourism
- learn how sustainable fishing can be achieved
- learn about some fishing methods and their impacts on fish populations
- learn about the roles of aquaculture in producing commercial species and in conservation
- learn about the methods used in aquaculture

CONTINUED

- learn about the impacts of the fossil fuel industry on marine ecosystems
- learn about the roles and impacts of renewable energy systems
- learn about the effects of plastic pollution on marine organisms
- learn about how farming can lead to pollution of marine ecosystems
- develop an understanding of how human activities are leading to climate change and its effects
- develop an understanding of how different methods can be used to conserve species and habitats.

GETTING STARTED

Imagine you are on a day trip to a beach with a group of other learners. You spend time diving, sailing and playing games on the beach.
You also bring a lunch to eat when you are there.

With another learner, discuss the following two questions. When you have finished, share your ideas with the rest of the class.

- How might your visit to the beach affect marine organisms?

- What could you do to reduce the negative effects of your visit?

MARINE SCIENCE IN CONTEXT

World Ocean Day

On 8 June 2019, over 2000 events to raise awareness of threats to marine ecosystems took place in over 140 different countries. World Ocean Day is an annual event that everyone around the world can join in with to celebrate and take action for all our oceans and seas. Figure 6.1 shows children and adults in Thailand at an event that illustrates the threat of plastic pollution in our oceans.

Figure 6.1: World Ocean Day event in Thailand to raise awareness about plastic pollution.

There are many conservation groups around the world that join in with World Ocean Day. Some of the groups are local groups based in one country, and others are international groups. All conservation groups recognise that the threats to our oceans and seas are greater than ever before. Many commercial species are under threat of extinction due to over harvesting. We call these species endangered species. Coastal habitats are being lost to make space for farming and tourist resorts. Pollution from farming and industry leaks into our oceans. The oceans are full of discarded plastics, packaging and fishing gear. The burning of fossil fuels in our cars, planes and power stations is releasing billions of tonnes of carbon dioxide gas every year. Excess carbon dioxide is changing our climate, making it warmer and causing sea levels to rise.

World Ocean Day helps to raise awareness of all the threats to our oceans and encourages everyone to play their part. If we continue to take our oceans and seas for granted, future generations will only know about whales, sea otters, dolphins, turtles and thousands of other species from films and books. Unless we act now, our oceans face an uncertain future.

CONTINUED

Discussion questions

1   In your opinion, what is the most important issue facing our oceans?

2   Think about your answer to the previous question. What do you think can be done to help stop further damage and repair the damage already done?

6.1 Human interactions with marine ecosystems

We all interact with the marine environment, even if we do not live close to the sea. We use the marine environment to provide us with food, energy and medicines. Coastal areas are places that many of us love to visit for holidays and recreation. Unfortunately, for many years we have damaged our marine world in many ways. In the past, people were often unaware of the damage being done to the natural world. In recent times, however, people have begun to understand how we have damaged marine ecosystems and how we now need to take action to prevent further damage.

The importance of marine ecosystems to humans

Ecosystem services are the things that we gain from ecosystems. These services can be obvious, such as food, building materials and energy. However, we also benefit from other services that are less clear. Many people enjoy experiencing the natural world. Recreation and tourism are examples of important services that marine ecosystems provide.

KEY WORD

ecosystem services*: the benefits that humans gain from ecosystems, such as food, recreation and coastal defences

Recreation and tourism

Our seas and oceans are areas of great beauty and interest. There are many reasons why people want to visit coastal areas. People want to experience the beautiful scenery, see animals, take part in sports, and even just relax on sandy beaches (Figure 6.2).

Figure 6.2: Recreational activities in coastal areas: **a** diving, **b** sailing and **c** enjoying beach activities.

Many holiday **resorts** have been developed in coastal areas. In the past, many resorts caused harm to the natural world by building on habitats and causing pollution. In recent years, however, ecotourism has become more popular. Ecotourism allows people to visit other areas but in a way that does not damage nature.

The growth of tourism has helped provide income for many countries with coastal areas. The Maldives, Seychelles and Sri Lanka, for example, all receive **foreign revenue** from tourist resorts. For many island nations, tourism has now replaced fishing as their main source of foreign revenue.

It is not only tropical coastal areas that people want to visit. Tourism companies provide opportunities to see everything from whale watching trips in Antarctica to diving in the warm clear waters of the Bahamas.

KEY WORDS

resort: an area that has been developed for tourists to visit

foreign revenue*: income that is brought into a country from abroad

---

Building materials and wood

In East Africa, South Asia, Southeast Asia and the Pacific, coral reefs have traditionally been mined for building materials. Pieces of coral reef are often used as bricks in houses or to repair roads. Coral can also be ground up to make cement. Because of the threats to coral reefs, the use of coral as a material for building is now discouraged.

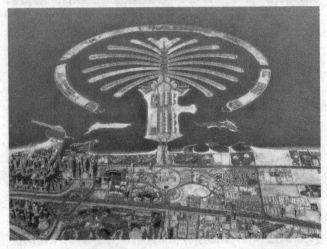

Figure 6.3: Artificially constructed Palm Island in Dubai, UAE.

Sand is often removed from beaches around the world to make cement and as part of land reclamation projects. China alone imports billions of tonnes of sand every year for construction projects. In Dubai, artificial islands have been created from over 5 million cubic metres of rock and 94 million cubic metres of sand from the deep sea in The Gulf (Figure 6.3). The massive global demand for sand is creating environmental issues.

ACTIVITY 6.1

Land reclamation in Singapore

Singapore is a small nation with a successful economy and a high standard of living. Because Singapore is so successful, it needs more land. Since it was founded as a nation, Singapore has carried out **land reclamation** projects to increase space.

1   Find a series of maps that show how Singapore has changed in size over its history.

2   Explain how this change in size has been achieved.

3   Explain how land reclamation has affected the environment in Singapore.

4   Explain how and why Singapore has moved to a much more environmentally sustainable method of land reclamation.

Summarise all your findings on two sides of A4 paper.

Self-assessment

Rate your work according to the following scheme:

☺   if it is well organised and has all of the information needed

☺   if it is reasonably well organised and has most of the information

☹   if it lacks organisation and has a lot of information missing.

KEY WORD

land reclamation: the conversion of natural areas, including wetlands and underwater areas, into land for development

For example, in Indonesia over 20 small, uninhabited islands have disappeared under the sea due to intensive sand mining.

Mangrove forests have traditionally been used by local people as a source of wood for building and fuels. Wood is an essential building material. Like sand, there has been a rapid increase in demand for wood over recent years. This has led to commercial over-harvesting of mangroves. In the future, alternative sources of wood will need to be found to reduce the deforestation of mangroves.

> **KEY WORD**
>
> **deforestation***: clearing of trees in forest areas to make way for development

Coastal protection

Many towns and cities are located close to the coast. These towns and cities began as fishing villages or ports for international trade. Human settlements in coastal areas are always at risk of flooding, erosion and damage from extreme weather. Sudden destructive events such as tsunamis and hurricanes can also threaten them.

Mangrove forests, seagrass beds, coral reefs and sand banks are some of the many natural structures that protect coastal communities from damage (Figure 6.4). These structures reduce wave energy, reduce erosion and act as natural barriers to flooding. In areas of Southeast Asia where there has been much mangrove deforestation, coastal areas have been severely affected by flooding.

Figure 6.4: Mangroves on an island in the Indus Delta outside of Karachi.

Medicines and medicinal plants

We have developed many medicines from plants and animals. Recently, scientists have researched the possibility of using marine organisms for developing new drugs. A range of invertebrate organisms, such as sponges, corals, sea squirts and molluscs, produce substances that might be useful as new medicines. These substances are often toxic in high doses but may be useful as drugs when in lower concentrations. Medicines for a wide range of diseases are being used or tested, including anti cancer medicines, painkillers and anti-inflammatory medicines.

For many years, people have used plants in mangrove forests as traditional medicines. Bacterial infections, parasite infestations, pain and diarrhoea have all been treated with plant extracts. Scientists in India recently identified over 50 plant species in mangrove forests producing chemicals that might be used to treat diseases. They also discovered that some plants make chemicals that act as antibiotics to kill bacteria. Many bacterial diseases are becoming resistant to current antibiotics, such as penicillin, so these plant-based antibiotics may offer new treatments. The increase in antibiotic-resistant bacteria is a huge problem for global human health.

> **KEY WORDS**
>
> **antibiotics**: drugs, usually produced by fungi, that kill bacteria
>
> **antibiotic-resistant bacteria**: bacteria that are not killed by antibiotics

Fisheries, food and nursery areas

A fishery is a difficult word to define, and it can have different meanings. We often refer to fishing businesses, or the whole industry of catching fish and seafood as fisheries. A fishery can also refer to the whole geographical area where fish and seafood are caught by the fishing industry. For example, the waters around the Maldives are the fishery for tuna.

We have traditionally harvested fish and other seafoods from our oceans for thousands of years. Seafood products are an important part of our diets and provide a rich source of protein and other essential nutrients. We harvest a wide range of species, from macroalgae such as kelp to top predator species such as swordfish. Communities throughout the world rely on sustainable harvesting of fish so that the fish populations are not negatively affected.

Over the twentieth and twenty-first centuries, fish stocks have fallen for two main reasons.

- The global human population has increased dramatically so the demand for fish and seafood has also increased. In 1900, the human population was approximately 1.6 billion; by 2020 this had grown to over 7.7 billion.

- Fishing methods have become increasingly intense and efficient. Fishing was once a local industry with little mechanisation. Fishing fleets now travel around the world and large trawlers have modern equipment to locate, catch and process fish.

KEY WORDS

fishery: a fishing business, industry for catching fish, or a geographical area where fish and seafood are caught

sustainable harvesting: methods of harvesting of marine species that do not reduce their populations over the long term

There is now a serious risk that the global demand for fish and seafood will damage fish populations so badly that none will be left. Figure 6.5 shows fishers emptying their net onto the deck. It is clear how many fish are taken in just one catch.

Figure 6.5: Fishers emptying their catch on a boat.

Nursery sites are areas such as kelp forests, seagrass meadows and mangroves where fish species breed, and juveniles (young fish) can escape from predators.

These areas are essential because they keep fish populations high so that we can continue to fish sustainably. If nursery sites are lost, fish populations decline and we lose a source of food. In Chapter 4, you learnt about the importance of kelp forests as nursery sites for ecologically important species. Kelp provides shelter and food for the many species that depend upon each other.

The impacts of human activities on marine ecosystems

Marine ecosystems provide us with many services. Unfortunately, our interactions with marine ecosystems can damage the marine environment. Our ever-increasing human population and demand for food, resources and energy is leading to direct and indirect consequences for marine ecosystems.

There are many direct effects of human activities, such as overfishing and damage to coral reefs from tourism and fishing. There are, however, other less obvious indirect effects, such as pollution from farming in inland areas, damage from container ships and pollution from the energy industry.

KEY WORD

overfishing: the harvesting of so many fish that their populations will no longer be sustainable in the future

Recreational activities and tourism

We have already looked at why people may want to visit coastal areas for recreation. Tourism is now a very big part of the economy of many nations. Although tourism brings in money, it does have negative impacts on the marine environment.

Habitat loss: if many people visit an area, there is a need for more hotel accommodation, food outlets, shops and other businesses. Because there are more job opportunities as tourist resorts develop, more people move to the area. These people will need more accommodation and services. When an area of coast starts to develop, valuable habitats such as mangrove forests and salt marshes are lost. Land reclamation projects may convert habitats into areas for resort development. Habitats can be lost to grow food for visitors. Figure 6.6 shows a tourist resort. There are many hotels and the beach itself has been developed. Large resorts such as this have a very serious effect on habitats and wildlife.

Figure 6.6: A large, highly developed holiday resort.

Recreational activities: visitors to beaches and other habitats trample and damage organisms, often without realising it. People may pick up interesting shells, or beautiful pieces of coral, to take home as souvenirs to remind them of their holidays. These cheap souvenirs are called trinkets and local businesses sell trinkets to tourists (Figure 6.7). This trade in marine organisms has a serious impact on coral reefs, Because of this, it is often illegal to remove coral.

Turtles, which lay their eggs in nests on beaches, are affected by beach obstacles such as deckchairs, and tourists can disturb their nests. The light and noise pollution from hotels and restaurants cause the turtles to lose direction when on the beaches. Light and noise pollution stop seals, sea otters and seabirds from living on built-up shores.

Figure 6.7: Trinket shop selling shells in Tamil Nadu, India.

Litter and waste plastic, dropped by careless people, can entangle organisms in the sea and on beaches.

Tourist boats and diving: many people want to go out on boat trips. However, large numbers of motorised boats cause oil pollution, and mammals such as manatees are damaged by collisions. All boats can physically damage shallow corals and seagrass beds, seriously affecting food webs. Diving around coral reefs and sunken wrecks is a very popular activity. Although most divers want to enjoy the natural world, they can harm marine habitats if they are not careful. Divers should avoid breeding sites and nursery sites and delicate coral should not be touched. Recreational fishing is a popular activity (Figure 6.8). However, fishers should not catch too many fish and must not discard gear that can kill turtles and dolphins.

Figure 6.8: Recreational fishers catching a marlin.

Infrastructure development

If an area of coast is developed as a resort, a port or a fishing industry, it attracts a greater number of visitors. This means that the infrastructure needs to be upgraded. The infrastructure of an area includes the basic facilities, services and installations needed for it to function. Figure 6.9 shows an aerial view of an island in the Maldives. A harbour has been developed, along with hotels, roads, shops, cafes and schools.

Some examples of infrastructure are listed here.

- Transport: new roads, airports and shipping routes need to be developed. This increases air pollution and leads to more habitat loss.

- Freshwater and electricity: there is a need for more freshwater and electricity. Many areas of the world already have a shortage of water. Resorts can come into conflict with local people and farms that need water for crops. Desalination plants are sometimes developed to produce freshwater from seawater. However, desalination plants can create environmental problems.

- Sewers and waste disposal: waste water, sewage and litter all increase when lots of people visit an area. Effective disposal methods need to be developed to prevent pollution of habitats and the ocean.

- Food: more food needs to be brought into the area when a population grows. More farmland is needed around the area, which puts pressure on natural habitats. Fishing also increases, putting fish populations at risk.

- Accommodation and services: when an area develops, more people will come to live there. More people means more accommodation, medical care, shops and schools.

Resource removal

Coastal areas are often sources of raw materials for the construction industry. There is a massive global demand for sand to make cement and concrete.

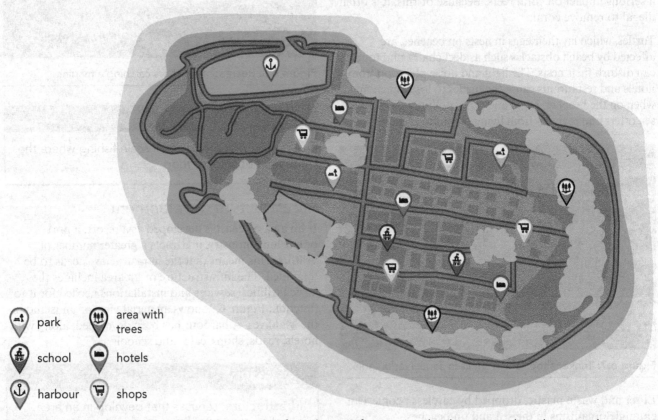

park		area with trees
school		hotels
harbour		shops

Figure 6.9: View of an island in the Maldives as seen from the air. Infrastructure development such as shops, roads, a harbour and other services are shown.

Sand is removed from beaches or the seabed by **dredging** (Figure 6.10). The removal of beach sand can lead to serious coastal erosion. Dredging sand from the seabed is also very destructive, causing habitat loss, damage to nursery sites and destruction of coral reefs. It also causes the water to become cloudy because sediment is stirred up. The cloudiness reduces light penetration and can block the gills of animals.

> **KEY WORD**
>
> **dredging:** the removal of sediment from the seabed, estuaries and shores

Figure 6.10: Sand being dredged from a sedimentary shore in China.

People sometimes remove mud from estuaries for use as a building material, often to make bricks. Estuaries are valuable ecological areas with many species that live in the mud or depend on it. The loss of mud affects tidal currents and leads to more soil erosion. It also damages seagrass beds because they are covered by sediment stirred up when mud is removed. Seagrass beds are important nursery sites for many marine animal species.

Wood is an important resource in the construction industry and wood from mangrove forests has traditionally been harvested for hundreds of years. In recent years, however, the global demand for wood has led to industrial logging of the mangroves and mass deforestation.

Blast fishing

Blast fishing is an extremely damaging method of fishing. Dynamite or home-made explosives are thrown into the water to cause an underwater explosion. This explosion causes the swim bladders of fish to burst so the fish lose buoyancy. Some fish float to the surface and are collected, but most sink to the seabed to decompose. Blast fishing kills all species close to the blast and destroys coral reefs, reducing them to rubble (Figure 6.11).

Figure 6.11: Coral reef that has been destroyed by blast fishing.

> **KEY WORD**
>
> **blast fishing:** the use of explosives to stun and kill fish; it is very destructive to coral reefs

It can take over 10 years for a coral reef to recover from one explosion and, when multiple explosions occur, the reefs may never recover. Many parts of the world have placed total bans on blast fishing, but the practice still occurs. Governments in Tanzania, the Philippines and Indonesia are working hard to stop blast fishing by educating local people, patrolling areas and even developing underwater sensors to identify when explosions occur. Scientists have estimated that blast fishing is the main cause of coral reef loss in the Indian Ocean and the Pacific Ocean.

Shrimp farms

There is a huge global demand for shrimp, encouraging many countries to develop shrimp **aquaculture**.

> **KEY WORD**
>
> **aquaculture:** the production of marine species by artificial methods in cages or tanks

By 2019, the global production of farmed shrimp was over five million tonnes. About three-quarters of these shrimp are grown in Asia, with the remaining quarter being grown in South and Central America. Shrimp farms need large, shallow pools called raceway pools (Figure 6.12). Raceway pools should be close to the sea.

Unfortunately, mangrove forests are ideal places for locating shrimp farms. This has led to massive deforestation of mangroves. It is estimated that 10% of all mangrove forest loss is due to shrimp farming. Shrimp farming can also pollute natural water (areas of sea, river and estuaries near to the shrimp farms) due to the outflow of wastes and chemicals. Diseases may spread from the farms into the natural populations. Conflict can arise between shrimp farmers and local people who have traditionally lived in areas where intensive shrimp farming now occurs.

Figure 6.12: Shrimp farms in Bangladesh.

Oil spills

There is a massive global demand for energy in the twenty-first century. Much of this energy comes from fossil fuels, such as oil, gas and coal. Some oil fields are located under land, but many are under the oceans. Oil platforms were developed to access the oil from deep under the oceans, often in areas with very harsh environmental conditions. Oil is transported around the world through pipelines and on oil tankers. Transportation and drilling for oil beneath the ocean brings a risk of oil leaking into the oceans. There have been many oil spills from ships and broken pipelines over the past 100 years. The *Deepwater Horizon* spill in the Gulf of Mexico in 2010 released over 600 000 tonnes of oil into the ocean.

Oil spills cause a lot of damage to ecosystems, including:

- death of birds and mammals (such as sea otters) due to feathers and fur becoming covered with oil

- death of fish and mammals due to suffocation

- poisoning of organisms due to toxins in the oil

- destruction of coastal areas

- loss of producer organisms due to lack of light in the water.

We will look at ways of reducing and removing oil spills in Section 6.5.

Endangered species, extinctions and sustainable resources

A sustainable resource is a natural resource that we can use that will still be available for future generations. To make sure that natural resources are not lost, we need to manage them carefully. Populations of many species in our oceans are in decline. Reasons for this include: overfishing, pollution, habitat loss and climate change. If marine species continue to decline, there will eventually be none left. When there are no members of a species left, it is said to be an extinct species. Extinctions are often natural events.

The International Union for the Conservation of Nature (IUCN) is a global organisation that monitors the populations of species and the states of habitats. It publishes a list of threatened species called the Red List (the list of threatened species produced by the IUCN). Scientists put species into the following groups depending on how healthy their populations are:

- least concern (LC) – there is no immediate risk to the species
- near threatened (NR) – species that could easily become threatened
- vulnerable (V) – species that could become at risk of extinction
- endangered species (EN) – species that are at a high risk of extinction in the wild
- critically endangered (CR) – species that are at an extremely high risk of extinction in the wild
- extinct in the wild (EW) – species that only survive in captivity, such as in aquaria or zoos
- extinct (EX) – species where no known individuals exist
- data deficient (DD) – species which have not been assessed or there is insufficient information.

Figure 6.13 shows the global catches of sharks and rays from 1950 to 2010. It is obvious that the catches of sharks and rays have increased, although there is a slight decrease in catches of rays from 2000 due to restrictions on catches. This increase in catch is typical of many commercially caught marine species and has led to decreases in populations.

Table 6.1 shows the number of shark and ray species in different habitats and their IUCN classifications in 2015. Out of 1030 species assessed, 308 are at some risk of extinction. To prevent the extinction of sharks and rays, the IUCN has a plan to stop the decline of shark and ray populations and maintain all shark and ray species by 2025. The plan has the following aims:

- save all shark and ray species
- manage shark and ray fisheries for sustainability
- ensure responsible trade in shark and ray products
- encourage responsible consumption of shark and ray products.

KEY WORDS

conservation: preventing extinction and restoring the numbers of endangered species; the protection and restoring of habitats

endangered species: species that are at risk of dying out in the wild

restrictions: limits placed on fishing intensity; they can be placed on fishing gear, times of fishing, seasons, species or mass of catch

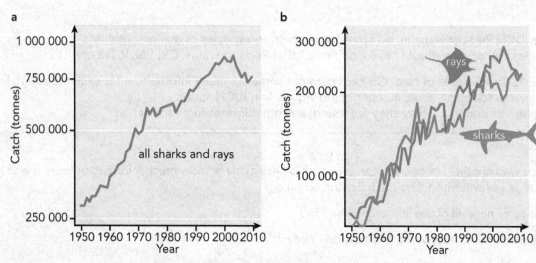

Figure 6.13: Annual catches of sharks and rays between 1950 and 2010: **a** Catch of sharks and rays; **b** Catches of sharks and rays shown separately.

Habitat type	IUCN Status					
	CR	EN	V	NR	LC	DD
coastal	16	28	83	75	104	188
pelagic	1	3	15	12	5	4
deep water	0	7	17	39	143	258
freshwater	3	7	1	1	2	18
Total	20	45	116	127	254	468

Table 6.1: IUCN status of sharks and rays.

The overall aim is to ensure that the populations of all sharks and rays are healthy, and that sustainable fishing can occur. A sustainable activity is an activity that can be continued at a rate that does not damage the environment and that does not put the resource at risk. Sustainable fishing is a desirable aim as it balances the need for employment within communities with the health of shark populations. If shark populations are at risk of extinction, the ecological food webs of the ocean will become damaged. If fishing for sharks is not controlled, there will be no fishing jobs left for future generations. In the long term, a sustainable approach to marine resources benefits both the environment and human populations.

KEY WORDS

sustainable resources: natural resources that we use in a way that ensures that they are replenished so that they will still be available in the future. For example, sustainable fishing is the harvesting of fish so that populations are not reduced in the long term and future generations will still be able to harvest fish.

Questions

1 a List three ways that humans benefit from marine ecosystems.
  b List three ways that humans negatively impact on marine ecosystems.
2 State what is meant by the term 'infrastructure', and explain what infrastructure will develop as a coastal community grows.
3 Look at Figure 6.13 and Table 6.1. Describe the changes in landings of sharks and rays between 1950 and 2010. Suggest reasons for these changes.

ACTIVITY 6.2

Conservation cards

Using the IUCN Red List website, do some research on five species of marine organism. Each species you choose should have a different IUCN Red List status: CR, EN, V, NR and LC.

Make five A5-sized pieces of card. On each card put some summary information for each organism. Include: common name, scientific name, number of individuals left, IUCN status, a photograph or drawing, where they are found, any other interesting information.

Peer assessment

Swap cards with another learner. You can rate each other's cards on how much information there is and how well the cards are presented. Use the following scheme:

☺ if the cards have all of the information needed

😐 if the cards have most of the information needed

☹ if the cards have little information.

6.2 Tourism

Tourism is now a main source of income for many nations, such as the Maldives, that have beautiful tropical coastlines (Figure 6.14).

Figure 6.14: A coastal resort in the Maldives.

Socioeconomic benefits of tourism

Socioeconomic effects are impacts on the living standards of human populations and the generation of money. In reality, the economy of an area is closely linked to social factors such as housing, health care and education. Tourism can increase employment, wealth and improve the living standards of local people. In 2019, over 1 600 000 tourists arrived in the Maldives (Figure 6.15). Tourism now accounts for 80% of the Maldivian economy. Over 80 000 people are employed in the tourist industry and four out of every ten jobs are involved with tourism. Economically, each visitor brings in over US$2000 to the Maldivian economy. Many other nations around the world

have also seen an increase in tourism and their economies may depend on tourism to earn foreign revenue. Because of the international response to the COVID-19 pandemic, there was a large fall in the number of international flights in 2020 and 2021. The economies of countries that rely on tourism have been very badly affected and many people have lost jobs and income.

Tourism brings the benefits of income and employment for local people, and it also improves infrastructure for the local area. Transport links need improving so better roads, ports and airlinks develop. Figure 6.16 shows the port of Caldera in Puntarenas, Costa Rica, an area that has developed as Costa Rica has increased its tourism industry.

Figure 6.16: The port of Caldera, Costa Rica, that has developed as tourism has increased.

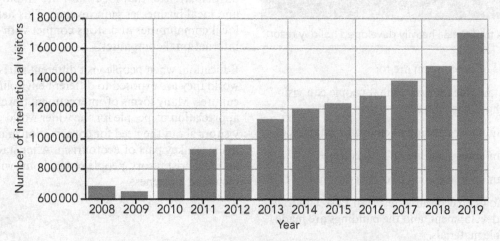

Figure 6.15: Growth of number of international tourists in the Maldives between 2008 and 2019.

As more people move into areas to work in the tourist industries, there is an increased need for housing, shops, schools and medical facilities. More training and education are often made available to provide a labour force for the tourist industry. Other businesses, such as food retailers and shops that sell goods to visitors, build up around tourist resorts. Diving schools, sailing businesses and recreational fishing businesses that cater for tourists also develop. With many more people living in an area, there is increased need for sewage treatment and freshwater.

Ecotourism

Figure 6.17 shows a beach in a traditional resort that grew up during the 20th century. The beach is very crowded, and the area around it has been heavily developed. While it is a great place for people to relax on their vacations, it was not originally developed with a view of working in harmony with the natural world. Over the late 20th century and early 21st century, resorts that do less damage to the natural world have been developed.

Figure 6.17: A traditional, heavily developed holiday resort.

The main aims of ecotourism are to:

- allow sustainable tourism so that people can visit areas without harming ecosystems
- develop an understanding of environmental issues
- develop an understanding of local cultures
- develop an understanding of conservation.

Figure 6.18 shows an ecotourist resort in East Timor. There is little development, and the buildings are made from sustainable materials.

Figure 6.18: An ecotourist resort in East Timor.

The impacts of tourism on marine areas

Traditional tourism and ecotourism can have positive and negative impacts on areas. Although ecotourism aims to prevent damage to the natural world, there can still be some negative impacts. A well-designed ecotourist resort, however, will be able to offset the negative impacts with positive ones.

Positive impacts

All forms of tourism can bring benefits to local areas.

Economic benefits: tourism brings foreign revenue into resort areas. In some resorts, however, hotels are often owned by international companies, and little of the money passes to the local community. Ecotourist resorts ensure that there is wide local participation so that local staff are employed, and local businesses gain revenue. This helps local communities and stops conflict with large international companies.

Education: when people visit different parts of the world they are exposed to different environments and cultures. Many forms of international travel increase the appreciation of people for the wider world. Educating visitors about the need for conservation and sustainable living is a key part of ecotourism. After staying in an ecotourist resort, people return home with an increased awareness.

Development of Marine Protected Areas (MPAs): these are areas where fishing and development is strictly regulated (Figure 6.19). Some areas have a no-take policy so that no fishing is allowed, but others allow limited catching of fish and development. Some MPAs allow tourist visits and diving trips to see conservation projects. The money raised from tourism is used to help fund the projects.

Providing funding for conservation organisations: ecotourism resorts often help to fund conservation organisations and form partnerships with them. The IUCN helps ecotourist businesses and conservation organisations to work together for the benefit of local people. Many resorts help to fund local projects, both directly with money raised from tourism and by encouraging guests to donate money.

> ### KEY WORD
>
> no-take policy*: a total ban on the harvesting of species in an area

Negative impacts

All forms of tourism can have negative impacts on marine environments. Ecotourism aims to offset the

negative impacts by minimising them and providing benefits to ecosystems and local people.

Competition for land and resources: developing a new resort can cause conflict, both with the environment and with the local communities. Hotels, restaurants and infrastructure all require land, and this may cause habitat loss. Mangrove forests are cleared and marshlands drained to make room for hotels. Ecotourist resorts try to minimise the loss of habitats and are not built in ecologically sensitive areas. Building materials, such as wood, do still need to be found and this can lead to deforestation. Ecotourist resorts try to reuse materials and only use renewable resources such as bamboo.

Developing a tourist resort increases the demand for freshwater and food. This can lead to the removal of lakes and rivers, and the loss of land for additional farming.

Existing industries may come into conflict with new tourist ventures. Fishing fleets can lose harbour areas and land may become too expensive for local people. Ecotourism can also threaten local businesses; for example, the development of a Marine Protected Area could lead to a ban on fishing. Resort development needs to be done so that it does not negatively impact on local people.

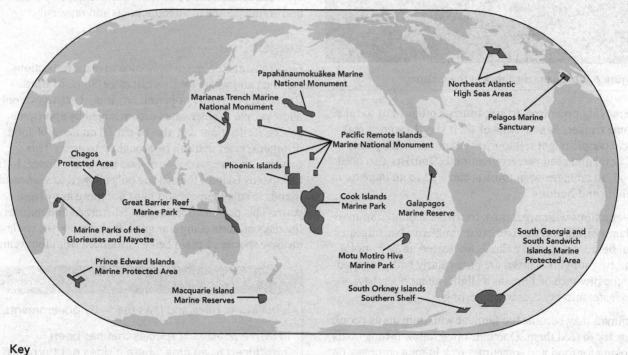

Key

■ Marine Protected Areas

Figure 6.19: Marine Protected Areas (MPAs) around the world.

Pollution: bringing large numbers of visitors into any area will increase the amount of waste produced. Sewage needs disposing of carefully as it will pollute natural waters if released without treatment. Litter and waste also need careful disposal, so they do not affect living organisms in the environment. Ecotourist resorts use methods to prevent pollution of water and encourage recycling of wastes such as plastic, paper and leftover food.

Damage to sensitive ecosystems: building any form of resort will affect natural ecosystems. Many ecotourists want to see rare species and so care needs to be taken to avoid harm to these ecosystems. The Galapagos Islands, off the coast of Ecuador, are a good example of a sensitive ecosystem that needs additional protection. These islands have very unusual species of animals and plants that could be affected by visitors introducing other species (Figure 6.20).

Figure 6.20: Iguana on a rock in the Galapagos Islands.

Removing organisms to sell: tourists often want to take home trinkets as souvenirs of their stay. In some areas, local people might sell tourists beautiful shells, pieces of coral and even preserved animals. Tourists also need food, so an increase in tourists can lead to an increase in fishing and hunting.

Interactions with organisms: tourists encounter animals when visiting and this can cause problems. Nesting sites can be trampled, and animals are scared away by noise and bright lights. Turtles are particularly badly affected by the presence of humans as lights affect how they navigate onto beaches when nesting.

Animals may become too familiar with humans as people may try to feed them. Dolphins often follow fishing boats looking for food and sometimes seek human company out of interest. Most interactions with dolphins are harmless but dolphins can act aggressively towards swimmers. If people feed and visit animals regularly, the animals learn

to keep returning to the same areas and change their natural behaviours. With some species it is important to stay well hidden if visiting an area to watch them.

Reducing the impact of tourism

The idea of ecotourism is to make sure there is no damage to the environment and that the positive impacts outweigh the negative ones. Table 6.2 summarises some of the measures that can be taken to reduce damage to the environment from tourism. Some of these actions are discussed here.

Education

Ecotourism raises awareness of conservation issues for guests and local communities. Often guests are given guidelines about how to behave around nature reserves and how to prevent harm to species. Many ecotourism resorts now have lectures from visiting scientists and students to inform guests about environmental issues, both locally and globally. Information packs are provided to guests to explain how to minimise waste, encourage recycling and reduce the energy they use.

Ecotourism companies can provide benefits for local people. Training in conservation methods is often provided for local communities and many resorts sponsor children and young people to attend schools and university.

Legislation

Governments can make legislation to place restrictions on when and where tourists can enter. Some Marine Protected Areas do not permit any tourist activity or only allow people to enter when accompanied by approved guides. Restrictions can also be placed on items of food or other species that can be brought into areas. This prevents invasive species or disease being introduced. In the Galapagos Islands, tourists are only allowed to visit certain islands in small groups and must not move away from paths. This prevents species being disturbed and reduces the risks of nests being trampled. It also stops the seeds of invasive species of plant being introduced from footwear.

KEY WORDS

legislation: rules and laws made by governments

invasive species: a species that has been introduced to an area where it does not normally live and is damaging the species that are normally found there

Method	Benefits	Problems
education	raises awareness of environmental issues reduces damage to environment because people understand what actions to take when visiting	relies on people cooperating and following guidelines
legislation	means that strong regulations are put in place and enforced	expensive to monitor that legislation is being followed may encourage people to break rules
planning	means that experts are brought in to design areas so that there is minimal environmental damage	costs are high
use of renewable energy and resources	reduces release of carbon dioxide and other pollutants reduced effect on the planet's climate using bamboo and other renewables for construction means fewer other resources are used	expensive to install renewable energy may not produce enough electricity at all times of year growing bamboo reduces available farmland so food prices rise
banning single-use plastics	reduces the amount of plastic entering oceans so fewer animals are damaged	expensive to install recycling facilities storage containers made from glass and metal are heavy
limiting motorised transport	reduces fossil fuel use reduces pollution	inconvenient for transport of goods and people

Table 6.2: Summary of methods that can be used to limit the impacts of tourists.

Planning

When a new resort is being developed, scientific studies of the local area need to be made. The state of ecosystems and possible impacts of development on any species should be assessed. A strategic plan is made which identifies the short, medium and long term goals of the project. Strategic plans give a clear focus of the aims and how they will be achieved and bring together information from many different experts such as environmentalists, business leaders and scientists.

The resort should be planned to ensure that:

* it will be sustainable
* it will not harm living species
* it will not pollute the area.

Use of renewable energy and resources

Humans have depended on the use of fossil fuels for energy for many years. This overreliance could be the cause of global warming, which we will cover in Section 6.8. To be a sustainable resort, hotels in the resort should reduce their use of energy from fossil fuels, and instead use renewable sources of energy. Solar panels, biofuels and wind turbines are often used to produce electricity. Figure 6.21 shows a hotel in Tamil Nadu, India, that is using solar power to generate electricity.

KEY WORDS

renewable sources: energy and materials that will not run out

solar panels*: devices that use solar energy to generate electricity

biofuel*: fuel that comes from crops which are grown as a source of fuel; examples include wood and alcohol

wind turbines: devices that use the energy of wind to generate electricity

Unfortunately, it is not easy to use renewable energy in all parts of the world. During winter in high or low latitude areas there is not enough sunlight to generate much electricity from solar panels. Biofuels, such as alcohol, are often produced from crops; this means that farmland is used for growing biofuels rather than food and can lead to an increase in food prices. Wind turbines only generate large amounts of electricity when it is windy and are damaged if it is too windy. Renewable energy resources are also expensive to install so government investment is often needed.

Building materials in resorts should be made from local materials. Wood can be taken from trees grown in special plantations and bamboo is a popular, rapid growing source of building material. The only problem with using bamboo is that farmland is converted into land used for growing bamboo, leading to an increase in food prices. The reuse of old building materials from demolished buildings is also encouraged.

Figure 6.21: An ecotourist lodge that is using renewable sources of energy to generate electricity.

Limiting water use

All resorts have a high demand for freshwater. If water is removed from lakes and rivers this can lead to severe water shortages in natural habitats. Ecotourist resorts minimise water wastage by encouraging guests to use showers rather than baths. Composting toilets that do not require water are often used, and rainwater is collected and stored in containers for when it is needed. Waste water is collected, cleaned and reused for other functions such as cleaning and watering plants (Figure 6.22). However, waste-water purification systems can be expensive to install.

Figure 6.22: Using waste water to water plants.

Educating people to minimise water use helps to ensure that everyone works together for the benefit of the environment.

Banning single-use plastic

Plastic bags and bottles are major pollutants in our oceans. Large pieces of plastic can trap turtles and dolphins underwater, causing them to suffocate. Smaller pieces are often mistaken for food, causing organisms to choke or blocking their intestines. In 2018, a dead pilot whale that washed up on a beach was found to have eaten 80 plastic bags. Many countries have now banned the use of single-use plastics to reduce littering and pollution. Education campaigns, such as the tunnel of polythene bags in Santiago, Chile, highlight plastic pollution in the oceans (Figure 6.23).

KEY WORD

single-use plastics: items made from plastic that are thrown away after using

Figure 6.23: Sculpture in Chile to raise awareness of plastic pollution.

Figure 6.24: The Bosca del Cabo Ecotourist Lodge.

There are a few problems when trying to reduce plastic usage. Alternative containers, made from glass and metal, could be used but these are very heavy when transporting water. Also, it can be difficult to enforce bans on single-use plastics in some shops.

Limiting motorised transport

Most cars, lorries and boats still use fossil fuels, contributing to global warming. Ecotourist resorts minimise the use of motorised vehicles by using car-sharing schemes and taking tours by bicycle or sailboats. Electrically powered vehicles are also increasingly popular. The carbon dioxide released by using aeroplanes to bring in visitors may be offset by planting fast growing plants (such as bamboo) that absorb carbon dioxide by photosynthesis.

However, car-sharing schemes can inconvenience people when travelling to the resorts and the costs of buying electric vehicles are often high. In addition, some motorised vehicles powered by fossil fuels are still needed for transporting large, heavy equipment.

An example of ecotourism

Figure 6.24 shows the Bosca del Cabo rainforest lodge, an ecotourist resort in Costa Rica.

This resort is a very good example of how ecotourism works with nature and the local community to enable sustainable tourism. Key features of ecotourism include the following.

- Support for conservation projects: the lodge supports the Osa Sea Turtle Conservation project, donating money towards beach patrols and conservation efforts. There are educational programmes and training schemes for local people and tourists, together with talks from marine biologists and students who work on the project.

- Minimising impact on the environment: building materials are reused when possible and local renewables, such as bamboo, are used for construction. The lodge filters waste water so that it does not pollute the natural water. **Biodegradable** soaps and cleaning products are used. Reusable bags are used for transporting goods. Paper, glass, metal, plastic and card are all recycled to reduce litter. The lodge donates food waste to farmers for feeding to animals, or uses food waste to make compost.

- Energy conservation: solar systems generate electricity and groups of guests are transported in vehicles to reduce the number of journeys made. The lodge uses low-energy light bulbs and guests are encouraged to minimise electricity use. The lodge engages in reforestation programmes to help capture carbon dioxide.

KEY WORD

biodegradable*: substances that are broken down naturally by bacteria and fungi

- Engagement with the local community: by using local food ingredients, money passes to all members of the community. Locally produced souvenirs and crafts are sold at the lodge and most staff are from the local area.

- Education: visitors can attend lectures about conservation projects and sustainability, and learn about the local culture. Staff are trained about conservation issues and local children are sponsored so they can attend a nearby school. Guests are encouraged to help with conservation projects and raise awareness with other people.

Ecotourism is a sustainable way that local communities can earn money to raise their standards of living without damaging the natural world. It also provides a way for people to visit areas of natural beauty and interest, and by doing so ensure that such areas are maintained.

Questions

4   State what is meant by 'ecotourism'.

5   Give three negative impacts of tourism on marine ecosystems.

6   Give advantages and disadvantages of the following strategies on reducing the impact of tourism:

   a   education

   b   limiting water use

   c   using renewable energy.

The impact of tourism in the Galapagos Islands

The Galapagos Islands are a group of volcanic islands in the Pacific Ocean that are part of the Republic of Ecuador. There are a total of 21 islands, all located 906 km off the coast of Ecuador, as shown in Figure 6.25.

Only four of the islands are inhabited by humans. The islands all contain many species that only live in the Galapagos. Charles Darwin visited the islands in 1835 while on his voyage around the world. In 1959, the Galapagos Islands were classed as a **national park** and tourism started to be developed on the inhabited islands. The ocean area surrounding the islands is now a protected marine reserve and a whale sanctuary. The United Nations recognises the areas as a **World Heritage Site** and a **biosphere reserve**.

> ### KEY WORDS
>
> **national park***: area of scientific interest where there are restrictions on development
>
> **World Heritage Site***: area of the world that is classed by UNESCO (The United Nations Educational, Scientific and Cultural Organization) as being of particular scientific or cultural interest
>
> **biosphere reserve**: an area that has been protected by UNESCO for the conservation of living organisms

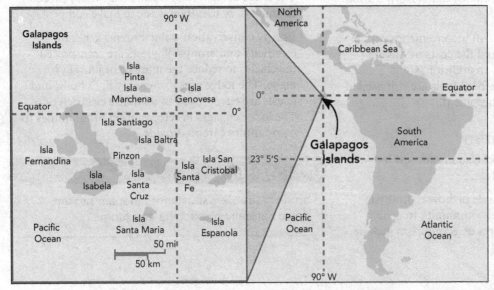

Figure 6.25: a Map showing location of the Galapagos Islands; **b** One of the Galapagos Islands.

There are several threats to life on the Galapagos Islands due to a rapidly growing human population and tourism. These threats include the following:

- Invasive species: an invasive species is a species that has been introduced to an area and is threatening the native species. When boats transport goods and people to islands they can accidentally carry other organisms that then escape into the islands' environment. Invasive predator species that have no predators of their own can rapidly reproduce and destroy native species. Rats, dogs, cats, ants and sheep are species that have been accidentally introduced to some of the islands. Dogs and cats kill birds and damage the nests of turtles. Rats attack baby tortoises and turtles, and have caused native species of rats to become extinct on some islands. Over 700 known species of plant have been accidentally carried to the islands and are at risk of outcompeting native species of plants on which native animals depend.

- Illegal fishing: local and foreign fishing boats have illegally targeted fish in the rich waters of the Galapagos. Sharks and sea cucumbers have been particularly badly affected.

- El Niño events: in 1997–1998, an El Niño event caused a warming of the waters leading to the death of many species of coral.

- Pollution: waste from increased hotel and resort development may pass into the seawater. Oil and chemicals can leak from visiting cruise ships.

Tourism provides a major source of income for the Galapagos Islands and over 150 000 people visit every year. Most visitors want to see the unique wildlife and to learn about the islands. Bird watching, horse riding and diving are all popular activities for tourists. As the number of tourists increases, more hotels have been built. Many workers have migrated from mainland Ecuador to work in the tourist industry. Because there is a shortage of farmland on the islands, more food has to be transported in.

The Galapagos National Park has introduced strategies to reduce the negative impacts of tourism. These include:

- Restrictions on development and travel: only four of the islands are developed and inhabited by humans. Resort development is only allowed in certain areas. Some islands can only be visited by scientific research teams or government officials.

- Restrictions on visitor numbers: on some islands, only a set number of people may visit the island at any one time. If damage occurs to an island, the visitor numbers are reduced.

- Management of boat routes and boat licensing: tour routes for cruise ships and local boats are set by the National Park. This prevents too many boats arriving at an island at any one time. Tour operators and fishing boats must apply for licences if they enter the National Park area.

- Entrance fees: all visitors must pay an entrance fee to the National Park. This money is used to fund conservation projects in the area.

- Education: the Charles Darwin Research Centre and the Galapagos Island National Park Interpretation Centre both educate visitors about the islands' natural history.

KEY WORDS

native species: species that are naturally found in an area

licences: permits for fishing issued by governments; they can be used to restrict the number or type of boats in an area

ACTIVITY 6.3

The Great Barrier Reef

The Great Barrier Reef, located off the Queensland coast of Australia, is an area of natural beauty visited by many tourists. Produce a poster to explain the impacts of tourism on the Great Barrier Reef and how these impacts are managed.

Peer assessment

Ask other learners to look at your poster. Ask them to rate the information it contains according to the following scheme for each of the points listed:

☺ if it is well organised and has all of the information needed

😐 if it is reasonably well organised and has most of the information

☹ if it lacks organisation and has a lot of information missing.

CONTINUED

My poster:

- describes the location of the Great Barrier Reef

- explains why there are many different species present on the Great Barrier Reef

- explains why tourists want to visit the Reef

- explains how tourism affects the Reef

- lists and explains some of the ways that threats to the Great Barrier Reef are reduced.

6.3 Fisheries

Humans have harvested fish and other seafoods from the oceans for a very long time and human communities have developed in many coastal regions. In this section we will look at the importance of the fishing industry, methods of fishing and the threat of overfishing.

The importance of marine organisms to humans

A trip to a fish market is essential for anyone who wants to be a marine scientist. It is always exciting to see the range of species on sale, as shown in Figure 6.26.

Seafood: a healthy, important food for humans

Fish and seafood products provide essential nutrients for humans. Tuna, for example, contains:

- protein, for growth and repair

- essential fatty acids, for a healthy nervous system

- vitamin A, for healthy eyes

- many B group vitamins, for respiration in cells

- minerals, such as calcium and iron, for healthy bones and blood.

KEY WORD

essential fatty acids*: fats that are essential in our diet

Figure 6.26: A fish market in Kolkata, India.

As human populations grow, the number of people employed in the fishing industry has also grown. Figure 6.27 shows a graph of seafood production from fishing and aquaculture. You can see that the overall demand for seafood products increases as the population increases. It is also obvious that, since the 1990s, aquaculture has increasingly been used to produce our seafood.

Fishing and economics

The fishing industry has expanded over the last hundred years to meet the demand for seafood. For many nations, fishing is a major part of their economy. Fishing ports have grown up in many coastal regions (Figure 6.28). The economy of these coastal regions depends on the sale of fish. Most large fishing ports began as small communities that gradually increased in size as fishing brought more money into the region.

As transport links and processing methods for seafood have improved, the global **export** of seafood has increased. This means that many nations now gain much of their foreign revenue from the export of seafood products. For some small island nations, the fishing industry is a major employer.

Figure 6.28: A fishing port in Sri Lanka.

In the Maldives, the fishing industry was the main part of the economy until the 1990s when tourism became the main source of revenue. Today, over 20 000 people in the Maldives are still employed in the fishing industry and the export of fish, such as tuna, is still important to the economy.

KEY WORD

export*: selling goods or services overseas

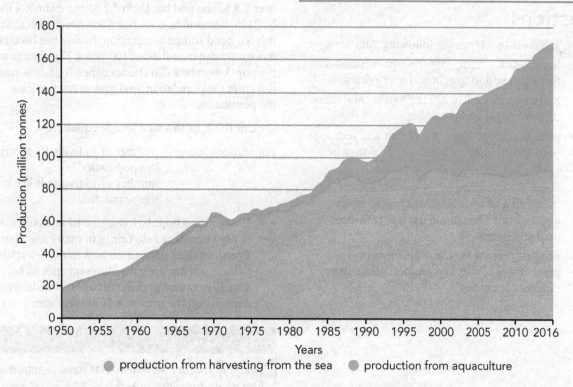

Figure 6.27: Increase in production of marine organisms from harvesting and aquaculture over time.

Country	Mass of fish and seafood caught by fishing fleet (tonnes)	Mass of fish and seafood produced by aquaculture (tonnes)	Total mass (tonnes)
China	17 800 000	63 700 000	81 500 000
India	5 082 332	5 703 002	10 800 000
United States	4 931 017	444 369	5 375 386
Bangladesh	1 674 770	2 203 554	3 878 324
Malaysia	1 584 371	407 887	1 992 258
Nigeria	734 731	306 272	1 041 458
United Kingdom	702 405	194 492	896 897
Sri Lanka	521 637	30 974	552 611
New Zealand	424 791	109 016	533 807
Kenya	171 391	15 360	186 751
Maldives	129 191	0	129 191

Table 6.3: Mass of seafood caught by fishing and produced by aquaculture.

Table 6.3 shows the mass of fish and seafood caught by the fishing fleets of some different nations in 2018. It also shows the mass of fish and seafood produced from aquaculture. You can see from the data that some countries have invested in aquaculture production to meet the demand for fish.

Questions

7   Use Table 6.3 to answer the following questions.

   a   State which country has the highest mass of fish and seafood caught by fishing fleets.

   b   State which country has the lowest total mass of fish caught and produced.

8   Calculate the percentage mass of fish and seafood produced in China by aquaculture, as shown in Table 6.3.

9   a   Rank the countries by the percentages of their fish and seafood that is produced by aquaculture. (You could use a spreadsheet to help you here.)

   b   Suggest reasons for the differences in percentages of fish and seafood produced by different countries.

Sustainable harvesting of marine species

Figure 6.29 shows the growth of the global human population since 1400 until 2020 and the projected increase until 2100. In 2020, the human population was over 7.8 billion and the United Nations estimates that by 2100 there will be over 10 billion people. Because fish is a good source of nutrition, fishing has become more intensive over the last 100 years. The change in the population of a fish species depends on how many fish enter the population, and how many fish leave the population.

We can think of this as a simple equation:

population change = number of individuals entering the population − number of individuals leaving the population

• Entry into a population is due to reproduction. A high breeding rate brings in many new fish. Breeding rates depend on how many **sexually mature fish** are present. Different species become sexually mature at different ages. Breeding also depends on the presence of nursery sites.

> **KEY WORD**
>
> **sexually mature fish:** fish that have reached an age when they can breed

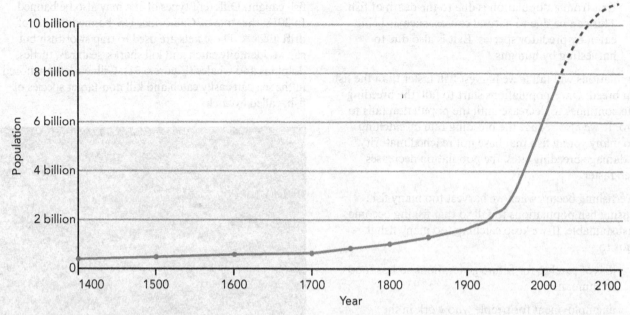

Figure 6.29: Growth of global human population from 1400 and predicted growth up to 2100.

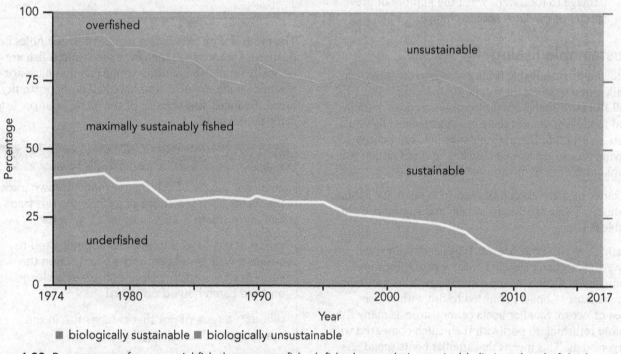

biologically sustainable ■ biologically unsustainable

Figure 6.30: Percentages of commercial fish that are overfished, fished up to their sustainable limit and underfished.

Figure 6.30 shows the changes in the percentages of commercial species of fish between 1974 and 2017. The categories (or groups) are: overfished, fished sustainably, or underfished. Sustainable fishing means that fishing is at the maximum level it can be without affecting the fish populations. Underfishing means that fishing does not affect the fish populations. The graph clearly shows that more and more species are being overfished, or fished at a maximum rate for sustainability.

- Exit from a population is due to the death of fish. This can be due to natural causes, such as being eaten by predator species. Exit is also due to harvesting by humans.

Populations will fall if we harvest fish faster than the fish can breed. Once populations start to fall, the breeding rate continues to decrease until the population falls to zero. If we also reduce the breeding rate by catching too many young fish that have not reached maturity, or damage breeding sites, the population decreases even faster.

Overfishing occurs when we harvest too many fish, causing fish populations to fall so that fishing becomes unsustainable. If we keep catching too many fish it leads to:

- loss of catches for future generations so less food for humans

- unemployment for people who work in the fishing industry

- damage to food webs when the number of prey species or predator species change.

Sustainable fishing

The aim of sustainable fishing is to harvest some fish while not damaging the fish population; this means fish will still be available for future generations of humans and food webs are not damaged. Sustainable fishing also ensures that there is a balance between people having jobs in the fishing industry, and not letting fish populations fall to unsustainable levels.

A range of methods can be used to regulate the fishing industry. These are discussed next and summarised in Table 6.4.

Restrictions on boat size, net types and mesh sizes: governments can place and enforce restrictions on commercial fishing. Many countries have restrictions on the sizes of boats permitted to fish within their area of ocean. Smaller boats cannot store as many fish before returning to port with their catch compared with larger boats. This means that smaller boats spend less time fishing, and fewer fish are caught. Large fishing companies may, however, use several boats at the same time unless restrictions are placed on the number of boats that can fish.

Net restrictions may reduce catches and control the sizes and species of fish caught. Maximum sizes can be set for cast nets and purse seine nets to reduce the numbers of fish caught. Different types of net may also be banned. In 2018, the state of California, US, banned the use of drift gillnets. These nets are used to trap swordfish but can accidentally catch and kill sharks, seabirds, turtles, dolphins and whales (Figure 6.31). Gillnets left anchored in the sea can easily catch and kill non-target species of fish, called bycatch.

Figure 6.31: Thresher shark that has been trapped in a gillnet.

The mesh size on nets is also regulated. If the holes in the mesh are too small then even the smallest fish are trapped. Small fish are often young fish that have not reached sexual maturity and have had no opportunity to breed. By increasing the size of the mesh, younger fish can pass through.

KEY WORDS

cast net: a type of fishing net that is thrown into the water from the shore or a boat; the net traps fish underneath it as it sinks into the water

purse seine nets: a type of fishing net used to create a wall of nets around a shoal; when the shoal is enclosed, the base of the net is closed and the catch hauled on board

gillnet*: a type of net that catches fish in the mesh by the head and gill operculum

bycatch*: the marine species caught that are non-target species

Method	Benefits	Problems
restricting boat sizes, net types, and mesh sizes	reduced catch reduced catch of juveniles reduced bycatch	needs monitoring by officials may encourage illegal fishing
quotas and licences	reduced catch can reduce the number of foreign fishing companies	may encourage dumping of excess catch can be too expensive for small fishing companies
closed seasons	increased reproduction of fish prevents fishing of breeding areas when fish aggregate	can cause conflict with traditional fishers can cause overfishing in periods outside the closed season
Marine Protected Areas (MPAs)	increases fish populations within the MPA fish spill over into other areas, increasing fish populations protects food webs and habitats	can cause conflict with local fishers if traditional fishing grounds are lost can cause overfishing in areas around the MPA can encourage illegal fishing in the MPA
international agreements	protects species that live in waters of many nations protects fish that live in open ocean areas	agreements are voluntary so not all nations sign difficult to monitor in areas not owned by any nation

Table 6.4: Summary of methods used to keep fishing sustainable.

Net restrictions do help to make fishing more sustainable by reducing the sizes of catch, targeting large fish, and reducing bycatch of non-target species. It can be difficult, however, to enforce restrictions on nets. Random fishing gear inspections must be carried out by government officials.

Quotas and licences: the setting of fishing quotas is a common method of preventing overfishing. Governments assess the state of fish populations and then decide how many fish can be harvested. Boat owners must purchase a licence from the government to take a set quota. Quotas help prevent overfishing but can be difficult to apply. There should be regular inspections of fishing boats to check that boats are not taking too many fish. Boat owners also need to keep a record of all their catches in logbooks. Many governments issue licences and permits to fish. Some governments ensure that some licences are reserved for small, local companies so that each company gets one licence. This stops large, wealthy companies buying up several licences.

Unfortunately, fishers often throw excess catch back into the ocean if they have exceeded quotas, resulting in a waste of fish. If licences need to be purchased to allow fishing, this favours bigger businesses rather than poorer fishers who perhaps cannot afford them. Using quotas and licences needs strict enforcement by authorities, both in dock areas and at sea.

Closed seasons: many fish, such as tuna, aggregate together at certain times of year to breed. During these periods, the fish can easily be caught as fishers know where to find them. Having closed seasons that prevent fishing during breeding seasons stops fishers deliberately targeting breeding grounds. It also makes sure that the fish have undergone a full breeding season before being harvested.

KEY WORDS

fishing quota: the maximum mass or number of a species that is allowed to be harvested

aggregate: the grouping together of organisms or objects

closed seasons: bans placed on fishing at certain times of year, usually the breeding seasons

In India, there is a ban on deep-water fishing with mechanised boats for 61 days during the monsoon period. But small, local boats that use traditional methods are still allowed to take small amounts of fish. The monsoon period coincides with the breeding seasons of most commercial fish. This ban has led to conflict between the government and the fishers in the state of Kerala where over one million people work in the fishing industry.

Like other restrictions, enforcing bans on fishing during certain times of year requires monitoring by government officials, which can be expensive. It may also cause fishers to overfish in the periods just before and just after the closed season.

Marine Protected Areas (MPAs): Figure 6.18 in Section 6.2 shows some of the MPAs around the world. MPAs are areas of ocean where species can live undisturbed. Marine organisms breed within them. Populations of marine organisms within the MPAs increase over time. Because the marine organisms can move to surrounding areas of ocean, marine areas outside the MPAs also benefit.

Figure 6.32 shows a shore on Ascension Island, an isolated island in the South Atlantic. The Ascension Island Marine Protected Zone was established in 2019. It is a 445 000 km² area of ocean and coastal areas that is home to a wide range of species. Some of these species are endangered. Within the area, certain activities are prohibited:

- Large-scale commercial fishing is banned in all areas of the MPA.

- All fishing is banned in all areas further than 12 km from the shore.

- Mineral extraction and sand removal is banned.

Figure 6.32: Ascension Island, the location of a large MPA.

Some activities are restricted:

- New coastline developments, such as the laying of cables, may be allowed if they have minimal impact.

- The release of waste from desalination plants and waste water treatment plants is permitted if there is minimal impact.

Some activities are permitted:

- Small local fishing operations, recreational fishing and sport fishing are allowed within the area at distances less than 12 km from the shore.

- Transit of supply ships to the island is permitted through the MPA; other ships may pass through, although fishing boats must remove all gear from the decks.

- Recreational activities such as diving and tourism are permitted under licence if there is minimal impact.

- Scientific research is permitted in the MPA if a licence is obtained.

MPAs can cause conflict with local people if they lose traditional fishing waters. MPAs also require constant monitoring by patrol boats and satellite tracking systems. Fishers often trawl close to the borders of MPAs where the fish have spilled over. Some fishers turn off satellite tracking systems to illegally enter the MPAs.

International agreements. most marine species that are caught commercially do not stay in one place. Fish do not respect national borders and move through waters that belong to many different nations. Many species are migratory, moving between different ocean areas of the world. This makes it difficult to have effective fishing regulations unless all nations work together. For example, when the breeding season approaches, all Atlantic bluefin tuna migrate to one of two areas – one is in the Western Mediterranean Sea and the other is in the Gulf of Mexico. To conserve the bluefin tuna, all countries that own waters around the breeding areas need to work together.

> ## KEY WORDS
>
> **satellite tracking systems:** the use of satellites to monitor the movement and positions of boats
>
> **international agreements:** agreements made between several countries on issues such as fish quotas

All countries with coastal waters have an **exclusive economic zone (EEZ)** that is the area of sea or ocean that extends 200 nautical miles from the coast. Beyond 200 nautical miles are the 'high seas', which do not belong to any nation state. This lack of ownership in the high seas makes it difficult to bring in regulations on large fishing fleets, which can travel thousands of miles and stay at sea for months.

- In 1966, the Convention on Fishing and Conservation of the Living Resources of the High Seas was signed by 39 countries. This international convention is an agreement to use international cooperation to stop overfishing of marine organisms in the high seas.

- The International Convention for the Regulation of Whaling (ICRW) was signed in 1946. It is an international agreement that was set up to prevent overhunting of whales and to bring about sustainable whale populations. By 2021, 88 different nations had signed the convention.

KEY WORD

exclusive economic zone (EEZ*): the area from a coastline up to 200 nautical miles out to sea that is owned and controlled by one country

---

International agreements are essential to prevent overfishing. The main problem is that they only apply to those nations that sign the agreements and signing is entirely voluntary. In 2019, Japan withdrew from the ICRW so it could resume commercial whaling.

Questions

10 Give three ways in which fishing can be restricted.

11 Explain how the Ascension Island MPA ensures sustainable fishing and does not cause conflict with local people.

12 Evaluate the effectiveness of using international agreements to ensure sustainable fishing.

Fishing methods

Different methods of fishing are used to catch different marine organisms. We can broadly separate the methods into two groups:

- netting and trapping
- angling.

Table 6.5 gives a summary of different fishing methods and their environmental impacts.

Netting and trapping

All these methods catch marine organisms by using nets or traps. Modern nets are usually made from nylon mesh.

Cast netting

Cast netting is a small-scale, simple, traditional fishing method (Figure 6.33). The nets are circular or conical with weights attached to the edge. A **handline** of rope is attached to the net, as shown in Figure 6.34.

KEY WORD

handline*: a nylon or rope line that is held in the hand at one end and attached to fishing gear at the other end

---

Figure 6.33: A fisher casting a cast net.

Fishing method	Summary of method	Environmental issues
cast netting	Circular net is thrown by hand over water to trap fish.	It has a low impact if done on a small scale. It is easy to release bycatch. Catch sizes are usually small.
trawling	Nets are towed behind boats. Pelagic trawling catches fish in the middle of water column. Benthic trawling drags the the net across the seabed.	Overfishing can occur when commercial fleets use large nets. Bycatch occurs, especially from benthic trawling. Benthic trawling destroys the seabed, coral reefs and habitats.
seining	Boat travels in a circle releasing the net like a vertical wall. The drawstring is pulled to close the base of the net.	Overfishing can occur when carried out on a large scale. Bycatch can occur when other species are attracted to shoals of fish.
tangle nets	Tangle nets are a form of gill net that traps fish in the mesh. Mesh sizes are set depending on the target species.	Gillnets are very environmentally damaging as they trap many non-target species. Lost gillnets can become ghost nets that entangle marine species.
basket traps	Traps are made that allow marine species to enter but not leave.	On a small scale, this has a low environmental impact. Traps can damage coral reefs.
longlining	A long nylon line is pulled behind a boat. The line has many barbed, baited hooks. Fixed lines can also be used at the surface and the seabed.	Commercial longlining can cause overfishing due to the long length of lines and many hooks. Bycatch is a major problem with turtles, seabirds and other species becoming attached to hooks. Lost longlines can entangle and snare species such as whales and turtles.
pole and line	A short line is attached to a barbless hook and a pole. Bait is thrown into the sea and water is sprayed on the surface. Fish are caught from the back of a boat and flicked onto the deck.	It is a low-impact method if not used intensively. There is low bycatch. Tuna caught by this method carry a premium price.

Table 6.5: Summary of fishing methods and environmental issues.

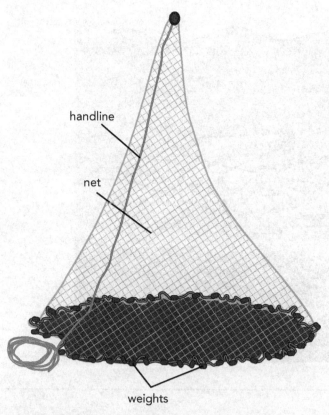

Figure 6.34: Diagram of a cast net.

The fisher stands on the shore, or on a boat, and throws the net onto the water so that it spreads out into a circle before landing on the water. The weights on the edge of the net make the net sink, trapping fish inside it. When the fisher starts to pull on the handline to pull in the net, the base of the net closes around the fish.

Cast netting is only used for catching smaller species of fish in coastal waters. There are a range of mesh sizes, depending on the size of the target species. Wide mesh sizes allow juveniles and small fish to escape. Cast netting is often used for catching bait fish that are then used to catch larger species such as tuna. This method does catch non-target species, but these are easily returned to the sea by the fisher.

Benefits of using cast netting:

- Cast netting is a traditional, cheap fishing method.

- Different mesh sizes mean that that juvenile fish or non-target species are not caught.

- Cast netting does not usually catch large quantities of fish, so is sustainable.

Drawbacks of using cast netting:

- It can only be used to catch relatively small species of fish.

- It is a method that requires skill and practice.

- Non-target species can be caught, but these are usually released.

Trawling

Trawling involves pulling a large net behind one or two boats. Fish are caught by the wide, open mouth as the net moves forward in the water and gather in the end of the net, which is called the cod end. Figures 6.35 and 6.36 on page 342 show pelagic trawling and benthic trawling. The sizes of trawling nets vary, from small nets used by local fishers to massive industrial sizes that can capture several tonnes of fish. Fishers can adjust mesh sizes for all types of trawling net so that smaller and juvenile fish can escape. Industrial-scale trawling is bad for the environment as it results in:

- overfishing

- the catch of non-target species, classed as bycatch

- and the loss of nets (which can then entangle other species).

KEY WORDS

trawling: a method of catching fish that involves towing a net through the water

pelagic trawling: the catching of fish by towing a net through the open water area; also called midwater trawling

benthic trawling: the catching of fish by towing a net along the seabed; also called bottom trawling

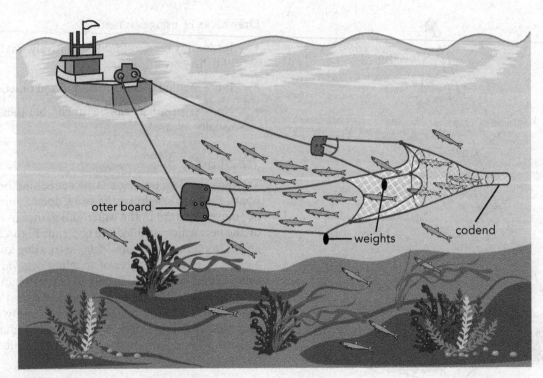

Figure 6.35: Diagram showing pelagic trawling.

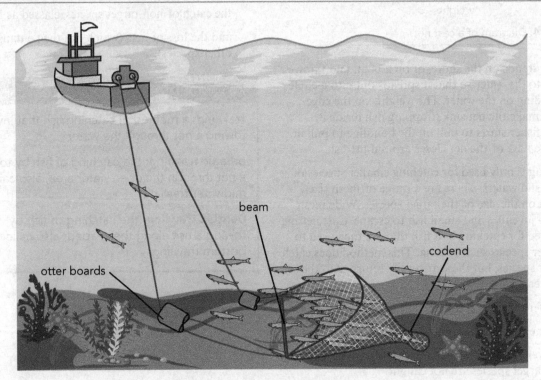

Figure 6.36: Diagram showing benthic trawling.

Pelagic trawling is where the net is towed through the water column. All the nets have ropes attached to either side of the mouth of the net. Sometimes, wooden or metal boards called otter boards are attached to the front of the net to keep the net open and help it to move in the correct direction. Weights and floats ensure that the net floats to the correct height in the water column. Pelagic trawls are used to catch species of fish that shoal such as herring and mackerel. If large nets are used, the result is overfishing and non-target species are caught. Because predator species such as sharks and dolphins are attracted to shoals of fish, sharks and dolphins can be caught in these nets and suffocate. Turtles are also killed by pelagic trawls.

KEY WORD

otter boards*: pieces of wood, metal, or plastic that are attached to a trawling net to keep it open and maintain its position in the water

---

Benthic trawling is the dragging of a weighted trawl net along the seabed. It is used to catch flatfish and crustaceans such as shrimps. The net is weighted so that it sinks. A wooden, metal or plastic beam is fixed across the mouth of the net to hold it open. Species from the seabed are pulled into the net as it is dragged along the seabed. Benthic trawling is very environmentally damaging as it destroys seabed habitats, wrecks coral and catches all the species that happen to be near the seabed. This results in a lot of bycatch (Figure 6.37).

Figure 6.37: Bycatch from a benthic trawl.

Seine nets

Purse seine fishing is a very old fishing method that is now used on a large scale by commercial fishing fleets (Figure 6.38). At the base of the net are metal hoops through which a rope runs. This rope acts as a draw string. Floats are attached to the top of the net. A boat sails around in a circle, releasing the net into the seawater to make a vertical wall of net around a shoal of fish. When the circle is complete, the drawstring rope is pulled in so that the base of the net is closed. The fish cannot swim downwards to escape. Fishers then haul the catch onto the boat, as shown in Figure 6.39. Although not as destructive as pelagic and benthic trawling, the industrial use of this method with very large nets causes severe overfishing. Bycatch is also a problem as dolphins, turtles and porpoises get caught up in the nets.

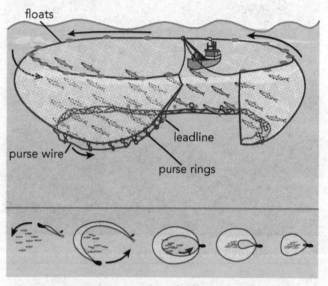

Figure 6.38: Diagram showing purse seine fishing.

Figure 6.39: Purse seine net being brought on board a boat.

Gillnets and tangle nets

Gillnets are vertical nets that are either suspended from the water surface by floats or secured into the seabed (Figure 6.40). They are usually placed into the water and left for several days. Fishers then harvest the trapped fish, which try to escape by swimming through the mesh in the net. If the fish are too large then only their heads pass through, and the gill operculum becomes stuck in the mesh. The size of mesh used depends on the target species. Small fish should be able to swim through the mesh and escape but large species may not get any part of the head through.

Figure 6.41: Sunfish caught in discarded gillnet.

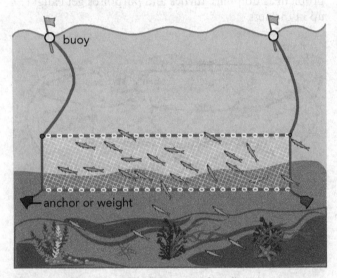

Figure 6.40: Diagram showing use of a gillnet.

In reality, all forms of gillnet are very damaging to the environment. Often non-target species become entangled and die. Animals that need to resurface, or move, to breathe are badly affected. Many dolphins, whales, seabirds, turtles and sharks are killed by gillnets every year. Because gillnets are left for a period a time, many are lost and end up as ghost nets which continue to kill thousands of marine animals every year. Many countries ban or strictly regulate the use of gillnets. Figure 6.41 shows a sunfish trapped in a lost gillnet.

Tangle nets are a modern form of gillnet that have a very small mesh. The mesh is so small that only the head and jaw of fish becomes caught, and bycatch can be untangled and released unharmed. These nets have been used successfully to catch salmon in parts of Canada.

KEY WORDS

ghost net*: discarded fishing gear that stays in the oceans aned continues to catch and kill marine organisms

tangle net: a type of net, similar to a gillnet, that catches fish in the mesh

Basket traps

For many hundreds of years, people all over the world have made traps to catch fish and other marine organisms. The general principle of any basket trap is the same – fish and other species enter the trap but then cannot get out. Figure 6.42 shows some lobster pots, which are cages that are lowered into the water and left for a period of time. The cages contain bait to attract lobsters. The lobsters move into the cages and then become stuck. Crabs and some species of fish are also caught using similar cages and baskets.

Some basket traps are permanent structures (Figure 6.43). Fish swim into the trap at high tide and become stuck. Widening the gaps between the bamboo canes allows smaller fish to escape. If used carefully, basket traps have a lower environmental impact compared with net fishing.

The main problems are overuse of basket traps (causing overfishing) and damage to reefs and the seabed if they are moved around by wave action and currents.

KEY WORD

basket trap: a basket or cage that allows marine organisms to enter but prevents them leaving

Figure 6.42: Lobster pots, a form of basket trap, stored at a harbour.

Figure 6.43: A fisher emptying a large, permanent basket trap.

Angling

Angling methods all use a fishing line and hook to catch marine organisms. Both commercial fishers and recreational anglers use angling. Modern fishing lines are made from nylon, and this can be an environmental problem if the lines are lost or discarded into the ocean.

KEY WORD

angling: the catching of marine organisms using hooks and lines rather than nets

Line fishing

Longline fishing is a commonly used method for catching fish. Fishers use longlines, both at the ocean's surface and anchored to the seabed.

Pelagic, or surface longlining uses long nylon fishing lines with barbed hooks attached to them, as shown in Figure 6.44. Each hook is usually tied to a small piece of line called a snood. Fishers can set the length of these snoods depending on the depth that the targeted fish swim. Bait is placed on the hooks to attract fish, and the lines are attached to floating buoys. Sometimes, the lines are left floating on the water and fishers return later to retrieve their catch. In most cases, fishing boats tow the lines to catch pelagic species such as tuna.

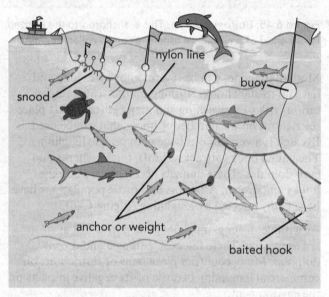

Figure 6.44: Diagram showing longlining; this method can catch many non-target organisms such as dolphins and turtles.

KEY WORDS

longline fishing: method of fishing that uses a long nylon line with many baited hooks attached; the line can be fixed in the water or towed behind a boat

snood*: small nylon lines that attach hooks to a longline

Fishers use bottom longlining (Figure 6.45) to catch fish living on the seabed, such as plaice and halibut. The line is anchored to the seabed for several days. Fishers then return to collect the catch.

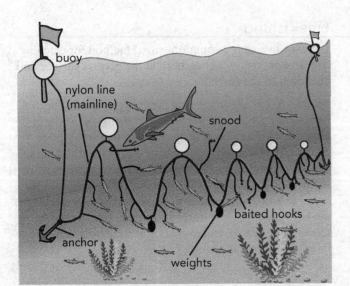

Figure 6.45: Bottom longline. This is anchored to the seabed for a period of time before fishers return to collect the catch.

Modern longlines can be several kilometres long and have up to 3000 hooks. Fishing on this scale brings a serious risk of overfishing and many governments place restrictions on the number of hooks that can be used. Bycatch is a very serious issue with pelagic longlining. The baited hooks attract seabirds, turtles, sharks and even dolphins. These animals become snared on the hooks and drown. Albatross and turtle populations have been badly affected by longlining (Figure 6.46).

As with net fishing, much longline gear is lost at sea every year. These lines can entangle and drown dolphins. Many countries place bans or restrictions on commercial longlining because of its negative impacts on the environment.

Figure 6.46: Turtle caught by hook on a longline.

Rod fishing

Pole and line fishing is one of the more sustainable fishing methods. It generally has a low rate of bycatch, and, if regulated, has a low risk of overfishing. The equipment is quite simple, consisting of a wood or fibreglass pole attached to a nylon line with a **barbless hook**.

Pole and line fishing is frequently used for catching tuna (Figures 6.47 and 6.48). The fishers search for a shoal of fish. When a shoal is located, they spray water over the surface of the sea. One person on the boat, called the **chummer**, throws **baitfish** into the water. The spray and baitfish attract the tuna who begin a **feeding frenzy**. The fishers stand at the back of the boat and catch the fish. When a fish is caught, it is flicked back onto the deck of the boat, easily detaching from the barbless hook.

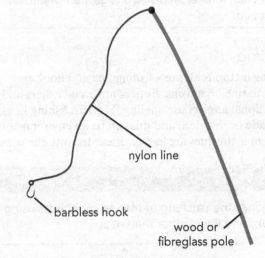

Figure 6.47: Pole and line used for tuna fishing.

Figure 6.48: Pole and line fishing for tuna.

Environmental campaigns have successfully encouraged the use of pole and line fishing for catching tuna. When it is sold, tuna caught this way carries a label to state that it has been caught in a sustainable method. This helps consumers to choose sustainable food.

ACTIVITY 6.4

Debating a ban on benthic trawling

Working with four other learners, have a debate on banning benthic trawling. Two learners will need to produce an argument proposing a ban on all forms of benthic trawling. Two learners will need to oppose the ban on benthic trawling. The fifth person will chair the debate. You will need to present the debate to an audience.

Peer assessment

The invited audience can vote on whether they feel they agree with the ban or oppose the ban. Each member of the audience can then use the following scheme shown here to decide on whether they felt that they had enough information to make a proper decision:

☺ if the argument was well organised and had all of the information needed

😐 if the argument was reasonably well organised and had most of the information

☹ if the argument lacked organisation and had a lot of information missing.

Fish aggregating devices

Fishers have long known that fish are attracted to floating objects. Small species of fish often seek shelter from predators and find food under floating pieces of wood. **Fish aggregation devices (FADs)** are artificial platforms that attract fish (Figure 6.49).

There are several key principles involved with FADs.

- A floating platform is attached to buoys. A long line hangs from the platform to a weight or anchor. Some FADs float freely and are not anchored.

- Producers such as macroalgae grow on the platform and the line. Microalgae also grow in the surrounding water.

- Small fish and other primary consumers are attracted to the FAD for food and shelter.

- A food web develops around the FAD. Larger, predatory species are attracted to the FAD by the presence of the small fish.

- Some species of larger marine organism, such as dolphins, learn that FADs are a rich source of food. They can use FADs as navigation devices.

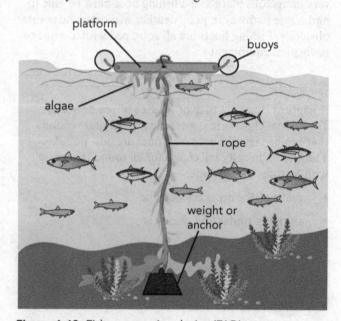

Figure 6.49: Fish aggregation device (FAD).

KEY WORD

fish aggregation device (FAD): a floating platform that is sometimes anchored to the seabed; used to attract fish

---

FADs are used all over the world to increase catches. However, there are some environmental concerns about using FADs as they can lead to overfishing and cause predator species to migrate to areas where they would not normally be found. Bycatch of turtles, dolphins and other marine mammals is also a problem as they can become entangled in the anchor lines.

Questions

13 State what is meant by the term 'bycatch'.

14 Describe the methods of:

  a   purse seining

  b   pole and line fishing.

15 Explain why pole and line fishing is a more sustainable fishing method compared with longlining.

Navigational aids

Fishers need to safely navigate between fishing grounds and harbours in all kinds of weather. The ocean can be a very dangerous place and a fishing boat must be able to find a safe pathway in poor weather, avoiding underwater obstacles. Fishing boats are all equipped with a range of navigation equipment.

Charts

A **nautical chart** is a map of an area of sea or ocean. Traditional charts are paper maps but digital versions that can be viewed on smartphones are now popular. The UK Admiralty sell charts for all round the world with features that include:

- maps of the areas of coastline
- shipping routes and channels
- water depths
- the locations of underwater obstacles such as reefs
- locations of navigation features such as buoys, lighthouses and docks
- safety notes for areas with strong or unusual currents, winds and weather patterns
- latitudes and longitudes
- a **compass rose**
- a scale bar to calculate distances.

Charts are used by sailors to safely plot journeys so that they avoid obstacles. Figure 6.50 shows two sailors looking at a nautical map of a harbour area.

Figure 6.50: A nautical chart.

Compass and compass rose

A compass is an essential piece of navigation equipment (Figure 6.51). It consists of needle that always points to **magnetic north**.

Figure 6.51: A compass. The red needle points to the magnetic north.

Sailors use a compass to determine the direction in which their boat is moving. When sailors plot a course, they use a compass together with a chart. A compass rose is shown on all nautical charts so the sailors can work out the direction the boat needs to move in (Figure 6.52). **True north** is a fixed point on the globe. Magnetic north moves slightly over time and is rarely totally aligned with true north. A modern compass rose shows the direction of true north and magnetic north so that sailors can adjust their compass bearings correctly.

KEY WORDS

magnetic north: the position that the needle in a compass points towards; it is rarely at the same position as true north

true north*: the geographical location of the North Pole; it is a fixed point on the globe

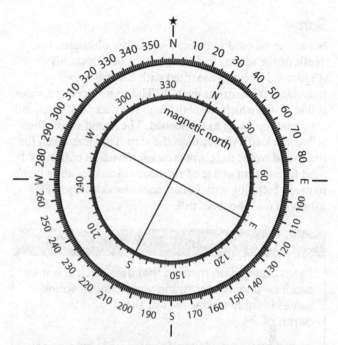

Figure 6.52: Chart showing a compass rose that shows the directions of magnetic north and true north.

Global Positioning System (GPS)

Most modern boats now rely on the Global Positioning System (GPS) for navigation. GPS uses satellites to map the position of a boat at any moment in time. This means that sailors know exactly where they are in the dark, or during fog when visibility is poor. Figure 6.53 shows a GPS screen on a ship used to navigate at night.

Figure 6.53: A GPS navigation system on a boat.

Sonar

Sonar can be used to detect underwater obstacles, the depth of the seabed and the position of fish shoals (Figure 6.54). Boats are fitted with a **sound wave transducer** underneath the hull. The transducer generates sound waves which travel through the water until they hit solid material such as the seabed. The sound waves then reflect back to a detector on the ship. The time taken for the sound waves to return is measured and a computer is used to make an image of the ocean. Sonar enables boats to avoid colliding with underwater obstacles and helps fishers to find shoals of fish.

> ### KEY WORDS
>
> **sonar:** navigation method that uses equipment to produce underwater sound waves; these sound waves identify obstacles, fish shoals and the depth of the sea
>
> **sound wave transducer*:** equipment on a boat that emits sound waves

Radar

Radar is a bit like sonar but uses radio waves in the air (Figure 6.55). A **radio wave emitter** sends out radio waves that then reflect off any solid objects. When these waves return, detectors on the ship pick up the returning waves and measure the time taken to bounce back. Boats use radar to identify obstacles, coastlines and other ships ahead of them. This prevents collisions. Radar is very useful in the dark and in foggy weather.

> ### KEY WORDS
>
> **radar:** navigation method that uses equipment to emit radio waves to identify obstacles, such as rocky reefs, around a ship
>
> **radio wave emitter*:** equipment on a boat that releases radio waves to help with navigation

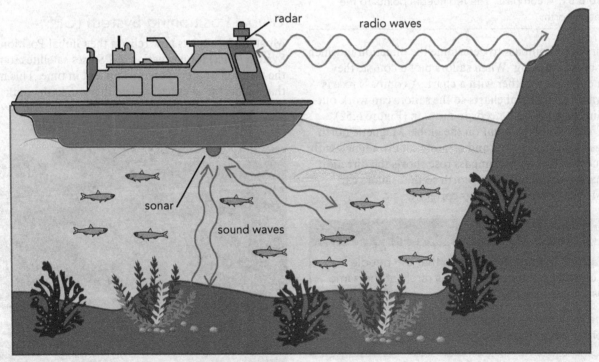

Figure 6.54: Sonar and radar operation on a boat.

Figure 6.55: Sailor using radar on a ship.

Questions

16 List three methods of navigation used on a ship.

17 Explain how an FAD works.

18 Explain how a ship could safely navigate to a harbour in foggy weather, avoiding obstacles above and below water.

6.4 Aquaculture

Figure 6.27 in Section 6.3 shows how the demand for fish and seafood products has increased over the last hundred years. It also shows a gap between the demand for seafood and what can we can sustainably harvest from the sea. We are becoming increasingly dependent on aquaculture as a method of growing fish and other marine species for consumption. Aquaculture will be vital in the future to prevent the loss of marine species due to overfishing. Aquaculture offers a range of benefits:

• It reduces dependence on harvesting wild species, preventing extinctions, and so can help to make fishing sustainable.

• If done on a large scale, it provides cheaper food to people in many parts of the world.

• It brings economic benefits to people when they produce and export species raised by aquaculture.

We do, however, need to be careful as there are some environmental costs to aquaculture. In Section 6.1, we discussed the effect of shrimp farming on mangrove forests. If aquaculture is not developed in sustainable ways, it can do great damage to the natural environment including:

• loss of habitats, such as mangrove forests

• pollution from wastes, pesticides and fungicides released into the natural water

• damage to wild stocks and food webs due to the escape of farmed organisms

• overfishing of species that are used for feeding the animals grown by aquaculture.

Species that are produced by aquaculture

People often think that aquaculture only produces fish and shrimp. There are, however, a wide range of different species produced. Figure 6.56 shows a few of the species. Species raised by aquaculture belong to several different groups, including:

• macroalgae seaweeds, such as kelp

• fish, such as salmon and grouper

• crustaceans, such as shrimp

• molluscs, such as mussels, oysters, scallops and even giant clams

• echinoderms, such as sea cucumbers.

Some species, such as bluefin tuna, are difficult to breed and raise in captivity. Scientists are researching how to use aquaculture on species that have so far not been produced commercially.

Figure 6.56: Some species produced by aquaculture: **a** kelp, **b** salmon, **c** shrimp and **d** mussels.

General methods of aquaculture

We can divide aquaculture methods into open systems and closed systems.

Open systems (Figure 6.57) are situated in natural water, often in coastal or estuarine areas. Organisms are usually kept in cages or nets. The natural movements of currents supplies oxygen and removes wastes. Because open systems are directly linked to the natural environment, operators must make sure that predators cannot enter the cages. They also need to ensure that pollutants do not leak out and organisms do not escape.

Closed systems are not directly connected to natural water (Figure 6.58). The organisms are placed in tanks so are not affected by predators. There is a very low risk that they will cause pollution of natural water or that organisms will escape. These systems are more expensive as they need constant filtering of the water. The oxygen concentration, salinity and water temperature must be constantly monitored.

KEY WORDS

open system*: method of aquaculture that uses cages and nets in natural, coastal waters

closed system*: method of aquaculture using tanks so that species are isolated from natural, coastal waters

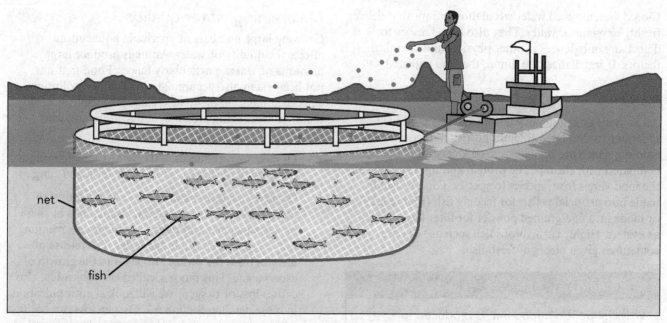

Figure 6.57: Open aquaculture system. A cage or net is placed into natural water.

Figure 6.58: A closed aquaculture system. The fish are all kept in tanks.

Requirements of aquaculture

Both open and closed aquaculture systems have similar requirements to enable mass production of organisms.

Selection of broodstock

Adults with desirable characteristics are selected for breeding. These organisms, called broodstock, are sometimes be taken from the wild. However, we should avoid reducing populations of wild organisms. Therefore we often take broodstock from animals that have been farmed. We select healthy, rapidly growing animals which will produce a high yield to maximise profits. This is called artificial selection. These artificially selected animals must not be allowed to escape. If they escaped, they could outcompete wild species or breed with wild organisms, introducing new characteristics into the wild.

> ## KEY WORDS
>
> broodstock: marine species that are used for breeding in aquaculture systems; they are usually artificially selected for rapid growth and high quality
>
> artificial selection: the selection of organisms with desirable characteristics for breeding programmes

Maintaining conditions

All species of marine organism need specific temperatures, salinities, light intensities and pHs to live and grow. Oxygen concentrations also must be kept high so that the organisms can respire. Open systems need to be located where there are water currents. The currents bring oxygenated water, and maintain the salinity, temperature and pH.

Closed systems need water circulation pumps that deliver freshly oxygenated water. They also have sensors to detect any imbalances in other physical and chemical factors. If imbalances are found, they are adjusted.

Food

All animals grown in aquaculture systems need feeding. Different species have different nutritional requirements. Salmon, which are predators, need a very different diet compared with shrimp. The protein and lipid content of the food varies from species to species. Food is usually made into artificial pellets for feeding fish (Figure 6.59), or made into fine-grained powder for filter feeders such as oysters. Highly carnivorous fish such as tuna are sometimes given pieces of fresh fish.

> ### KEY WORD
>
> artificial pellets*: food that is produced for aquaculture; it contains the correct balance of nutrients for the species being farmed

There are environmental issues with the manufacture of food pellets, especially pellets for top predators. Sometimes, small species of fish such as anchovies and sardines are overfished to produce food pellets, and this is not sustainable. Recently, to improve sustainability, plant-based and insect-based protein pellets have been developed. Pellets made from the waste trimmings of processed fish, such as fins and heads, are also used.

Figure 6.59: Artificial pellets using in fish aquaculture.

Maintaining water quality

Growing large numbers of species in aquaculture affects the quality of water. Animals produce large amounts of waste, particularly faeces. Food that has not been eaten also accumulates and causes pollution. This accumulation of waste creates problems for both the organisms being grown in aquaculture and wild species if the waste escapes.

- Disease spread: faeces and other waste encourages the growth of disease-causing bacteria and fungi.

- Oxygen loss: faeces and waste food is a source of food for decomposer bacteria. Populations of these bacteria increase and respire at a high rate, meaning that oxygen levels fall in the water. The release of nitrates from the wastes also leads to the growth of excess algae. This process, called eutrophication, also causes loss of oxygen. We will look at eutrophication in more detail in Section 6.7. Oxygen loss can occur within the tanks of closed systems and in the natural waters surrounding open systems.

The methods used to prevent the build-up of waste depend on whether the aquaculture system is open or closed.

- Open systems: in open systems, waste falls through the mesh of nets causing environmental problems (Figure 6.60). To minimise build-up of waste, feeding needs to be controlled and too much food should not be given. Organisms are fed frequently but just a little food at one time. The nets and cages need to be placed where there are good water currents to remove waste and bring in freshly oxygenated water.

- Closed systems: in closed systems, water is constantly circulated and filtered (Figure 6.61). Oxygen is also bubbled into the water. The waste collected by the filtration systems is removed so that it does not cause pollution. The waste can be used as fertiliser because it is rich in nutrients.

> ### KEY WORD
>
> eutrophication: the release of nutrients into water that causes the production of algal blooms which die and decay; eventually this leads to a loss of oxygen in the water

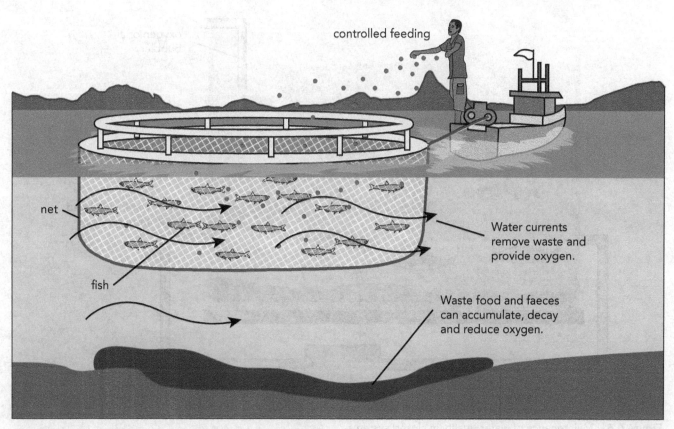

controlled feeding

net

fish

Water currents remove waste and provide oxygen.

Waste food and faeces can accumulate, decay and reduce oxygen.

Figure 6.60: Maintenance of water quality in open systems.

Separating sizes to prevent cannibalism

Cannibalism occurs when organisms eat members of their own species. Predatory species of fish, such as salmon, eat smaller, younger fish if there is not enough food. If fish are overcrowded, they may eat the fins of other fish, weakening them and increasing the risk of disease. There are two main methods used to prevent cannibalism:

* providing enough food through regular feeding
* separating fish of different sizes and ages into different cages or tanks.

> **KEY WORD**
>
> **cannibalism:** the practice of eating members of the same species

Prevention of disease spread

Growing large numbers of one species in a small area leads to the easy spread of diseases and **parasites**. Figure 6.62 shows sea lice that are attached to the skin of a salmon.

Diseases and parasites kill organisms and result in poorer quality products with lower sale prices. Diseases and parasites can also spread to wild populations, causing environmental damage. There are several methods used to reduce disease spread.

* Low stocking densities: diseases spread when fish are close to each other. Overstocking also causes stress, which weakens the immune system of fish so that they cannot fight infections as easily. Having a low stocking density is one of the best ways of reducing disease spread and parasite transmission.

> **KEY WORD**
>
> **parasites:** organisms that live and feed on a host organism, causing damage to the host

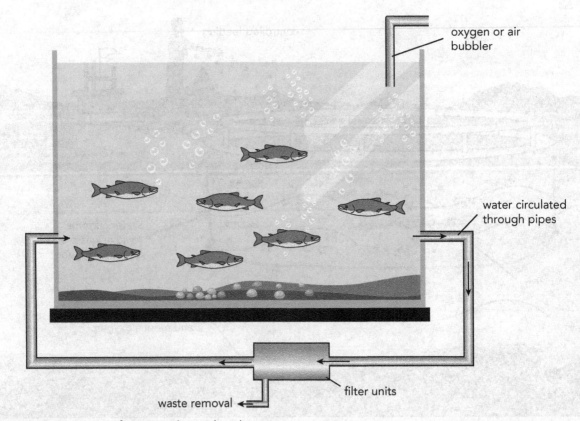

Figure 6.61: Maintenance of water quality in closed systems.

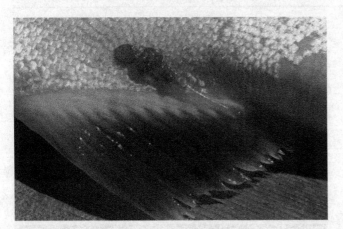

Figure 6.62: Lice on the skin of a salmon.

- Drug treatment: pesticides to kill parasites and antibiotics to kill bacteria can be added to the water. This reduces the risks of parasite and disease spread but may harm the environment. The overuse of antibiotics has led to bacteria becoming resistant. In open systems, the drugs leak into wild populations of organisms. These drugs can also accumulate in the bodies of the species being farmed, posing a risk to people who eat them. Sometimes, using chemicals is the only option for controlling a disease but we should minimise their usage.

- Biological control: Figure 6.63 shows a ballan wrasse, which is a species of fish used to control sea lice in farmed salmon. Ballan wrasse are cleaner fish that eat the sea lice living on salmon. Using cleaner fish is a more environmentally friendly method of reducing parasites than using chemical pesticides.

KEY WORD

biological control*: the use of organisms, often predator species, to remove parasites and other harmful organisms

Figure 6.63: A Ballan wrasse; these fish are used in aquaculture as they eat parasites.

Using aquaculture to repair environmental damage

We can use aquaculture to raise organisms for release into the wild. Endangered species, for example, can be bred in captivity and then released. In North America, salmon produced by aquaculture are released into rivers to increase populations. Coral and mangroves are now being grown using aquaculture to repair environmental damage.

Figure 6.64: Coral being raised by aquaculture for repair of reefs.

Coral reef aquaculture: Figure 6.64 shows coral being grown on a frame near the island of Cozumel, Mexico. Coral polyps are grown in indoor tanks and then transported onto frames in open water. When larger colonies have formed, they are transplanted onto reefs that have been damaged by fishing or storms. Coral aquaculture is a very successful method of repairing

reefs. It is, however, expensive, labour intensive and needs skilled, trained workers. The coral must first be produced in laboratories and then monitored after being placed in open ocean nursery areas.

Mangrove replanting: many thousands of square kilometres of mangrove forest have been lost over the last 100 years. Cuttings are small pieces of plants that we can use to grow new plants. To regrow mangrove forests, we can take cuttings of mangrove trees. These cuttings are grown in laboratories and conservation areas until they grow into small trees. The small trees are then transplanted in areas of mangrove where trees have been lost (Figure 6.65).

Figure 6.65: Mangroves being replanted to repair mangrove forests.

Mangrove aquaculture is an effective method for slowing the loss of mangrove forest. Many countries now have mangrove planting schemes, providing income for local people. However, mangrove aquaculture is expensive and takes many years to have a visible effect. It also requires skilled, trained workers.

KEY WORD

cuttings*: small pieces of plant that are taken from a parent plant and then used to develop lots of identical plants

Questions

19 List four types of marine organism that are produced by aquaculture.

20 a State the difference between open and closed aquaculture systems.

   b Compare how water quality is maintained in open systems compared with closed systems.

21 Explain why the following practices help to ensure that aquaculture is sustainable:

   a using plant-based food pellets rather than fish-based pellets

   b keeping a low stocking density

   c not over-feeding fish

   d keeping cages of detritivores such as crabs and lobsters underneath fish cages.

ACTIVITY 6.5

Sustainable aquaculture

Work with a group of other learners for this activity. Each group member needs to choose a different species.

Imagine that you have been asked to set up a new aquaculture system for a named species in a coastal area. On a large piece of paper, design your aquaculture system so that it will produce large numbers of organisms without harming the environment. Annotate all the features to explain their function.

You will need to consider:

- how to keep organisms of different ages separate

- how to provide food, clean water and oxygen, and how you will monitor them

- how to prevent escape of organisms and entry of predators

- how to prevent pollution of the environment

- how to prevent disease.

Peer assessment

Work with other learners to make a display of all the different systems you have devised.

CONTINUED

Rate all the posters by adding sticky notes with smiling faces from the following scheme:

☺ if the aquaculture system would work well and there is an excellent explanation

😐 if the aquaculture system would work reasonably well and there is some explanation

☹ if the aquaculture system would not work well and there is no explanation.

6.5 Energy from the seas

The growing human population brings with it a huge demand for energy. We need energy to run our cars, light our homes, cook our food, even power our phones. Over the last hundred years, much of the energy has come from burning fossil fuels such as oil, gas and coal. We have extracted oil and gas from deep in the ground below our oceans for many years. This fossil fuel industry does, however, have an environmental cost. Recently, we have begun to use our oceans to generate energy from renewable methods such as wind or wave power.

Oil and its uses

Figure 6.66 shows some oil that has been extracted from underground. It is often called crude oil or petroleum when in this state.

Crude oil is a thick, yellow-black liquid and is actually a mixture of several thousand different chemicals. It is a fossil fuel found deep underground in the Earth's crust. Oil is formed from algae and zooplankton that died millions of years ago. These organisms did not decompose and instead were buried under rock. Over time, intense heat and pressure turned the remains of these dead organisms into oil. Because oil is produced from long dead organisms, we call it a fossil fuel.

KEY WORDS

wave power: a method of generating electricity using energy from wave action

crude oil (petroleum)*: the natural oil that is removed from under the ground; it is a mixture of many different chemicals

Figure 6.66: Crude oil, a thick yellow-black liquid that is a mixture of many chemicals.

Many of the chemicals in oil are rich sources of energy so we can use them as a fuel. When we burn fossil fuels, we release the energy that the organisms built into their bodies millions of years ago. Fossil fuel **combustion** also releases carbon dioxide gas into the atmosphere. We will look at some of the problems caused by the release of carbon dioxide in Section 6.8. Oil is also used in the manufacture of plastics.

The extraction and transport of oil

Oil is buried deep underground and we do not find it everywhere around the world. Figure 6.67 shows a map of the locations of some of the main deposits of oil around the world. Each deposit is called an **oilfield**.

Many oilfields are located under the ocean. We have designed oil platforms (Figure 6.68) to extract oil from areas far from coasts and in very deep water. First, a metal platform is set up on the surface of the water. A drill is then used to sink a hole through the rock of the seabed deep into the Earth's crust. When the drill reaches the oilfield beneath the seabed, the oil is pumped up to the platform at the surface.

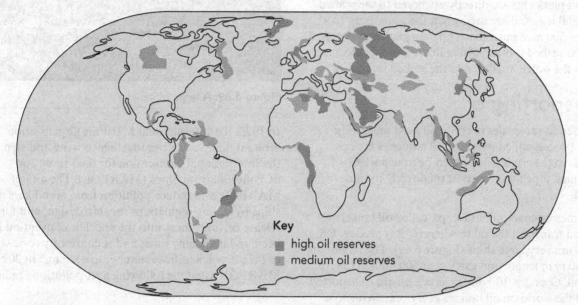

Key
■ high oil reserves
■ medium oil reserves

Figure 6.67: Map of some of the major oilfields around the world (United States not included).

Figure 6.68: An oil platform.

Fixed oil platforms are directly anchored to the seabed with metal legs and are used when the water is up to a depth of 500 m. Semi-submersible oil platforms are used when the seabed is over 3000 m deep. These platforms float on the water, anchored to the seabed by chains.

Transporting oil

The different molecules in crude oil need separating using a process called refining. Oil refineries are based on land, so the crude oil needs to be transported. Sometimes, pipelines transport oil directly to sites on land.

Sometimes we load oil onto ships, called oil tankers, that then transport the oil to wherever it is needed. Oil tankers are very large ships (Figure 6.69). The largest are over 400 m in length and carry over 500 million dm³ of crude oil. Over 3×10^{11} dm³ of crude oil are transported around the world on oil tankers every year. With so much transport of oil around the world, often in very severe weather, there is a high risk of oil leaking into the environment. There have been many major oil spills over the last century, causing a great deal of damage to the environment.

To reduce the risk of oil spills, modern ships and oil tankers must be built to the standards of the International Convention for the Prevention of Pollution from Ships (MARPOL).

> ### KEY WORDS
>
> oil refinery*: industrial complex that separates out the different molecules in crude oil, such as petrol and diesel
>
> MARPOL: a series of standards for ships to prevent pollution of the oceans and seas

Figure 6.69: A large oil tanker.

In 1973, the International Maritime Organization brought many countries together to write and sign the International Convention for the Prevention of Pollution from Ships (MARPOL). The aim of MARPOL is to reduce pollution from oil tankers and ships by setting regulations for ship design, and for the release of substances into the sea. The convention has been updated many times and is constantly reviewed to take new scientific research into account. In 2021, MARPOL listed the following anti-pollution regulations.

- All oil tankers must be fitted with double hulls. This means that if there is a collision, there is less chance of oil leaking into the water.

- To reduce pollution, the holds of tankers can only be washed out when at special collection sites in ports. The hold of an oil tanker is the large tank where oil is kept. The holds need cleaning out regularly by flushing water through them. If waste water is dumped into the sea, this also releases oil into the sea.

- Sewage release from all ships (not just oil tankers) must be controlled. Waste from toilets on all ships must not pass directly into the sea. Waste is stored in tanks and then removed when in port.

- Garbage disposal must be controlled on all ships. Waste material such as plastics, glass and card should be returned to port and disposed of on land.

Oil spills

Marine environments can be harsh, with storms and huge waves. Drilling for oil and transporting oil brings the risk that some oil may be spilt. There have been many oil spills over the last hundred years. Table 6.6 shows some of these oil spills and the volumes of oil lost.

There are two main causes of oil spills:

- leakage from pipelines or the drilling area

- leakage from oil tankers that have been damaged, usually due to collisions.

When oil is released into water it does not dissolve and most of the oil forms a layer across the surface. Wave action breaks the oil into small droplets that mix with deeper water. Some of the oil droplets join together to form a thick, tar-like substance that sinks to the seabed.

Question

22 Use Table 6.6 to answer the following questions:

a   Which oil spill, listed in Table 6.6, released the most oil?

b   Describe the pattern in the amount of oil lost from the spills over time. Suggest reasons for the pattern.

Impacts of oil spills

Oil spills have devastating impacts on marine organisms and habitats (Figure 6.70). They harm organisms that live in the open ocean and have severe effects on coastal ecosystems when oil washes up on shores.

Year	Location	Cause	Mass of oil lost (tonnes)
1903	UK	A ship carrying oil (*Thomas W. Lawson*) sank in harsh weather. This is the first major oil spill at sea.	c. 7400
1967	UK	An oil tanker (*Torrey Canyon*) collided with rocks near the Scilly Isles, causing widespread environmental damage.	between 80 000 and 119 000
1970	Canada	An oil tanker (*SS Arrow*) ran aground in Nova Scotia, causing widespread environmental damage.	c. 10 330
1974	Chile	An oil tanker (*VLCC Metula*) ran aground near Tierra Del Fuego, causing widespread environmental damage.	c. 50 000
1978	France	An oil tanker (*Amoco Cadiz*) collided with rocks near Brittany, France, releasing the largest oil slick up to that time.	c. 225 000
1983	Iran	An oil tanker collided with a platform, releasing a large oil slick.	c. 260 000
2009	Australia	An oil platform developed a major leak in the Timor Sea, releasing a very large amount of oil close to coral reefs.	between 4000 and 30 000
2010	US	An explosion on the *Deepwater Horizon* oil platform in the Gulf of Mexico caused the largest ever oil spill.	between 492 000 and 627 000

Table 6.6: Some of the oil spills between 1903 and 2014.

Figure 6.70: Crude oil that has washed up on a rocky shore.

The crude oil harms marine organisms in a variety of ways.

Coating fur and feathers: Figure 6.71 shows a seabird covered in oil after an oil spill. The oil sticks to the feathers of birds and to the fur of mammals such as sea otters. Because oil does not dissolve in water, it is very difficult to wash off. The fur and feathers lose their insulating effect, and the animals often die because their body temperature cools too much. **Hypothermia** is the name for this overcooling of the body.

KEY WORDS

hypothermia*: the overcooling of the body of an organism that can result in death

Figure 6.71: Seabird coated with crude oil.

After an oil spill, conservationists and volunteers try to save birds and mammals covered with oil (Figure 6.72). The animals need to be carefully washed in special detergents to remove the oil and are then left to recover before being released.

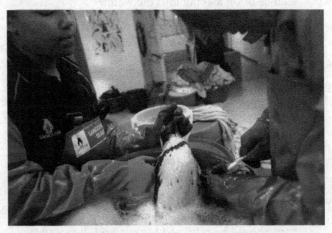

Figure 6.72: Volunteers cleaning oil from a penguin.

Poisoning by oil: oil is a mixture of many chemicals. Some of these chemicals are poisonous and kill animals that ingest them. The oil is sometimes ingested directly when organisms swim through the spill. However, birds also consume the oil when they preen their feathers. Some chemicals in oil stick inside the bodies of organisms. When predators eat these organisms, the predators are also eating lots of chemicals. After oil spills people sometimes report that fish tastes of chemicals. This shows that the chemicals released from an oil spill can work their way up food chains, even to humans.

Disrupting food chains: because oil forms a large coating over the surface of the water, it reduces the amount of light for marine producers. In the open ocean, photosynthesis by microalgae reduces, so less energy is brought into food chains. On coastal areas, oil covers seaweeds such as kelp so that they cannot photosynthesise.

If the rate of photosynthesis slows, the productivity of an ecosystem reduces. If there are fewer producers, there will be less food for primary consumers, and the whole food web is affected.

Minimising the effects of oil spills

Although oil may not seem to be a natural substance, it is actually made from the natural organic molecules found in living organisms. Over a long period of time, bacteria in the ocean and on shores decompose oil. In the short term, however, we must take action to minimise environmental damage from an oil spill.

When a large oil spill is reported, there has to be a rapid response to clean it up. Several methods are used to stop further spread of oil and then to remove it.

Figure 6.73 shows a **boom** to prevent oil spreading. Booms are long floating barriers placed on the surface of the water. Boats tow booms into place and position them around the oil to prevent it spreading towards coastal areas. Some booms absorb oil from the water so that the oil can then be disposed of.

Figure 6.74: Use of a skimmer to remove oil.

Figure 6.75 shows a ship spraying chemicals called **dispersants** onto an oil spill. Dispersants cause oil to break up into tiny droplets and scatter through the water. They remove the oil from the surface and cause it to sink into deeper water. Unfortunately, the oil droplets are toxic to fish and coral. Oil that settles on the seabed also takes a long time to decompose in the cold conditions at seabed depth.

Figure 6.75: Use of dispersant sprays to remove oil.

Figure 6.73: Use of a boom to contain an oil spill.

Skimmers are devices that are towed across the water on cables or fixed to boats. They scoop up surface water and remove the oil (Figure 6.74). Skimmers are often made of a rotating drum that is coated with material that sticks to the oil.

KEY WORDS

boom: device that is floated on the surface of water in an effort to contain an oil spill

skimmer: device that is used to absorb oil from the surface of water

dispersants: chemicals that are sprayed onto an oil spill to break up the oil into smaller droplets that are carried away

Controlled burning of the oil on the ocean's surface may remove it (Figure 6.76). Although it looks very dramatic, burning can remove oil effectively but it does pollute the atmosphere. Burning oil produces waste gases such as sulfur dioxide and carbon dioxide and also releases a lot of smoke particles. It cannot be done in windy conditions or very close to coastal areas.

Figure 6.76: Burning oil from the surface of water.

The advantages and disadvantages of using fossil fuels

We have used fossil fuels for many years as a source of energy. They are used to power our cars, trucks, trains and aeroplanes. Many power stations burn fossil fuels to generate the electricity we all need for our everyday lives. There are many advantages and disadvantages to using fossil fuels.

Advantages

Constant energy supply: as long as we have a supply of fossil fuels such as oil and gas, we can use them to generate electricity or power our vehicles. The demand for power and electricity is now higher than ever because of the number of electrical items we use. Fossil fuels give us a constant supply of electricity that is unaffected by weather or other factors. Fossil fuels are generally a reliable source of energy. If we have a supply of fossil fuels, we can generate enough electricity for a whole country.

Energy density: this is a measure of how much energy is present in a set mass or volume of a substance. Fossil fuels are very energy dense. This means that only a small mass or volume of fuel is used to generate a lot of power. This is very important for aeroplanes and heavy vehicles that need to have a large amount of energy contained in as small a space as possible. The calorific value of most fossil fuels is high, so a lot of energy is released when they are burnt. For example, a typical car can travel over 500 km on a full tank of petrol.

> ### KEY WORD
>
> **energy density:** a measure of how much energy is contained within a set mass or volume of a substance; energy dense substances have a lot of energy within a small mass

Relatively cheap price: fossil fuels are often cheap to buy. They may not seem to have a low price when we purchase them, but some of the price we pay at the petrol stations or shops is tax taken by governments. Compared with many other forms of fuel (such as nuclear power or hydroelectric power), fossil fuels are relatively cheap to buy and are easy to use.

Stable to transport and use: fossil fuels are generally stable chemicals that are easily transported through pipelines and in tankers or transport trucks. They are highly flammable but, as long we are careful, they can be transported safely.

Disadvantages

Fossil fuels are non-renewable: 'renewable' means that something can be easily replaced. Fossil fuels are an example of non-renewable energy as they cannot be replaced easily once we have used them up. Fossil fuels are the products of millions of years of geological activity so are not going to be replaced in our lifetimes. There is also only a limited amount of fossil fuel on the planet. So, once we have used all the fossil fuels, we will have to find alternative forms of energy.

> ### KEY WORD
>
> **non-renewable energy:** energy sources that will eventually run out, such as fossil fuels

Burning fossil fuels releases pollution: burning fossil fuels is highly polluting.

When fossil fuels are combusted, they release carbon dioxide gas. Carbon dioxide is a greenhouse gas and the constant burning of fossil fuels is leading to an increase in the atmospheric carbon dioxide concentration. This increase of carbon dioxide leads to global warming (Section 6.8).

Other polluting gases, such as sulfur dioxide, are also produced from fossil fuel combustion. Sulfur dioxide is a gas that dissolves in the water in clouds to form sulfuric acid. When the clouds move over land and precipitation occurs, they release acid rain, which kills trees, poisons lakes and kills fish. Particles of carbon are also released into the atmosphere in the smoke from combustion. These particles are harmful to ecosystems.

> **KEY WORD**
>
> acid rain*: rain that is made acidic due to the release of pollutants such as sulfur dioxide

Extracting fossil fuels causes environmental damage: we have already looked at the impacts of oil spills on the marine environment. Fossil fuels are mostly found underground and we need to extract them. To extract oil and gas, we drill deep into the ground. We can extract solid coal by underground mining. Extracting oil, gas and coal from the ground can be very damaging to the environment (Figure 6.77). Large oil spills occur when oil platforms explode, pipes burst and oil tankers run aground. There is also a steady leak of small amounts of oil from pipes that have broken seals. Drilling into the seabed is very damaging, destroying coral reefs and stirring up sediment. The disturbance of the seabed leads to habitat loss for benthic (seabed) organisms.

Figure 6.77: Deforestation due to acid rain formed from the burning of fossil fuels.

There are difficulties with extracting the fuels: because fossil fuels are non-renewable, the amount of oil and gas left underground falls each year. As the amount of underground oil falls, scientists search even harder for new oil fields. However, these new oil fields are often beneath very deep ocean or are in remote areas such as underneath the Arctic Ocean. Drilling for oil in deep water far from land is very dangerous for workers and risks oil spills. As extraction becomes more difficult, the costs rise and the price of oil increases.

Renewable energy

As we begin to understand the damage caused by the overuse of fossil fuels, humans have turned to alternative ways of generating power. We are using more renewable sources of energy to generate electricity. During this century there will be a massive increase in the use of renewable energy sources because fossil fuels will run out and we need to reduce pollution. The marine environment is ideal for generating electricity from renewable energy sources such as wind, waves and tides.

Figure 6.78 shows a wind turbine farm based off the coast of the UK. The wind spins the turbines, and this movement is used to generate electricity. Electrical cables under the sea then transmit the electricity back to land. Coastal areas are often very windy so are ideal locations to place the turbines.

Figure 6.78: Wind turbines being used to generate electricity.

Figure 6.79 shows a wave power electricity generator. This floats on the water surface and moves up and down with the waves. The up and down motion is then used to generate electricity, which is transmitted through cables to land.

Figure 6.79: Wave power electricity generator.

Figure 6.80 shows the La Rance power station in France. This power station is built across a river estuary. Under the water are turbines, which turn when the tide moves in and out (Figure 6.81). The movement of these turbines is used to generate electricity. The La Rance power station is the oldest tidal power station in the world and was built in 1966. Smaller tidal power stations are now being developed all round the world.

Figure 6.80: The La Rance tidal power station in France.

Figure 6.81: A turbine in the La Rance power station.

> KEY WORD
>
> tidal power*: a method of generating electricity using energy from tidal movements

Advantages and disadvantages of renewable energy sources

Compared with using fossil fuels, there are several advantages and disadvantages with using renewable sources of energy.

Advantages

- Renewables are an infinite energy source, which means that they will not run out. There will always be wind, waves and tides to power generators.

- Renewables do not produce carbon dioxide gas so do not contribute to global warming.

- There is less reliance on fossil fuels. If more electricity is generated using renewable sources, there is less need to use fossil fuels. This means that there is less carbon dioxide produced.

- There is much less pollution as there is no smoke or sulfur dioxide. There is no risk of oil spills or leakage from pipelines or tankers.

Disadvantages

- Installation and maintenance costs can be high. Therefore it takes a long time to recover the costs of setting up and running a renewable energy power station.

- Renewable energy systems cannot be set up everywhere. Wind turbines need an area with high winds. Tidal systems must not block the entry of boats in river estuaries. Wave power systems need to have waves with high energy. Electricity generation is not always reliable: for example, wind turbines only generate electricity when it is windy.

- Extreme weather conditions damage renewable energy systems. Wind turbines are damaged if the wind speed is too high.

- Wind turbines need to be strongly fixed into the seabed. This requires drilling into the seabed and using concrete to secure the turbine. The seabed can be damaged by securing wind turbines – although probably no more than when using oil platforms to drill for oil.

- Birds have been killed and injured by wind turbines. Tidal systems and wave systems may block the migration routes of animals and prevent them reaching breeding and feeding grounds.

- Underwater cables need to be laid to conduct electricity back to land. These cables damage the seabed and may produce magnetic fields that affect the navigation of animals.

- Wind farms can be very unsightly. Having many wind turbines, wave power systems and tidal systems can result in fewer tourists visiting an area. This reduces the income that a local community could receive from tourism.

Renewable energy sources will become increasingly important over the next century. We are now more aware of the damage caused by fossil fuels to the environment and the need to find alternatives. The stocks of fossil fuels will also continue to fall. However, the marine environment offers us a wide range of possibilities to reduce our dependence on oil and gas.

ACTIVITY 6.6

Can we use more renewables to generate our electricity?

1   Do some research to find out how electricity is generated in your country. How much of it is generated from coal, oil and gas? How much of it comes from renewables? Are there any other ways of generating electricity, for example nuclear power or hydroelectric dams? Summarise your findings on one page of A4 paper.

2   What might the benefits and drawbacks be for your country of reducing fossil fuel use and increasing the use of renewables? Would it be possible to use solar, wind and tidal power in your country? Summarise this on one page of A4 paper.

3   Make a simple questionnaire to find out the views of other learners and teachers on the use of fossil fuels and renewables. Find out if other people are aware of where power comes from and the effects of fossil fuel use.

Self-assessment

Review your summaries. Do you think that your findings are accurate? Did your questionnaire generate interesting results, or would you change the questions if you did it again?

Questions

23 Give two uses of oil.

24 State what the MARPOL standards are and explain why they are important.

25 Compare the benefits and drawbacks of using renewable fuels compared with using fossil fuels.

6.6 Plastic pollution

Since the 1950s there has been a massive growth in the production and use of plastics. There are many different types of plastic and all of them are produced by humans, usually from chemicals in fossil fuels. By 2021, around 50 kg of plastic were manufactured every year per human on the planet. Plastics are used for packaging goods, and to make carrier bags, car parts, toys, computers and medical equipment. We can find plastics in almost every part of the world, and we all see them every day.

The main problem with plastics is that they often do not breakdown naturally. This resistance to decay is made worse because so many plastic items are used just once and then discarded. Our planet now has a massive quantity of discarded straws, water bottles and other plastic items. Much of this waste plastic finds its way into our oceans.

Plastic pollution and marine ecosystems

It is estimated that between 1 million and 8 million tonnes of plastic waste enters the oceans and seas every year. This means there are now over 80 million tonnes of waste plastic in the marine environment. Plastic bottles and other wastes litter our shores and travel all around the world on ocean currents. These plastics cause many problems to marine organisms.

Microplastics

When pieces of plastic are exposed to sunlight and are moved around by waves they break up into smaller pieces of plastic. Tiny particles of plastic that are less than 5 mm in size are called microplastics (Figure 6.82). Some of these microplastics come from waste water that has been used for washing clothes that contain plastic, such as synthetic fleece. Other microplastics result from larger pieces of plastic in the ocean that have broken up.

> **KEY WORD**
>
> **microplastics:** pieces of plastic that are less than 5 mm in diameter

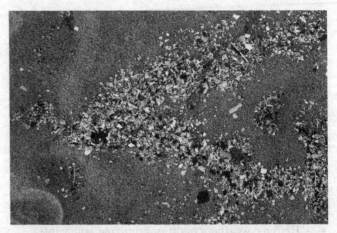

Figure 6.82: Plastics and microplastics washed up on a beach.

Microplastics absorb toxins from the water. The microplastics are eaten by filter-feeding animals such as crustaceans and molluscs and stick inside their bodies. When predators eat these organisms, the plastics then pass to the predator. This means that plastics and any toxins work through food chains to reach top predators.

Consumption of plastic by organisms

In 2021, Scientists listed over one thousand marine organisms known to ingest plastic. Many species of sea turtles eat jellyfish (Figure 6.83). But floating plastic bags can look like jellyfish and many sea turtles die after eating plastic bags by mistake. Whales and dolphins are also killed by eating plastics. In 2018, a dead whale in the Philippines was found to have over 40 kg of plastic in its stomach. When organisms consume plastic, it blocks the gut and causes animals to starve.

Figure 6.83: Turtle swimming by a plastic bag. Turtles often consume plastic bags mistaking them for jellyfish.

Adult seabirds hunt for food and then return to their nests to feed their young. The adult birds are attracted to pieces of plastic that they then feed to the chicks. This plastic blocks the guts of the chicks, causing their death. Figure 6.84 shows waste plastic masks that were collected from a harbour area in Italy during the response to the COVID-19 pandemic. Over three billion face shields and facemasks were discarded worldwide every day and much of this ended up in the marine environment.

Figure 6.85: A diver removing discarded fishing gear.

Figure 6.84: Some of the discarded plastic masks that were collected from a coastal area in Italy. These masks were discarded during the international response to the Covid-19 pandemic.

Entangling animals

Large plastic items, such as discarded fishing lines, nets and ropes, can trap organisms (Figure 6.85). Dolphins, turtles and seabirds can become entangled in lines and nets and drown because they cannot return to the surface to breathe. Fish also become entangled, damaging their skin so it easily become infected. Trapped fish are easy prey for predator species or starve to death because they cannot feed. Discarded and lost fishing tackle that continue to trap organisms are known as ghost nets.

Ocean garbage patches

Figure 6.86 shows the main ocean gyres in the oceans. You learnt about ocean gyres in Section 1.4. An ocean gyre is a region where strong currents circle around a central area. There are five main ocean gyres:

- North Pacific gyre
- South Pacific gyre
- Indian Ocean gyre
- North Atlantic gyre
- South Atlantic gyre.

The currents around the gyres concentrate waste plastics and other refuse in the centre of the gyre to create garbage patches. All the ocean gyres have a garbage patch, but the Great North Pacific garbage patch is the largest. It is hard to estimate how large it is, but it may have an area of over 1.5 million square kilometres.

KEY WORD

garbage patch: area within an ocean gyre where plastic and other garbage accumulates

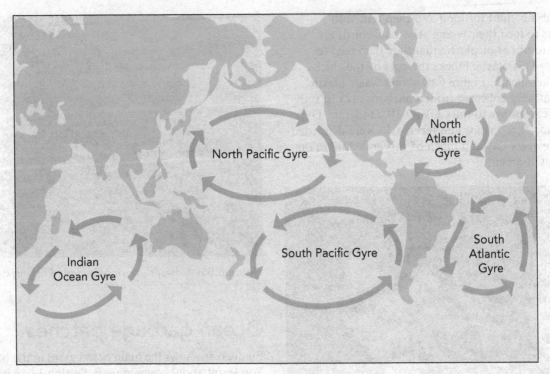

Figure 6.86: Map showing the ocean gyres.

In 2018, the Great North Pacific garbage patch was estimated to contain more than 1.8 trillion items of plastic, mostly pieces larger than 5 mm in length. The types of plastic present include discarded fishing gear, plastic bottles, pens, cigarette lighters, mobile phones and large masses of microplastic (Figure 6.87).

Scientists think that much of the plastic waste comes from coastal areas of China, Indonesia and the Philippines. Dumping of waste from cargo ships is another major source of the waste.

Figure 6.87: Plastic waste floating in a garbage patch.

Reducing the size of the garbage patches

Cleaning up the garbage patches is a priority for conservation organisations, but this is going to be difficult. There are two main strategies to reduce the size of the patches:

- removing the existing waste

- preventing more waste reaching the garbage patch.

Removing the existing waste is not easy. The gyres are difficult to reach and sending people to work there is dangerous. A non-profit organisation called The Ocean Cleanup uses booms to capture the waste from the surface and prevent more waste from entering by catching it before it reaches the centre of the gyre (Figure 6.88).

After capture by the booms, the waste is channelled into a collection net. Refuse ships then regularly empty the net and remove the waste. Researchers are working to ensure that the collection methods do not harm marine animals. They are also designing stronger booms to cope with the extreme weather conditions of the open oceans.

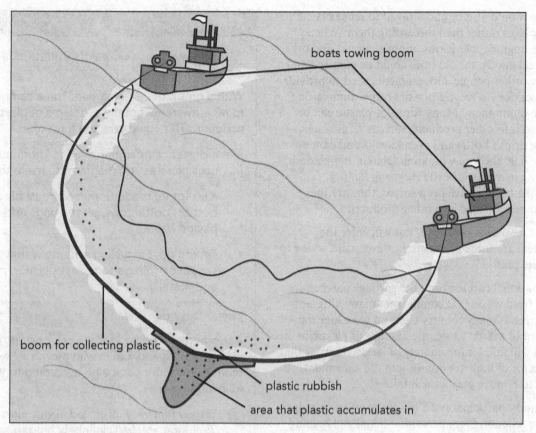

Figure 6.88: Method of removing plastic garbage from the ocean using booms.

We can reduce the size of the garbage patches by limiting the amount of plastic that enters the oceans in the first place. Several approaches can be taken to reduce the use of plastic and discourage the discarding of plastic.

- Government legislation: single-use plastics can be banned, and charges or taxes can be introduced. For example, handing out free plastic carrier bags in supermarkets is now banned in many countries. Some countries have introduced a charge on plastic carrier bags to encourage customers to reuse sustainable bags. More and more supermarkets use paper bags or reusable bags made from plant materials. Drinking straws and plastic bottles are often banned or taxed to reduce their use.

- Education: many people are unaware of the damage done by plastics. Some charity groups hold awareness events to highlight this and encourage people to help out. Most people try to protect the natural world if they know how their actions affect it. Figure 6.89 shows a sculpture of a killer whale made from single-use plastic and over 40 000 bottle tops on a beach in Mumbai, India. Events such as this

Figure 6.89: Sculpture made from discarded plastic to raise awareness of plastic pollution.

raise awareness of pollution and may stop people throwing away plastic waste.

- Reduce, reuse, recycle: manufacturers and shops can reduce the use of plastic packaging.

People should also be encouraged to reuse plastic carrier bags rather than discarding them. When people upgrade televisions, mobile phones and other electrical goods, the old ones could be repaired and used by other people. Governments need to provide more services to recycle plastics rather than letting people dump them. Many forms of plastic can be recycled into other products, such as refuse bags, bricks, drinks bottle and even kayaks and canoes. Figure 6.90 shows a woman in Dhaka, Bangladesh, working in a plastic bottle recycling factory. After the bottles have been sorted, they are then sent to be reformed into other products.

If less plastic waste is produced, less will enter the oceans. There are some problems, however, with trying to reduce waste plastic.

- International cooperation: the garbage patches are made from waste that comes from many different countries. If every country signs up to reduce the amount of plastic waste, the amount of plastic in the ocean will fall. Unfortunately, if large countries that have a lot of industry do not join the agreement, plans to remove plastics will fail.

- Voluntary participation: a lot of the effort to reduce plastic relies on every person on the planet helping a little bit. If everyone reduces their plastic waste, we will clean up the oceans quickly. However, not everyone is fully aware of what happens to the plastic bottles they throw on the ground, or the drinking straws they use. Education and awareness are very important to make sure that everyone plays a part. It is, however, not always possible to reach everyone with information.

Figure 6.90: Woman in Bangladesh recycling plastic bottles.

ACTIVITY 6.7

Raising awareness of plastic pollution in our oceans

With a group of other learners, run a campaign to raise awareness of the problems of plastic pollution. This could take the form of:

- a poster campaign that gives information and uses pictures and diagrams to make the points

- a sculpture made from discarded plastic bottles, bottle tops, plastic bags and other plastic waste

- setting up a recycling scheme within your school or college to collect plastics, paper and metal.

Peer assessment

Ask other learners to look at your posters, or your sculpture and join in with recycling. Ask them to rate your campaign according to the following scheme:

☺ if they feel very informed about plastic pollution and will definitely help to reduce it

😐 if they feel partly informed about plastic pollution and will try to help reduce it

☹ if they do not really understand about plastic pollution and will not try to help reduce it.

6.7 Eutrophication

The demand for human food increases every year. Most of our food is produced by farming and, to meet demand, intensive farming methods are often used. Intensive farming, however, can cause severe pollution of rivers, oceans and seas.

KEY WORD

intensive farming*: methods of farming that produce large amounts of crops or animals; often relies on mechanisation and the addition of fertilisers and pesticides

Fertiliser use

Traditionally, crop fields have been fertilised by adding animal faeces and dead waste plant material. The faeces and waste is slowly broken down by bacteria and fungi in the soil, releasing nutrients for the crops.

Modern fertilisers are mixtures of the chemical nutrients that are essential for crop growth. We add fertilisers to fields to increase crop yields (Figure 6.91). A typical fertiliser contains nitrates, phosphates, potassium, magnesium and other mineral ions. Fertilisers makes crops grow more quickly so more food can be produced. However, adding too much fertiliser can be very damaging to freshwater and marine environments.

Figure 6.92: Massive algal bloom along coastline of China.

Once eutrophication gets out of control, it leads to a loss of oxygen, so animals suffocate and die. There are several stages that occur during eutrophication, shown in Figure 6.93.

Stages of eutrophication

- Fertiliser that has been added to fields dissolves in rainwater to form a solution.

- The fertiliser solution runs off into a river, a lake or the sea.

- The fertiliser solution increases the availability of elements such as nitrogen and phosphorus in the water.

- Algae grow very rapidly, producing an algal bloom.

- When there are large numbers of algae, less light is able to pass through water. Algae in deeper water are unable to photosynthesise and die.

- Dead algae sink and are decomposed by bacteria.

- Decomposer bacteria respire aerobically, very rapidly, using oxygen from the water.

- Oxygen levels in the water drop.

- The lack of oxygen means that animals such as fish cannot respire and so they die.

Figure 6.91: Farmers adding fertiliser to fields in China.

Eutrophication is the process by which algae grow rapidly when a body of water has a lot of mineral ions added to it. The large quantity of algae produced is called an algal bloom. Figure 6.92 shows an area of coastline in China where an excess of algae have grown due to fertiliser in the water.

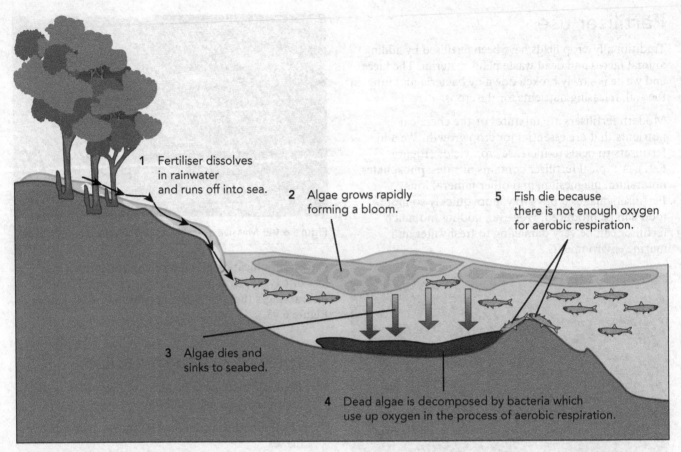

Figure 6.93: The stages of eutrophication.

Sewage pollution

Releasing untreated sewage into rivers, lakes and oceans also leads to a loss of oxygen. Sewage is liquid or solid waste, such as human or animal faeces. If sewage enters water without first being treated, the number of decomposer bacteria in the water increase rapidly. These bacteria use up a lot of the oxygen in the water for aerobic respiration. The oxygen concentration of the water falls, so animals are unable to respire and die.

Questions

26 State why fertilisers contain nitrates and magnesium.

27 Explain why oxygen levels in the water of an estuary near farmed fields reduce after fertiliser has been added to the fields.

28 Suggest why adding animal faeces and rotting plant material results in less eutrophication of water compared with adding chemical fertilisers.

6.8 Understanding climate change

The Earth is estimated to be over 4.5 billion years old. Over this time, the proportions of gases in the atmosphere have changed a lot. When the Earth first formed, there was a large amount of carbon dioxide in the atmosphere and very little oxygen.

Around 2.3 billion years ago, bacteria evolved that could photosynthesise. These bacteria removed a lot of carbon dioxide from the atmosphere and replaced it with oxygen. The carbon dioxide levels gradually fell, and the oxygen levels increased. The climate of the planet also changed. We now know that gases in the atmosphere, such as carbon dioxide, have a very important effect on our climate. Over the last 335 million years there has been an overall decrease in the level of carbon dioxide in our atmosphere and a decrease in the average temperature of the Earth.

The greenhouse effect

Based on our distance from the Sun, scientists estimate that the average temperature of the Earth should be about −18 °C. However, the actual average temperature is +14 °C because of the greenhouse effect (Figure 6.94).

The greenhouse effect produces warming due to the presence of greenhouse gases in the Earth's atmosphere. Three of the main greenhouse gases are:

- carbon dioxide
- methane
- water vapour.

These greenhouse gases affect the Earth's temperature:

- Radiation from the Sun hits the Earth's atmosphere.
- Some of the radiation passes through the atmosphere and hits the Earth; this radiation is absorbed by the oceans and land.

- Some of the radiation hitting the planet is reflected back to the Earth's atmosphere.
- The greenhouse gases in the atmosphere reflect some of the radiation back down to the surface of the planet, trapping the radiation; this warms the planet.

The greenhouse effect is a natural effect, and it maintains the temperature of our planet at a level suitable for life.

> **KEY WORD**
>
> **greenhouse effect:** the natural warming effect that occurs when radiation is reflected back to the planet by greenhouse gases in the atmosphere

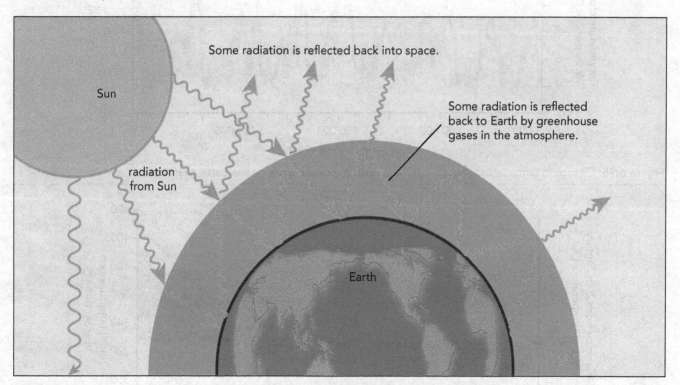

Figure 6.94: The greenhouse effect. Radiation from the Sun enters the Earth's atmosphere. Some radiation passes back into space but some is reflected back to Earth by greenhouse gases in the atmosphere.

The enhanced greenhouse effect and climate change

Figure 6.95 shows the changes in atmospheric carbon dioxide and average global temperature over the past 800 000 years. You can see from this graph that the two lines follow the same pattern. This means that, generally, the Earth is warmer when there is more carbon dioxide in the atmosphere.

Over the past century, we have seen an increase in the amount of carbon dioxide in the atmosphere and also an increase in the average temperature of the Earth. Figure 6.96 shows how carbon dioxide levels and the average temperature have changed since 1880. The average

temperature on the graph is a measure of how different the temperature is each year compared with the average temperature over the whole of the twentieth century. As carbon dioxide levels have increased, so too has the global temperature. Because of the increase in carbon dioxide gas, our planet is now experiencing an enhanced greenhouse effect. The rise in temperature resulting from the enhanced greenhouse effect is called global warming.

> **KEY WORD**
>
> **enhanced greenhouse effect:** the artificial warming that occurs due to the release of excess carbon dioxide and methane into the atmosphere

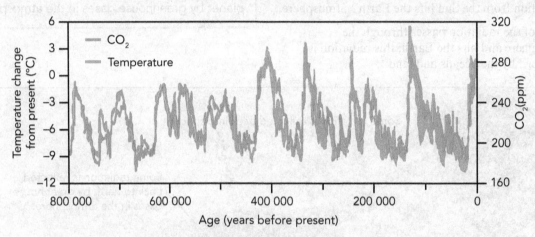

Figure 6.95: Change in temperature and atmospheric carbon dioxide levels on the Earth over time.

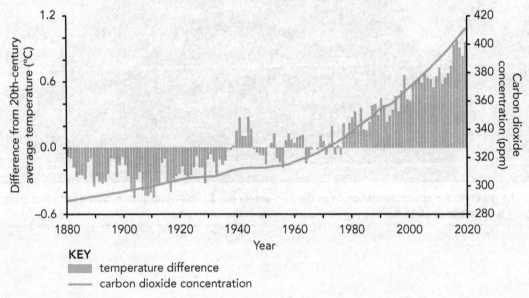

KEY
temperature difference
carbon dioxide concentration

Figure 6.96: Changes in temperature and atmospheric carbon dioxide concentrations between 1880 and 2020.

Climate change

Climate change is the long-term change in weather patterns across the planet. It includes changes in temperature, rainfall patterns and the frequency of storms. The cause of climate change is still being discussed by scientists as it is difficult to find one factor that is the definite cause. However, over the past 50–60 years, there has been an increase in global temperatures and a change in weather patterns. The increased release of greenhouse gases from human activities is now thought to be the leading cause of climate change and global warming. However, volcanic activity and changes in the activity of the Sun may be factors that also contribute to climate change.

The two main greenhouse gases released from human activity are carbon dioxide and methane. Figure 6.97 shows processes that remove and release carbon dioxide from the atmosphere.

Carbon dioxide is removed from the atmosphere by:

- photosynthesis by producer organisms
- carbon dioxide gas dissolving in the oceans.

Many processes, however, release carbon dioxide:

- volcanic eruptions
- respiration of living organisms and decomposition of dead material
- oceans releasing some dissolved carbon dioxide
- combustion of fossil fuels
- deforestation – this reduces the number of producer organisms that photosynthesise and also releases carbon dioxide from the decomposition of dead trees
- forest fires.

The amount of fossil fuel (oil, gas and coal) that is burnt has increased dramatically over the last 150 years.

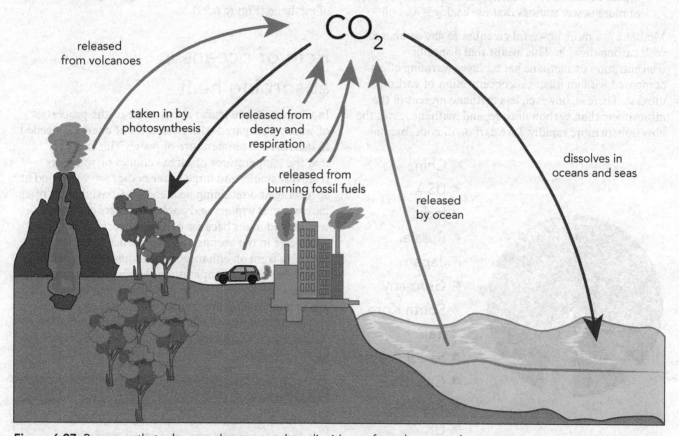

Figure 6.97: Processes that release and remove carbon dioxide gas from the atmosphere.

This means that more carbon dioxide is now being released into the atmosphere compared with the carbon dioxide being removed from the atmosphere. In 1990, over 22 000 000 000 kilograms of carbon dioxide were released from fossil fuel combustion. In 2017, this had increased to over 37 000 000 000 kilograms.

Figure 6.98 shows the percentage of this carbon dioxide released by different countries in 2017. You can see from this pie chart that nearly half of the carbon dioxide released was from three countries, with China accounting for nearly 30% of the total.

There are many reasons why fossil fuel combustion has increased:

- more cars and trucks using petrol and diesel
- more transport of goods on ships using diesel
- more aeroplanes transporting people around the world using kerosene
- higher demand for electricity, leading to the building of more power stations that use coal, gas and oil.

Methane is a more powerful greenhouse gas compared with carbon dioxide. This means that a specific concentration of methane has a bigger warming effect compared with an identical concentration of carbon dioxide. There is, however, less methane present in the atmosphere than carbon dioxide, and methane leaves the atmosphere more rapidly. Like carbon dioxide, methane

levels have risen over the last hundred years, rising especially rapidly over the last 20 years.

Methane release comes from a variety of natural and human sources:

- wetland areas are the largest natural source, and it is released when areas of frozen wetland near to the poles thaw
- animals that live in natural environments, especially detritivores, such as termites
- decaying natural vegetation
- fossil fuel production by humans
- agriculture, especially rice farming and cattle farming
- waste food and other waste materials in rubbish tips.

The increasing human population means there is now a high demand for food and large amounts of food waste are produced every day. Cattle and rice farming have also increased, releasing large amounts of methane (Figure 6.99).

Role of oceans in absorbing heat

In Chapter 2, you learnt about some of the properties of water. Compared with land, a lot of energy is needed to increase the temperature of water. This means that the temperatures of large volumes of water are relatively stable, and large water bodies are very good at absorbing and retaining heat energy. Coastal areas often have warmer winters and cooler summers compared with inland areas because of this property of water. The water in the oceans and seas reduces some of the warming from an enhanced greenhouse effect, helping to stabilise global temperatures. However, because our oceans absorb much of the additional heat energy, they are also increasing in temperature. This temperature rise in the oceans will affect photosynthesis, alter food chains, cause ice to melt and lead to **thermal expansion** of water bodies.

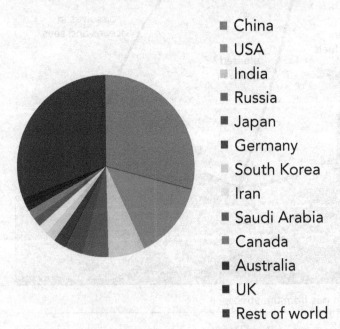

- China
- USA
- India
- Russia
- Japan
- Germany
- South Korea
- Iran
- Saudi Arabia
- Canada
- Australia
- UK
- Rest of world

Figure 6.98: Pie chart showing the proportions of carbon dioxide gas released by different countries in 2017.

> KEY WORD
>
> **thermal expansion:** the expansion of water in the oceans and seas due to an increase in temperature

Figure 6.99: Agriculture releases methane gas: a cattle farming; b rice farming.

Thermal expansion, sea level rises and the melting of ice

One of the risks of global warming is a rise in sea level. A rise in sea level will result in widespread flooding and loss of coastal habitats. Humans in coastal communities could also lose their homes. Figure 6.100 shows the increase in sea levels between 1993 and 2021.

There are two reasons why global warming increases sea levels:

- thermal expansion of water
- melting of land ice.

As water heats up, it expands. This means that the same mass of water will take up a bigger volume. It is estimated that about 42% of the sea level rises that have occurred over the last century are due to the thermal expansion of water.

Ice sheets are massive sheets of frozen water that cover land. They are only found in Greenland in the Northern Hemisphere and in Antarctica in the Southern Hemisphere. It is estimated that 70% of the world's freshwater is locked up in the ice sheet over Antarctica.

> ## KEY WORD
>
> ice sheet: large masses of frozen water that cover land masses; the main ice sheets are located in Greenland and Antarctica

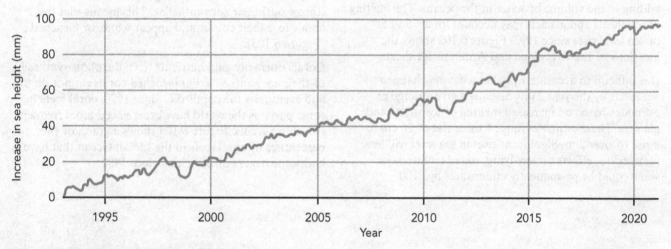

Figure 6.100: Change in sea levels since 1993.

Glaciers, such as the Eqi glacier in Greenland, are permanent masses of ice that slowly move along the ground (Figure 6.101). They are found in polar regions or regions with high mountains. Pakistan is the country with the greatest number of glaciers; it has at least 7000 glaciers.

KEY WORD

glacier: a permanent, land-based sheet of ice that slowly moves along the ground

Figure 6.101: The Eqi glacier in Greenland.

In the cold winter months, ice sheets form over Greenland and Antarctica. Parts of these sheets naturally melt during warmer months. However, as global temperatures rise, the rate of ice formation becomes lower compared with the rate of ice melting. Water from the melted ice runs into the oceans, increasing the ocean volume. Glaciers also melt, further adding to the volume of water in the oceans. The melting of ice sheets and glaciers may account for around 58% of sea level rises since 1993. Figure 6.102 shows the locations of the Greenland and Antarctic ice sheets.

It is difficult to accurately predict what may happen to sea levels by the year 2100. Scientists give a range of estimates based on increased melting of ice sheets and glaciers. These estimates range from a rise of 26 cm to a rise of over 2 m. Significant rises in sea level will have very serious effects on low-lying, island countries as some could be permanently underwater by 2100.

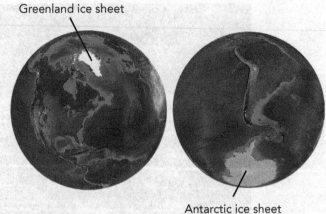

Greenland ice sheet

Antarctic ice sheet

Figure 6.102: The locations of the Greenland and Antarctic ice sheets.

Impacts of increasing greenhouse gases on marine ecosystems

If we continue to release large quantities of greenhouse gases, there are many possible impacts on marine ecosystems.

Continued melting of ice sheets and glaciers, and thermal expansion of water, will increase sea levels. Coastal habitats will be lost. This habitat loss will lead to extinctions of species and disruption of food webs. Human settlements will be lost, and land that is used now for farming, industry and tourism will be flooded. Low-lying, island countries, such as the Maldives, are at risk of severe flooding.

When coral polyps are placed under environmental stress, due to pollution or temperature rises, they expel (throw out) their zooxanthellae. This means that the corals lose their colour and appear white, or bleached (Figure 6.103).

Corals normally gain nutrients from the photosynthesis of their zooxanthellae but bleached corals cannot do this and eventually the corals die. Since 1990, coral reefs in some parts of the world have experienced more frequent bleaching events. Figure 6.104 shows a graph of the percentage of coral reefs in the Indian Ocean that have had some degree of bleaching since 1980.

Figure 6.103: Corals that have expelled their zooxanthellae and become bleached.

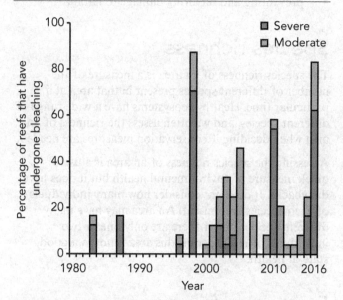

Figure 6.104: Graph showing percentage of coral reefs in the Indian Ocean that had bleaching events between 1980 and 2016.

Seawater has a pH of around 8.1 to 8.2. Carbon dioxide is an acidic gas. This means that as more carbon dioxide dissolves in seawater, the pH of the seawater becomes lower (less alkaline). This lower pH is a problem for organisms that use calcium carbonate as part of their skeletons. For example, the reduced alkalinity of seawater causes coral reefs to erode, leading to slower growth and loss of the reef area.

Molluscs have thinner shells in seawater which is less alkaline, so are less protected from predators and physical damage.

As water warms up, smaller amounts of gases are able to be dissolved. An increase in water temperature leads to a reduced concentration of oxygen in the oceans, so marine organisms will be less able to respire. Larger, active organisms, such as tuna, will be affected most because they have a high oxygen demand.

As the climate changes, marine species that are adapted for cooler waters will shift their range further towards the poles to find water of the temperature they prefer. They will be replaced in their traditional waters by species better adapted for warmer water. Scientists have found already that in the North Atlantic, cod and halibut are becoming rarer in southerly areas, but are caught more frequently in more northerly areas. Warm water species, such as swordfish and bluefin tuna, have also been sighted more frequently in northern waters.

Migration patterns may no longer be suitable for species that rely on the presence of food in certain places at certain times of year. For example, humpback whales traditionally migrate to polar waters when rich populations of krill appear after the ice starts to melt. If the ice melts earlier, the fear is that the whales will arrive in the polar waters too late for the sudden increase in krill. This may lead to starvation for the whales.

Global warming will cause habitat loss and disruption of food chains. New competitor organisms, predators and parasites may also expand their range from other areas of the oceans. All these factors will lead to extinction of organisms. For example, those organisms that rely on ice sheets for a habitat, such as polar bears, may risk extinction.

Global warming and climate change may affect the weather systems of the planet. Some areas will experience more storms and excess rainfall while other regions will have droughts. If glaciers melt and release freshwater into the oceans, the salinity of the oceans can decrease. These changes in salinity can affect ocean current systems. An increase in storms may damage coral reefs, causing a loss of habitats for many species.

ACTIVITY 6.8

Playing our part in reducing climate change

We can all play a role in reducing the release of carbon dioxide and methane. Do some research to design a school that minimises the release of carbon dioxide and methane. There are lots of things that you can think about: recycling, low-energy light bulbs, reducing waste, sharing transport, and encouraging walking or cycling to school.

Draw out a large plan of the school you have designed, with notes to explain how your school will reduce the release of greenhouse gases.

Self-assessment

Rate your work according to the following scheme for each of the points listed below:

☺ if the design gives more points than the ones on the list

☻ if the design gives most of the points on the list

☹ if the design gives few of the points on the list.

I have thought about:

- reducing the amount of electricity used
- finding ways to reduce air conditioning and central heating
- reducing car usage
- reducing waste production
- reducing waste food.

Questions

29 Give four negative impacts of global warming.

30 Compare the greenhouse effect with the enhanced greenhouse effect.

31 Explain why global warming can lead to an increase in sea levels.

6.9 Conservation strategies

Humans are the dominant species on the planet, and we are currently doing more damage to the planet than any other species has ever done. We need to try to repair some of the damage already done and prevent further damage so that future generations can enjoy the marine environment.

Conservation is the attempt to prevent and repair environmental damage and it has two main objectives:

- preventing the extinction of species and increasing populations
- preventing and repairing damage to habitats.

Species richness

The species richness of an area is a measure of the number of different species present in that area at a particular time. Healthy ecosystems have a wide range of different species, and we often assess the richness of an area when deciding if conservation measures are needed.

Assessing the species richness of an area is a useful, quick measure of environmental health but it does have drawbacks. It does not consider how many individuals of each species are present. An area may have many different species but, if there are only one or two individuals of each species, this area is not in a good state of health.

Strategies for preserving species richness

We can use several methods to maintain different species in an area. Three methods often used in marine ecosystems are:

- making sure that harvesting of species is sustainable
- using aquaculture to grow species
- setting up protected areas.

Sustainable harvesting

In Section 6.3 we looked at measures taken to maintain stocks of commercial species.

We harvest many species of seaweed (macroalgae), plants and animals from the oceans. However, if we overharvest, stocks of marine organisms fall and food chains are damaged. Measures that we can take include:

- setting quotas for harvesting

- restricting the number of days on which fishers can work

- having closed seasons when species cannot be harvested

- having closed areas where we cannot remove species

- preventing the use of some methods or use of certain equipment

- requiring the use of licences and permits to fish.

Tuna populations around the Maldives are fished sustainably. This is due to the banning of all fishing methods other than pole and line and the strict use of quotas and licences.

There are advantages and disadvantages to permitting sustainable harvesting.

Advantages:

- Local people can still earn money from harvesting species.

- Local communities can maintain a traditional occupation, so communities are not lost.

- Species will maintain their populations for future generations of humans and for the health of ecosystems.

- Local people will help if they are getting some benefits from the conservation measures.

Disadvantages:

- It can be difficult to monitor and enforce regulations.

- Some overfishing may still occur making populations unsustainable.

Aquaculture of species

In Section 6.4 you learnt about the use of aquaculture to produce commercial and endangered species. Aquaculture can help to meet the demand for species and so prevent overfishing. We also use aquaculture to replenish stocks of endangered species such as coral and giant clams (Figure 6.105). Giant clam farming has been very successful in reducing the number of clams harvested from the sea commercially. Also, we can use the farmed clams to replenish wild populations.

Figure 6.105: A giant clam farm in Fiji.

There are advantages and disadvantages to using aquaculture as a method of conservation.

Advantages:

- There is less pressure to harvest wild organisms so less overfishing.

- Aquaculture can bring money into local economies.

- Organisms can be grown using aquaculture and released into the wild.

Disadvantages:

- Aquaculture can release pollutants into the marine environment.

- Aquaculture can require the harvesting of species from the ocean, which are then used to feed the species being grown; sometimes species harvested from the ocean are also used for broodstock.

- Organisms raised by aquaculture can introduce diseases into wild populations when released.

Setting up protected areas

MPAs and national parks are set up to conserve populations of endangered species as well as the rest of the ecosystem. You learnt about the use of MPAs to prevent loss of fish stocks in Section 6.4. There are many MPAs and national parks around the world, including the Galapagos Islands (off Ecuador) and the Great Barrier Reef (off Australia). MPAs and national parks control activities within their boundaries. Different MPAs and national parks have different levels of control depending on how important the conservation work is.

Possible regulations include:

- bans on harvesting all species in some areas – limited harvesting may be permitted in other areas but restrictions may be placed on catches, the species harvested, fishing gear used and the time of year that harvesting is allowed
- bans on drilling for minerals from the seabed
- bans on extraction of oil and gas
- bans or restrictions on the use of renewable energy systems such as wind turbines
- bans or restrictions on tourism
- bans or restrictions on the passage of boats through the areas.

There are advantages and disadvantages to setting up MPAs and national parks.

Advantages:

- Species can reproduce and increase their populations in these areas.
- Habitats and food chains are preserved so a wide variety of species are conserved in an area.
- Species within the protected area will 'spill over' into surrounding areas helping to increase populations elsewhere in the oceans.

Disadvantages:

- Conflict can occur with local people who may lose traditional fishing grounds.
- High fish populations around an MPA or national park can encourage fishers to harvest species near the area.

Conservation projects

There are many conservation projects around the world. Some projects focus on preventing the extinction of one species, while others protect a whole area or habitat.

Coral farming

We use three methods of aquaculture to grow coral.

- Small pieces of coral are removed from a reef, placed into nursery tanks and grown until large enough to transplant onto reefs.

- Coral larvae are collected from a reef during the spawning season. The larvae are placed into nursery tanks and allowed to settle onto small pieces of concrete, plastic or rock. The corals are then grown until large enough to transplant onto reefs.
- Coral broodstock is allowed to spawn in an aquaculture system. The larvae are collected and settle onto concrete, plastic or rock. When large enough, the corals are then transplanted onto reefs.

Coral farming (Figure 6.106) is now used all round the world to help repair coral reefs damaged by blast fishing, pollution and from predation by crown of thorns starfish. As a method of reef conservation, coral farming has advantages and disadvantages.

Advantages:

- Coral farming has successfully helped to repair many coral reefs.
- Coral farming provides work for local people, improving the economy.

Disadvantages:

- Coral farming is time consuming and expensive.
- Coral farming requires trained, skilled workers.
- Transplantation of corals is not always effective and requires the farming of many corals.
- To be effective, the underlying cause of the reef damage also needs to be stopped; for example, blast fishing must be banned.

Figure 6.106: Coral farm in the Federated States of Micronesia.

Turtle conservation

There are seven species of sea turtle and nearly every species is at some risk of extinction. In the last 30 years, the population of all sea turtles in the East Pacific fell by 90%. Sea turtles face many threats including:

- bycatch – turtles are caught in fishing nets and on longlines
- illegal catching – turtles are caught for food or for trading their eggs and shells
- habitat loss – beaches where turtles nest have been developed and built over
- consumption of plastics – turtles are killed as they confuse waste plastic with jellyfish
- climate change and pollution – global warming could alter the ratio of males and females and affect food chains.

Many different conservation groups work to help turtle populations. These groups are sometimes funded by governments, but others depend on donations and volunteer workers. Methods of conservation include reducing the release of plastics into the ocean, and removing waste fishing nets and gear from oceans. Some groups protect beaches used by nesting turtles, and rear turtles safely in captivity before releasing them into the sea.

Figure 6.107 shows volunteers on a beach in Indonesia releasing baby turtles that have been raised in **captive breeding programmes.** The volunteers remove turtle eggs from nests once the females have returned to the seas. The eggs are then incubated away from predatory birds and mammals that eat turtle eggs. The baby turtles are raised in tanks until they are ready to be taken to the sea and released. Volunteers release the turtles close to the water so that they are not eaten by predatory birds.

Figure 6.107: Turtles being released as part of a conservation project in Indonesia.

Figure 6.108 shows information signs around a beach in Thailand. Access to the beach is restricted during the months when turtles nest there. Tourists are allowed to visit the area at night, when accompanied by guides, to see turtles laying eggs or eggs hatching. Turtles are confused by bright white lights and blue or green lights, so the beaches are lit by red light. In many areas of the world, red light is the only light allowed on beaches that turtles use for nesting.

Figure 6.108: Information and warning signs near a beach where turtles nest in Thailand. Note that the area is illuminated with red light which does not confuse the turtles.

There are advantages and disadvantages of these methods of turtle conservation.

Advantages:

- Incubating the eggs in captivity means that more hatch and fewer are eaten by predators.
- Releasing the turtles into the sea means that fewer are eaten by predators when trying to reach the sea.
- Protecting the nesting sites means that turtles still have breeding areas.
- Lighting beach areas with red light means that the turtles are not confused by bright lights.

KEY WORD

captive breeding programme*: the production of offspring from endangered species in zoos, aquaria and safari parks; the aim is to help prevent extinctions

Disadvantages:

- Out in the oceans, turtles are still at risk from being caught or trapped in fishing gear.

- Raising the turtles and installing red lights are expensive.

Removal of invasive species

An invasive species is an organism that causes ecological or economic harm in a new environment where it is not native. We have, unfortunately, introduced many species to areas of the world where they are not native. Often these invasive species damage native species. Figure 6.109 shows the most widely known invasive species in the world, the lionfish.

Figure 6.109: A lionfish; a species that is classed as an invasive species in many parts of the world.

Lionfish are native to coral reefs in the Indo-Pacific area. They are popular aquarium fish and were transported to aquaria all round the world. In the mid-1990s, some lionfish escaped into the waters near Florida. No-one knows how they escaped – perhaps people discarded them as unwanted pets, or they may have escaped when a hurricane destroyed an aquarium. By 2015, lionfish were sighted far up and down the Atlantic coastline of North America, throughout the Caribbean Sea and in the Gulf of Mexico (Figure 6.110).

The spread of lionfish could cause an ecological disaster. These fish have few predators and the species of grouper that do eat them have been overfished. Lionfish eat a wide range of reef species and quickly become the dominant species on a coral reef. They are aggressive fish and force other fish species out. It is estimated that they could be reducing the species richness of coral reefs by 80%.

There are several methods being tested to reduce lionfish populations:

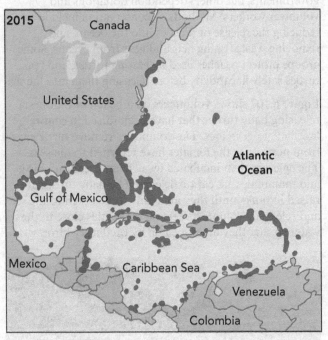

Figure 6.110: Map of the East coast of North and Central America showing areas where lionfish were seen in 1995 and 2015.

- setting baited traps that only lionfish can enter

- encouraging divers to catch lionfish (Figure 6.111); the Florida Keys National Marine Sanctuary licences divers to use spearfishing for lionfish

Figure 6.111: Diver catching lionfish with a speargun.

- encouraging local people to catch lionfish commercially as a food; in some countries, governments run promotional campaigns to suggest ways of cooking lionfish
- in Cuba, scientists have been trying to train sharks to eat lionfish.

There are advantages and disadvantages of these methods of removing lionfish.

Advantages:

- Trapping and catching lionfish reduces the populations of lionfish. This will prevent other species from becoming extinct.
- Promotional campaigns to encourage people to eat lionfish is a cheap method of encouraging people to reduce lionfish populations.

Disadvantages:

- Traps can catch other species if not carefully designed to only attract lionfish.
- Divers and fishers can damage the coral reef.
- Lionfish seem to change their behaviour to avoid divers when they are regularly hunted.

Questions

32   State what is meant by the term 'species richness'.

33   Explain why methods to cull lionfish are being introduced in the Caribbean Sea.

34   Explain why setting up an MPA may be a better way of conserving a population of sharks compared with raising sharks using aquaculture and then releasing them into the wild.

SUMMARY

Humans gain a range of services from marine ecosystems, such as recreation, tourism, building materials and fisheries; humans can have negative impacts on marine ecosystems, such as pollution, land development and oil spills.

Sustainable resources are resources that we can continue to use.

Tourism is an important part of many coastal economies but can have negative impacts on marine ecosystems.

Ecotourism is an ecologically sustainable form of tourism that promotes environmental and cultural understanding; negative impacts of ecotourism can be reduced by education, planning, legislation, use of renewables, limiting water use, banning single-use plastics and limiting motorised transport.

Marine organisms are an important source of food for many people but may be over-harvested due to the increasing human population.

Sustainable harvesting is harvesting marine organisms while ensuring that there are still organisms present for future generations; this can be achieved by methods including restrictions, using quotas, closed seasons, setting up Marine Protected Areas and making international agreements.

There are many different methods of fishing, each with different environmental impacts: methods include cast netting, trawling, purse seining, tangle nets, basket traps, line fishing and rod fishing.

Fish aggregating devices (FADs) are floating platforms that attract fish and are used by fishers to increase catches.

Boats have a range of navigation aids including charts, compasses, GPS, sonar and radar.

CONTINUED

Aquaculture is a method of producing marine species for commercial or environmental purposes; it is used to reduce the overfishing of wild fish stocks and increase their populations.

A range of marine organisms are produced by aquaculture: seaweeds, fish, crustaceans, molluscs, echinoderms; open aquaculture systems are located in natural water bodies, and closed systems use tanks that are separate from natural water.

Aquaculture systems need: selection of rapidly growing organisms, broodstock, methods of maintaining conditions, water filtration to prevent eutrophication, prevention of disease spread, prevention of predators.

Aquaculture can be used to grow coral and mangroves to restock natural areas.

Oil is a fossil fuel that is found under the seabed; oil has a range of functions including uses as fuels and in the manufacture of plastic.

Oil drilling and transport carries a risk of oil spillage; MARPOL lists standards for ship design that reduce oil pollution: oil tankers must have double hulls, tankers cannot wash out holds at sea, sewage must not be released at sea and garbage must not be disposed at sea.

Oil spills can coat the fur and feathers of animals, poison animals and prevent photosynthesis so that food chains are damaged; the impacts of oil spills can be minimised by using booms, skimmers, dispersant sprays, and burning off the oil.

Fossil fuels are non-renewable fuels that will eventually run out, but they are difficult to extract and produce carbon dioxide gas when combusted; advantages include: they are a constant energy supply, have a high calorific value and are easy to transport and use.

Marine renewable energy systems generate electricity using energy from wind, wave power and tidal power; these systems are more sustainable than fossil fuels as they will not run out, do not release carbon dioxide and are less polluting; but they are expensive to install, may not be useable in all locations, may not give a constant supply of electricity and can damage marine organisms.

Plastic pollution is major problem in marine ecosystems and impacts include: microplastics entering food chains, large plastics entangling animals, large plastics blocking the guts of animals; plastics take a very long time to break down so are not removed from the sea easily; ocean gyres accumulate plastic waste to form garbage patches; plastic pollution can be reduced by legislation to ban single-use plastics, by education and by increased recycling.

Modern farming methods use fertilisers to increase crop yields; fertilisers run off into natural bodies of water and cause eutrophication.

Eutrophication has several stages including: fertiliser increases algal growth, algae die, some of the dead algae are decomposed by bacteria, the bacteria respire and use up oxygen in the water, and eventually fish and animals die due to lack of oxygen.

The levels of carbon dioxide and methane in the atmosphere are increasing due to fossil fuels burning, agriculture and increased waste; carbon dioxide and methane are greenhouse gases that reflect radiation back to the planet; increasing carbon dioxide and methane in the atmosphere produces an enhanced greenhouse effect leading to global warming.

Global warming may be causing climate change, sea level rises, coral bleaching, reduced oxygen concentration of water, extinction of species, increases in extreme weather and changes in distribution of species.

Sea level rises are due to thermal expansion of water and increased melting of ice sheets and glaciers; the oceans absorb heat energy and so help to maintain the thermal stability of global temperatures.

CONTINUED

Conservation aims to prevent the extinction of species and maintain ecosystems.
Species richness is a measure of how many different species are in an area at one time.
Species richness can be maintained by: sustainable harvesting, aquaculture of endangered and commercial species, setting up national parks and MPAs, farming coral, protecting turtles and culling invasive species.

CASE STUDY PROJECT

Zoos, aquaria and conservation

Before the second half of the twentieth century, zoos and public aquaria were places of entertainment that people visited to see animals. Figure 6.112 shows a drawing of a zoo in the nineteenth century in the UK. Animals were kept in very small cages and tanks. They had little to keep them stimulated and conditions were cruel. These animals existed only for the entertainment of humans.

Figure 6.112: A drawing of a nineteenth century zoo. Animals were kept in small, cruel enclosures and were there to entertain humans.

In the later twentieth century, the focus of zoos and public aquaria changed from being places of entertainment for humans to places for educating people and running conservation programmes. The enclosures for animals were made larger and more stimulating. Animals born in the zoos were used in breeding programmes to increase populations in the wild. Today, money from zoos and aquaria supports conservation programmes in all areas of the world. Figure 6.113 shows fish in an aquarium at Singapore Zoo. This modern zoo has space for animals in their enclosures. It provides the animals with stimulation. The aim is to allow the animals to experience what they might experience in the wild, or as close to this as possible.

Figure 6.113: Fish in an aquarium at Singapore Zoo.

Singapore Zoo helps with over 50 conservation projects around the world. The zoo is involved with conserving over 100 different endangered species and provides veterinary care for thousands of animals. In partnership with the Cambodian Government, it has helped to save the critically endangered Cambodian River Terrapin (Figure 6.114). The zoo is a centre of education for all ages, from young children up to older people, including post-doctoral research scientists. It plays a leading role in publicising global issues such as ocean plastic and climate change.

CONTINUED

Figure 6.114: Conservation of the Cambodian River Terrapin.

Sadly, some zoos and aquaria still have cruel conditions for the animals. Fortunately, however, many zoos and aquaria now play vital roles in helping with conservation.

Your task is to investigate the roles of zoos and aquaria in marine conservation. Most zoos and aquaria have informative websites that fully explain their roles. You could pick somewhere that is close to where you live, or somewhere that is based in another country.

Work as a pair to produce a large poster to focus on the following three aspects.

1 Use your poster to explain how the zoo or aquarium helps to support:

- **ex situ conservation** (looking after animals within the zoo)

- and **in situ conservation** (looking after animals in their own habitats).

2 Produce a fact file on one or two species that the zoo or aquarium helps to conserve. Alternatively, you could focus on an ecosystem that the zoo or aquarium helps to conserve. Explain why this conservation is important, what is being done, and how successful the project is. This fact file should form part of your poster.

3 Use your poster to give some information about the roles of marine scientists in zoos and aquaria. This information will be useful for people thinking about careers in marine science.

Peer assessment

Ask other learners to look at your poster. They should read it and decide if your poster affects how they think about zoos and aquaria. Ask them to rate your work according to the following scheme:

☺ if they feel fully informed to decide on how zoos and aquaria work in conservation

😐 if they feel that they would need more information to think about the roles of zoos and aquaria

☹ if they think that there is not enough information to make a decision about zoos and aquaria.

Also, ask other learners to provide written or verbal feedback in the form of 'two stars and a wish'. They can describe two things about your poster that they liked, and give one suggestion for improvement: 'It could be even better if…'

KEY WORDS

ex situ conservation*: conserving a species by removing it from its natural habitat and placing it in a protected area such as a zoo or aquarium

in situ conservation: the conservation of a species while it is still in its natural habitat

Look at the ratings on your case study poster from the other learners.

* How do you think that you could improve your poster?

* How could you make a better review of the value of all zoos and aquaria?

* Was it enough to look at only one zoo or aquarium?

* Does the information from the zoo's website or aquarium's website only show the positives, and did you take this into account when you made your poster?

* Did making this poster inspire you to get involved with volunteer conservation programmes?

EXAM-STYLE QUESTIONS

1 a Give three ways in which humans depend on marine ecosystems. [3]

b A tourism company decides to convert an existing tourist resort into an ecotourist resort. The tourism company decides that the resort should convert from using electricity generated by fossil fuels to electricity generated by renewable energy sources in the local area. Solar power, wind power and wave power systems are installed.

i State two negative impacts of tourism on a coastal area. [2]

ii The cost of installing the equipment is US$750 000.

The mean electricity bill when using fossil fuels is US$25 000 per year.

Calculate how long it will take the resort to recover the cost of installing the equipment. State the unit. [2]

iii Explain why using renewable energy is better for the environment compared with using fossil fuels. [3]

iv Suggest a reason why using renewable energy sources to generate electricity may not be a reliable method for the resort. [2]

[Total: 12]

2 Table 1 shows the catch of seabream using longlining in an area of Pacific Ocean between 2008 and 2020.

Year	Catch (tonnes)
2008	1260
2010	1350
2012	1025
2014	875
2016	755
2018	585
2020	495

Table 1

COMMAND WORDS

give: produce an answer from a given source or recall / memory

state: express in clear terms

calculate: work out from given facts, figures or information

explain: set out purposes or reasons / make the relationships between things evident / provide why and / or how and support with relevant evidence

suggest: apply knowledge and understanding to situations where there are a range of valid responses in order to make proposals / put forward considerations

CONTINUED

a i Calculate the mean rate of change of catch between 2008 and 2020. Show your working. Give your answer to three significant figures. [3]

ii Draw a line graph of the catch of seabream between 2008 and 2020. Join the points with ruled, straight lines. [5]

iii Describe the change in catch between 2008 and 2020. [2]

iv Suggest two reasons for the change in catch between 2010 and 2020. [2]

b i Describe the process of longline fishing to catch fish that live near the surface. [4]

ii Explain the environmental impacts of longline fishing. [4]

c Sketch a diagram of a fish aggregation device (FAD), labelling the platform and the float. [3]

[Total: 23]

COMMAND WORDS

describe: state the points of a topic / give characteristics and main features

sketch: make a simple freehand drawing showing the key features, taking care over proportions

3 Figure 1 shows an aquaculture system used to produce trout in coastal waters.

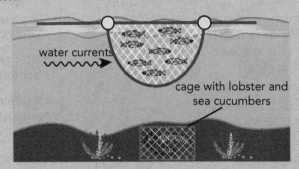

water currents

cage with lobster and sea cucumbers

Figure 1

a i Explain the purpose of the net. [2]

ii Ballan wrasse are also kept with the trout. Ballan wrasse eat parasites such as sea lice that live on trout.

Explain why keeping ballan wrasse with the trout is a more sustainable method compared with adding pesticides. [3]

b Scientists investigated the effect of different feeding methods on oxygen levels and algae levels in the surrounding water. They fed the fish with the same mass of food every day for two weeks but with different feeding frequencies. After the two weeks, the level of algae and the concentration of oxygen in the water were measured. Their results are shown in Table 2.

Feeding method	Algae level (arbitrary units)	Oxygen concentration (%)
1 kg of feed five times a day	15	12
2.5 kg of feed twice a day	25	8
5 kg of feed once a day	75	4

Table 2

CONTINUED

    i   Describe the effect of different feeding methods on the level of algae and oxygen concentration of the water. [2]

    ii Explain the results shown in Table 2. [4]

  c Cages of detritivore organisms such as lobsters and sea cucumbers are placed under the nets to help maintain the quality of the water.

    i   Define the term 'detritivore'. [1]

    ii Suggest reasons why keeping the cages with lobsters and sea cucumbers is of benefit to the aquaculture system. [3]

[Total: 15]

COMMAND WORD

define: give precise meaning

4 Crude oil is often transported around the world on oil tanker ships.

Two of the MARPOL regulations for oil tanker design are:

- Oil tankers must have a double hull.
- Sewage release must be controlled.

  a Give two uses of crude oil. [2]

  b Explain how these two MARPOL regulations reduce damage to marine ecosystems. [4]

  c Oil spills can have many impacts on marine ecosystems.

    Give three negative impacts of oil spills on marine organisms. [3]

  d Conservationists investigated the effect of using dispersant and skimmers on the removal of an oil slick. They released a slick of oil on the surface of some water in a tank. They then measured the length of time taken to remove the oil when using: skimmers only, dispersant sprays only, skimmers and dispersant sprays together, and burning the oil. The results are shown in Table 3.

Method of oil removal	Time taken to remove oil / hours
skimmers only	8.0
dispersants only	6.5
skimmers and dispersants	6.5
burning	2.5

Table 3

    i   State the method that removed the oil in the shortest time. [1]

    ii Give two factors that the scientists would need to keep the same when testing each method. [2]

    iii Calculate the percentage decrease in time taken to remove the oil when using skimmers and dispersants compared with skimmers only. [2]

    iv Suggest an explanation for the effect of using skimmers with dispersants. [2]

    v Suggest how the scientists could make the experiment more reliable. [1]

  e Discuss the benefits of using one named renewable source of energy to generate electricity compared with using fossil fuels. [4]

[Total: 21]

COMMAND WORD

discuss: write about issue(s) or topic(s) in depth in a structured way

CONTINUED

5 A student investigated the effect of climate change on sea level rises.

They placed water at a temperature of 4 °C into a tank and added five ice cubes. The height of the water immediately after adding the ice cubes was 25 cm. This was tank A.

They then filled a second tank with water at a temperature of 4 °C up to a height of 25 cm. Five ice cubes were placed on a plastic shelf, as shown in Figure 2. This was tank B.

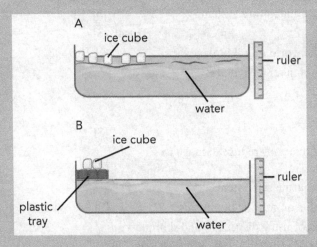

Figure 2

Both tanks were placed into an incubator at 30 °C and the height of the water measured over time.

a i Figure 3 shows a graph of how the height of the water in tank A changed over time.

Predict the change in water height of the water in tank B by drawing the expected results for tank B on Figure 3. [2]

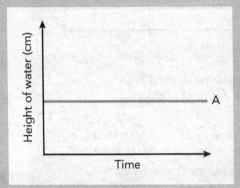

Figure 3

ii State two reasons why increasing the temperature causes a rise in the height of the water in the tank B. [2]

COMMAND WORD

predict: suggest what may happen based on available information

CONTINUED

   b i Give the names of two greenhouse gases. [2]

     ii Describe three negative effects, other than sea level rises, of global warming on marine ecosystems. [3]

[Total: 9]

6 Kelp is often harvested from rocky shores. The presence of kelp on a rocky shore may increase the species richness of the shore.

   a Plan an investigation to compare the species richness of a rocky shore where kelp is harvested with a rocky shore where kelp is not harvested. [8]

   b Suggest why large amounts of kelp increases species richness. [2]

[Total: 10]

SELF-EVALUATION CHECKLIST

After studying this chapter, think about how confident you are with the different topics. This will help you to see any gaps in your knowledge and help you to learn more effectively.

I can	Needs more work	Getting there	Confident to move on	See Section
outline the importance of marine ecosystems to humans and the impact of humans on these ecosystems				6.1
explain the importance of tourism to economies and the impact of tourism on marine ecosystems				6.2
explain the aims of ecotourism and how different strategies reduce the impacts on marine ecosystems				6.2
explain the importance of marine organisms as a food supply for humans				6.3
explain the need for sustainable harvesting of marine organisms and the methods that can be used to prevent overfishing				6.3
describe different methods of fishing and their impacts on the marine environment				6.3
explain how FADs increase fish catches				6.3
describe the use of different navigational aids on boats, including charts, compasses, GPS, sonar and radar				6.3
describe the social, environmental and commercial roles of aquaculture				6.4

CONTINUED

I can	Needs more work	Getting there	Confident to move on	See Section
list species that are produced by aquaculture and describe the differences between open and closed systems				6.4
outline the key methods used in all forms of aquaculture				6.4
describe how oil is extracted from under the sea, how it is transported, and explain how MARPOL regulations reduce the risk of marine pollution				6.5
describe the impacts of oil spills on marine organisms and the methods that can be used to reduce their impacts				6.5
discuss the advantages and disadvantages of using fossil fuels and using renewable energy systems				6.5
describe the impacts of plastic pollution on marine ecosystems and the strategies that can be used to reduce these impacts				6.6
explain how ocean gyres form garbage patches and how these garbage patches can be reduced				6.6
explain how the use of fertilisers in intensive farming can lead to eutrophication in marine ecosystems				6.7
explain the causes of climate change, including the roles of carbon dioxide release from fossil fuels and methane release from agriculture				6.8
explain the effects of climate change on marine ecosystems, including the causes of sea level rises				6.8
describe the roles of conservation and evaluate different conservation strategies				6.9

> Glossary

Command words

Below are the Cambridge International definitions for command words which may be used in exams. The guidance text provides some additional explanation on the meaning of these words, written by the authors of this coursebook.

The information in this section is taken from the Cambridge International syllabus (0697) for examination from 2024.

You should always refer to the appropriate syllabus document for the year of your examination to confirm the details and for more information. The syllabus document is available on the Cambridge International website www.cambridgeinternational.org.

calculate: work out from given facts, figures or information

guidance: You will need to do some maths to arrive at the answer. Include any units and show your working.

compare: identify / comment on similarities and / or differences

guidance: Use the provided marks to determine how many points of comparison you need to provide. Try not to repeat the same points within your answer – each mark will only be given once.

define: give precise meaning

guidance: Try to word your definitions precisely with all major identifying features. This is a concise response that should not be longer than a sentence.

describe: state the points of a topic / give characteristics and main features

guidance: Commonly confused with 'explain', 'describe' means 'what is happening'. This could mean describing data (i.e. it increases or decreases), a process, or the meaning of a term. Do not try to write about how or why something is happening.

determine: establish an answer using the information available

guidance: This may involve using numerical data or other information to answer the question, such as if an outcome is possible or likely using the information provided.

discuss: write about issue(s) or topic(s) in depth in a structured way

guidance: These are generally longer answers and require the use of details to support your knowledge about a topic. In general, responses to 'discuss' questions require the use of many well-written sentences.

evaluate: judge or calculate the quality, importance, amount, or value of something

guidance: You need to create an opinion or choose a side about the topic in question. You then need to support your opinion using details from either your background knowledge or information provided in the question.

explain: set out purposes or reasons / make the relationships between things clear / say why and / or how and support with relevant evidence

guidance: These questions require you to write about why or how something happens. It is important to provide reasons and clear connections within your answer. Unless expressly stated, it is not necessary to outline what is happening, just why or how.

give: produce an answer from a given source or recall / memory

guidance: Generally a short response that may not even need a complete sentence. They may require you to recall something from memory or locate something on a graph or data set.

identify: name / select / recognise

guidance: This requires a brief, direct response.

outline: set out the main points

guidance: While you can use a paragraph to answer an 'outline' question, a detailed, bulleted list is also appropriate. Include enough detail to clarify each point.

predict: suggest what may happen based on available information

guidance: These questions do not expect you to get the information through recall. Rather, the expectation is that you can use background information in conjunction with the information or data provided in the question to make a best guess about what may happen next. For example, you may see 'predict' when discussing data, behaviour of organisms, or the conditions in the ocean.

sketch: make a simple freehand drawing showing the key features, taking care over proportions

guidance: Use a pencil to draw the process or graph being requested. Make sure to label major features as necessary. If data is provided, make sure your proportions are appropriate to represent the numbers given, for example when sketching trophic pyramids.

state: express in clear terms

guidance: This indicates that the response should be short. This can be used when you identify important data points on a graph, provide the term that matches a definition, or in other situations where only a one-word or two-word response would be appropriate.

suggest: apply knowledge and understanding to situations where there are a range of valid responses in order to make proposals / put forward considerations

guidance: 'Suggest' asks you to combine information from the question with other information learned during the course. 'Suggest' questions often have a wide variety of responses that could be used to produce a successful answer. Make sure you provide a clear line of reasoning for the suggestion being made.

Key words (syllabus)

abiotic factors: the non-living, physical and chemical factors that affect an organism in its environment

abyssal plain: the generally flat ocean floor, usually at depths of 3000–6000 m

accuracy: a measurement result is described as accurate if it is close to the true value

acidic: a solution containing H^+ ions in water; such a solution has a pH below 7

aerobic respiration: the release of energy from glucose, using oxygen, by cells

aggregate: the grouping together of organisms or objects

alkaline: a solution containing OH^- ions in water; such a solution has a pH above 7

angling: the catching of marine organisms using hooks and lines rather than nets

animals: multicellular organisms; animal cells have nuclei but do not contain chloroplasts, cell walls or permanent vacuoles; examples include fish, mammals and reptiles

annelids: a group of invertebrate organisms that have bilateral symmetry, a segmented body and setae that stick out from segments; examples include lugworms and fan worms

anomalies: data or results that do not fit a general trend or pattern

anomalous results: results that do not fit the expected pattern or trend. When results have been repeated, an anomaly is a result that is significantly different from two or more similar values

anomalous values: values that are very different from other results and do not fit the normal pattern

antennae: sensory organs that stick out from the head of an organism; crustaceans have two pairs of antennae

antibiotic-resistant bacteria: bacteria that are not killed by antibiotics

antibiotics: drugs, usually produced by fungi, that kill bacteria

aquaculture: the production of marine species by artificial methods in cages or tanks

arbitrary units: units that are relative to each other; for example, we can measure the mass of fish in arbitrary units where one arbitrary unit is the mass of one sardine

Archaea: a domain containing single-celled organisms similar in structure to bacteria; the Archaea may have more features in common with Eukarya than with Bacteria

artificial selection: the selection of organisms with desirable characteristics for breeding programmes

asexual reproduction: a single organism producing exact copies of itself

atmosphere: layer of gases surrounding the surface of the Earth

atmospheric dissolution: the dissolving of atmospheric gases in water

atoll: a coral island that has formed around a central lagoon

bacteria: a group of single-celled organisms that do not have nuclei; bacteria are different from organisms in the Archaea group (see Section 3.3)

bar chart: a graph showing the relationship between a categoric variable and a quantitative variable

barrier reef: ridge of coral separated from land by a lagoon

basket trap: a basket or cage that allows marine organisms to enter but prevents them leaving

benthic trawling: the catching of fish by towing a net along the seabed; also called bottom trawling

benthic zone: the seabed and the water directly above it bilateral symmetry: the body shape of organisms that can be divided along the body midline to make reflections (mirror images) of each other

binocular vision: having two eyes positioned on an organism so that objects can be seen by both eyes

binomial system: the system we use to give scientific names to organisms, referring to them by their genus and species; for example, *Carcharodon albimors* is the great white shark

bioluminescent: the biochemical release of light by living organisms

biomass: the mass of living matter; it is usually measured as dry mass

biotic factors: the living factors that affect an organism in its environment

birds: animals that have skin (covered by feathers) and lungs; the young develop inside hard-shelled eggs

blade: the photosynthetic organ of kelp; it is similar to the leaf of a true plant

blast fishing: the use of explosives to stun and kill fish; it is very destructive to coral reefs

boom: device that is floated on the surface of water in an effort to contain an oil spill

broodstock: marine species that are used for breeding in aquaculture systems; they are usually artificially selected for rapid growth and high quality

camouflage: the blending of an organism with its environment so that prey or predators are less able to detect it

cannibalism: the practice of eating members of the same species

carbohydrates: organic molecules containing carbon, hydrogen and oxygen; they are used as a source of energy in living organisms

carnivore: animals that obtain energy by eating other animals

cast net: a type of fishing net that is thrown into the water from the shore or a boat; the net traps fish underneath it as it sinks into the water

cell membrane: the outer boundary of the cytoplasm of cells; it controls the movement of substances in and out of cells

cell wall: strong layer found around the outside of plant, bacterial and some algal cells; it prevents cells bursting if water enters the cytoplasm

cellulose: a carbohydrate found in the cell walls of plants and some algae

chlorophyll: the green chemical found inside chloroplasts; it absorbs light energy for photosynthesis

chloroplasts: organelles that perform photosynthesis; they are found in plant cells and some algal cells

classification (classifying): placing organisms into groups based on shared features

climate change: the changing of weather patterns due to increased global temperatures

closed seasons: bans placed on fishing at certain times of year, usually the breeding seasons

cnidaria: a group of invertebrate organisms that have radial symmetry, tentacles and stinging cells; examples include sea anemones and coral polyps

combustion: the burning of a substance using oxygen; it is also called oxidation

community: all the organisms in an area at a specific time

compass: navigation equipment that contains a magnetic needle that always points to the north

compass rose: a diagram on charts that shows the directions of north, south, east and west

compound: a substance formed by the chemical combination of two or more elements in fixed proportions

compound eye: a type of eye that is divided into thousands of individual light receptor units

conclusion: a statement summarising findings in an investigation

condensation: the process of a gas turning into a liquid, visible as droplets of liquid on a surface or as a cloud in the air

conservation: the process of a gas turning into a liquid, visible as droplets of liquid on a surface or as a cloud in the air

continental shelf: part of the continental plate extending from the coast/shore in shallow waters with little or no slope

continental slope: the steeper slope from the continental shelf to near the abyssal plain

continuous data: numerical data that can have 'in-between' values

convection current: the transfer of thermal energy (heat energy) by the motion of a fluid

convergent plate boundary: two tectonic plates move towards each other

coordinates: a pair of numbers used to identify a point

core: the very hot, dense centre of the Earth

correlation: a pattern between two variables; this may be due to a causal link between them but a correlation is not proof of cause

crust: outermost solid layer of the Earth

crustaceans: invertebrate animals that have segmented bodies, skeletons on the outside of the body, jointed limbs, compound eyes and two pairs of antennae; examples include crabs, lobsters, shrimp and barnacles

(sea or ocean) current: continuous flow of seawater in a particular direction

cyanobacteria: a type of bacteria that are producer organisms

cytoplasm: the substance that makes up most of the cell volume around the organelles; it is the site of chemical reactions such as protein synthesis (making proteins)

data: information such as numbers or descriptions relating to measurements or observations

decomposer: microorganism that digests and breakdown dead organisms and organic waste; they often recycle nutrients in ecosystems

density: the relationship between the mass of a substance and the volume it occupies: density = mass ÷ volume

dependent variable: the variable we measure in an investigation

detritivore: animals that obtain energy from eating dead organic material

detritus: solid remains and waste from living organisms

diatoms: microalgae that have chloroplasts and delicate skeletons made from silica

diffusion: the random movement of particles (or molecules) from an area of higher concentration to an area of lower concentration (down a concentration gradient); it is a passive process, not requiring the input of energy

dinoflagellates: microalgae that have chloroplasts, two flagella and cell walls

directly proportional: a positive correlation when the ratio between the independent and dependant variables is constant, for example, doubling the independent variable also doubles the dependent variable

discrete data: numerical data that can only be recorded as whole numbers or integers

dispersants: chemicals that are sprayed onto an oil spill to break up the oil into smaller droplets that are carried away

dissolve: the process of a solid mixing into a liquid

divergent plate boundary: two tectonic plates move apart, forming new land between them

domain: the highest taxonomic rank; the three domains are the Archaea, Eukarya and Bacteria

dredging: the removal of sediment from the seabed, estuaries and shores

earthquake: a sudden shaking of the ground, usually caused when two plates suddenly slip against each other

echinoderms: invertebrate animals that have pentaradial symmetry, tube feet and spines; examples include starfish, sea cucumbers and sea urchins

ecosystem: all the organisms in the area along with their environment

ecotourism: tourism that does not harm ecosystems; it aims to protect ecosystems and educate tourists about the environment and local cultures

El Niño: a warm current that develops off the coast of Ecuador, usually in December, which can cause widespread death within local food chains

element: a substance which cannot be further divided into simpler substances by chemical methods; all elements are listed on the Periodic Table

endangered species: species that are at risk of dying out in the wild

energy density: a measure of how much energy is contained within a set mass or volume of a substance; energy dense substances have a lot of energy within a small mass

enhanced greenhouse effect: the artificial warming that occurs due to the release of excess carbon dioxide and methane into the atmosphere

environment: the abiotic and biotic factors that influence an organism in its habitat

Equator: an imaginary line drawn round the Earth, halfway between the North Pole and the South Pole

erosion: the wearing away of rock along the coastline

estuary: a partially enclosed, tidal, coastal body of water; it is where freshwater from a river meets the saline water of the ocean

ethical considerations: planning to avoid harm or damage to living organisms during investigations

Eukarya: a domain containing organisms that are all composed of cells with nuclei; examples include plants, animals and protoctists

eutrophication: the release of nutrients into water that causes the production of algal blooms which die and decay; eventually this leads to a loss of oxygen in the water

evaporation: a process occurring at the surface of a liquid, involving the change of state from a liquid into a vapour but at a temperature below the boiling point / a practical technique used to separate a dissolved solid from a liquid

exoskeleton: a hard, rigid covering on the outer surface of the body of many invertebrate animals such as crustaceans

external fertilisation: the process by which fertilisation occurs outside the body

extinct species: species that have died out and no longer exist

extinction: the loss of a species from the planet

extrapolation: extending a line on a line graph beyond the range of data collected

fertile: organisms that are able to breed

fertilisers: chemical substances added to fields to increase crop growth; they contain mineral nutrients including nitrates, phosphates and magnesium

filtration: a practical technique used to separate a solid from a liquid

fins: structures which stick out from the surface of a fish's body; they are used to balance, steer and thrust the fish forward

fish: animals that have skin (covered with scales) and gills; they reproduce using external fertilisation

fish aggregation device (FAD): a floating platform that is sometimes anchored to the seabed; used to attract fish

fishery: a fishing business, industry for catching fish, or a geographical area where fish and seafood are caught

fishing quota: the maximum mass or number of a species that is allowed to be harvested

flagella: microscopic tails attached to some animal cells and some protoctists; they are used for movement

food chain: a diagram showing the flow of energy from one organism to the next, beginning with a producer

food web: the interactions between all the food chains in an ecosystem

fossil fuels: energy-rich fuels that are extracted from underground; they were produced from plants and protoctists that lived millions of years ago

freeze: the change of a liquid into a solid; during this process heat is given out to the surroundings

freshwater: water that has very low concentrations of salts; it is used for drinking water

garbage patch: area within an ocean gyre where plastic and other garbage accumulates

gas bladders: organs found in kelp and other seaweeds; they contain gases and are used for floatation

gas exchange structure: organs or structures, such as lungs and gills, that exchange oxygen and carbon dioxide

geomorphology: the study of the physical features of the surface of the Earth and their relation to its geological structures and processes

gills: gas exchange structures that are often used by marine organisms

glacier: a permanent, land-based sheet of ice that slowly moves along the ground

Global Positioning System (GPS): a network of artificial satellites forming a navigation and location system

global warming: the long-term increase in temperature of the planet

gradient: the rate of change in a variable, calculated by dividing the change in y-value by the change in x-value

gravity / gravitational pull: the force that exists between any two objects with mass

greenhouse effect: the natural warming effect that occurs when radiation is reflected back to the planet by greenhouse gases in the atmosphere

greenhouse gases: atmospheric gases that reflect radiation back to the Earth; examples include carbon dioxide, methane and water vapour

gyre: a large system of rotating ocean currents

habitat: the area where an organism lives and interacts with its environment and other organisms

haemoglobin: protein that contains iron and is used to transport oxygen in blood

herbivore: animal that obtains energy by eating plants

hierarchy: arrangement or placing of groups of organisms into smaller groups

histogram: a graph showing the frequency of a continuous variable

holdfast: the part of kelp that anchors it to a substrate

horizontal migration: the movement of organisms from one geographical place to another geographical place

human error: an incorrect result due to incorrectly reading a result or measurement

hypothesis: an explanation of an observation that we can test through experiments or further observations

ice sheet: large masses of frozen water that cover land masses; the main ice sheets are located in Greenland and Antarctica

increment: (of a measuring instrument) the smallest interval on the scale

independent variable: the variable that is being changed in an investigation

infrastructure: services that develop in an area, including roads, rail links, sewers, water supplies, schools, hospitals and shops

ingest: the taking in of food or other material

insoluble: the description of a substance that does not dissolve in a particular solvent

insulation: a layer wrapped around a body that prevents heat loss; fur and feathers insulate the bodies of mammals and birds

intercept: the value on an axis when a line meets the axis

internal fertilisation: the process by which fertilisation occurs inside a living organism

international agreements: agreements made between several countries on issues such as fish quotas

interpolation: estimation of values between two known values

intertidal zone: area of shore over which the tide flows; periods of time are spent exposed to the air and periods of time are spent submerged (under the water)

interval: the gap between separate measurements for the independent variable

invasive species: a species that has been introduced to an area where it does not normally live and is damaging the species that are normally found there

inversely proportional: a negative correlation when the ratio between the independent and dependant variables is constant, for example, doubling the independent variable halves the dependent variable

invertebrates: animals that do not have a backbone

iron: a metallic element with magnetic properties

kelp: large, multicellular organism that grows in coastal areas; it photosynthesises to produce glucose

kinetic energy: the energy possessed by objects or particles due to movement

kingdom: a domain can be divided into kingdoms; marine kingdoms include animals, plants and protoctists

land reclamation: the conversion of natural areas, including wetlands and underwater areas, into land for development

large permanent vacuole: a large structure found in plant cells that consists of a membrane surrounding fluid called sap; it stores water and other substances

larvae: intermediate form of an organism that occurs before the organism reaches adulthood; they often have different diets and locations compared with adult organisms

lateral line: a sensory organ that stretches along the body of fish; it detects vibrations in the water

latitude: the distance from the Equator to the North Pole or South Pole, on a scale where 0° is at the Equator and 90° is at the pole

legislation: rules and laws made by governments

licences: permits for fishing issued by governments, they can be used to restrict the number or type of boats in an area

life cycle: the stages that an organism passes through from its beginning until it reaches sexual maturity

light intensity: the quantity of visible light; this is greatest at the surface of the ocean and reduces as depth increases

light penetration: the depth light is able to reach in a body of water

line graph: a graph showing the relationship between two quantitative variables

line of best fit: a line drawn on a graph to show the general trend in the data plotted

lipids: organic molecules containing carbon, hydrogen and oxygen; they are used in living organisms for energy, insulation and are a source of fat-soluble vitamins

litter: waste materials, such as plastic bottles, that have been discarded

logical sequence: a series of steps or events which we place in a suitable order to complete a task successfully

longitude: the distance east or west from the Prime Meridian on a scale where 0° is at the Prime Meridian and 180° is on the opposite side of the Earth from the Prime Meridian

longline fishing: method of fishing that uses a long nylon line with many baited hooks attached; the line can be fixed in the water or towed behind a boat

macroalgae: large, multicellular algae such as kelp

magma: hot semi-liquid rock found below or within the crust

magnetic field: a region of space around the Earth in which a magnet experiences (feels) a force

magnetic north: the position that the needle in a compass points towards; it is rarely at the same position as true north

mammals: animals that have skin covered by fur or hair, lungs and the young develop within the female body

mantle: the region of the Earth found between the crust and the core

marine snow: particles of organic material that fall from surface waters to the deeper ocean

MARPOL: a series of standards for ships to prevent pollution of the oceans and seas

melt: the change of a solid into a liquid; during this process heat is taken in from the surroundings

melting point: the temperature at which a solid turns into a liquid; it has the same value as the freezing point

mental maps: memory maps of landmarks that animals learn when making migrations

microalgae: microscopic, single-celled algae that are part of the phytoplankton; examples include dinoflagellates and diatoms

micronutrients: essential nutrients that are needed in small amounts

microplastics: pieces of plastic that are less than 5 mm in diameter

midnight zone: the deepest layer of ocean where no light can penetrate

migration: movement of animals from one region to another, usually in response to changes in the seasons

minerals: nutrients that are needed by living organisms; examples include calcium and iron

mitochondria: cell organelles that perform aerobic respiration

mixture: two or more substances mixed together but not chemically combined – the substances can be separated by physical means

molecule: a group of atoms held together by sharing electrons between atoms in the molecule

molluscs: group of invertebrate organisms that have bilateral symmetry, a shell and an unsegmented body; examples include squid, octopuses and scallops

moon: a natural satellite of a planet

mutualistic relationship: ecological relationship between different species where both benefit

nares: small pits on the head of fish that detect chemical scents in the water

native species: species that are naturally found in an area

nautical chart: a map that helps sailors to plot a course without colliding with obstacles

navigate: the process of plotting a course from one place to another

navigation: the finding of direction so that animals can move from one place to another

neap tides: tides experienced during the first and last quarters of the Moon with lower high tides and higher low tides than usual

neutral: having a pH that equals 7

non-renewable energy: energy sources that will eventually run out, such as fossil fuels

nucleus: large cell structure that contains chromosomes made from DNA; it controls cell activities

nursery site: a habitat that is used for breeding or where the young live

nutrients: chemicals that provide what is needed for organisms to grow, repair damaged cells or tissues, release energy or for their metabolism

observations: an aspect of the world around us that we notice

ocean trench: a deep underwater valley formed when oceanic crust slides below continental crust

oil platform: mechanical structure that is used to extract oil from under the seabed

oil spill: the release of large amounts of oil from a pipeline, platform or tanker

oil tanker: large ship that is used to transport large volumes of crude oil

olfaction: the detection of chemical scents

omnivore: animals that obtain energy from eating producers and other animals

operculum: protective covering of the gills; found in bony fish

orbit: the path of an object as it moves around a larger object

overfishing: the harvesting of so many fish that their populations will no longer be sustainable in the future

parasites: organisms that live and feed on other organisms, causing them harm

particle theory: a theory which describes the bulk properties of the different states of matter in terms of the movement of particles (atoms or molecules) – the theory explains what happens during changes in physical state

pelagic trawling: the catching of fish by towing a net through the open water area; also called midwater trawling

pelagic zone: the total volume of water in the ocean or sea that is not in contact with land

pentaradial symmetry: a type of radial symmetry, usually found in echinoderms, where the shape of an organism is arranged along five lines of symmetry

pH scale: a scale running from 0 to 14, used for expressing the acidity or alkalinity of a solution; a neutral solution has a pH of 7

photosynthesis: the process by which plants produce carbohydrates from carbon dioxide and water using energy from light

pie chart: a chart showing the proportions of different parts making up the total

pitch: the movement of the head of a fish up or down in the water

plants: multicellular organisms; plant cells contain nuclei, chloroplasts and permanent vacuoles and are surrounded by cells walls; examples include seagrasses

pneumatophores: adapted root structures of some mangroves that stick up from the soil and water; they are used for gas exchange

polar zones: the area north of the Arctic Circle or south of the Antarctic Circle

pole and line fishing: a fishing method that catches fish with a pole, line and hook; also known as rod and line fishing

population: the number of organisms of the same species in a specific area at the same specific time

precipitation: water that falls from the atmosphere to the Earth's surface as rain, sleet, snow or hail

precision: quantitative – how close the measured values of a quantity are to each other; qualitative – descriptions or observations that closely match the characteristics being recorded

predator: animal that hunts, catches and eats other animals

prevailing winds: the direction from which winds usually blow at a particular location

primary consumer: organism at the second trophic level of a food chain; a primary consumer obtains energy from eating producers

producer: an organism that makes its own organic nutrients; generally using energy from sunlight, through the process called photosynthesis

productivity: the rate of production of new biomass, usually through photosynthesis; biomass refers to any cells and tissues produced by organisms as they grow

profile: the angle of slopes along a shore

prop roots: adapted root system of mangroves with vertical roots that stick out from the stem and look like stilts

proteins: organic molecules containing the elements carbon, hydrogen, oxygen and nitrogen; they are used for cell growth and repair in living organisms

protoctists: organisms that have cells with nuclei; some species are unicellular and others are multicellular; some species are similar to plants and others are similar to animals; examples include seaweeds (such as kelp) and other algae

purse seine nets: a type of fishing net used to create a wall of nets around a shoal; when the shoal is enclosed, the base of the net is closed and the catch hauled on board

pyramid of biomass: a diagram that shows the biomass at each trophic level

pyramid of energy: a diagram that shows the energy at each trophic level

pyramid of number: a diagram that shows the number of organisms at each trophic level

quadrat: square frame that is used in ecological investigations to sample areas

qualitative data: data recorded as words, descriptions or categories

quantitative data: data recorded as numerical values

radar: navigation method that uses equipment to emit radio waves to identify obstacles, such as rocky reefs, around a ship

radial symmetry: the shape of organisms, such as cnidaria, where the body can be divided equally around a central point

range: the upper and lower values for the independent variable

recreational fishing: small-scale fishing where the fish are not sold for food

renewable sources: energy and materials that will not run out

replicates: two or more trials of the same experiment, using the same materials and apparatus

reptiles: animals that have skin (covered with scales made from keratin) and lungs; the young develop inside hard-shelled eggs

resort: an area that has been developed for tourists to visit

respiration: the chemical reactions in cells that break down nutrient molecules and release energy for metabolism

restrictions: limits placed on fishing intensity; they can be placed on fishing gear, times of fishing, seasons, species or mass of catch

rhizome: a swollen plant stem that may be buried under sediment; it provides stability and is used for asexual reproduction

rip current: a narrow powerful current moving from a beach out to the ocean

roll: circular, rolling movement of the body of a fish as it moves forwards

salinity: a measure of the quantity of dissolved salts in ocean water; represented by parts per thousand (ppt)

salts: ionic compounds that can be made by the neutralisation of an acid with an alkali

sampling: fairly assessing a small number of a group or population

satellite: any object that orbits a planet

satellite tracking systems: the use of satellites to monitor the movement and positions of boats

scale: the regular markings and values showing measurements on equipment

scales: small, rigid plates found on the skin of most fish; they protect the skin from damage and reduce water loss

seagrass: true plants that are found in the marine environment; they have adaptations for surviving underwater

seasonal: events that occur at certain times of the year

secondary consumer: organism at the third trophic level; a secondary consumer obtains energy from eating primary consumers

sedimentary shore: coastal shores that are composed of particles of sediment; the particles can range in size from silt to pebbles

sedimentation: the settling of sand or silt particles onto a shore

sediments: small fragments of rock, such as gravel, sand and silt

segmented body: a body that is divided up into separate sections; annelids and crustaceans have segmented bodies

setae: bristles or hairs that are present on the segments of annelids

sewage: liquid or solid waste, such as faeces, that is mixed with water and discarded

sexual reproduction: organisms producing male and female sex cells, which fuse to produce offspring with characteristics from both parents'

sexually mature fish: fish that have reached an age when they can breed

silica: a glass-like substance used to produce the cells of diatoms

single-use plastics: items made from plastic that are thrown away after using

skimmer: device that is used to absorb oil from the surface of water

socioeconomic: factors that relate to the economy and standards of living of an area.

soluble: the description of a substance that dissolves in a particular solvent

solute: a substance that dissolves in a liquid (the solvent) to form a solution

solution: formed when a substance (solute) dissolves into another substance (solvent)

solvent: the liquid that dissolves the solid solute to form a solution; water is the most common solvent

sonar: navigation method that uses equipment to produce underwater sound waves; these sound waves identify obstacles, fish shoals and the depth of the sea

species: organisms that are able to breed and produce fertile offspring

species richness: the number of different species in an area

spring tides: tides experienced during a new Moon and full Moon with higher high tides and lower low tides than usual

starch: a complex carbohydrate made of many glucose sugar molecules joined together; it is used as a long-term energy storage molecule by plants and some protoctists

stinging cells: cells that can inject a toxin into other organisms; they are used to catch food and to defend against predators (also called nematocysts)

stipe: the stem of kelp that holds the blades upright in the water

structural adaptations: physical structures of organisms that have evolved to enable them to survive

subsidence: the sinking of land

substrate: hard surface to which organisms can attach – rock is an example

subtidal zone: area of shore that is permanently submerged by water

sugars: simple carbohydrates, such as glucose, that provide living organisms with a source of immediate energy

sunlight zone: the upper layer of the ocean, generally the top 200 m, where there is sufficient light for photosynthesis to occur; also known as the epipelagic zone

supercontinent: a large landmass thought to have broken up into several of the current continents

supratidal zone: part of the shore that is furthest from the sea; it is rarely covered by the tide but receives spray from wave action

surface run-off: water flowing over land to return to rivers and oceans (can occur on natural surfaces such as rocks, soil and vegetation, or artificial surfaces such as roads and buildings)

sustainable harvesting: methods of harvesting of marine species that do not reduce their populations over the long term

sustainable resources: natural resources that we use in a way that ensures that they are replenished so that they will still be available in the future. For example, sustainable fishing is the harvesting of fish so that populations are not reduced in the long term and future generations will still be able to harvest fish.

tangle net: a type of net, similar to a gillnet, that catches fish in the mesh

tectonic plates: large sections of crust

temperate zones: the area between the Tropic of Cancer and the Arctic Circle, and the area between the Tropic of Capricorn and the Antarctic Circle

tentacles: long, slender, flexible organs that stick out from the body of an organism; used in feeding or gas exchange

terrestrial forests: areas of forest that are fully on land

tertiary consumer: organism at the fourth trophic level; a tertiary consumer obtains energy from eating secondary consumers

theory: an explanation of observations that have been repeatedly tested and confirmed through observation and experimentation

theory of plate tectonics: a theory developed in the 1960s that helps explain the formation of some of the important features on the Earth's surface and how the continents move

thermal expansion: the expansion of water in the oceans and seas due to an increase in temperature

thrust: the forward force that pushes a fish through the water; the caudal fin gives thrust

tidal amplitude: half the difference in height between high tide and the following low tide

tides: the rising and falling of the sea in regular cycles, caused by the gravitational attraction between the Earth, the Moon and the Sun

tourism: recreational visits to an area that brings money into local economies

transect: a line taken across a habitat to see how organisms change along the line; line transects investigate organisms touching a rope and belt transects investigate the species in an area by the side of the rope

trawling: a method of catching fish that involves towing a net through the water

trend: a general pattern in data showing an increase, decrease or remaining constant, when smaller changes are ignored

trophic level: the position occupied by an organism in a food chain

tropical zones / tropics: the region between the Tropic of Cancer and the Tropic of Capricorn, between which the Sun moves directly overhead during a year

tsunami: a fast-moving wave with a long wavelength, created by ocean floor displacement or landslide

tube feet: small, muscular, tubular structures that are used by echinoderms for moving around

twilight zone: the layer of ocean below the sunlight zone where there is some light but not enough for photosynthesis to occur; typically extends from 200 m to 1000 m; also known as the mesopelagic zone

universal indicator: a mixture of indicators that has different colours in solutions of different pH

unsegmented body: a body that is not divided into segments; for example, molluscs and cnidarians have unsegmented bodies

upwelling: the movement of cold, nutrient-rich water from deep in the ocean to the surface

valid: an investigation that only changes the independent variable and keeps all other variables constant as much as possible

variable: factors in an investigation that can be changed, or that change as a result of changes we make in an investigation

vertebrates: animals that have a vertebral column (backbone)

vertical migration: the movement of organisms between the sunlight zone and twilight zones of the oceans

viscous: describes a liquid that flows slowly

vitamins: nutrients that are required by living organisms; they are manufactured or produced by living organisms; examples include vitamin A and vitamin C

volcanic islands: islands formed when volcanic eruptions result in the formation of an island or group of islands

volcanoes: part of the Earth's crust from which lava erupts

waste water: discarded water that has been used for purposes such as washing and cleaning

water cycle: the cycle of processes by which water circulates between the Earth's oceans, atmosphere, and land; it involves precipitation, drainage and run-off into streams and rivers, and return to the atmosphere by evaporation

wave power: a method of generating electricity using energy from wave action

wind turbines: devices that use the energy of wind to generate electricity

World Ocean: all the oceans, which are interconnected to encircle the world

yaw: the side-to-side movement of the head of a fish

zooxanthellae: a type of algae that lives inside coral polyps; the algae benefits the coral and the corals benefit the algae

Key words (non-syllabus)

acid rain: rain that is made acidic due to the release of pollutants such as sulfur dioxide

artificial pellets: food that is produced for aquaculture; it contains the correct balance of nutrients for the species being farmed

atom: the smallest particle of a substance that can take part in a chemical reaction

axis: the imaginary line between the Earth's North Pole and South Pole

baitfish: small species of fish that are caught and then used to attract tuna

barbless hook: a hook that does not have a barb and is commonly used to catch tuna

behavioural adaptations: behaviours of organisms that have evolved to enable them to survive

biodegradable: substances that are broken down naturally by bacteria and fungi

biofuel: fuel that come from crops which are grown as a source of fuel; examples include wood and alcohol

biological control: the use of organisms, often predator species, to remove parasites and other harmful organisms

biosphere reserve: an area that has been protected by UNESCO for the conservation of living organisms

boiling point: the temperature at which a liquid boils

breakwater: a barrier which reduces the energy in waves before waves reach the coast

buoy: a floatation device, sometimes used to mark shipping lanes and the location of fishing gear

bycatch: the marine species caught that are non-target species

captive breeding programme: the production of offspring from endangered species in zoos, aquaria and safari parks; the aim is to help prevent extinctions

chummer: the person on a boat who throws bait to attract tuna when pole and line fishing

closed system: method of aquaculture using tanks so that species are isolated from natural, coastal waters

crude oil (petroleum): the natural oil that is removed from under the ground; it is a mixture of many different chemicals

cuttings: small pieces of plant that are taken from a parent plant and then used to develop lots of identical plants

deforestation: clearing of trees in forest areas to make way for development

degrees Celsius (°C): unit used to measure temperature in the metric system

deposition: the settling and laying down of sediment or particles onto a landmass by water bodies

desalination plants: industrial sites that produce freshwater from salt water

ecosystem services: the benefits that humans gain from ecosystems, such as food, recreation and coastal defences

endoskeleton: a skeleton that is found inside the body, such as the bones inside a whale

essential fatty acids: fats that are essential in our diet

ex situ conservation: conserving a species by removing it from its natural habitat and placing it in a protected area such as a zoo or aquarium

exclusive economic zone (EEZ): the area from a coastline up to 200 nautical miles out to sea that is owned and controlled by one country

export: selling goods or services overseas

feeding frenzy: rapid feeding that occurs when many tuna swim around food

filter feeders: organisms whose method of feeding involves extracting small particles from water

foreign revenue: income that is brought into a country from abroad

fringing reef: the coral reef that forms around the sides of a volcanic island

genetic diversity: range of genetic variation in a population

ghost net: discarded fishing gear that stays in the oceans aned continues to catch and kill marine organisms

gillnet: a type of net that catches fish in the mesh by the head and gill operculum

handline: a nylon or rope line that is held in the hand at one end and attached to fishing gear at the other end

hemisphere: half of a sphere; the Earth can be considered to be made of two hemispheres divided by the Equator

high water neap tide mark: point on the shore reached by the highest neap tide

high water spring tide mark: point on the shore reached by the highest spring tide

humidity: the amount of water vapour in the air

hybrid: animal produced from the breeding of two different species; they are rarely fertile

hydrothermal vent: cold ocean water seeps into the Earth's crust and is superheated by underlying magma; this heated water is forced through vents (gaps) in the ocean floor and as it cools dissolved minerals solidify and form a chimney-like structure

hypothermia: the overcooling of the body of an organism that can result in death

immune system: the system in the body that destroys infections

in situ conservation: the conservation of a species while it is still in its natural habitat

intensive farming: methods of farming that produce large amounts of crops or animals; often relies on mechanisation and the addition of fertilisers and pesticides

ions: charged particles made from an atom or group of atoms

lagoon: area of shallow water separated by land from the sea or ocean

latent heat energy: energy absorbed or released by a substance during a change in its physical state

lava: molten rock that erupts from the Earth's crust

low water neap tide mark: point on the shore reached by the lowest neap tide

low water spring tide mark: point on the shore reached by the lowest spring tide

meniscus: the upward or downward curve at the surface of a liquid where it meets a container

metamorphosis: the change of a larva into a different form of larva or into an adult organism

mid-ocean ridge: mountain ranges formed deep in the ocean that extend for hundreds of miles either side of the parting plates

national park: area of scientific interest where there are restrictions on development

no-take policy: a total ban on the harvesting of species in an area

oil refinery: industrial complex that separates out the different molecules in crude oil, such as petrol and diesel

oilfield: a large deposit of crude oil found under the ground

open system: method of aquaculture that uses cages and nets in natural, coastal waters

otter boards: pieces of wood, metal, or plastic that are attached to a trawling net to keep it open and maintain its position in the water

oxygen minimum layer: the layer within the ocean where the concentration of dissolved oxygen is at its lowest; typically found in the twilight zone

Pangea: a large landmass thought to have broken up to create all the current continents

pesticides: chemicals that are used to kill pests such as sea lice

phases of the Moon: the changes in the observed shape of the Moon caused by changes in the amount of the visible surface of the Moon

physical state: solid, liquid and gas are the three states of matter in which any substance can exist, depending on the conditions of temperature and pressure

pipelines: large metal tubes that are used to transport oil from one place to another

polysaccharide: long chain of sugar molecules bonded together; examples are starch and cellulose

Prime Meridian: a line from the North Pole to the South Pole through the Royal Observatory in Greenwich, England

radio wave emitter: equipment on a boat releases radio waves to help with navigation

snood: small nylon lines that attach hooks to a longline

solar panels: devices that use solar energy to generate electricity

Solar System: eight planets and their moons in orbit around the Sun

sound wave transducer: equipment on a boat that emits sound waves

subduction: the downwards movement of one plate beneath another

surface area: the outer part or exposed area of a material

taxonomic rank: the different classification levels, such as kingdom or phylum

temperature gradients: changes in temperature as ocean depth increases; polar regions have more gradual changes in temperature with increasing depth compared to tropical regions

thermocline: the zone between two layers of water with different temperatures; where the temperature rapidly decreases as depth increases

tidal power: a method of generating electricity using energy from tidal movements

tidal range: difference in height between high tide and the following low tide

transform plate boundary: two tectonic plates try to slide past each other

true north: the geographical location of the North Pole; it is a fixed point on the globe

turbidity: cloudiness in water due to particles, which reduces the transmission of light

turbulence: the movement of water

water vapour: water in the air that has evaporated

World Heritage Site: area of the world that is classed by UNESCO (The United Nations Educational, Scientific and Cultural Organization) as being of particular scientific or cultural interest

zonation: the distribution of the different species of a community into separate areas, which are created by variations in the environment

> Acknowledgements

The authors and publishers acknowledge the following sources of copyright material and are grateful for the permissions granted. While every effort has been made, it has not always been possible to identify the sources of all the material used, or to trace all copyright holders. If any omissions are brought to our notice, we will be happy to include the appropriate acknowledgements on reprinting.

Thanks to the following for permission to reproduce images:

Cover Reinhard Dirscherl/GI; *Inside* **Introduction** Zero Creatives/GI; **Experimental Skills** Giordano Cipriani/GI; Cimmerian/GI; Rishik Rajpal/EyeEm/GI; Chris Clor/GI; Trey Thomas/GI; Monty Rakusen/GI; malerapaso/GI; **Unit 1:** Cavan Images/GI; Kryssia Campos/GI; Mark Garlick/GI; Andrzej Wojcicki/GI; Christopher Swann/SPL; Undefined Undefined/GI; NASA Earth Observatory/GI; Demetri2K/GI; **Unit 2:** Carlos Chavez/GI; Itsabreeze Photography/GI; MB Photography/GI; Alfred Pasieka/GI; Anton Petrus/GI; James Osmond/GI; Leonello Calvetti/GI; PeterHermesFurian/GI; Rainer Lesniewski/GI; Dante Fenolio/SPL(x2); Natural History Collection/Alamy Stock Photo; Carlyn Iverson/SPL; Martyn F. Chillmaid/SPL; Oversnap/GI; **Unit 3:** Qi Yang/GI; Paul Souders/GI; Cameron D Smith/GI; Brent Durand/GI; Xia Yuan/GI; Ed Reschke/GI; Anadolu Agency/GI; VW Pics/GI; JohnPitcher/GI; Wildestanimal/GI; Paul Souders/GI; Enrique Aguirre Aves/GI; ElojoTorpe/GI; Mike Powles/GI; Indianoceanimagery/GI; Gerard Soury/GI; Rodrigo Friscione/GI; Whitepointer/GI; Humberto Ramirez/GI; George Karbus Photography/GI; Choksawatdikorn/GI; Gustavo Frindt/GI; JustineG/GI; Gerard Soury/GI; Brent Durand/GI; Paul Starosta/GI; Lachlan Dunwoodie/GI; Damocean/GI; Aleksei Permiakov/GI; Ed Reschke/GI; Gerard Soury/GI; Catherine McQueen/GI; Little Dinosaur/GI; VW Pics/GI; TheSp4n1sh/GI; Tonygeo/GI; Allexxandar/GI; Paul Starosta/GI; Ed Reschke/GI(x2); Viviana Delidaki/GI; Douglas Klug/GI; Zhengshun Tang/GI; Albert Lleal Moya/GI; Ed Reschke/GI; Adek Berry/GI; Burke/GI; **Unit 4:** Sellwell/GI; Mixa/GI; Fajrul Islam/GI; Rodrigo Friscione/GI; Dallas Stribley/GI; Hiroshi Higuchi/GI; Brett Monroe Garner/GI; Christa Dr LÃ¼Decke/GI; Dorling Kindersley/GI; Placebo365/GI; Little Dinosaur/GI; Scubazoo/SPL; Ed Reschke/GI; Ron Sanford/GI; **Unit 5:** Sunphol Sorakul/GI; Cavan Images/GI; Mangiwau/GI; Marcin Smok/GI; Andrey Nekrasov/GI; Morten Falch Sortland/GI; Stephen Frink/GI; Georgette Douwma/GI; Massimiliano Finzi/GI; NASA/SPL; Ahmed Areef/GI; ImageBroker/Andrey Nekrasov/GI; Kiyoshi Hijiki/GI; GeographySouthWest/GI; The Photolibrary Wales/Alamy Stock Photo; ChoksaWatdikorn/GI; Wildestanimal/GI; Hdere/GI; Dante Fenolio/SPL; Jeff Rotman/SPL; Herve Conze, ISM/SPL; SPL/SPL; Ashley Cooper/SPL; Karsten Schneider/SPL; Dan Wright/GI; DR Neil Overy/SPL; Sirachai Arunrugstichai/GI; Michael Zeigler/GI; Bastianas/GI; Alan Barker; Feifei Cui-Paoluzzo/GI; CE Jeffree/GI; Robert Brook/GI(x2); Ed Reschke/GI; Roy James Shakespeare/GI; John Lawson/GI; Nature Photographers Ltd/Alamy Stock Photo; Dante Fenolio/SPL; Somnuk Krobkum/GI; Humberto Ramirez/GI; Dante Fenolio/SPL; TorriPhoto/GI; Oxford Scientific/GI; Photost0ry/GI; Anake Seenadee/GI; Csaba Tökölyi/GI; Sirachai Arunrugstichai/GI; Oxford Scientific/GI; Stephen Frink/GI; Federica Grassi/GI; Emma Holman/GI; Humberto Ramirez/GI; Gerard Soury/GI(x2); Federica Grassi/GI(x2); Terry Hughes et al. (2018) Global warming transforms coral reef assemblages, Nature; **Unit 6:** Piola666/GI; Romeo Gacad/GI; VW Pics/GI; DimaBerkut/GI; Dario Cingolani/GI; Thomas Philip Galvez/GI; Bloomberg /GI; Jeff Rotman/Nature Picture Library/SPL; Kolderal/GI; NurPhoto/GI; Kelly Dalling/GI; China Photos/GI; Jeff Rotman/SPL; Majority World/GI; Fig. 6.12 from data at IUCN SSG, Source: Duval et al. 2014; Saowakhon Brown/GI; Fig. 6.14 data source WorldBank / TradingEconomics.com; Gianfranco Vivi/GI; Scubazoo/SPL; Sirachai Arunrugstichai/GI; Atlantide Phototravel/GI; Chris & Monique Fallows/SPL; Carolyn Cole/GI; Leisa Tyler/GI; Nature Production/SPL; Claudio Reyes/GI; Roy Toft; Wolfgang Kaehler/GI; India Photography/GI; Fig. 6.26 data from Global Seafood Alliance; EyesWideOpen/GI; Don Kelsen/GI; Fig. 6.29 data The Food and Agriculture Organization (FAO) of the United Nations, The State of World Fisheries and Aquaculture 2020, Sustainability in Action; SolvinZankl/SPL; Barry Lewis/GI; NurPhoto/GI; VW Pics/GI; Pedro Narra/SPL; Ullstein Bild/GI; Education Images/GI; Thierry Falise/GI; John Birdsall Social Issues Photo Library/SPL; Hulton Deutsch/GI; Cheryl Chenet/GI; Artpartner-Images/GI; Monty Rakusen/GI; Monty Rakusen/GI; Portland Press Herald/GI; Future Publishing/GI; Bloomberg/GI; Wolfgang Kaehler/GI; Tim Pannell/GI; Bloomberg Creative Photos/GI; Natalie Fobes/GI; Santiago Urquijo/GI; James R.D. Scott/GI; JordiRamisa/GI; John Harper/GI; Bloomberg/GI; MCT/GI; David McNew/GI; Pierre-Philippe Marcou/GI; Rodger Bosch/GI; Mario Tama/GI; Win McNamee/GI; South China Morning Post/GI; Bloomberg/GI; Régis Bossu/GI; Matt Cardy/GI; Dan Suzio/SPL; C. Sappa/GI; AFP/GI; Kontrolab/GI; Dante Fenolio/SPL; Laura Lezza/GI; Anadolu Agency/GI; Brent Durand/GI; Arun Sankar/GI; SOPA Images/GI; VCG/GI; Hong Wu/GI; Fig. 6.94 data from NOAA; Fig. 6.94 data from climate.gov NOAA; Brazil Photos/GI; Athanasios Gioumpasis/GI; Data source: Satellite sea level observations.Credit: NASA's Goddard Space Flight Center; Education Images/GI; NASA/SPL; Alexis Rosenfeld/GI; Ullstein Bild/GI; VW Pics/GI; NurPhoto/GI; Sirachai Arunrugstichai/GI; Benjamin Lowy/GI; Fig. 6.108 based on data from USGS, Reef, NOAA; Alexis Rosenfeld/GI; Biblioteca Ambrosiana/GI; Chris McGrath/GI; Tang Chhin Sothy/GI

Key: GI= Getty Images; SPL= Science Photo Library

> Index